Funding for Research, Study and Travel

Latin America and the Caribbean

Funding for Research, Study and Travel
Latin America and the Caribbean

Edited by Karen Cantrell and Denise Wallen

Phoenix • New York
ORYX PRESS
1987

The rare Arabian Oryx is believed to have inspired the myth of the unicorn. This desert antelope became virtually extinct in the early 1960s. At that time several groups of international conservationists arranged to have 9 animals sent to the Phoenix Zoo to be the nucleus of a captive breeding herd. Today the Oryx population is over 400 and herds have been returned to reserves in Israel, Jordan, and Oman.

The Oryx Press
2214 North Central at Encanto
Phoenix, Arizona 85004-1483
Published simultaneously in Canada

Printed and Bound in the United States of America

∞ The paper used in this publication meets the minimum requirements of American National Standard for Information Science—Permanence of Paper for Printed Library Materials, ANSI Z39.48, 1984.

Library of Congress Cataloging-in-Publication Data

Cantrell, Karen.
Funding for research, study and travel.

Bibliography: p.
Includes index.
1. Latin America—Study and teaching—Research grants—United States—Directories. 2. Research grants—United States—Directories. 3. Latin America—Study and teaching—Scholarships, fellowships, etc.—United States—Directories. 4. Scholarships—United States—Directories. 5. Exchange of persons programs, American—Latin America—Directories. 6. Exchange of persons programs, Latin American—United States—Directories. I. Wallen, Denise. II. Title.
F1409.95.U6C36 1987 001.4'4'09729 87-22053
ISBN 0-89774-326-1

Table of Contents

Acknowledgements

There are many people whose help we have valued in the preparation of this directory and whom we wish to thank. Our colleagues at The University of New Mexico are continuously supportive. We would like to thank the reference librarians at the university's Zimmerman Library, especially Barbara Rosen, Reference Library Specialist, and Maria Teresa Marquez, the Assistant Department Head of Government Publications and Maps, for their time and expertise. We would like also to thank Jimmy Diecker of the university's Latin American Institute for his assistance. Joanne Hazlett of the National Science Foundation User Assistance Section provided valuable assistance and information which is much appreciated. We also offer thanks to the many association, corporation, federal, foundation, library, and museum program officers and staff assistants who patiently answered our many questions and provided us with the information necessary to compile this directory. Finally, special thanks to Sue Johnson, Sam Mongeau, Susan Slesinger, and the staff of Oryx Press.

July, 1987

Introduction

Funding for Research, Study, and Travel: Latin America and the Caribbean is designed to facilitate the search for sponsored research, study, and travel support for students and professional scholars interested in pursuing work in or concerning the countries of 393 programs alphabetically by sponsor, the directory includes programs offered by private and corporate foundations, government agencies, foreign sources, associations and organizations, institutes and centers, museums and libraries, and professional societies. Each funding program profile includes available information essential to securing support: address, telephone number, program purpose and activities, samples of previously funded projects, eligibility and limitations, fiscal information, application information, and deadlines.

The directory is designed to provide sufficient detail to steer applicants in the right direction in the search for funding. This directory should act as a starting point for such a search. The potential applicant is advised, however, to confirm all profile contents prior to proposal development. This means that current funding priorities, the availability of funding, and deadlines should be confirmed with the sponsor.

The funding opportunities listed in this directory provide support for a variety of research activities and methodologies. Applied, basic, and clinical research project support is included, as is funding for field research. Research and study in a variety of disciplines is covered, including work in the arts and humanities, the social and behavioral sciences, and the sciences and engineering. The listings include opportunities for biomedical, medical, and legal research and study. Support for work of particular interest to Latin America and the Caribbean is covered, including funding for demonstration, research, or study projects in: democratization; economic development, growth, and stabilization; education; the growth and transformation of institutions, both public and private; health and health care delivery; human rights and judicial reform; marine research and oceanography; population; tropical agriculture and ecology; social change; and urbanization.

Geography and history dictate parallel interests for the United States and the countries of Latin America and the Caribbean. Indeed, the U.S. government is currently preparing a variety of projects and programs in celebration of the Columbian Quincentenary, the 500th anniversary of the discovery and subsequent colonization of the New World. These activities are indicative of U.S. interests in the area, and many federal agencies (and other institutions) are funding special initiatives in support of the Columbian Quincentenary. This directory serves the interest and intent of the Columbian Quincentenary, the celebration of all the countries of the New World, by facilitating the search for support for both research and travel in Latin America and the Caribbean and study about the area. We encourage interested individuals to use this directory as a *starting point* in their search for sponsored research support. Additional sources of information on funding are included in a bibliography at the end of this volume.

How to Use This Directory

Funding for Research, Study and Travel: Latin America and the Caribbean is composed of a Program Profiles section, a Subject Index, a Sponsor Type Index, a List of Sponsoring Organizations, and a Bibliography.

PROGRAM PROFILES SECTION

Each entry in this section is composed of all or some of the following elements: accession number; sponsoring organization name; department or division name; street address with city, state, zip, country, and telephone number; the program title; for federal programs, the *Catalog of Federal Domestic Assistance* program number; a program description which briefly details the purpose of the program; a sample grants statement which lists programs recently funded by the sponsor; a statement of program eligibility/limitations describing any special requirements or restrictions for each program; special fiscal arrangements; application information; deadline information; the subject terms assigned to each entry which create the Subject Index; and a statement of any additional, useful information that does not fit into one of the listed categories.

Accession Number **Program Sponsor** **Division/Department Name**

257. National Science Foundation
Directorate for Biological, Behavioral, and Social Sciences, Division of Biotic Systems and Resources
1800 G Street, NW
Washington, DC 20550
(202) 357-9734

Program Title **Address Information**

Ecology Program
CFDA Program Number 47.051
Program Description The Ecology Program provides support for research on relationships within and between communities of animals and plants in terrestrial and inland aquatic habitats. These include studies of plant-animal, predator-prey interactions and symbioses, as well as studies of the effects of key species on communities. The program also supports research on microbial ecology of soils and sediments, and paleoecology. Emphasis is placed on multi-species interactions at the community level.

Catalog of Federal Domestic Assistance Program No. **Program Description**

Sample Grants

Sample Grants Foreign travel and activity support of a study of the environmental hardships for rainforest trees in abandoned Amazon pastures, $82,647 to Penn State University Central Office (1986). Foreign travel and activity support of a study of the role of fine roots and Mycorrhizae in the cycling of P in Brazilian tropical forest and agroecosystems, $186,239 to Colorado State University (1986). Foreign travel and activity support of a study of group foraging in spiders, $125,000 to Miami University Hamilton Campus (1986). Foreign travel and activity support of collaborative research on the role of interspecific aggression in structuring Amazonian bird communities, $62,746 to Princeton University and $29,889 to the University of Illinois at Urbana (1986). Foreign travel support for a study of Amazon fires in an ancient and current-day context, $16,044 to Penn State University Central Office (1986).

Eligibility/ Limitations

Eligibility/Limitations The most frequent recipients of support for research are academic institutions and nonprofit research groups. In special circumstances, grants are also awarded to other types of institutions and to individuals. In these cases, preliminary inquiry should be made to the appropriate program officer before a proposal is submitted. Support may be provided for projects involving a single scientist or a number of scientists. Awards are made for projects confined to a single disciplinary area and for those that cross or merge disciplinary interests.

Fiscal Information

Fiscal Information Level of support varies from project to project. Although most grants are for much shorter periods, up to five years of support may be requested. Grant funds may be used for paying direct and indirect costs necessary to conduct research or studies. Institutions are required to share in the cost of each research project. This may be accomplished by a contribution to any cost element, direct or indirect.

Application Information

Application Information Address inquiries to the program director. Guidelines are contained in the publication "Grants for Research and Education in Science and Engineering."

Deadline(s)

Deadline(s) Deadlines and target dates for receipt of proposals are published in the NSF *Bulletin.*

Additional Information

Additional Information Proposals for specialized research equipment, doctoral dissertation research, and research conferences and workshops will also be considered.

Subject Term(s)

Subject Term(s) Doctoral Dissertation Support; Individuals, Eligibility of; Seminars and Conferences; Publication Support; Ecology; Equipment Acquisition

SUBJECT INDEX

The most effective way to access specific funding programs is by searching the Subject Index. Index terms have been assigned to programs. All subject terms are displayed with the applicable program and the program's accession number listed alphabetically under each term.

Dominance
The Harry Frank Guggenheim Foundation, 108-09

Dominica
National Science Foundation, 301-03

Dominican Republic
Agency for International Development, 3
Council for International Exchange of Scholars, 53
National Science Foundation, 301-03

Drug Abuse
National Institute on Drug Abuse, 248

Earth Sciences
National Science Foundation, 276-83

Earthquake Mitigation
National Science Foundation, 271

Eastern Caribbean
Agency for International Development, 3

Subject Term → **Ecology**
Agency for International Development, 3
American Museum of Natural History, 19
National Geographic Society, 224
National Science Foundation, 257-58, 260 ← **Sponsor Name & Accession No.**
National Wildlife Federation, 313
Jessie Smith Noyes Foundation, 324
University of Florida, 373

SPONSOR TYPE ORGANIZATION

This index is broken into six different sponsor types with the name of the program sponsor and the program's accession number listed under each type. The six sponsor types are: Corporation; Federal; Foundation; Museum/ Library; Nonprofit Organization; and Professional Society.

Sponsor Type ——→ **Federal**

Agency for International Development, 1-4
Department of Education, 65-73
Department of State, 74-76
Fogarty International Center, 84
Institute of International Education, 127
National Cancer Institute, 158-59
National Endowment for the Arts, 161-82
National Endowment for the Humanities, 183-222
National Eye Institute, 223
National Heart, Lung, and Blood Institute, 225-27
National Institute of Allergy and Infectious Diseases, 229-30
National Institute of Arthritis, Musculoskeletal and Skin Diseases, 231
National Institute of Child Health and Human Development, 232-33
National Institute of Dental Research, 234-35
National Institute of Diabetes and Digestive and Kidney Diseases, 236-38
National Institute of Environmental Health Sciences, 239
National Institute of General Medical Sciences, 240-43
National Institute of Mental Health, 244
National Institute of Neurological and Communicative Disorders and Stroke, 245
National Institute on Aging, 246
National Institute on Alcohol Abuse and Alcoholism, 247
National Institute on Drug Abuse, 248

Sponsor Name & Accession No. ——→ National Science Foundation, 251-312

Smithsonian Institution, 352-57
United States Information Agency, 368-69

LIST OF SPONSORING ORGANIZATIONS

This index alphabetically lists all sponsors with address.

National Institute on Drug Abuse
5600 Fishers Lane
Rockville, MD 20857

National Research Council
2101 Constitution Avenue, NW
Washington, DC 20418

Sponsoring Organization ——→ **National Science Foundation**
1800 G Street, NW
Washington, DC 20550

National Wildlife Federation
1412 Sixteenth Street, NW
Washington, DC 20036

The Needmor Fund
1730 Fifteenth Street
Boulder, CO 80302

Program Profiles

1. Agency for International Development

320 Twenty-first Street, NW
Washington, DC 20523

Contracts and Grants

Program Description The Agency for International Development (AID) administers foreign economic assistance programs of the U.S. government. It operates from headquarters in Washington, DC, through field missions and representatives in approximately seventy developing countries in Africa, Asia, Latin America and the Caribbean, and the Near East. AID's purpose is to help people in the Third World acquire the knowledge and resources to build the economic, political, and social institutions needed for a better life. This assistance covers many diverse areas including agriculture, rural development, nutrition, family planning, health, education and human resources, energy, and science and technology. The United States, through AID, leads an international effort to help Third World countries meet the challenges of development through programs that emphasize four major thrusts: use of market forces, policy dialogue, institution building, and technology transfer. AID awards contracts and grants to appropriate, "responsible" institutions in order to implement these programs.

Sample Grants To support a program to develop cooperative relationships with African, Caribbean, and Latin American health institutions, $897,000 to Morehouse College (1985). To conduct research on the stage of malaria parasites within the blood, $1,922,604 to the University of Missouri (1985). To improve the potential for cultivation of lesser known native palm species for use as a tropical oil seed, $137,366 to the New York Botanical Garden (1985). To provide support for a program in the testing of three pine species in Central America and Mexico, $132,570 to North Carolina State University (1985). To assist a natural resource management project in the Dominican Republic, $655,000 to Michigan State University (1985).

Eligibility/Limitations Universities, firms, and nonprofit institutions are eligible to compete for AID contracts and grants.

Fiscal Information Contracts and grants vary according to the scope of the program or project. In 1985 contracts and grants awarded for work in Latin America totaled over $287 million.

Application Information AID announces projects in the *Commerce Business Daily.*

Deadline(s) Deadlines are announced in the *Commerce Business Daily.*

Subject Term(s) Development; Developing Countries; Economic Development; International Development

2. Agency for International Development

International Development Intern Program, Recruitment Division, M/PM/R
Washington, DC 20523
(202) 647-1850

International Development Intern Program

Program Description The Agency for International Development's (AID) programs are so diverse and far-reaching that highly specialized talents and years of professional experience are required to plan and administer them. For that reason, in 1968 the agency initiated the International Development Intern (IDI) Program. This entry-level program trains qualified persons to become career Foreign Service Officers who will assume positions of increasing responsibility for planning, implementing, and managing AID's foreign economic assistance programs. Interns develop the specialized talents AID's programs require, and are immersed in the professional international development network to which they will belong. Applications are requested for the following targeted areas: administrative management officers, accountants, education/human resources development officers, health/population/nutrition officers, housing/urban development officers, program economists, and project development officers.

Eligibility/Limitations Selection for the IDI program is based upon competitive screening. Candidates are evaluated in terms of academic record, related overseas and domestic professional experience, and other relevant factors. For most target positions, a graduate degree in one of the following is required: agriculture, agricultural economics, economics, education, housing/urban development, international relations, population planning, public health/nutrition, public or business administration, or other closely related disciplines. Two or more years of pertinent professional experience are required for most target positions. Foreign language proficiency is required for tenure in the Foreign Service. IDIs must have foreign language proficiency or they will receive training after employment. Preferred languages are French, Spanish, and certain other languages, such as Arabic, spoken in developing countries. Candidates must be U.S. citizens.

Fiscal Information Appointments range from FP6 to FP3 ($20,142 to $50,393).

Application Information To apply, send resume to the address listed above. An application packet will be sent to each applicant tentatively deemed eligible for the program. This set of applications must be returned by the date indicated in the instructions accompanying the packet.

Deadline(s) There are two intern classes a year, spring and fall, with approximately ten months' lead time for competitive screening, interviews, and security and medical clearances. Inquiries are accepted on a year-round basis.

Additional Information This program was cancelled in 1985 for budgetary reasons. Hiring has been reactivated but will continue to be quite limited and in the specific target areas listed above.

Subject Term(s) Development; International Development; Developing Countries; Internships; Economic Development

3. Agency for International Development

Office of the Science Advisor
Room 720, SA-18
Washington, DC 20523
(703) 235-3669

Program in Science and Technology Cooperation

Program Description The Program in Science and Technology Cooperation (PSTC) is a Congressionally-mandated activity of the U.S. Agency for International Development (AID). It seeks to stimulate new and innovative research on problems that confront developing countries. The program is administered by the Office of the Science Advisor (AID/SCI) and is currently implemented by a system of highly competitive research grants which undergo scientific peer review. PSTC seeks new *research* in the natural sciences, such as biology and chemistry, and in engineering. By research, the program means the testing of a scientific hypothesis or the development of a new technology through organized observation in an experimental setting (laboratory or field). Innovative findings that can be readily applied to serious developing country problems are accorded highest priority. AID/SCI received over 2,300 preproposals during its first five cycles of open competition. Based on this experience and on U.S./developing country meetings on specific new technologies, AID/SCI has identified six areas of investigation, so-called "Research Modules," for special emphasis and priority funding: (1) *Biotechnology/Immunology* in human and/or animal systems, including recombinant microbiology, monoclonal antibodies, and related immunological techniques for better and more rapid diagnosis, immunotherapy, vaccine development, and related health applications. (2) *Plant Biotechnology*, including tissue culture research, protoplast fusion, somaclonal variation, and recombinant microbiology to enhance food crops; also improvement of drought tolerance and enhancement of resistance to disease, insecticides, and/or herbicides, e.g., through studies of gene expression, transfer and regulation. (3) *Chemistry for World Food Needs*, particularly biochemical growth regulation in plants and animals, soil chemistry, soil-plant-animal relationships (biochemistry), innovative agricultural and food chemistry, studies of natural pesticides from plants, and the chemistry of integrated aquaculture systems. (4) *Biomass Resources and Conversion Technology*, emphasizing improved, renewable production and innovative efficient use of woody biomass and tropical grasses (including cane and bamboo) for fuels, fodder, and higher value chemicals; new and simpler methods to identify economically useful biomass products and byproducts. (5) *Biological Control* of (a) human schistosomes and their snail vectors, and (b) plant crop viruses and their arthropod vectors, emphasizing ecologically acceptable interruption of disease transmission based on microorganism-host-vector relationships, genetics, biochemistry (e.g., juvenile hormones, pheromones), immunology, natural predation, and pathobiology. (6) *Diversity of Biological Resources*, emphasizing innovative *research* on terrestrial and aquatic plant/animal/microbial species of economic promise for development. This includes: new methods for identifying economically useful species and products, restoration and optimization of habitat for species and ecosystem maintenance and productivity, and development of new molecular-genetic methods for the above. Conventional breeding, taxonomic studies, and distribution surveys are normally excluded. AID/SCI also occasionally supports selected, innovative research in the following two broader areas: (1) Engineering technology—structural/materials research, mechanical engineering, and electrical engineering, including low-cost information and computer technology. (2) Atmospheric, Marine, and Earth Sciences—meteorology, hydrology, geology, seismology, remote sensing for natural resource analysis, and the better utilization and preservation of coastal zones. Research which does not fall substantially within any of the foregoing areas will be rejected. Specifically, the program does *not* fund: planning or policy studies, operations research, international conferences, core support for organizations, travel or training grants, social sciences research, surveys or evaluations, baseline data collection, routine mapping, literature reviews, or the preparation of manuals.

Eligibility/Limitations PSTC gives highest priority to submissions from scientists in those developing countries which receive U.S. AID development assistance, including Barbados, Belize, Bolivia, Costa Rica, Dominican Republic, the Eastern Caribbean, Ecuador, El Salvador, Grenada, Guatemala, Haiti, Honduras, Jamaica, Panama, and Peru. Cooperation with U.S. scientists is encouraged, but not required. Applicants may be affiliated with universities, nonprofit or for-profit organizations, and/or government laboratories. The grants competition is also open to U.S. investigators and scientists from middle income countries (e.g., Brazil, Colombia, Mexico, Paraguay, Venezuela) when the research is particularly relevant, unusually innovative, and there is strong linkage with developing countries. PSTC does not continue projects previously funded by, or more appropriate to, other components of AID, e.g., conventional applications of known techniques or traditional technology transfer. PSTC does not support projects whose benefits are limited to a single country; such projects are normally part of AID's bilateral programs. PSTC does not fund research on topics of predominant interest to developed countries.

Fiscal Information For the entire length of a project, grants range from a few thousand dollars up to a total of $150,000, including overhead, if any. PSTC grants are nonrenewable, except for selected investigators who can recompete for funding through the normal PSTC review process. Training and travel may be included to achieve the purposes of a well-defined research project, but not as independent objectives outside of a definitive research protocol.

Application Information Preproposals are required. These should be concise, up to three pages long, and describe in English, in specific terms: the project title; the research module in which the project fits; the investigators, their institutional affiliations, and the full mailing address and telephone number of the principal investigator; the project objectives (a one to three sentence description); the project duration and proposed starting date; the research rationale and proposed workplan; what is new or innovative about the proposed research; the relevance to and impact of the proposed research on international development; collaborative arrangements, if any; and a brief budget. Further information on preproposal format is available from the Office of the Science Advisor. Following an internal review of preproposals, selected investigators will be invited to submit a full proposal.

Deadline(s) Preproposals may be submitted to the Office of the Science Advisor at any time, although only one formal review of preproposals is scheduled per year. The next deadline for receipt is February 1.

Subject Term(s) Developing Countries; Economic Development; Natural Sciences; Biology; Chemistry; Engineering; Barbados; Belize; Bolivia; Costa Rica; Dominican Republic; Eastern Caribbean; Ecuador; El Salvador; Grenada; Guatemala; Haiti; Honduras; Jamaica; Panama; Peru; Brazil; Colombia; Mexico; Paraguay; Venezuela; Biotechnology; Immunology; Genetics; Aquaculture; Agriculture; Ecology; Food Systems; Schistosomiasis; Meteorology; Hydrology; Geology; Seismology; Remote Sensing

4. Agency for International Development

OSDBU/MRC, Room 648, SA-14
Washington, DC 20523
(703) 235-1720

Unsolicited Proposals

Program Description The Agency for International Development (AID) administers foreign economic assistance programs of the U.S. government. AID's purpose is to help people in the Third World acquire knowledge and resources to build the economic, political, and social institutions needed for a better life. This assistance covers many diverse areas including agriculture, rural development, nutrition, family planning, health, education and human resources, energy, and science and technology. AID encourages the submission of unsolicited proposals which contribute new ideas consistent with and contributing to the accomplishment of AID's objectives. However, the requirements for contractor resources are normally quite program specific, and thus widely varied, and must be responsive to the host-country needs. Further, AID's projects are usually designed in collaboration with the cooperating country. These factors can limit both the need for, and AID's ability to use unsolicited proposals. Therefore, prospective offerors are encouraged to contact AID technical personnel to determine AID's mission and needs as related to the offeror's proposal before preparing and submitting a formal unsolicited proposal.

Eligibility/Limitations An "unsolicited proposal" is a written offer to perform a proposed task or effort, initiated and submitted to the government by an offeror without solicitation by the government, with the objective of obtaining funding. Advertising material, commercial product offerings, contributions, or technical correspondence will *not* be considered as unsolicited proposals.

Application Information Guidelines for submitting unsolicited proposals to AID are available on request.

Deadline(s) No deadlines are listed.

Additional Information For research proposals, prospective applicants should contact AID, Washington, DC, 20523, Attention: S&T/RUR, Room 309, SA-18; all other proposals should be submitted to the address listed above.

Subject Term(s) Development; International Development; Developing Countries; Economic Development

5. American Alpine Club

113 East 90th Street
New York, NY 10028
(212) 722-1628

Research Grants

Program Description The research committee of The American Alpine Club administers funds derived from the income of two endowments: The Arthur K. Gilkey

Memorial Research Fund and The Roger L. Putnam Research Fund. Through these funds the club is able to support modest requests to assist research activities. Projects must be within the scope of the club's charter, and may include all alpine research problems. Projects for research grants are considered in terms of their scientific or technical quality, contribution to scientific endeavor germane to mountain regions, and in terms of the purposes for which the club was established.

Eligibility/Limitations Individuals involved in alpine research are eligible to apply. Each grantee is required to submit a formal report at the end of the grant period; a copy will be sent to the editor of The American Alpine Journal for publication consideration. Written acknowledgment to The American Alpine Club is required in such publication.

Fiscal Information Most grants are in the $200 to $500 range.

Application Information Application forms are available from the club.

Deadline(s) Applications must be received by the research committee on or before March 1.

Subject Term(s) Individuals, Eligibility of; Alpine Research; Mountain Regions

6. American Association for the Advancement of Science

1776 Massachusetts Avenue, NW
Washington, DC 20036

Science, Engineering and Diplomacy Fellows Program

Program Description The American Association for the Advancement of Science (AAAS) Science, Engineering and Diplomacy Fellows program is designed to make practical contributions to the more effective use of scientific and technical knowledge in the foreign affairs and development programs of the U.S. government, to demonstrate the value of science and technology in working on important societal problems, and, more generally, to provide a unique, internationally oriented, public policy learning experience. Fellows spend one year working either in the Bureau of Oceans and International Environmental Scientific Affairs of the Department of State (STATE), or in one of the bureaus of the Agency for International Development (AID). Individuals who are selected will work on scientific and technical subjects in international affairs. These will be in foreign policy for STATE and in international development for AID. The program includes an orientation on foreign affairs, executive branch, and congressional operations, and seminars on issues involving science and technology and public policy held throughout the year.

Eligibility/Limitations A prospective fellow must demonstrate exceptional competence in some area of science or engineering; be cognizant of the ways in which science and technology affect a broad range of international development and foreign policy issues; be articulate, literate, and able to work effectively with decision makers and others outside of the scientific and engineering communities; exhibit willingness and flexibility to tackle problems in a number of nonscientific areas; demonstrate sensitivity toward political, economic, and social issues; and, perhaps most important, have some experience and/or a strong interest in applying knowledge toward the solution of problems in the area of foreign affairs/international development. Applications from individuals in any area of science or engineering are welcome.

Fiscal Information In cooperation with the State Department and the Agency for International Development, the AAAS will select two or more fellows (one for STATE and one or more for AID). The individuals will serve a one-year appointment at a salary consistent with education level and experience, if possible, but not exceeding the GS-12 range ($31,600 to $41,100). Appointments may be made at a lower level for awardees whose educational level and experience do not warrant GS-12 according to U.S. government rules. Details of stipend level and arrangements will be available to finalists. Fellows serving in the Department of State will be employees of STATE and fellows serving in AID will receive their stipends from AAAS. A formal security clearance will be initiated after selection.

Application Information Application information about the program is available from the association.

Deadline(s) Applications must be received by February 15.

Subject Term(s) Fellowships; Individuals, Eligibility of; Science and Technology; Public Policy; International Affairs; Foreign Policy; Foreign Affairs; International Development

7. American Association of University Women Educational Foundation

2401 Virginia Avenue, NW
Washington, DC 20037
(202) 728-7630

American Fellowships—Dissertation Fellowships

Program Description Dissertation Fellowships are available for women in any field who will complete all required course work and examinations for the doctorate, except the dissertation defense, by December 31. It is expected that the fellowship will be used for the final year of doctoral work and that the degree will be received at the end of the fellowship year.

Eligibility/Limitations Women who are citizens of the United States or hold permanent resident status are eligible to apply for the final year of doctoral work. There is no restriction as to place of study.

Fiscal Information Awards are for $10,000 for a twelve-month period beginning July 1. Fellows are expected to devote full time to their projects during the fellowship year.

Application Information Application forms are available to individuals only from the AAUW Educational Foundation Programs Office by written request from August 1 to November 1. No telephone requests will be honored.

Deadline(s) Final date for postmark of completed applications is November 15.

Subject Term(s) Doctoral Dissertation Support; Women, Eligibility of

8. American Association of University Women Educational Foundation

2401 Virginia Avenue, NW
Washington, DC 20037
(202) 728-7630

American Fellowships—Postdoctoral

Program Description Postdoctoral fellowships are available to women who hold a doctoral degree and wish to pursue research. These awards are limited to five restricted, endowed fellowships: The Founders Fellowship for a distinguished scholar's postdoctoral research in any field; the Palmer Fellowship for postdoctoral research in any field; the Berliner Fellowship for postdoctoral research in physics, chemistry, or biology; the Curie Fellowship for postdoctoral research in chemistry, physics, or radiology; and the Seibert Fellowship for postdoctoral research in the biological or medical sciences.

Eligibility/Limitations Women who are citizens of the United States or hold permanent resident status and who have achieved distinction or promise of distinction in their fields are eligible to apply. There are no restrictions as to an applicant's age or place of study. Postdoctoral fellowships are not awarded for the revision of the dissertation nor for tuition for additional course work. Preference is given to women who have held the doctorate at least three years. Fellows are expected to devote full time to their projects during the fellowship year.

Fiscal Information Postdoctoral fellowships carry an award of $15,000 for a twelve month period of research except for the Founders Fellowship which carries an award of $20,000.

Application Information Application forms are available to individuals between August 1 and November 1 only from the AAUW Educational Foundation Programs Office by written request. No telephone requests will be honored.

Deadline(s) The final date for postmark of completed applications is November 15.

Additional Information Additional research and project grants for AAUW members are available. Contact the Programs Office for additional information.

Subject Term(s) Fellowships; Postdoctoral Support; Women, Eligibility of; Social Sciences; Humanities; Physics; Chemistry; Biology; Medical Sciences; Radiology

9. American Council of Learned Societies

228 East 45th Street
New York, NY 10017-3398
(212) 697-1505

ACLS/Ford Fellowships

Program Description These fellowships support humanistic research, broadly defined, on social issues which bear on the following questions: (1) the various meanings of equality and their relationship to a socially just society; (2) intergenerational responsibility—the obligation of the young to the old, the old to the young, and of both to generations yet unborn; (3) the concept of governance, with emphasis on centralization and decentralization and the division of power and authority among levels and branches of government; and (4) the cultural and philosophical assumptions implicit in concepts and practices of crime and punishment.

Eligibility/Limitations Fellows must devote a minimum of six continuous months (to a maximum of twelve) to full-time work on their projects. Applicants must be citizens and permanent residents of the United States, hold the doctorate or its equivalent (scholarly maturity as demonstrated by professional experience and publications) as of the deadline that has been set. The conditions of the awards should make them of particular interest to scholars whose teaching loads restrict time for research, those whose normal places of work are remote from repositories of research materials, and those independent scholars who have no institutional support for their research and writing.

Fiscal Information Awards do not exceed $15,000; they are intended primarily for the provision of free time, although amounts for travel, for clerical or research assistance, or for the reproduction or purchase of materials are allowable. Support of dependents may be included.

Application Information General inquiries and requests for application forms should be addressed to the Office of Fellowships and Grants. In requesting application forms the prospective applicant should state the highest academic degree held and the date the degree was received, citizenship or permanent residence, academic or other position, field of specialization, proposed subject of research or study, and the period of time for which support is requested.

Deadline(s) The deadline for receipt of applications is September 30.

Subject Term(s) Fellowships; Individuals, Eligibility of; Humanities; Social Sciences; Social Issues; Aging; Governance; Criminal Justice; Law

10. American Council of Learned Societies

228 East 45th Street
New York, NY 10017-3398
(212) 697-1505

Fellowships

Program Description These awards provide support for scholars engaged in research in the humanities; research in the social sciences with a predominantly humanistic emphasis will also be considered. Fields or specializations supported include philosophy (including the philosophy of law and science), aesthetics, philology, languages, literature and linguistics, archeology, art history and musicology, history (including the history of science), law and religion, cultural anthropology, and folklore.

Sample Grants A fellowship was awarded in support of study of cultural expression in developing societies in African and Caribbean nations (1983).

Eligibility/Limitations Fellows must devote a minimum of six continuous months (to a maximum of twelve) to full-time work on their projects. Applicants must be citizens and permanent residents of the United States, hold the doctorate or its equivalent (scholarly maturity as demonstrated by professional experience and publications) as of the deadline that has been set. The conditions of the awards should make them of particular interest to scholars whose teaching loads restrict time for research, those whose normal places of work are remote from repositories of research materials, and those independent scholars who have no institutional support for their research and writing.

Fiscal Information Awards do not exceed $15,000; they are intended primarily for the provision of free time, although amounts for travel, for clerical or research assistance, or for the reproduction or purchase of materials are allowable. Support of dependents may be included.

Application Information General inquiries and requests for application forms should be addressed to the Office of Fellowships and Grants. In requesting application forms the prospective applicant should state the highest academic degree held and the date the degree was received, citizenship or permanent residence, academic or other position, field of specialization, proposed subject of research or study, and the period of time for which support is requested.

Deadline(s) The deadline for receipt of applications is September 30.

Subject Term(s) Fellowships; Individuals, Eligibility of; Humanities; Social Sciences; Anthropology; Literature; Art History; Musicology; Philology; Linguistics; Archeology; Philosophy; Aesthetics; Language; History; Law; Religion; Folklore; History of Science

11. American Council of Learned Societies

228 East 45th Street
New York, NY 10017
(212) 697-1505

Fellowships for Recent Recipients of the Ph.D.

Program Description These awards provide support for scholars engaged in research in the humanities; research in the social sciences with a predominantly humanistic emphasis will also be considered. Fields or specializations supported include philosophy (including the philosophy of law and science), aesthetics, philology, languages, literature and linguistics, archeology, art history and musicology, history (including the history of science), law and religion, cultural anthropology, and folklore.

Eligibility/Limitations These awards are limited to scholars whose Ph.D. degree has been conferred in the year of and not more than two calendar years prior to the competition to engage in research. Fellows must devote a minimum of six continuous months (to a maximum of twelve) to full-time work on their proposals. Proposals for dissertation revision as well as those for work on other projects are appropriate. Applicants must be citizens and permanent residents of the United States.

Fiscal Information Fellowships do not exceed $10,000; they are intended primarily for the provision of free time, although amounts for travel, clerical or research assistance, or for the reproduction or purchase of materials are allowable.

Application Information General inquiries and requests for application forms should be addressed to the Office of Fellowships and Grants. In requesting application forms the prospective applicant should state the highest academic degree held and the date the degree was received, citizenship or permanent residence, academic or other position, field of specialization, proposed subject of research or study, and the period of time for which support is requested.

Deadline(s) The deadline for receipt of applications is September 30.

Subject Term(s) Fellowships; Postdoctoral Support; Humanities; Social Sciences; Philosophy; Aesthetics; Language; Literature; Law; Religion; Philosophy; Art History; Musicology; Linguistics; Archeology; History; History of Science; Anthropology; Folklore

12. American Council of Learned Societies

228 East 45th Street
New York, NY 10017
(212) 697-1505

Grants for Travel to International Meetings Abroad

Program Description These grants support the participation of scholars in humanistic disciplines in international meetings held outside North America.

Eligibility/Limitations Applicants must read papers or have a major, official role in the meeting. Preference is given to the reading of scholarly papers over the performance of bureaucratic functions, to youth over age, and to scholars who have not held travel grants over those who have received grants in the past. Applicants must be citizens and permanent residents of the United States and hold the doctorate or its equivalent. Applications may not be submitted by scholars who were awarded travel grants in competitions taking place in either the current or the two preceding calendar years.

Fiscal Information Financial assistance will approximate an amount not less than one-half of the most economical airfare available between major commercial airports. Award amounts are usually between $500 and $1,000. The use of U.S. flag carriers is required.

Application Information Address inquiries to the Travel Grant Office of the ACLS setting forth the name, dates, place, and sponsorship of the meeting, as well as a brief description of the nature of the applicant's scholarly interests and proposed role in the meeting.

Deadline(s) Deadlines for applications are Oct 1 for meetings January-June; March 1 for meetings July-December.

Subject Term(s) Individuals, Eligibility of; Travel Support Abroad; Humanities

13. American Council of Learned Societies

228 East 45th Street
New York, NY 10017-3398
(212) 697-1505

Grants-in-Aid

Program Description The purpose of Grants-in-Aid is to provide funds in support of significant humanistic research. Grants are to be used exclusively to advance specific programs of research in progress by contributing to the scholar's essential personal expenses for that purpose.

Sample Grants Support for a study of art and iconography of monumental sculpture at Copan and Quirigua (1984-85). Support for a study of the mural painting tradition of Teotihuacan (1984-85). Support for a study of British-American competition for petroleum in Latin America, 1910-1930 (1983-84). Support for an economic history of eighteenth century Mexico (1983-84). Support for a study of the Quechuan Memorial Mourning ceremony (1983-84).

Eligibility/Limitations Applicants must be citizens and permanent residents of the United States and hold the doctorate or its equivalent.

Fiscal Information Stipends will not exceed $3,000 and should be expended within one year after acceptance. Awards for living expenses at home to relieve the applicant of the necessity of teaching beyond the conventional academic year will be made only in exceptional cases. Allowable expenses may include personal travel and maintenance away from home while gaining access to materials, research or clerical assistance and reproduction or purchase of materials.

Application Information General inquiries and requests for application forms should be addressed to the Office of Fellowships and Grants. In requesting application forms the prospective applicant should state the highest academic degree held and the date the degree was received, citizenship or permanent residence, academic or other position, field of specialization, proposed subject of research or study, and the period of time for which support is requested.

Deadline(s) The deadline for receipt of applications is December 15.

Subject Term(s) Individuals, Eligibility of; Humanities; Social Sciences

14. American Heart Association

7320 Greenville Avenue
Dallas, TX 75231
(214) 750-5453

Grants-in-Aid

Program Description The American Heart Association's Grants-in-Aid Program supports research activities broadly related to cardiovascular function and disease, stroke, or to related fundamental problems. Support is available for all basic disciplines as well as for epidemiological and clinical investigations which bear on cardiovascular problems. Limited funds are available for support of research in the basic sciences irrespective of apparent direct application to the field of cardiovascular disease.

Eligibility/Limitations Eligible applicants include citizens of the United States or foreign nationals with permanent resident or exchange visitor status who hold a doctorate and will be engaged in essentially full-time research in an area supported by the association. Grants for research to be performed outside the United States are limited to principal investigators who are U.S. citizens. Grants are awarded for work in accredited universities, colleges, medical and dental schools, schools of public health, accredited hospitals and laboratories, including governmental research laboratories, and other nonprofit research institutions where basic facilities and staff for the specific research project elected by the applicant are available.

Fiscal Information While there is no declared dollar value limit that may be awarded to an investigator and institution, available funds for individual new grants, including 10% overhead, currently average $32,000 per year. For the coming year, new grants will not exceed $30,000 per year, plus 10% overhead, for a maximum of three years.

Application Information For information and applications contact the Division of Research Programs at the above address.

Deadline(s) Applications must be received no later than midnight on October 1.

Subject Term(s) Foreign Nationals, Eligibility of; Cardiovascular Research; Medical Sciences

15. American Institute of Nutrition

9650 Rockville Pike
Bethesda, MD 20814
(301) 530-7050

AIN Nestle Postdoctoral Nutrition Fellowship

Program Description These fellowships promote full-time postdoctoral involvement in nutrition research by young scientists holding recognized doctoral degrees in specializations such as nutrition, biochemistry, medicine, dentistry, or other fields closely related to nutrition. Research programs proposed in the fellowship application shall emphasize basic nutrition research, using human or animal models, and shall have pertinence to increasing knowledge in the area of maternal-child nutrition. The research shall deal with basic nutrition research (e.g., digestibility, bioavailability, absorption, metabolism, nutrient requirements, nutrient interactions) pertinent to mother-child nutrition. The scientific quality of the research proposed will be a major criterion for the award. Research aimed at food production and processing for commercial purposes will not be considered.

Eligibility/Limitations Candidates shall be citizens of the United States or Canada. They shall hold a doctoral degree or expect to receive the degree before July 1 of the year in which the award is given. Preference will be given to applicants who are recent recipients of their doctoral degree. The award may not be used for study leading to a scholastic or professional degree. The research may be conducted abroad. Continuation of effort in the institution from which the doctoral degree was obtained will not be a negative factor.

Fiscal Information The program shall involve one award annually, each for a maximum of three years, although applications for one- or two-year programs will also be considered. The annual stipend provided by the fellowship grant will be $16,000. An additional amount of $5,000 will be made available to the host institution to cover allowances on behalf of the fellow, for items including health insurance, research equipment and supplies, and travel to scientific meetings. The host institution will also receive an overhead fee of 10% of the stipend.

Application Information For application forms write The American Institute of Nutrition at the address listed above.

Deadline(s) The deadline for applications is February 1.

Subject Term(s) Fellowships; Postdoctoral Support; Canadian Nationals, Eligibility of; Nutrition

16. American Museum of Natural History

Office of Grants and Fellowships
Central Park West at 79th Street
New York, NY 10024
(212) 873-1300, Ext. 517

Collection Study Grants

Program Description These grants provide financial assistance to enable predoctoral and recent postdoctoral investigators to study any of the scientific collections at the American Museum. These collections represent the fields of vertebrate zoology, invertebrate zoology, paleozoology, anthropology, and mineral sciences.

Eligibility/Limitations Predoctoral and recent postdoctoral investigators are eligible to apply. Grants are not available to investigators residing within daily commuting distance of the American Museum. Only one Collection Study Grant will be awarded to an individual.

Fiscal Information The awards partially support travel and subsistence while visiting the American Museum; the visit is expected to be four days or longer in duration. The maximum amount of the award is $400.

Application Information Applicants for Collection Study Grants should first contact the appropriate museum department to discuss the feasibility of the proposed visit. Approval by the department chairman is required. These grants require a special application form which must be requested *by name* from the Office of Grants and Fellowships.

Deadline(s) Applicants may submit their forms at any time during the year and may expect a decision within two months of submission.

Additional Information Applicants requiring larger grants for collection study may apply instead to one of the other grant programs offered by the museum.

Subject Term(s) Predoctoral Support; Postdoctoral Support; Museums; Anthropology; Zoology; Paleozoology; Collections Study, Museums; Mineral Sciences

17. American Museum of Natural History

Office of Grants and Fellowships
Central Park West at 79th Street
New York, NY 10024
(212) 873-1300, Ext. 517

Curatorial Fellowships

Program Description These fellowships bring to the museum individuals holding the doctoral degree or its equivalent to assume all the duties, responsibilities, and activities of members of the curatorial staff for a limited term. Appointees are expected to engage in an active research program and to participate in exhibition planning, educational activities, management of collections, and administration of their department to varying degrees.

Eligibility/Limitations Fellowships are available to individuals holding the doctoral degree or its equivalent.

Fiscal Information Fellowship appointments are non-tenured, may not exceed a five-year period, and are renewable annually. Limited support for relocation, research, and publication costs is generally offered.

Application Information Museum departments compete for curatorial fellowship positions, and once a position is awarded, the department receiving it recruits for candidates as it would for a tenure track curatorship. Hence announcements stating qualifications and application procedures for a curatorial fellowship opening will appear in journals appropriate to the field.

Deadline(s) Application deadlines appear in announcements for fellowship openings.

Subject Term(s) Fellowships; Individuals, Eligibility of; Curatorships, Museums; Museums

18. American Museum of Natural History

Office of Grants and Fellowships
Central Park West at 79th Street
New York, NY 10024
(212) 873-1300, Ext. 517

Frank M. Chapman Memorial Grants

Program Description The Frank M. Chapman Memorial Grants support and foster research in ornithology, both neontological and paleontological, from a broad and international point of view. Research projects need not be carried out at the American Museum.

Eligibility/Limitations Advanced graduate students and postdoctoral researchers who are commencing their careers are eligible to apply.

Fiscal Information Awards range from $200 to $1,000 and average $550.

Application Information Application forms and additional information are available from the museum.

Deadline(s) Applications must be postmarked on the prescribed form by January 15.

Subject Term(s) Graduate Support; Postdoctoral Support; Ornithology

19. American Museum of Natural History

Office of Grants and Fellowships
Central Park West at 79th Street
New York, NY 10024
(212) 873-1300, Ext. 517

Lerner-Gray Grants for Marine Research

Program Description The Lerner-Gray Grants for Marine Research provide financial assistance to highly qualified persons starting careers in marine zoology. Support is limited to projects dealing with systematics, evolution, ecology, and field-oriented studies of marine animals. Awards are not made to support research in botany and biochemistry.

Eligibility/Limitations Advanced graduate students and postdoctoral researchers who are commencing their careers are eligible to apply.

Fiscal Information Awards range from $200 to $1,000 and average $550.

Application Information Application forms and additional information are available from the museum.

Deadline(s) Applications on prescribed forms must be postmarked by March 15.

Subject Term(s) Graduate Support; Postdoctoral Support; Marine Zoology; Field Research, Support of; Ecology; Marine Research

20. American Museum of Natural History

Office of Grants and Fellowships
Central Park West at 79th Street
New York, NY 10024
(212) 873-1300, Ext. 517

Research and Museum Fellowships

Program Description These fellowships provide support to recent postdoctoral investigators, established scientists and other scholars to carry out a specific project within a limited time period. The project must fit into the areas of vertebrate zoology, invertebrate zoology, paleozoology, anthropology, mineral sciences, astronomy, or museum education. The program is designed to advance the training of the participant by having her/him pursue a project in association with museum professionals in a museum setting.

Eligibility/Limitations Fellowships are available to candidates with a doctoral degree or its equivalent.

Fiscal Information These awards offer salary or stipend and modest expenses to a scholar while in residence at the American Museum or one of its field stations, to carry out a specific project within a prescribed time period. The period is usually for one year, but may be more or less in accordance with the nature of the project.

Application Information Interested researchers should obtain a special Research-Museum Fellowship application form from the Office of Grants and Fellowships.

Deadline(s) Applications must be postmarked by January 15.

Subject Term(s) Fellowships; Individuals, Eligibility of; Postdoctoral Support; Collections Study, Museums; Zoology; Paleozoology; Anthropology; Mineral Sciences; Astronomy; Museums

21. American Museum of Natural History

Office of Grants and Fellowships
Central Park West at 79th Street
New York, NY 10024
(212) 873-1300, Ext. 517

Theodore Roosevelt Memorial Grants

Program Description These grants offer financial support to individuals for research on the fauna of North America and adjoining regions in any phase of wildlife conservation or natural history related to the activities of the American Museum.

Eligibility/Limitations Grants are intended principally to assist advanced predoctoral candidates and postdoctoral researchers, although there are no formal educational restrictions for application. Research projects need not be carried out at the American Museum.

Fiscal Information Awards range from $200 to $1,000 and average $550.

Application Information Application forms are available from the Office of Grants and Fellowships.

Deadline(s) Applications on prescribed forms must be postmarked by February 15.

Subject Term(s) Predoctoral Support; Postdoctoral Support; Individuals, Eligibility of; Wildlife Conservation; Natural History

22. The American Musicological Society
201 South 34th Street
Philadelphia, PA 19104-6313

Noah Greenberg Award

Program Description The Noah Greenberg Award was established by the trustees of the New York Pro Musica Antiqua in memory of their founder and first director. The award is intended as a grant-in-aid to stimulate active cooperation between scholars and performers by recognizing and fostering outstanding contributions to historically-aware performance and to the study of historical performing practices.

Eligibility/Limitations Both scholars and performers may apply, since the award may subsidize the publication costs of articles, monographs, or editions, in addition to supporting public performance, recordings, or other projects. Applicants need not be members of the society.

Fiscal Information The award will be given annually, provided at least one of the entries is judged by the committee to be of sufficient distinction and appropriate to the intention of the award. The award will consist of a sum up to $2,000; normally, there will be a single award but it may, at the committee's discretion, be divided.

Application Information Applicants should submit a brief description of the project for which funding is sought, and a budget, together with any accompanying materials (such as relevant articles or tapes of recent performances) which might help the committee to evaluate the proposal. Applications should be sent to the chair of the award committee.

Deadline(s) Applications should be submitted by April 1.

Subject Term(s) Musicology; Individuals, Eligibility of

23. The American Numismatic Society
Broadway at 155th Street
New York, NY 10032
(212) 234-3139

Graduate Fellowships

Program Description Each year the American Numismatic Society awards a fellowship in support of a doctoral dissertation which employs numismatic evidence. Applicants may be from the fields of classical studies, history, archeology, art history, economic history, or related disciplines.

Eligibility/Limitations Applicants must be graduate students who have completed the general examinations (or the equivalent) for the doctorate, be writing a dissertation in which the use of numismatic evidence plays a significant part, and have attended one of the American Numismatic Society's Graduate Seminars prior to the time of application.

Fiscal Information One award of $3,500 is granted annually.

Application Information Information and application materials may be obtained from the society.

Deadline(s) Applications must be completed by March 1.

Subject Term(s) Doctoral Dissertation Support; Fellowships; Humanities; Social Sciences; Numismatics

24. American Philosophical Society
104 South Fifth Street
Philadelphia, PA 19106
(215) 627-0706

Daland Fellowships for Research in Clinical Medicine

Program Description The American Philosophical Society awards a limited number of Daland Fellowships for research in clinical medicine including the fields of internal medicine, neurology, psychiatry, and pediatrics. The Daland Committee interprets "clinical medicine" broadly. For example, the research need not necessarily be associated directly with patients. It is predicted, however, that the work will have clinical significance.

Eligibility/Limitations These fellowships are designed for qualified persons who have held an M.D. degree for less than six years. The society expects that essentially 100% of the fellow's time will be devoted to research. With the cognizance of the Daland Committee, teaching or clinical service of limited amount is permitted.

Fiscal Information The term of the fellowship is one year, with renewal for one year if satisfactory progress is demonstrated. Stipends are $10,000 for the first year and $11,000 for the second year. With the knowledge of the Daland Committee, additional salary may be granted by the institution at which the fellow is located, from another fellowship, or from a similar award during the tenure of the Daland Fellowship. The society provides no funds for institutional overhead.

Application Information Application is by nomination. Application forms and additional information are available from the society.

Deadline(s) The deadline for receipt of new applications is September 1. The deadline for receipt of renewal applications is October 15.

Subject Term(s) Fellowships; Postdoctoral Support; Medical Research; Clinical Medicine

25. American Philosophical Society

104 South Fifth Street
Philadelphia, PA 19106
(215) 627-0706

Michaux Research Grants in Silviculture

Program Description The Michaux Fund was established in 1855 to contribute to the progress of agriculture and silviculture in the United States. In practice, silviculture is broadly defined to include forestry, forest botany, and the history of forestry and botany.

Sample Grants Projects have included studies of palms, azaleas, ornamental trees, everglade woody plants, and plants of Central America.

Fiscal Information Grants average over $2,800, with some grants over $5,000. Eligible expenses are not only necessary travel, hotel and meals, computer time, consumable supplies not normally available on campus for scientists, and xeroxing or microfilm, but also research assistants, equipment, supplies, and typing.

Application Information Application should be made on forms available from the society.

Deadline(s) Deadline for receipt of application is February 1.

Subject Term(s) Forestry; Botany; Agriculture

26. American Philosophical Society

104 South Fifth Street
Philadelphia, PA 19106
(215) 627-0706

Research Grants

Program Description The American Philosophical Society makes grants towards the cost of scholarly research in all areas of knowledge except those in which support by government or corporate enterprise is more appropriate and regularly available. "Scholarly research," as the term is used here, covers most kinds of scholarly inquiry by individuals. It does not include journalistic or other writing for general readership; the preparation of textbooks, casebooks, anthologies, or other materials for classroom use by students; or the work of creative and performing artists.

Sample Grants Research grant in support of carbon dates for excavations in the upper Zana Valley, Peru (1983). Research grant in support of a project on mass-produced stone tools, Maya site of Colha, Belize (1983).

Eligibility/Limitations Applicants are normally expected to have a doctorate, but applications will be considered from persons who display equivalent scholarly preparation and achievement. Grants are rarely made to persons who have had the doctorate less than a year; and never for predoctoral study or research. Applications may be made by residents of the United States, by American citizens on the staffs of foreign institutions, and by foreign nationals whose research can only or best be carried on in the United States. Applicants expecting to use materials or conduct interviews in a foreign language must possess the necessary competence in the language or languages involved. It is the society's long-standing practice to encourage research by younger and less well-established scholars.

Fiscal Information The maximum grant that will be made is $3,500, and this amount will be approved only in exceptional cases. The maximum grant for a full professor is $2,500.

Application Information For application forms briefly describe your project and proposed budget in a letter to the Committee on Research.

Deadline(s) Deadlines are December 1, February 1, April 1, August 1, and October 1.

Subject Term(s) Individuals, Eligibility of; Foreign Nationals, Eligibility of; Humanities; Social Sciences

27. Amoco Foundation

200 East Randolph Drive
Chicago, IL 60601
(312) 856-6306

Program Description Since Amoco Foundation was organized in 1952, it has maintained a commitment to improve the social and economic development in areas where Amoco Corporation operates. The foundation also emphasizes and promotes excellence in education. Since 1980, Amoco has made a major commitment to urban neighborhood organizations working in areas of housing, jobs, energy, and education to help residents stabilize and improve their communities. With operations in more than forty countries, Amoco strives to be an ambassador of goodwill in foreign lands. In support of this policy, the Amoco Foundation makes grants overseas to hospitals, schools, museums, and other institutions in areas where the company has operations. Local and national groups that are dedicated to improving conditions for the citizens in the host country also receive foundation support.

Sample Grants Support for Caribbean/Central American Action, Washington, DC, $10,000 (1982). Support for the Caribbean Institute of Alcoholism (1985). Support for the Field Museum-Trinidad Archaeological Project (1985).

Eligibility/Limitations Amoco Foundation makes its domestic contributions only to organizations exempt from federal income tax under Section 501(c)(3) of the Internal Revenue Code, and that are not private foundations as defined in Section 509(a) of the code. It does not normally make grants to organizations that already receive operating support through United Way, to primary and secondary schools, or to religious, fraternal, social, or athletic organizations. Endowment grants are not provided for any purpose.

Fiscal Information In 1985 the foundation awarded $23 million in grants, with about half of the total awarded in support of education.

Application Information All requests for grants or other information about the foundation should be directed to the address listed above. Requests for funding must be submitted in writing and should include: a brief description of the organization; a specific purpose for requesting the grant and the benefits it is expected to make possible; the amount of the grant requested and plans to evaluate its effectiveness; budget information including an annual report and a copy of the latest IRS Form 990 report; and a copy of letter(s) from the Internal Revenue Service declaring that the organization is exempt from federal income taxes under Section 501(c)(3) and is not a private foundation under Section 509(a) of the Internal Revenue Code.

Deadline(s) Application deadlines are not announced.
Subject Term(s) Education; Development

28. The Annenberg/CPB Project

1111 Sixteenth Street, NW
Washington, DC 20036
(202) 955-5251

Demonstration Projects

Program Description The Annenberg/CPB Project was created in 1981 to enhance the quality and availability of higher education through the use of telecommunication and information technologies. With funding provided by The Annenberg School of Communications to the Corporation for Public Broadcasting (CPB), the project seeks to develop new course materials, tools, and delivery systems that increase opportunities for those who wish to obtain a college-level education, especially to the baccalaureate level. To achieve that end, the project provides funds to explore new applications of electronic technologies, including broadcast television and radio, videotape and audiotape, computers either alone or networked, videodisc, compact disc, or any combination of these or other newly developed technologies. In an effort to focus on what higher education needs that these technologies might make possible, the project has worked with leaders in the field to identify areas where new approaches might be welcomed because they hold the promise of having perceptible positive impact on students' educational experiences. Several areas of particular promise have emerged. (1) Reshaping courses, disciplines, and majors—demonstration projects might design resources and teaching strategies to test what is possible and desirable within or across disciplines at the level of course, major, or discipline. (2) Fostering improvements in students' skills across a curriculum—by using new technologies, it may be possible to develop tools and teaching ideas to encourage students' underlying skills, including their ability to write, to reason, to quantify, and to work collaboratively. (3) Increasing access to a baccalaureate degree—telecommunication and information technologies have the potential to enable students to enter, accelerate, and/or complete degree programs. These suggestions, however, are not meant to be restrictive. The project remains open to all good ideas.

Eligibility/Limitations Any group or institution, profit or nonprofit, is eligible to apply. In unusual circumstances, an individual may initiate a proposal but prior discussion with the project staff is recommended. All projects are expected, either in the short or long run, to have the potential to improve the education of nontraditional learners who, because of constraints on time, resources, or available options, are unable to work toward an undergraduate degree by attending regularly scheduled campus-based classes.

Fiscal Information The project has funding of $10 million a year.

Application Information All applicants must submit a preliminary application, a brief document that describes the proposed concept and provides basic information about need, innovation, and key personnel. Preliminary applications may be submitted either for projects that are ready to move swiftly to completion or for those that need development funds. The preliminary applications are screened by the project's staff and discussed with the Annenberg/CPB Council. Based on that evaluation, the most promising projects are then asked to submit a full proposal.

Deadline(s) Preliminary applications will be accepted at any time. Action on them is keyed to the meetings of the Annenberg/CPB Project Council in April, July, and December. For submission dates for each council meeting, contact the project's staff.

Subject Term(s) Radio; Television; Education

29. The Annenberg/CPB Project

1111 Sixteenth Street, NW
Washington, DC 20036
(202) 955-5251

Materials Development Projects

Program Description The Annenberg/CPB Project was created in 1981 to enhance the quality and availability of higher education through the use of telecommunication and information technologies. With funding provided by The Annenberg School of Communications to the Corporation for Public Broadcasting (CPB), the project seeks to develop new course materials, tools, and delivery systems that increase opportunities for those who wish to obtain a college-level education, especially to the baccalaureate level. To achieve that end, the project provides funds to develop innovative, academically rigorous course materials. When the project speaks about "materials development projects," it means college-level courses that can be taken for credit by students who find it difficult to participate in regularly scheduled, campus-based courses. The range of possible subject areas mirrors the undergraduate curriculum, and all good ideas are encouraged, although the project has determined that it might make a special contribution by developing introductory courses that are particularly difficult to teach well. Three broad areas have emerged as fields particularly worth tackling. They are the sciences, including such fields as biology, astronomy, and the history of science and technology; cultural and cross-cultural studies, including both the American experience and that of other regions of the world; and business, including management and public administration, designed to enlarge the understanding of the liberal arts student.

Eligibility/Limitations Any group or institution, profit or nonprofit, is eligible to apply. In unusual circumstances, an individual may initiate a proposal but prior discussion with the project staff is recommended. All projects are expected, either in the short or long run, to have the potential to improve the education of nontraditional learners who, because of constraints on time, resources, or available options, are unable to work toward an undergraduate degree by attending regularly scheduled campus-based classes.

Fiscal Information The project has funding of $10 million a year.

Application Information All applicants must submit a preliminary application, a brief document that describes the proposed concept and provides basic information about need, innovation, and key personnel. Preliminary applications may be submitted either for projects that are ready to move swiftly to completion or for those that need development funds. The preliminary applications are screened by the project's staff and discussed with the Annenberg/CPB Council. Based on that evaluation, the most promising projects are then asked to submit a full proposal.

Deadline(s) Preliminary applications will be accepted at any time. Action on them is keyed to the meetings of the Annenberg/CPB Project Council in April, July, and December. For submission dates for each council meeting, contact the project's staff.

Subject Term(s) Radio; Television; Education

30. The Arca Foundation

1425 Twenty-first Street, NW
Washington, DC 20036
(202) 822-9193

Grants

Program Description The Arca Foundation supports a wide variety of organizations that are struggling for social and economic justice. The foundation seeks to sustain these organizations in their different missions of analysis and outreach to a wider public. In general, whenever feasible, the foundation will support: projects that address problems of powerlessness, with emphasis on the constituencies—such as the poor—most affected; projects that create movement towards greater equity and equal opportunity; work that takes on abuses of power; program activities that embody risk-taking and innovation around social issues; organization-building that empowers those left out and left behind; projects that encourage and develop citizen participation and full citizenship in all its possibilities; and U.S.-based projects that promote a foreign policy based on human rights. Presently, the principal focus of the foundation is on projects that promote a U.S. foreign policy seeking peace and based on human rights. In 1985 grants focused heavily on U.S. policies towards the Central American region.

Sample Grants In support of a travel delegation to Central America organized by the Inter-American Dialogue, $15,000 to Aspen Institute for Humanistic Studies, Washington, DC (1985). For the purpose of protecting the rights of Central American refugees in the U.S. and keeping the issues of U.S. involvement in the region alive for a public dialogue, $10,000 to Central American Resource Center, Austin, Texas (1985). For work assisting Nicaragua's Indians' efforts to negotiate a peace settlement with the government, $7,500 to Indian Law Resource Center, Washington, DC (1985).

Eligibility/Limitations Organizations are eligible to apply.

Fiscal Information Most awards range from $5,000 to $20,000.

Application Information While The Arca Foundation welcomes all inquiries, grant application information should be made by letter, whenever possible. Applicants are requested to submit a brief two- or three-page summary of the project with budget figures and proof of tax-exempt status, if your application has such status. There should be a clear identification of the problem, the project's goals and strategies for achieving such goals, the proposed solution and the value that such a project adds to our social system. If the program or idea falls within the foundation's primary areas of interest and passes a screening process, the foundation will contact the applicant and ask that a formal proposal be submitted.

Deadline(s) The deadline for submitting proposals, once requested by the foundation, is March 15 for the spring board meeting and September 15 for the fall board meeting.

Subject Term(s) Human Rights; Peace; Foreign Policy; Central America

31. Association for Women in Science, Inc.

2401 Virginia Avenue, NW, Suite 303
Washington, DC 20037
(202) 833-1998

AWIS Predoctoral Awards

Program Description These awards support predoctoral students in any field of the sciences, including the social sciences. One award is specifically designated for a student working toward a doctorate in physics.

Eligibility/Limitations These awards support women at the predoctoral level of study. Successful candidates have traditionally been at the dissertation level of their graduate work.

Fiscal Information Four awards of $500 each can be used for any aspect of doctoral education, including books, housing, research, tuition, equipment, etc. U.S. citizens may use the money for studies either in the U.S. or abroad. Non-U.S. citizens must be enrolled in a U.S. institution of higher education to be eligible.

Application Information Application forms are available from the association at the address above between September 1 and December 15 of each year.

Deadline(s) The deadline for receipt of all materials is January 15.

Subject Term(s) Women, Eligibility of; Predoctoral Support; Doctoral Dissertation Support

32. Leo Baeck Institute

129 East 73rd Street
New York, NY 10021
(212) 744-6400

LBI/DAAD Fellowships

Program Description The intent of the fellowship is to assist doctoral students in their dissertation and/or academics in the preparation of a scholarly essay or book that requires a period of research in the libraries, archives, or research institutions in the

Federal Republic of Germany. The research must be in the field of study served by the LBI, i.e. the social, communal, and intellectual history of German-speaking Jewry.

Eligibility/Limitations Applicants must be U.S. citizens. Doctoral candidates and academics affiliated with an accredited institution of higher education are eligible to apply.

Fiscal Information One six-month fellowship, (alternatively two three-month fellowships), is available per year. The fellowship consists of a monthly stipend in the amount of DM 1400.- to cover expenses during the time abroad. The entire period of the fellowship must fall within one calendar year. Support for travel or family members is not available.

Application Information For further information and application guidelines, contact the institute.

Deadline(s) Applications for the fellowship must be submitted to the institute not later than March 15.

Subject Term(s) Fellowships Abroad; Doctoral Dissertation Support Abroad; Jewish Studies

33. Bancroft Prize

Columbia University
202A Low Library
New York, NY 10027
(212) 280-3810

Bancroft Prize

Program Description Under the terms of the will of the late Fredric Bancroft, provision is made for prizes to be awarded to the authors of distinguished works in either or both of the following categories: American History (including biography) and Diplomacy. The word "American" is interpreted to include all the Americas, North, Central, and South.

Eligibility/Limitations The award is for works first published in the previous year. The awards are confined to works originally written in English or of which there is a published translation in English. Volumes of papers, letters, and speeches of famous Americans, unless edited by the author, are not eligible. Autobiography comes within the terms of the prize, but books reporting on recent personal experiences of Americans, within a limited area both in time and geographically, are not considered eligible. Previous winners of the Bancroft Prize are eligible for an award in a later year.

Fiscal Information Two annual prizes of equal rank in the value of $4,000 are awarded.

Application Information Works submitted in competition may be sent to the Bancroft Prize Committee at the address listed above, preferably as published. It is requested that four copies be furnished and that the address should state that the books are for the Bancroft Prize Competition. A letter should accompany the books so that acknowledgment may be made.

Deadline(s) Works should be submitted prior to November 1. However, page-proof copy may be submitted after November 1, provided the work will be published after that date and before December 31. (Page-proof copy will not be accepted for any work which will have a publication date earlier than November 1.)

Subject Term(s) History; Diplomacy; Awards and Prizes

34. Benton Foundation

1776 K Street, NW, Suite 900
Washington, DC 20006
(202) 429-7350

Grants

Program Description The Benton Foundation is a private grant-making foundation committed to increasing public understanding and use of communications in our democracy. The foundation is concerned with the communications policy issues raised by new technologies, and encourages public participation in the policy debate. The foundation also supports innovative uses of the media that broaden public understanding of complex issues. Finally the foundation offers educational and training opportunities to nonprofit groups that seek greater access to the new tools of communications.

Sample Grants To improve the public outreach and communications ability of the center, $7,500 to Central American Refugee Center, Washington, DC (1985). To support news coverage and background features on Central America, $25,000 to National Public Radio, Washington, DC (1985). For partial support for bringing an Ecuadorian journalist to the U.S. to learn about American print and broadcast journalism and its adaptability to Ecuador, $1,000 to Eisenhower Exchange Fellowships, Inc., Philadelphia (1985). To support media activities on human rights in Central America and the plight of refugees in the U.S., $5,000 to Central American Refugee Center, Washington, DC (1986).

Eligibility/Limitations Priority is given to projects of national or regional significance. Grants are usually made to educational, charitable, or civic nonprofit groups. The foundation does not ordinarily support books, periodicals, or newsletters. Contributions to capital fund drives or for general operating support are not likely to be considered.

Fiscal Information The trustees anticipate the foundation will make grants totaling approximately $500,000 annually. Grants range in size from $500 to $30,000. In addition, the foundation contributes board and staff assistance to projects to which it is committed.

Application Information Grant applicants are asked to submit in letter form a brief description of their project, including a statement of goals, the personnel to be involved, budget, and funds requested. If further information is required, it will be requested by program staff.

Deadline(s) Funding decisions are made by the board of directors, which normally meets in March, June, and November.

Additional Information While the foundation encourages film and television productions, a relatively small grants budget limits such support. However, two such grants are awarded annually to works that are judged to contribute to international peace and understanding.

Subject Term(s) Media; Public Affairs; Education; Peace

35. Bermuda Biological Station

Ferry Reach 1-115, Bermuda
(809) 297-1880

Grants-in-Aid

Program Description Only 700 miles from the east coast of the U.S., Bermuda is located on some of the world's northernmost coral reefs and surrounded by deep ocean. Significant research opportunities are presented by Bermuda's diversity of ecological communities: from limestone caves and mangroves to coral reefs and the Sargasso Sea. Thus, the Bermuda Biological Station (BBS) is uniquely situated—and excellently equipped—for highly productive marine field research. Moderate air and water temperatures make BBS a year-round magnet for independent and collaborative research involving disciplines as diverse as marine invertebrate zoology, reef ecology, chemical and physical oceanography, animal physiology and carbonate geology. Well-equipped laboratories, a modern research vessel, comfortable on-station housing, and a supportive staff combine to maximize the productivity of even brief field visits.

Fiscal Information Grants-in-Aid range from $200 to $2,200 each and are available to help defray the costs of BBS in-house charges. Please note that applicants are expected to provide part of their funding from sources other than the BBS. Station grants are intended to help defray the costs of BBS in-house charges such as housing, lab fees, and boat rental. They do not cover salary, personal expenses, supplies, or air fare.

Application Information Grant proposals should be concise and contain the following: an abstract of the proposed research; background objectives, methods and significance of proposed research, including justification for choosing Bermuda as a site (4-6 pages); curriculum vitae; and a budget (including expected support from BBS and other sources). The proposal or a request for additional information should be sent, via *international air mail*, to the director of the station.

Deadline(s) Applications for grants-in-aid should be submitted to the director by March 1 or October 1 for summer or winter projects respectively.

Subject Term(s) Marine Research; Field Research, Support of; Oceanography; Ocean Sciences

36. Boehm Foundation

500 Fifth Avenue
New York, NY 10110-0296
(212) 354-9292

Program Description The Boehm Foundation supports programs which assist the development of human democratic rights both at home and abroad. Since its inception in the early 1960s the primary emphasis of the foundation has been social justice and support for democracy. The foundation continues to voice its concern in the field of race relations as well as its support of other under-represented groups of citizens seeking to exercise their constitutional rights. Specific areas of interest have always included issues of peace, human rights, education, and government accountability. Since 1983 the foundation has increased support for programs promoting peace, disarmament, and anti-nuclear activities. The national debate over United States foreign policy in Central America has prompted an additional focal point for financial aid.

Sample Grants To support investigation of the impact of U.S. corporate activities and economic programs on Haiti, $1,500 to Columbia University (1983). In support of a special report on Chile, ten years after the military coup, $2,500 to the North American Congress on Latin America (NACLA), New York (1983).

Eligibility/Limitations The foundation does not make grants to individuals. The foundation supports well established, recognized organizations as well as newer, experimental, and "grass roots" approaches to the problems of an ever more complex world.

Fiscal Information Grants average between $1,500 and $3,000.

Application Information No formal grant application forms are available. Proposals should be presented in a letter briefly outlining the objectives and significance of the project, the plans for carrying the project to completion and the qualifications of the organization and personnel concerned. A preliminary budget and letter proving tax-exempt status should be included.

Deadline(s) The foundation board meets once a month.

Subject Term(s) Social Justice; Human Rights; Peace; Education; Disarmament; Central America; Foreign Policy Studies

37. The Brookings Institution

1775 Massachusetts Avenue, NW
Washington, DC 20036
(202) 797-6000

Research Fellowships in Economic Studies

Program Description The Brookings Institution awards a limited number of resident fellowships for policy-oriented predoctoral research in economics. The fellowships are designed for doctoral candidates whose dissertation topics are directly related to public policy issues and thus to major interests of the institution. Current Brookings research in economics includes the general fields of economic growth, international economics, human resources, industrial organization, regulation, public finance, monetary economics, and economic stabilization. Essential criteria for the award are relevance of the topic to the Brookings research program and evidence that the research will be facilitated by access to the institution's resources or to federal government agencies.

Eligibility/Limitations Only candidates nominated by graduate departments can be considered for these fellowships; applications from individuals not so nominated cannot be accepted. Candidates must have completed the preliminary examinations for the doctorate not later than February 15.

Fiscal Information The fellowships carry a stipend of $10,000, payable on a twelve-month basis, for eleven months of research in residence at Brookings and one month of vacation. The institution will provide supplementary assistance for typing and other essential research requirements in an amount not to exceed $500, plus access to computer facilities. Fellows will be expected to pursue their research at Brookings beginning between July 1 and September 1. Fellows are protected by the institution's health insurance policies during the period of their appointment.

Application Information Candidates are nominated by letters addressed to the Economics Studies Program at the address listed above. One or two candidates may be nominated by any department from among the present or recent graduate students of the department.

Deadline(s) Nominations must be received not later than December 16.

Subject Term(s) Economics; Fellowships; Predoctoral Support

38. John Carter Brown Library

Brown University
Box 1894
Providence, RI 02912
(401) 863-2725

National Endowment for the Humanities Fellowships

Program Description Long-term fellowships funded by the National Endowment for the Humanities are available in support of research appropriate to the holdings of the John Carter Brown Library, an internationally known, constantly growing body of primarily historical sources pertaining to the Americas prior to 1830. Numerous works dealing with Native Americans in North and South America, including both printed and manuscript works on Indian languages, offer opportunities for work in anthropology, archeology, and linguistics.

Eligibility/Limitations Applicants must hold a doctorate and be American citizens or have been resident in the U.S. for the three years immediately preceding the term of the fellowship.

Fiscal Information Fellowships consist of either two six-month awards, carrying a stipend of $13,750 each, or a single twelve-month award with a stipend of $27,500. Fellows are expected to be in regular residence at the library and to participate in the intellectual life of Brown University. Therefore, preference may be given to applicants able to take up the fellowship during the course of the academic year.

Application Information Application forms may be obtained from the director of the library.

Deadline(s) Applications should be postmarked no later than February 1.

Subject Term(s) Fellowships; Library Research; Foreign Nationals, Eligibility of; Humanities; History; Anthropology; Archeology; Linguistics; South American Indians

39. John Carter Brown Library

Brown University
Box 1894
Providence, RI 02912
(401) 863-2725

Research Fellowships

Program Description Fellowships support scholars engaged in research appropriate to the resources of the library, an internationally known, constantly growing body of primarily historical sources pertaining to the Americas prior to 1830. Numerous works dealing with Native Americans in North and South America, including both printed and manuscript works on Indian languages, offer opportunities for work in anthropology, archeology, and linguistics.

Eligibility/Limitations Fellowships are open to Americans and foreign nationals who are engaged in predoctoral, postdoctoral, or independent research. Fellows are expected to be in regular residence at the library and to participate in the intellectual life of Brown University. Therefore, preference may be given to applicants able to take up the fellowship during the course of the academic year.

Fiscal Information Fellowships range from one to four months with a monthly stipend of $800. (Foreign nationals are advised that the monthly stipend may not be sufficient to cover all of a fellow's travel and living expenses.)

Application Information Application forms are available on request.

Deadline(s) Applications should be postmarked no later than February 1.

Additional Information One appointment each year, for up to three months, will be reserved for the recipient of the Jeannette D. Black Memorial Fellowship. This fellowship is awarded to a scholar with a particular interest in research on the history of cartography or to one who intends to make considerable use of early maps in his or her research.

Subject Term(s) Fellowships; Predoctoral Support; Postdoctoral Support; Individuals, Eligibility of; Foreign Nationals, Eligibility of; History; Anthropology; Archeology; Linguistics; South American Indians; Library Research; Cartography

40. Mary Ingraham Bunting Institute of Radcliffe College

34 Concord Avenue
Cambridge, MA 02138
(617) 495-8212

The Berkshire Summer Fellowship

Program Description The Mary Ingraham Bunting Institute of Radcliffe College and the Berkshire Conference of Women Historians announce a fellowship in support of research and writing in history by women historians.

Eligibility/Limitations Women historians at the postdoctoral level are eligible to apply. Preference will be given to women who do not have access to libraries in the Cambridge/Boston area.

Fiscal Information The fellowship stipend is $2,500 for the summer. Recipients must be in residence for at least one month during the period June 15 through September 1. Office space and access to the libraries and other facilities of Radcliffe College and Harvard University are also provided.

Application Information Inquiries and requests for application guidelines should be made to the Berkshire Fellowship Program and the Bunting Institute.

Deadline(s) The application deadline is March 16.

Subject Term(s) Women, Eligibility of; History

41. Mary Ingraham Bunting Institute of Radcliffe College

34 Concord Avenue
Cambridge, MA 02138
(617) 495-8212

The Bunting Fellowship Program

Program Description These fellowships are designed to support women who wish to pursue independent study in academic and professional fields, in creative writing, in the visual and performing arts, and in music and thereby advance their careers.

Sample Grants Fellowship award to study women and development programs in the Caribbean, 1975-1985 (1986-87).

Eligibility/Limitations Women scholars, professionals, creative writers, poets, visual and performing artists, and musicians at various levels of career development are eligible to apply. The applicant must have received the doctorate at least two years prior to appointment, or have equivalent professional experience for non-academic applicants.

Fiscal Information Award of the fellowship carries a stipend of $16,000 for a one-year appointment, office or studio space, auditing privileges, and access to libraries and other resources of Radcliffe College and Harvard University. Residence in the Boston area is required during the fellowship appointment.

Application Information For information and application forms contact the fellowship program of the institute.

Deadline(s) Applications and recommendations must be postmarked by October 15.

Additional Information Affiliation with the institute is also available. Affiliation appointment is without stipend for one or two semesters with office/studio space and other resources available to all fellows.

Subject Term(s) Fellowships; Postdoctoral Support; Women, Eligibility of; Social Sciences; Humanities; Individuals, Eligibility of

42. Mary Ingraham Bunting Institute of Radcliffe College

34 Concord Avenue
Cambridge, MA 02138
(617) 495-8212

The Peace Fellowship

Program Description The Peace Fellowship is designed to support women actively involved in finding peaceful solutions to conflict or potential conflict among groups or nations.

Fiscal Information The fellowship carries a stipend of $16,000 for the year plus additional funds for research and travel.

Application Information For information and application contact the fellowship program of the institute.

Deadline(s) Application postmark deadline is March 16.

Subject Term(s) Fellowships; Women, Eligibility of; Peace

43. Mary Ingraham Bunting Institute of Radcliffe College

34 Concord Avenue
Cambridge, MA 02138
(617) 495-8212

The Science Scholars Fellowship Program

Program Description These fellowships are designed to support women scientists who wish to pursue independent study in the following science fields: physical and mathematical, environmental, engineering, biological, and psychological.

Eligibility/Limitations Women scientists at any level in their careers who have received the doctorate at least two years prior to appointment are eligible to apply.

Fiscal Information Award of the fellowship carries a stipend of $20,000 plus research expenses. Two-year appointments are awarded to recipients affiliated with a laboratory; one-year appointments are awarded to recipients who do not require a laboratory affiliation. Office space, auditing privileges, and access to libraries and other resources of Radcliffe College and Harvard University are provided. Residence in the Boston area is required during the fellowship appointment.

Application Information For information and application forms contact the fellowship program of the institute.

Deadline(s) Applications and recommendations must be postmarked by October 15.

Subject Term(s) Fellowships; Women, Eligibility of; Mathematical Sciences; Physical Sciences; Environmental Sciences; Engineering; Biological Sciences; Psychology

44. Business and Professional Women's Foundation

2021 Massachusetts Avenue, NW
Washington, DC 20036
(202) 293-1200

Sally Butler Memorial Fund for Latina Research

Program Description This fund supports research on a range of issues of importance to women, although economic and employment issues and issues of concern to Latinas are a priority for funding. This program's goals include assisting women scholars of Latin American descent or citizenship at crucial points in their careers; facilitating understanding among women of the Americas; and supporting research which promotes equity for Latinas.

Eligibility/Limitations Applicants must be Latin American women by descent or citizenship, including women in the Caribbean, North, South, and Central American regions. Applicants must be postdoctoral scholars or doctoral candidates whose proposal for research has been approved by academic authorities in an accredited graduate school. Predoctoral candidates must have completed all coursework and passed their qualifying exams. Individuals able to demonstrate that the proposed research will be conducted under standards of scholarship recognized at the doctoral level may also apply. Predoctoral candidates must have completed all coursework and passed their qualifying exams.

Fiscal Information Awards range from $500 to $3,000. The average fellowship award is $2,000. Fellowship support is for direct research costs and applicants may request any level of funding between $500 and $3,000. Grants are made directly to the award recipient; institutional overhead is not a permissible cost.

Application Information Applications are available between September 1 and December 15. To receive an application form applicants must send a one-page letter including a concise statement about the proposed research subject and the applicant's academic level. Candidates should indicate Latina background in the initial letter. Applications will be sent only after eligibility is ascertained.

Deadline(s) Applications must be postmarked on or before January 1. Letters of reference, mailed directly by the recommender to the foundation, also must have a January 1 postmark. Only completed applications with the required supporting materials will be considered.

Subject Term(s) Predoctoral Support; Postdoctoral Support; Women, Eligibility of; Foreign Nationals, Eligibility of; Individuals, Eligibility of; Fellowships; Latin American Women, Eligibility of; Women's Studies; Latinas

45. Carnegie Corporation of New York

437 Madison Avenue
New York, NY 10022
(212) 371-3200

Strengthening Human Resources in Developing Countries

Program Description In its grant program to strengthen human resources in developing countries Carnegie Corporation is dedicated to the development of healthier, better-educated individuals. While the geographic perspective of the program is worldwide, the foundation's primary focus is the English-speaking nations of sub-Saharan Africa and the English-speaking Caribbean. The principal emphasis of the program is the health of women and children. Nutrition and adolescent fertility are of particular concern. Fostering cooperation among scientific counterparts in developed and developing countries is a priority.

Sample Grants Toward a conference on parliamentarians of the Commonwealth Caribbean on population and development, $20,000 to Inter-American Parliamentary Group on Population and Development (1985). Toward planning a series of meetings of prominent private and governmental officials from the Commonwealth Caribbean and North America on regional development issues, $7,500 to Caribbean Resources Development Foundation (1985). To expand its program on child survival in Mexico and the English-speaking Caribbean and to augment it with a study of adolescent fertility, $500,000 to the Population Council (1985). Toward a conference on the political economy of health and disease in Africa and Latin America, $10,000 to the Social Science Research Council (1985).

Eligibility/Limitations The corporation makes grants primarily to organizations based in the United States, and emphasizes the role of the U.S. scientific, technical, and policy communities in the search for effective educational strategies in the areas of concentration. The program does not provide individual fellowships for postgraduate, diploma, or degree work. Training, however, may be a component of a funded project.

Fiscal Information The corporation commits around $20 million each year in grants, primarily for the people of the United States.

Application Information Program policy statement and guidelines are available on request. There is no formal procedure for submitting a proposal. All that is necessary for preliminary consideration is a statement describing the project's aims, methods, personnel, and the amount of financial support required.

Deadline(s) No deadlines are announced.

Subject Term(s) Developing Countries; Health; Women and Children; Nutrition; Fertility; Caribbean

46. Center for Advanced Study in the Behavioral Sciences

202 Junipero Serra Boulevard
Stanford, CA 94305
(415) 321-2052

Postdoctoral Fellowships

Program Description The center awards residential postdoctoral fellowships each year to scientists and scholars who show exceptional accomplishment or promise in their respective fields. In most cases candidates for fellowships are nominated by well-known scholars, academic administrators, and former fellows. The center provides the mechanism by which distinguished and very promising scholars working in universities and related institutions can increase their competence, broaden their perspectives, and, in a specially designed setting, do the original work for which they are already prepared.

Eligibility/Limitations The fellowship award entails a period of residence in the vicinity of the center, normally beginning in September and extending from seven to twelve months. In most cases the fellow contributes to the cost of the stipend, which is based on the academic salary for the year preceding residence at the center. In determining the composition of each group of fellows, several criteria are considered, including age and sex distribution and diversity in terms of discipline and institution, as well as the special needs of any collaborative project planned for a particular year. Naturally the individual preferences of prospective fellows play a major role in the formation of each cohort.

Fiscal Information The award carries arrangements for financial support at a level that protects fellows from serious financial sacrifice and enables their families to participate in the fellowship year, plus secretarial, library, research, editorial, and instructional services, and convenient access to computing and photocopying facilities.

Application Information The normal process of selection begins with nomination and proceeds through a moderately complex set of evaluations. Any scholar is entitled to nominate another person for consideration as a fellow, but the preponderance of nominations come from well-known scholars, academic administrators, former fellows, and directors of the center's summer institutes. Periodically, requests for nominations are sent to graduate deans of most universities, department heads, college presidents, and former fellows.

Deadline(s) Nominations are accepted at any time.

Subject Term(s) Fellowships; Postdoctoral Support; Behavioral Sciences

47. The Center for Field Research

680 Mount Auburn Street, Box 403
Watertown, MA 02172
(617) 926-8200

Private Grants for Field Research

Program Description The Center for Field Research exists to strengthen and refine public understanding of the world's natural and human resources, and of their interdependence, through participant funding of significant scholarship in the sciences and humanities. To these ends EARTHWATCH, a private volunteer research corps, was created in 1971 to enable "participant funding"—whereby qualified members of the public both join research expeditions as co-workers and help underwrite expedition costs. The center defines "field research" broadly, to include any research in the sciences and humanities that directly addresses primary sources—whether natural, artifactual, or archival—and especially favors projects of clear scholarly and public value. The center neither awards nor distributes grants. All funds are distributed by EARTHWATCH, on recommendations by the center, and derive from the contributions of the working volunteers.

Sample Grants Support for a project in open ocean mariculture: developing a new food source for Caribbean countries (1985). Support for a project reconstructing South Central Andean prehistory (1986). Support for a project on overwintering biology of the monarch butterfly in Mexico (1985). Support for a project on the breeding biology of the leatherback sea turtle, St. Croix, U.S. Virgin Islands (1986). Support for a project on the archeology of empire: the Royal Navy dockyard and fortifications, Bermuda (1986).

Eligibility/Limitations Awards principally support advanced postdoctoral scholars of any nationality. Women and minority applicants are encouraged to apply. Research teams supported must include qualified volunteers from EARTHWATCH.

Fiscal Information Grants range from $5,000 to $85,000 and average $18,000. Grants cover all expenses for maintaining research teams (including both scholarly staffs and volunteers) in the field, the travel of the principal investigator to and from the field, plus expendable and leased or rented field equipment. Faculty salaries, university overhead, or major (capital) equipment purchases are not allowed.

Application Information The application procedure is designed to be informal and straightforward. There are three stages involved. In a preliminary proposal, outline the project in two or three pages. After submission of the preliminary proposal, candidates will hear from the center staff in thirty days. Eligible projects will be invited to submit a full proposal which will be scheduled for peer review. Approved projects are recommended to EARTHWATCH for publication and funding. Questions regarding the application procedure, eligibility requirements, or submission deadlines should be directed to a program officer at the center.

Deadline(s) Preliminary proposals should be submitted nine to twelve months before project date. Full proposals should be submitted nine months before project date.

Subject Term(s) Postdoctoral Support; Foreign Nationals, Eligibility of; Field Research, Support of

48. The Edna McConnell Clark Foundation

250 Park Avenue
New York, NY 10017
(212) 986-7050

Program Description The basic goal of the Edna McConnell Clark Foundation is to improve conditions for persons who are poorly or unfairly served by the established institutions of society. To do so effectively, the foundation seeks basic adjustments in the way institutions and agencies work to meet social needs and opportunities to make a difference where other funding is not available. One of the interests of the foundation is supported by its program in tropical disease research which has two major emphases. The foundation seeks the reduction of schistosomiasis (snail fever) by supporting research on the immunology of the disease to help develop a vaccine and studies on the epidemiology of the disease to develop or test cost-effective control strategies. The foundation seeks the prevention of the two major infectious causes of blindness, onchocerciasis and trachoma by supporting: research on the immunology of *Onchocerca volvulus*; studies on immunology and pathogenesis of *Chlamydia trachomatis* in order to understand the immune response to infection, develop better diagnostic tests, and develop a vaccine; and studies on the epidemiology of blinding trachoma in order to develop effective control strategies.

Sample Grants To conduct epidemological studies in two Brazilian communities using an index case-cluster method, $10,000 to Fundacao de Apoio Universitario, Pelotas, Brazil (1984). To study the pathogenesis of invasive amebiasis, $24,000 to Centro de Investigacion y de Estudios Avanzados del Instituto Polytecnico Nacional, Mexico City, Mexico (1984). To study the etiology of respiratory infections in young children, $8,864 to Fundacao Oswaldo Cruz, Rio de Janeiro, Brazil (1984).

Eligibility/Limitations The foundation does not consider proposals for capital purposes, endowments, deficit operations, scholarships, or grants to individuals.

Fiscal Information The foundation's fund balance is $265 million. Annual grants total approximately $15 million with the majority of grants falling between $10,000 and $250,000.

Application Information To apply, grant seekers should write a brief letter describing the program for which they are seeking funds. It will be reviewed by the program director. If the proposed work seems to fit the program's goals, the program director will ask for more information and a proposal.

Deadline(s) Proposals are acted upon by the trustees of the foundation at one of their five regular meetings each year.

Subject Term(s) Tropical Diseases Research; Schistosomiasis; Trachoma; Onchocerciasis

49. Columbia Foundation

1090 Sansome Street
San Francisco, CA 94111
(415) 986-5179

Program Description The Columbia Foundation is currently focusing its grant program on projects that address critical issues and offer promise of significant positive impact in the following areas: preservation of the natural environment; enhancement of urban community life and culture; the interdependence of nations and understanding among people from different cultures; reversal of the arms race worldwide; and protection of basic human rights.

Sample Grants To support Dialogo de Todas las Americas, a cultural dialogue involving twenty-five leading artists and writers from Latin America in a meeting with their U.S. and Canadian counterparts, $5,000 to National Institute for Dialogo de Todas Las Americas, New York (1985). To support an exhibition titled "Border Reality," a multi-media art event focusing on the U.S./Mexican border, $2,000 to Galeria de la Raza, San Francisco (1985).

Eligibility/Limitations The foundation considers applications from regional or local projects located in the San Francisco Bay Area community. National or international projects are considered regardless of location. However, priority is assigned to California-based efforts. The foundation generally does not provide support for endowments, building campaigns, ordinary operating budgets of established organizations, individual fellowships or scholarships, nor to agencies that are wholly supported by federated campaigns heavily subsidized by government funds. The foundation will consider grants only to organizations certified by the IRS as "public charities."

Fiscal Information Grants range in size from $5,000 to $100,000.

Application Information Preliminary inquiry by letter to the executive director at the address listed above is preferred. A full proposal will be requested if the application is to be considered further by the foundation. Foundation profile and grants list are available on request.

Deadline(s) Grant applications are accepted on an ongoing basis. The board of directors meets four times each year.

Subject Term(s) Environment; Cultural Awareness; Human Rights

50. Compton Foundation

10 Hanover Square
New York, NY 10005
(212) 510-5040

Program Description The foundation's directors determine funding priorities. The areas of interest given precedence may change from time to time when, in the opinion of the directors, adjustments are appropriate in response to social change, unanticipated needs of the community, or emerging opportunities. At present, the foundation's priorities include: (1) *Global-Human Survival.* In a world in which most problems have become increasingly interrelated and universal in dimension and in which the survival of human life under conditions worth living is in jeopardy, the foundation is concerned with the prevention of nuclear holocaust and the elimination of elements that tend to cause conflict and war. The foundation's interests include the control of armament; the scholarly development of knowledge and understanding intended to help resolve complex global issues; individual rights and human dignity; the control of population growth; environmental quality; and the preservation of natural resources. (2) *Education.* The foundation has a particular interest in promoting equal educational opportunity through grants to selected schools, colleges and universities, and related service organizations. By providing funding for fellowship programs in areas of special interest—world order, peace, and population, for example—the foundation seeks to strengthen research programs and teaching in these areas at major university centers. (3) *Social Welfare and Social Justice.* The foundation's interest and support in the area of social justice stress the provision of adequate social, health, and youth services at the community level. (4) *Culture and the Arts.* The objectives of this program are to improve the quality of life in the United States; to promote community participation in cultural affairs; to encourage the development of creative talent in the arts; and to improve the quality of cultural institutions. (5) *Religion.* Funding occasionally is provided for research on selected significant issues. More often, however, a few small grants are made for church and religious programs.

Sample Grants For support of a doctoral dissertation on international migration and rural village development: a study of the interaction between Mexico-U.S. migration and socio-economic change in rural Mexico, funds to the University of California at Berkeley (1983).

Eligibility/Limitations The Compton Foundation makes grants only to organizations and institutions that qualify under requirements of the federal Tax Reform Act of 1969. No grants are awarded to individuals.

Fiscal Information Grants range from $100 to $125,000.

Application Information The Compton Foundation has no application forms. Inquiries may be made by writing a concise letter clearly stating the objectives of the proposal, the means by which they are to be accomplished, the qualifications of the personnel involved, and a budget. Evidence of the organization's status under provisions of the Internal Revenue Code should be included. Prospective applicants are encouraged to determine before making an application that the proposal is relevant to the foundation's interests. An annual report, delineating the foundation's interests and grant-making policies, and significant grants made, is available on request from the foundation.

Deadline(s) Not announced.

Subject Term(s) Human Rights; Environment; Arms Control; Education; Peace; Population; Social Justice

51. Corporation for Public Broadcasting

Assistant to the Vice President, Telecommunications
1111 Sixteenth Street, NW
Washington, DC 20036
(202) 955-5216

National Radio Program Production

Program Description The Corporation for Public Broadcasting (CPB) has available a fund to support national radio program production. Through this program fund, the CPB supports public radio system projects of high quality, diversity, excellence, and innovation obtained from diverse sources, with strict adherence to objectivity and balance in programming of a controversial nature. Proposals for all programming types are encouraged, including arts and performance, news and information, and specialized audience programming. Priorities are for projects that may not succeed initially in the public radio program marketplace; will take programmatic risks; will yield at least one major new service or series; and will increase the national audience targeted by the producer.

Sample Grants Support for The Latin American News Service, a nationally-distributed radio service focused exclusively on Latin American countries and the U.S., El Paso, Texas (1987). Support for "Dreams of Rio," a dramatic series set in Brazil incorporating the "magical realism" so often described by Latin American writers, ZBS Foundation, Fort Edward, New York (1987).

Eligibility/Limitations Any individual, association, foundation, institution, partnership, corporation, or other business entity may submit a proposal.

Fiscal Information No floor or ceiling exists on the amount of funds available for an individual project. CPB will evaluate all proposals from a "cost-for-product" perspective. Although not the major or only consideration in making final choices, awards to otherwise equal proposals may be determined by budget factors.

Application Information Questions should be addressed to and completed forms should be returned to the Assistant to the Vice President, Telecommunications, at the address listed above.

Deadline(s) Proposals must be *actually* received by the Assistant to the Vice President, Telecommunications, by the close of business (5:30 p.m.) on September 9.

Subject Term(s) Media; Radio

52. Corporation for Public Broadcasting

Program Fund
1111 Sixteenth Street, NW
Washington, DC 20036
(202) 293-6160

Program Fund

Program Description The program fund of the Corporation for Public Broadcasting (CPB) announces an open solicitation process through which independent producers and public television stations may submit proposals for the development and production of programs for public television. Proposals may be submitted in three areas: news and public affairs; cultural and children's; and drama and arts. Submissions need not be limited to these areas, however. The open solicitation is an open call for programs of high quality, diversity, creativity, excellence, and innovation from diverse sources. All subjects are eligible, and will be measured by criteria heavily weighted toward a project's broadcast potential for public television and its relevance to the American people.

Eligibility/Limitations Independent producers and public television stations are eligible to submit program proposals. Submissions from women and minorities are encouraged, as are coproductions between independent producers and public television stations. The open solicitation requires projects to conform to traditional broadcast lengths, e.g., 28 minutes, 58 minutes, etc. Proposed programs must be visual, of more than local or regional interest, and must adhere to accepted technical, ethical, and artistic or journalistic standards. The credentials of the production team and whether or not a subject has received, or is likely to receive, adequate coverage elsewhere are also factors in the selection process.

Fiscal Information There are no restrictions on the amount of funds that may be requested, although the program fund reviews all budgets submitted and encourages producers to obtain other sources of funding. Major projects inevitably require several funding sources because the total cost places too great a demand on program fund resources.

Application Information Open solicitation guidelines and submission requirements are available from the CPB.

Deadline(s) Open solicitation proposals are preselected by staff for review by an advisory panel three times each year. The closing dates for submissions are January 10, May 2, and September 6. Proposals not received at CPB by close of business (5:30 p.m.) on the closing date will be held for consideration in the next funding round. There will be no exceptions. Packages received after the closing date but postmarked on or before said date are not acceptable.

Subject Term(s) Individuals, Eligibility of; Public Television, Program Development; Television

53. Council for International Exchange of Scholars

Eleven Dupont Circle, NW, Suite 300
Washington, DC 20036-1257
(202) 939-5401

Fulbright Scholar Program—Faculty Grants for Lecturing

Program Description The Fulbright Scholar Program serves two primary purposes. It enables Americans to learn firsthand about other countries and cultures and it promotes academic and professional development. Some seven hundred awards are offered in support of university lectureships; many of these also offer some opportunity for research. In 1987-88 lectureships were available in various fields in Argentina, Bahamas, Bolivia, Brazil, Chile, Colombia, Costa Rica, Dominican Republic, Ecuador, El Salvador, Guatemala, Haiti, Honduras, Jamaica, Mexico, Nicaragua, Panama, Paraguay, Peru, Trinidad/Tobago, Uruguay, and Venezuela.

Eligibility/Limitations Prospective applicants should have United States citizenship at the time of application. For lecturing, usually a doctoral degree at the time of application and postdoctoral college or university teaching experience at the level and in the field of the lectureship is required. In some programs, language proficiency may be required. Persons who have lived abroad for the full ten-year period immediately preceding the time of application are ineligible. In general, preference is given to persons who have not already had lecturing or research grants. A previous grantee may, however, apply for a second award if three years have elapsed between the end of the first grant period and the beginning of the second. In accordance with a new ruling by the Board of Foreign Scholarships, scholars who have already held two (or more) Fulbright scholar awards are no longer prohibited from making application. Such applicants should bear in mind, however, that preference will be given to those who have not participated in the program and who do not have substantial recent experience abroad.

Fiscal Information Grant benefits include: round-trip travel for the grantee and for a principal dependent of a grantee whose appointment is for a full academic year; a maintenance allowance, paid either in local currency, in dollars, or in local currency with a dollar supplement (allowance amounts vary by grant category, the country and duration of the grant, and family status); incidental allowances for baggage, for books and services essential to the assignment, and for travel within the host country; housing (or housing allowance) in certain countries; and tuition allowance in certain countries (where available, tuition reimbursement is provided for tuition costs of accompanying dependents enrolled in elementary or secondary schools of the host country).

Application Information Only one application may be filed in an annual competition, but applicants may name up to three alternate countries. To obtain an application form and more detailed information, write or call the council.

Deadline(s) Application deadline for faculty lectureship awards to Latin America is June 15. A brochure is produced in November announcing awards for which there are insufficient numbers of candidates. For those unfilled awards, applications will continue to be accepted. Applications will also be accepted for some lecturing awards after the announced deadline. Interested persons may inquire at any time during the year.

Subject Term(s) Faculty Support Abroad; Argentina; Bahamas; Bolivia; Brazil; Chile; Colombia; Costa Rica; Dominican Republic; Ecuador; El Salvador; Guatemala; Haiti; Honduras; Jamaica; Mexico; Nicaragua; Panama; Paraguay; Peru; Trinidad and Tobago; Uruguay; Venezuela; Lectureships Abroad

54. Council for International Exchange of Scholars

Eleven Dupont Circle, NW, Suite 300
Washington, DC 20036-1257
(202) 939-5401

Fulbright Scholar Program—Faculty Grants for Lecturing/Research

Program Description The Fulbright Scholar Program serves two primary purposes. It enables Americans to learn firsthand about other countries and cultures and it promotes academic and professional development. Some awards are designed to combine both lecturing and research. In 1987-88 lecturing/research awards were available in various fields in Argentina, Barbados, Brazil, Costa Rica, Ecuador, El Salvador, Honduras, Mexico, and Panama.

Eligibility/Limitations Prospective applicants should have United States citizenship at the time of application. For lecturing, usually a doctoral degree at the time of application and postdoctoral college or university teaching experience at the level and in the field of the lectureship is required. In some programs, language proficiency may be required. Persons who have lived abroad for the full ten-year period immediately preceding the time of application are ineligible. In general, preference is given to persons who have not already had lecturing or research grants. A previous grantee may, however, apply for a second award if three years have elapsed between the end of the first grant period and the beginning of the second. In accordance with a new ruling by the Board of Foreign Scholarships, scholars who have already held two (or more) Fulbright scholar awards are no longer prohibited from making application. Such applicants should bear in mind, however, that preference will be given to those who have not participated in the program and who do not have substantial recent experience abroad.

Fiscal Information Grant benefits include: round-trip travel for the grantee and for a principal dependent of a grantee whose appointment is for a full academic year; a maintenance allowance, paid either in local currency, in dollars, or in local currency with a dollar supplement (allowance amounts vary by grant category, the country and duration of the grant, and family status); incidental allowances for baggage, for books and services essential to the assignment, and for travel within the host country; housing (or housing allowance) in certain countries; and tuition allowance in certain countries (where available, tuition reimbursement is provided for tuition costs of accompanying dependents enrolled in elementary or secondary schools of the host country).

Application Information Only one application may be filed in an annual competition, but applicants may name up to three alternate countries. To obtain an application form and more detailed information, write or call CIES.

Deadline(s) Application deadline for research and lecturing awards to Latin America is June 15. A brochure is produced in November announcing awards for which there are insufficient numbers of candidates. For those unfilled awards, applications will continue to be accepted. Applications will also be accepted for some lecturing awards after the announced deadline. Interested persons may inquire at any time during the year.

Subject Term(s) Faculty Support Abroad; Argentina; Barbados; Brazil; Costa Rica; Ecuador; El Salvador; Honduras; Mexico; Panama; Lectureships Abroad

55. Council for International Exchange of Scholars

Eleven Dupont Circle, NW, Suite 300
Washington, DC 20036-1257
(202) 939-5401

Fulbright Scholar Program—Faculty Grants for Research

Program Description The Fulbright Scholar Program serves two primary purposes. It enables Americans to learn firsthand about other countries and cultures and it promotes academic and professional development. Some three hundred grants are offered in support of research in most disciplines. In 1987-88 grants for research were available in Argentina, Belize (tentatively), Bolivia, and Ecuador.

Eligibility/Limitations Prospective applicants should have United States citizenship at the time of application. A doctorate at the time of application, or comparable professional qualifications is required. In some programs, language proficiency may be required. Persons who have lived abroad for the full ten-year period immediately preceding the time of application are ineligible. In general, preference is given to persons who have not already had lecturing or research grants. A previous grantee may, however, apply for a second award if three years have elapsed between the end of the first grant period and the beginning of the second. In accordance with a new ruling by the Board of Foreign Scholarships, scholars who have already held two (or more) Fulbright scholar awards are no longer prohibited from making application. Such applicants should bear in mind, however, that preference will be given to those who have not participated in the program and who do not have substantial recent experience abroad.

Fiscal Information Grant benefits include: round-trip travel for the grantee and for a principal dependent of a grantee whose appointment is for a full academic year; a maintenance allowance, paid either in local currency, in dollars, or in local currency with a dollar supplement (allowance amounts vary by grant category, the country and duration of the grant, and family status); incidental allowances for baggage, for books and services essential to the assignment, and for travel within the host country; housing (or housing allowance) in certain countries; and tuition allowance in certain countries (where available, tuition reimbursement is provided for tuition costs of accompanying dependents enrolled in elementary or secondary schools of the host country).

Application Information Only one application may be filed in an annual competition, but applicants may name up to three alternate countries. To obtain an application form and more detailed information, write or call the council.

Deadline(s) Application deadline for faculty research awards to Latin America is June 15. Applications for research normally are not accepted after the deadline. Interested persons may inquire at any time during the year.

Subject Term(s) Faculty Support Abroad; Argentina; Belize; Bolivia; Ecuador

56. Council for International Exchange of Scholars

Eleven Dupont Circle, NW, Suite 300
Washington, DC 20036-1257
(202) 939-5401

Fulbright Scholar Program—Junior Lecturing and Junior Research

Program Description The Fulbright Scholar Program serves two primary purposes. It enables Americans to learn firsthand about other countries and cultures and it promotes academic and professional development. These awards are designed primarily for younger scholars who are recent Ph.D.s, or advanced Ph.D. candidates. In 1987-88 these awards were available in Argentina (junior research) and Brazil (junior lecturing).

Eligibility/Limitations Prospective applicants should have United States citizenship at the time of application. In some programs, language proficiency may be required. Persons who have lived abroad for the full ten-year period immediately preceding the time of application are ineligible. In general, preference is given to persons who have not already had lecturing or research grants. A previous grantee may, however, apply for a second award if three years have elapsed between the end of the first grant period and the beginning of the second. In accordance with a new ruling by the Board of Foreign Scholarships, scholars who have already held two (or more) Fulbright scholar awards are no longer prohibited from making application. Such applicants should bear in mind, however, that preference will be given to those who have not participated in the program and who do not have substantial recent experience abroad.

Fiscal Information Grant benefits include: round-trip travel for the grantee and for a principal dependent of a grantee whose appointment is for a full academic year; a maintenance allowance, paid either in local currency, in dollars, or in local currency with a dollar supplement (allowance amounts vary by grant category, the country and duration of the grant, and family status); incidental allowances for baggage, for books and services essential to the assignment, and for travel within the host country; housing (or housing allowance) in certain countries; and tuition allowance in certain countries (where available, tuition reimbursement is provided for tuition costs of accompanying dependents enrolled in elementary or secondary schools of the host country).

Application Information Only one application may be filed in an annual competition, but applicants may name up to three alternate countries. To obtain an application form and more detailed information, write or call the council.

Deadline(s) Application deadline for research and lecturing awards to Latin America is June 15. A brochure is produced in November announcing awards for which there are insufficient numbers of candidates. For those unfilled awards, applications will continue to be accepted. Applications will also be accepted for some lecturing awards after the announced deadline. Interested persons may inquire at any time during the year.

Subject Term(s) Postdoctoral Support Abroad; Predoctoral Support Abroad; Argentina; Brazil

57. Council for International Exchange of Scholars

Eleven Dupont Circle, NW, Suite 300
Washington, DC 20036-1257
(202) 939-5404

Fulbright Scholar-in-Residence Program

Program Description This program supports American colleges and universities hosting a visiting scholar in the humanities or social sciences, or in scientific or professional specializations with a strong international focus. Of particular interest for the current program are proposals to bring foreign specialists in the fields of communications, education, U.S. constitutional law and related subjects, as well as foreign scholars in U.S. studies (history, literature, and politics).

Eligibility/Limitations American colleges and universities are eligible to apply.

Fiscal Information Grants support visiting scholars for all or part of the academic year. The program provides roundtrip travel for the grantee, and for awards for the full academic year, one accompanying dependent; a maintenance allowance; and incidental allowances. The host institution is expected to share in the support of the visiting scholar.

Application Information Detailed program guidelines, proposal forms and further information are available on request.

Deadline(s) The deadline for receipt of proposals is November 1.

Subject Term(s) Visiting Professorships, Support of; Social Sciences; Humanities; Foreign Nationals, Eligibility of

58. Council for International Exchange of Scholars

Eleven Dupont Circle, NW, Suite 300
Washington, DC 20036-1257
(202) 939-5458

Regional Awards: American Republics Research Program

Program Description This program offers up to twenty research awards, each for six months, in any discipline for one or more countries of the Caribbean, Mexico, or South America. Applications are encouraged from scholars whose projects involve collaboration with colleagues in the host country and who are willing to give occasional lectures.

Eligibility/Limitations Applicants for non-English-speaking countries should have sufficient language ability to conduct the proposed research.

Fiscal Information The grant carries an award of approximately $1,800 to $3,000 per month (in U.S. dollars or local currency), depending on country and number of dependents. In addition, international travel for grantee, and in some countries, tuition reimbursement for accompanying K-12 children up to $8,000 is awarded.

Application Information Additional information and application guidelines are available from the council.

Deadline(s) The application deadline is June 15.

Subject Term(s) Faculty Support Abroad; Individuals, Eligibility of; Caribbean; Mexico; South America; American Republics

59. Council for International Exchange of Scholars

Eleven Dupont Circle, NW, Suite 300
Washington, DC 20036-1257
(202) 939-5464

Regional Awards: Central American Republics Research and Lecturing Program

Program Description The Council for International Exchange of Scholars (CIES) offers an expanded program of Fulbright awards for research and lecturing with Belize, Costa

Rica, El Salvador, Guatemala, Honduras, Nicaragua, and Panama. Up to fifteen awards are offered for from three to nine months of research in any field in one or several countries of the area (fields may be restricted in some countries). Awards for lecturing in a variety of fields are offered for periods of from six to twelve months.

Eligibility/Limitations With few exceptions, lecturing awards require good to fluent Spanish.

Fiscal Information Awards carry stipends of from $1,800 to $2,600 per month (in U.S. dollars), plus an initial allowance of $1,635 to $1,820 to cover such items as international travel, excess baggage, settling in, books and services. Tuition reimbursement for accompanying K-12 children is offered up to $12,000 for grants over nine months, or $8,000 for shorter grants. Deductions may be made if the host institution provides local salary, international travel, or housing.

Application Information Additional information and application guidelines are available from CIES.

Deadline(s) The application deadline is June 15.

Subject Term(s) Faculty Support Abroad; Individuals, Eligibility of; Central America; Belize; Costa Rica; El Salvador; Guatemala; Honduras; Nicaragua; Panama; Lectureships Abroad

60. Council for International Exchange of Scholars

Eleven Dupont Circle, NW, Suite 300
Washington, DC 20036-1257
(202) 939-5414

Spain Research Fellowships

Program Description Approximately twenty postdoctoral fellowships of three to ten months' duration will be awarded for research under the Agreement of Friendship, Defense, and Cooperation between the U.S. and Spain. Fields of preference are: anthropology, archeology, arts, communications, economics, education, geography, history, law, linguistics, literature, logic, philosophy, political science, psychology, and sociology.

Eligibility/Limitations Competence in oral and written Spanish is required, according to the needs of the proposed research project. The doctorate is required at the time of application.

Fiscal Information Fellowships carry an award of approximately $1,200 to $1,800 per month, the total to be based on the number of accompanying dependents; $1,000 for books and settling-in expenses; round-trip travel for grantee, and, if the grant period is seven or more months, for one accompanying dependent.

Application Information Special application forms are available from the council.

Deadline(s) Application deadline is January 1.

Subject Term(s) Fellowships; Postdoctoral Support Abroad; Spain

61. Council on Foreign Relations

58 East 68th Street
New York, NY 10021
(212) 734-0400

International Affairs Fellowships

Program Description The fellowships, for individuals from the government, business, professional, and academic communities, seek to bridge the gap between analysis and action in foreign policy by supporting a variety of policy studies and active experiences in policy-making. Academic and other professionals from the private sector spend their fellowship tenures in public service, while opportunities for the systematic assessment of key issues in foreign policy, in a research environment, are given to government officials on leave. Since the focus of the program is the provision of a contrasting career experience for the young and exemplary foreign policy professional, a change of residence is generally required. The competition is multidisciplinary, past recipients having included scholars and practitioners representing the fields of political science, economics, history, anthropology, sociology, psychology, philosophy, law, journalism, business, and government.

Eligibility/Limitations The program is open to all men and women holding American citizenship between the ages of twenty-seven and thirty-five (inclusive) in the calendar year of their application. The program does not fund predoctoral or postdoctoral scholarly research, work toward a degree, nor the completion of projects on which substantial progress has been made prior to the fellowship period. For the academic applicant, while the Ph.D. or its equivalent is not a firm requirement, given the caliber of candidates, those who have not yet completed their doctorate and first professional "tour of duty" do not fare well. Similarly, successful candidates from government or business communities generally hold advanced degrees and possess a solid record of work experience in the international field.

Fiscal Information The stipend is determined according to individual budget statements in consultation with the program administration. Within the fixed maximum, the program generally will attempt to meet the major portion of a fellow's current income. If necessary, modest supplementary funding may be sought from outside sources to close the gap, at least partially, between the stipend ceiling and the fellow's earnings. The program does not provide support for research assistance or computer time, and fellows are responsible for arranging their own housing, insurance, benefits, and travel. The duration of the fellowship is one year. Short-term projects are not eligible for consideration. No extensions are granted.

Application Information Interested individuals who feel that their backgrounds and goals mesh with those of the program are encouraged to forward a brief outline of their proposal, the ways in which they intend to carry it out, and a curriculum vitae to the Director, International Affairs Fellowship Program at the address listed above. After internal council review, an invitation to apply, application forms, and supplementary information on procedures will be sent to those satisfying the preliminary requirements.

Deadline(s) The deadline for nominations is September 15; applications are due by October 31.

Subject Term(s) Fellowships; Individuals, Eligibility of; Foreign Policy Studies; Policy Analysis; International Affairs

62. Council on International Educational Exchange

The International Student Identity Card Scholarship Fund
205 East 42nd Street
New York, NY 10017
(212) 661-1414

The International Student Identity Card Scholarship Fund

Program Description In 1981, the Council on International Educational Exchange (CIEE) established a scholarship fund in support of U.S. students planning an educational study or service experience in the developing countries of Africa, Asia, and Latin America. The fund provides direct support to university and high school students who would otherwise be unable to take part in such educational study or service experience.

Eligibility/Limitations Scholarships will be granted to U.S. citizens and permanent residents sixteen years of age or older who are: (1) participating in a reciprocal exchange program in developing countries; (2) studying in a developing country; or (3) participating in a service project (either in a group or as an individual) in a developing country. Awards are made only to high school and undergraduate level students. Length of overseas projects must be a minimum four weeks, maximum one year (to accommodate intersession projects, this may be reduced to three weeks). Applications must be sponsored by nonprofit institutions or organizations in support of individual students.

Fiscal Information Scholarships awarded usually will be as a subsidy for travel to and from the project site. Awards will not exceed the cost of minimum, round-trip transportation.

Application Information Official application forms and additional information are available from the scholarship fund.

Deadline(s) Awards are made on a twice-yearly basis. Applications for April awards, for projects beginning during the period June 1 through December 31, must be received by CIEE no later than March 31; applications for November awards, for projects beginning during the period January 1 through July 15 of the following year, must be received by CIEE no later than October 31.

Subject Term(s) Undergraduate Support Abroad; Secondary Student Support Abroad; Developing Countries

63. Cummins Engine Foundation

Mail Code 60814, Box 3005
Columbus, IN 47202-3005
(812) 377-3114

Program Description The foundation gives special consideration for funding to programs in three major categories: youth and education; equity and justice; and quality of life. In the area of youth and education, the foundation seeks ways to help young people grow up to be full participants in a complex world. In equity and justice, the foundation's focus is on those who face discrimination, are dispossessed, or are poorly served by society. The foundation also encourages opportunities for leadership development among women and minorities. A limited number of grants is made annually to promote economic development and human rights abroad. In quality of life, the foundation looks for programs that refresh the spirit and enhance the general environment in communities where Cummins and its subsidiaries have manufacturing plants. The foundation also seeks new and unusual ways to support the arts and artists.

Sample Grants For an economic development organization promoting self-help and employment opportunities for low-income people in Latin America, the Caribbean, and remote areas of North America, $5,000 to Accion International, Cambridge, MA (1984).

Eligibility/Limitations Cummins does not support political causes or candidates, or sectarian religious activities. No grants are made to individuals. The foundation makes virtually all its local grants in communities where Cummins and its subsidiaries have manufacturing plants.

Fiscal Information Grant awards range from $500 to $30,000.

Application Information A preliminary proposal should include a brief description of the problem being addressed, specifically what the program hopes to achieve, operating plan and cost, description of key leadership, and how one will be able to tell whether or not the program worked. Upon receipt of the proposal, the foundation staff will respond regarding the possibility of funding.

Deadline(s) Inquiries and proposals may be submitted in writing at any time during the year, though to be on the agenda for a specific meeting, proposals should be received no later than the first of the previous month. The foundation directors meet in February, July, September, and December to consider new programs and approve grants. The staff has authority to make small grants from its discretionary budget between meetings.

Subject Term(s) Education; Economic Development; Human Rights; Social Justice

64. Eben Demarest Fund

111 Yorkshire Road
Pittsburgh, PA 15208

Program Description The income of the Eben Demarest Trust is to be paid to a man or a woman gifted in one of the arts, or to an archeologist. Such a person must be one who wishes to devote himself or herself to art or archeology without "dependence upon the public sale of his work or necessary approval of his ideal or action by those to whom it is generally known, in order to gain his livelihood" and has no other income from any source equal to the income accruing from the trust. The word art is used in its broadest sense and includes any form of literature, the pictorial or plastic arts, music, dancing, acting, etc.

Eligibility/Limitations The beneficiary is preferably (but not necessarily) to be an American citizen. The grant is almost always given to a mature candidate who has already produced work in a chosen field.

Fiscal Information The annual income from the trust is at the present time approximately $7,000 a year.

Application Information Unsolicited applications from individuals will not be accepted. However, the Eben Demarest Council will consider applications from organizations or institutions in behalf of an unusually gifted person.

Deadline(s) June 1 is the deadline by which all correspondence with the sponsor and supporting sponsors must be completed for applications for the following calendar year.

Subject Term(s) Foreign Nationals, Eligibility of; Archeology; Fine Arts; Literature

65. Department of Education

Center for International Education, Advanced Training and Research Branch, Office of Assistant Secretary for Postsecondary Education
Seventh and D Streets, SW, ROB-3
Washington, DC 20202
(202) 732-3283

National Resource Centers and Fellowships Program for Language and Area or Language and International Studies

CFDA Program Number 84.015

Program Description Project grants to centers are awarded to promote instruction in those modern foreign languages, area studies, and international studies critical to national needs by supporting the establishment, strengthening, and operation of such programs at colleges and universities. Fellowships are awarded to meet the needs of the United States for experts in modern foreign languages, area studies, and world affairs by supporting advanced study at institutions for higher education.

Sample Grants Support for the University of Wisconsin/Latin American Studies Center which offers courses in many disciplines at the undergraduate level in all participating campuses; the Madison and Milwaukee campuses offer extensive graduate and some professional training programs in Latin American Studies as well (1985).

Eligibility/Limitations Accredited American colleges and universities are eligible to apply. Applying institutions must provide evidence of existing resources and institutional commitment to language and area and international studies through a curriculum that provides instruction dealing with a particular world area and its languages, with comparative world area studies, or with the international aspects of professional or other fields of study. Fellowship candidates must be citizens or nationals of the United States or resident aliens training in modern foreign languages and/or related area studies programs. Training must be undertaken at a graduate school which has a quota of Foreign Language and Area Studies Fellowships (FLAS).

Fiscal Information Grants are awarded to centers for twelve month periods, subject to renewals of two years. Fellowship awards are made for the academic year; if summer fellowships are issued, they will be for a summer session in which the equivalent of an academic year's foreign language study is completed. The range of awards to centers is from $70,000 to $170,000; fellowships for the academic year are for $7,500 (average rate of assistance).

Application Information Eligible institutions may submit proposals for the funding of centers only, fellowships only, or both when the announcement of a new competition is issued in the Federal Register. Application forms and guidelines for the submission of proposals are available from the Advanced Training and Research Branch.

Deadline(s) Deadline for receipt of applications is early December.

Subject Term(s) Fellowships; Foreign Nationals, Eligibility of; Area Studies; International Studies; Languages, Research and Study

66. Department of Education

Center for International Education, International Studies Branch, Office of Assistant Secretary for Postsecondary Education
Seventh and D Streets, SW, ROB-3, Room 3053
Washington, DC 20202
(202) 732-3292

Summer Seminars Abroad (Fulbright Exchange)

CFDA Program Number 84.018

Program Description This program is designed to increase mutual understanding between the people of the United States and those in other countries by offering qualified American teachers and other educational personnel the opportunity to participate in short-term training seminars abroad.

Eligibility/Limitations Teachers at different levels in varying subject fields, social studies supervisors, and curriculum directors are eligible to apply for seminars abroad. Applicants must have at least a bachelor's degree and be citizens of the United States at the time of application; they must have at least two years of successful full-time teaching experience; and they must be employed currently in the subject field. Evidence of good health and emotional maturity and stability is required.

Fiscal Information Grants to study abroad provide round trip transportation to some countries. Maintenance is provided for seminars in Brazil. No dependents are to accompany grantees participating in seminars.

Application Information Applications should be submitted on forms available on request from the International Studies Branch, Center for International Education. Program regulations and guidelines are detailed in "Opportunities Abroad for Educators" available from the International Education Program.

Deadline(s) Applications must be received by December 30 of the year preceding the grant during an academic year to attend a seminar overseas.

Subject Term(s) Seminars and Conferences

67. Department of Education

Center for International Education, Office of Assistant Secretary for Postsecondary Education
Seventh and D Streets, SW, ROB-3, Room 3928, (Mail Stop 3308)
Washington, DC 20202
(202) 732-3298

Fulbright-Hays Training Grants—Doctoral Dissertation Research Abroad

CFDA Program Number 84.022

Program Description This program is designed to provide opportunities for graduate students to engage in full-time dissertation research abroad in modern foreign language and area studies. The program is designed to develop research knowledge and capability in world areas not widely included in American curricula. Awards will neither be available for projects focusing primarily on Western Europe nor in countries where the United States has no diplomatic representation.

Sample Grants Support for project on the history of a Colombian coffee municipality, 1870-1970 (1985). Support for a project on Congress and the role of ideology in the making of U.S. foreign policy toward Costa Rica and Honduras (1986). Support for a project on Brazilian capital markets since 1964 (1986).

Eligibility/Limitations Institutions of higher education may apply on behalf of doctoral students. Candidates for Doctoral Dissertation Research Fellowships must: (a) be a citizen or national of the United States; (b) be a permanent resident of the United

States; (c) provide evidence from the Immigration and Naturalization Service that he or she is in the United States for other than a temporary purpose with the intention of becoming a citizen or permanent resident; or (d) be a resident of the Trust Territory of the Pacific Islands; (e) be a graduate student in good standing at an institution of higher education who, when the fellowship period begins, has been admitted to candidacy in a doctoral degree program in modern foreign languages and area studies at that institution; (f) plan a teaching career in the United States upon graduation; and (g) possess adequate skills in the language(s) necessary to carry out the dissertation research project.

Fiscal Information Grants generally range from $2,825 to $36,000 with an average award of $15,473. Awards are made for at least six but not more than twelve months.

Application Information Candidates for dissertation research fellowships apply directly to the institutions at which they are enrolled in a Ph.D. program, not to the Department of Education. Students should send requests for application forms to the office of the graduate dean or his or her representatives at the graduate schools at which they are enrolled.

Deadline(s) Generally, applications must be received by the last week in October or the first week in November of the year preceding the year of study.

Subject Term(s) Foreign Nationals, Eligibility of; Doctoral Dissertation Support Abroad; Area Studies; Languages, Research and Study

68. Department of Education

Center for International Education, Office of Assistant Secretary for Postsecondary Education
Seventh and D Streets, SW, ROB-3, Room 3928
Washington, DC 20202
(202) 732-3301

Fulbright-Hays Training Grants—Faculty Research Abroad

CFDA Program Number 84.019

Program Description These grants are designed to help universities and colleges strengthen their programs of international studies through selected opportunities for research and study abroad in foreign languages and area studies; to enable key faculty members to keep current in their specialties; to facilitate the updating of curricula; and to help improve teaching methods and materials. Awards will not be available for projects focusing primarily on Western Europe or in countries where the United States has no diplomatic relations.

Sample Grants Support for a project on transnational integration and industrial development in Brazil (1985). Support for a project on the presidency, bureaucracy, and policy in Mexico (1985). Support for a project on household energy consumption in the middle income oil importing countries of Central America and the Caribbean: a case study of Costa Rica (1986).

Eligibility/Limitations Institutions of higher education may apply on behalf of faculty. Candidates for Faculty Research Abroad awards must: (a) be a citizen or national of the United States; (b) be a permanent resident of the United States; (c) provide evidence from the Immigration and Naturalization Service that he or she is in the United States for other than a temporary purpose with the intention of becoming a citizen or permanent resident or (d) be a resident of the Trust Territory of the Pacific Islands; (e) be employed by an institution of higher education; (f) have been engaged in teaching relevant to his or her foreign language or area of specialization for the two years immediately preceding the date of the award; (g) propose research relevant to his or her modern foreign language or area specialization which cannot be conducted in the United States, or for which a foreign country or region provides superior research facilities and will contribute to the development or improvement of the study of modern foreign languages or area studies in those fields needed for a full understanding of the area, regions, or countries in which the modern foreign languages are commonly used; (h) is not preparing for dissertation research for a Ph.D.; and (i) possess adequate skills in the language or languages necessary to successfully carry out the project.

Fiscal Information Financial provisions include a stipend in lieu of salary; cost of air fare for award recipient only; baggage allowance; project allowance to purchase expendable materials, services, and supplies. The amount of project assistance generally ranges from $7,158 to $52,107, with an average award of $21,500, for projects that last from three to twelve months.

Application Information Faculty members may address requests for general information to the Advanced Training and Research Branch, Department of Education, but should obtain application forms from the appropriate office at their employing institutions. Applications should be submitted directly to the institution, not to the branch.

Deadline(s) Generally, applications must be received by the last week in October or the first week in November of the year preceding the year of study. Exact deadline is announced in the Federal Register.

Subject Term(s) Foreign Nationals, Eligibility of; Faculty Support Abroad; Area Studies; Languages, Research and Study

69. Department of Education

Center for International Education, Office of Assistant Secretary for Postsecondary Education
Seventh and D Streets, SW, ROB-3
Washington, DC 20202
(202) 732-3294

Fulbright-Hays Training Grants—Group Projects Abroad

CFDA Program Number 84.021

Program Description This program provides grants to educational institutions to conduct overseas group projects in research, training, and curriculum development.

Eligibility/Limitations Higher education institutions, private nonprofit educational organizations, state departments of education, and consortia of these eligible parties may apply. Individuals participating in group projects must be: (1) citizens or nationals of the United States, and (2) faculty members in foreign language or area studies, experienced educators responsible for conducting, planning, or supervising programs in foreign language or area studies at the elementary, secondary, or junior college levels, or graduate students or upperclassmen who plan teaching careers in foreign language, area studies, or world affairs.

Fiscal Information Grant funds may be used for international travel; maintenance allowances; purchase of artifacts, books, or other teaching materials; rent for instructional facilities in the country of study; project-related travel in the overseas area; and clerical and professional services in the country of study. Awards range from $20,000 to $225,000, with an average award of $72,777, for projects ranging from six weeks to twelve months.

Application Information Specific guidelines for preparation of proposals as published in the Federal Register are available upon request from the Office of International Programs. The standard application forms as furnished by the federal agency and required by OMB Circular No. A-102 must be used for this program.

Deadline(s) Generally, applications must be received by the first week in November of the year preceding the year of overseas activity.

Subject Term(s) Faculty Support Abroad; Graduate Support Abroad; Area Studies; Languages, Research and Study

70. Department of Education

Center for International Education, Office of Assistant Secretary for Postsecondary Education
Seventh and D Streets, SW, ROB-3
Washington, DC 20202
(202) 732-3283

Undergraduate International Studies and Foreign Language Programs

CFDA Program Number 84.016

Program Description The purpose of these awards is to (1) assist institutions of higher education to plan, develop, and carry out a comprehensive program to strengthen and improve undergraduate instruction in international studies and foreign languages and (2) assist associations and organizations to develop projects that will make an especially significant contribution to strengthening and improving undergraduate instruction in international studies and foreign languages. Projects integrating Master's degree programs with undergraduate training are eligible for support.

Eligibility/Limitations Accredited colleges and universities, and public and nonprofit private agencies and organizations are eligible to apply.

Fiscal Information Funds may be used for instructional costs of international studies programs; administration, lectures, and conferences; library facilities and staff; and for staff travel. Grants range from $10,025 to $76,000, with an average award of $46,269, and are awarded for twelve month periods, subject to renewals of one or two years.

Application Information When funds are available for support of new programs, announcements are issued in the Federal Register. Application forms and guidelines for submission of proposals are available from the Undergraduate International Studies and Foreign Language Program, International Education Program, Office of Postsecondary Education.

Deadline(s) A closing date for receipt of applications generally appears in the Federal Register in September.

Subject Term(s) International Studies; Education, Undergraduate; Foreign Language Programs; Seminars and Conferences; Travel Support

71. Department of Education

International Education Program, Division of Advanced Training and Research
Seventh and D Streets, SW, ROB-3
Washington, DC 20202
(202) 732-3297

International Research and Studies

CFDA Program Number 84.017

Program Description This program supports the conduct of research and study designed to improve and strengthen instruction in modern foreign languages, area studies, and related fields. Funding priorities are established by the Secretary of Education and most recently have focused on the following areas: (1) improved teaching methodologies for modern foreign languages, (2) foreign language proficiency testing, and (3) foreign language acquisition processes. In addition, the secretary has urged the proposal of projects involving the use of computers for improving foreign language instruction and for projects involving the development of instructional materials for uncommonly taught foreign languages.

Eligibility/Limitations The program provides grants to public and private agencies, organizations, institutions, and individuals.

Fiscal Information The length of assistance depends on the project, but is generally twelve to thirty-six months. Project awards range from $6,000 to $100,000, with an average award of $40,000.

Application Information The standard application forms as furnished by the federal agency and required by OMB Circular No. A-102 must be used for this program.

Regulations, guidelines, and literature pertaining to this program may be obtained from the Advanced Training and Research Branch.

Deadline(s) Deadlines are announced in the Federal Register.

Subject Term(s) Individuals, Eligibility of; Area Studies; Languages, Research and Study

72. Department of Education

Office of Assistant Secretary for Postsecondary Education
Seventh and D Streets, SW, ROB-3
Washington, DC 20202
(202) 732-3305

Fulbright-Hays Training Grants—Foreign Curriculum Consultants

CFDA Program Number 84.020

Program Description This program is designed to benefit American education at all levels by helping institutions bring specialists from other countries to the United States to assist in planning and developing curricula in modern foreign language and area studies.

Eligibility/Limitations American institutions eligible to apply for these grants are as follows: state departments of education, local public school systems, institutions of higher education accredited by a nationally recognized accrediting agency or association, private nonprofit educational organizations, or a consortium of these institutions. Foreign educators participating in the consultant program are required to have at least five years of experience as an educator in foreign language and/or area studies and appropriate related experience in curriculum planning and development, preparation of teaching materials, or teacher training; speak English fluently; and have an exchange visitors visa.

Fiscal Information Grant awards range from $16,890 to $21,787 with an average of $20,000. Grants finance costs of international travel to and from the U.S. assignment via Washington, DC, for the consultant only; unaccompanied baggage allowance for a maximum of 300 pounds round trip; cost of health and accident insurance, for consultant only, under a government contracted group insurance policy; 70% of a $1,300 monthly maintenance allowance and an accompanying dependents' allowance. Funds from the grantee institution will provide 30% of the $1,300 monthly maintenance allowance and other project-related expenses for the consultant in the U.S. Length of assistance ranges from eight to ten months.

Application Information The standard application forms as furnished by the federal agency and required by OMB Circular No. A-102 must be used for this program. Proposals for a grant should be submitted to the Application Control Center, Department of Education, Washington, DC, 20202.

Deadline(s) The deadline for receipt of applications is generally the first week in November of the year preceding the year of consultancy.

Additional Information This program was not funded in FY 1987.

Subject Term(s) Consultant Services

73. Department of Education

Office of Assistant Secretary for Postsecondary Education, International Studies Branch
400 Maryland Avenue, SW (Room 3053, ROB-3)
Washington, DC 20202
(202) 732-3291

Business and International Education

CFDA Program Number 84.153

Program Description The program awards grants in support of projects which promote innovation and improvement in business international education curricula and serve the needs of the business community.

Eligibility/Limitations Accredited institutions of higher education are eligible to apply. Applying institutions must enhance international academic programs and provide appropriate services to the business community to expand commercial activities abroad.

Application Information Application forms and guidelines are available from the International Studies Branch. This program is subject to the provisions of OMB Circular No. A-110.

Deadline(s) Eligible institutions may submit proposals for funding of projects when the announcement of a new competition appears in the Federal Register.

Subject Term(s) Education, Business; Business

74. Department of State

Center for the Study of Foreign Affairs, Foreign Service Institute
1400 Key Boulevard
Washington, DC 22209
(703) 235-8830

Diplomat in Residence Program

Program Description From its beginning, the Diplomat in Residence (DIR) program has been based on the assumption that the campuses of America's colleges and universities reflect the nation's changing moods and values, and indeed are frequently the places where these changes are initiated. Senior Foreign Service personnel, who normally spend much of their careers overseas, stand to profit greatly from living in an American academic environment for a reasonably protracted period. This enables them to get to know faculty and students on a level that would not be possible during a brief visit. The presence of an experienced diplomat in the academic world can be a stimulating experience for that institution. The diplomat constitutes a special kind of resource, one that is frequently not otherwise available—a resident reservoir of practical experience in the nuts and bolts of diplomacy, able to draw on twenty or more years of experience in the Foreign Service to explain how our foreign relations are actually conducted.

Eligibility/Limitations Colleges and universities are eligible to apply. Precedence is usually given to institutions outside the Washington, DC, area, to those not having had a DIR before, and to institutions in the process of creating new programs in the area of foreign affairs.

Fiscal Information The Department of State pays the diplomat's salary and travel expenses, while the diplomat pays for his or her housing and other personal expenses. The host institution is expected to provide an office, telephone, other normal office supplies, and access to a secretary. The department also expects the receiving institution to help document the personnel file of the DIR with a record of activities and performance.

Application Information An application form is available for institutions interested in participating in the DIR program. Inquiries may be sent to the Diplomat in Residence Program, at the address listed above. Selection of an institution is done by and through the Foreign Service Institute. The program is not advertised. Knowledge of its existence is normally spread by word of mouth. As a rule, presidents of universities formally request that their institutions be considered. There have been more requests than the department has been able to honor.

Deadline(s) No application deadlines are announced.

Subject Term(s) Diplomacy; Education; Foreign Policy

75. Department of State

Intern Coordinator
P.O. Box 12209, Rosslyn Station
Arlington, VA 22209
(703) 235-9375

Paid Summer Student Internships

Program Description The Department of State and its constituent bureaus and offices in Washington annually sponsor various internships under which a limited number of highly qualified college or university junior, senior, and graduate students have the opportunity to gain first-hand knowledge of American foreign affairs. The purpose of the intern program is to encourage students to consider careers in the field of foreign affairs and to aid the department in the fulfillment of its mission. Interns are assigned to junior-level professional duties which may include such activities as conducting research, preparing reports, drafting replies to correspondence, working in computer science, analyzing international issues, and assisting in cases related to domestic and international law.

Eligibility/Limitations These internships are considered to be an adjunct to an applicant's education and therefore are open only to currently enrolled students who are taking at least one-half of a full-time academic workload, and who will be returning to continue their education immediately upon completion of their internships. An applicant must be a continuing college or university junior, senior, or graduate student. An applicant is considered a junior if he or she has completed all sophomore credits (sixty semester hours or ninety quarter hours) by the time an internship is begun and will be entering the junior year in the semester or quarter immediately following the completion of an internship. Applicants for Legal Intern positions must have at least two years of law school. The applicant must also: be a U.S. citizen, have completed some academic studies relevant to the type of work the applicant wishes to perform in the department, and be able to pass through background investigation.

Fiscal Information The Paid Summer Intern Program begins in May and ends in September each year. Candidates selected for the program will be appointed to positions at the GS-4 through GS-9 grade levels based on their individual qualifications.

Application Information All applicants must submit a completed Standard Form 171, a certified copy of college or university transcripts, two letters of endorsement only from faculty members, and a 500- to 750-word autobiography, which includes a statement of the applicant's objective in seeking an internship and discusses relevant studies and involvement in area issues. All applicants must indicate in their applications the bureaus or offices (maximum of three) in which they are interested. In addition, applicants are requested to submit a completed Office of Personnel Management (OPM) Form 1386 which may be obtained by writing the Intern Coordinator at the address listed above.

Deadline(s) The deadline for receipt of Paid Summer Internship applications is November 1.

Subject Term(s) Internships

76. Department of State

Intern Coordinator
P.O. Box 12209, Rosslyn Station
Arlington, VA 22209
(703) 235-9375

Presidential Management Internships

Program Description The purpose of the Presidential Management Intern program is to attract to the Federal Service outstanding men and women who have a clear interest in, and commitment to, a career in the analysis and management of public policies and programs. Duties assigned to such interns may include management analysis, personnel management, budget analysis, systems analysis, international trade, and grant/policy analysis.

Eligibility/Limitations Applicants must be U.S. citizens who have demonstrated both exceptional academic ability and a commitment to public sector management. Applicants must have received or must expect to receive imminently an appropriate college or university advanced degree.

Fiscal Information All interns are appointed at the GS-9 level regardless of prior work experience or federal employment. Presidential Management Interns receive two-year excepted Civil Service appointments, which may be extended for one additional year. Interns are eligible for promotion to GS-ll after successfully completing one year of service, and to GS-12 after completing the second year.

Application Information Colleges and universities submit nominations for the program based on competitive selection procedures. The Office of Personnel Management (OPM) then determines the eligibility of each nominee, and ultimately 200 finalists are selected each year. Each participating federal agency makes selections from among the finalists in accordance with its staffing needs. Interested applicants should contact their faculty advisors if they wish to apply for the program.

Deadline(s) Those selected must be appointed before October 1 of the calendar year during which they are selected.

Subject Term(s) Internships

77. The William H. Donner Foundation, Inc.

630 Fifth Avenue, Room 2452
New York, NY 10111
(212) 765-1695

Program Grants

Program Description The foundation supports projects in three fields: U.S.-Canadian relations, ocean and inland water resources, and nutrition education. The ocean and inland water resources program has two primary objectives—to strengthen the analysis, debate, and formulation of national ocean policies that guide the management of the nation's coastal zone; and to encourage a critical examination of the institutional arrangements which govern the way surface water and groundwater are managed, especially in areas of the country where water supplies are considered "scarce." The nutrition education program supports nutrition education opportunities available to the medical profession and the public.

Sample Grants To develop a management plan for La Amistad Park, $100,000 to Fundacion de Parques Nacionales, San Jose, Puerto Rico (1984).

Eligibility/Limitations The foundation makes grants to tax-exempt organizations.

Fiscal Information The foundation does not fund construction or renovation of buildings, capital campaigns, annual charitable drives, individuals, research and travel, operating deficits, or loans.

Application Information Applicants should determine first if their project falls into one of the foundation's program fields and within the program criteria. Next, the applicant should send the foundation a letter outlining briefly the proposed project.

Deadline(s) After an initial screening, those proposals that appear most promising are submitted to the board of trustees for consideration at meetings usually held in February, May, and October.

Subject Term(s) Natural Resources, Water

78. Dumbarton Oaks Center for Byzantine Studies

1703 Thirty-second Street, NW
Washington, DC 20007
(202) 342-3232

Fellowships

Program Description Dumbarton Oaks offers fellowships in the areas of Byzantine studies (including related aspects of late Roman, early Christian, western medieval, Slavic, and Near Eastern studies), Pre-Columbian studies, and the history of landscape architecture.

Sample Grants A fellowship in support of study on the cultural revolution in Maya civilization: the Cerros architecture (1982-83).

Eligibility/Limitations Fellowships are available for scholars who at the time of application hold a doctorate (or appropriate final degree) or who have established themselves in their field and wish to pursue their own research. Applications will also be accepted from graduate students who expect to have the Ph.D. in hand prior to taking up residence at Dumbarton Oaks. (Successful applicants will revert to the status and stipend of junior fellows if the degree has not been conferred.)

Fiscal Information Fellowships are normally awarded for the academic year from September 15 until June 1, during which recipients are expected to be in residence at Dumbarton Oaks and to devote full time to their fellowship projects, without undertaking other major activities. Applications are also accepted for either the first (September 15-January 20) or the second (February 1-June 1) term or for shorter periods. The maximum annual stipend (which is prorated for shorter periods) is $9,000, to which is added $1,250 for each dependent who accompanies the recipient and is without other means of support. Fellows also receive: (a) furnished housing or housing allowance adjusted to need; (b) an expense account of $500 for the academic year for approved research expenses (such as typing, since secretarial and other support services are not provided); and (c) lunch in the Fellows Building on weekdays. Fellowships are not renewable, but initial application may be made for two successive years (two annual fellowships and an intervening summer fellowship, part of which may be spent away from Dumbarton Oaks). Applications from former fellows are accepted but reappointments are not normally made (except for fellows previously appointed for less than three months) before five years have elapsed since the tenure of the previous fellowship.

Application Information There is no application form. Application guidelines are available from the assistant director.

Deadline(s) Applications for all awards are due on or before November 15.

Additional Information Inquiries concerning long-term appointments, which are occasionally made for senior scholars, on both a full- and part-time basis, should be addressed to the director of Dumbarton Oaks. Dumbarton Oaks also makes grants to assist with scholarly projects in the three fields with which it is concerned. These can cover expenses such as travel, photography, supplies, and occasionally modest stipends to replace salary otherwise lost. Preference is given to projects for limited periods of time conducted in cooperation with other institutions.

Subject Term(s) Fellowships; Postdoctoral Support; Pre-Columbian Studies; Individuals, Eligibility of

79. Dumbarton Oaks Center for Byzantine Studies

1703 Thirty-second Street, NW
Washington, DC 20007
(202) 342-3232

Junior Fellowships

Program Description Dumbarton Oaks offers fellowships in the areas of Byzantine studies (including related aspects of late Roman, early Christian, western medieval, Slavic, and Near Eastern studies), Pre-Columbian studies, and the history of landscape architecture.

Sample Grants A junior fellowship in support of a study of monuments at Piedras Negras: illustration and analysis of the carvings and texts of an ancient Maya center (1982-83). A junior fellowship in support of a study of ancient Maya writing (1983-84). A junior fellowship in support of a stylistic analysis of Recuay stone sculpture of north highland Peru (1983-84).

Eligibility/Limitations Junior fellowships are available for students who at the time of application have fulfilled all preliminary requirements for a higher degree and are working on a dissertation or final project under the direction of a faculty member at their own university. In exceptional cases applications will be accepted from students before fulfilling preliminary requirements.

Fiscal Information Junior fellowships are normally awarded for the academic year from September 15 until June 1, during which recipients are expected to be in residence at Dumbarton Oaks and to devote full time to their fellowship projects, without undertaking other major activities. Applications are also accepted for either the first (September 15-January 20) or the second (February 1-June 1) term or for shorter periods. The maximum annual stipend (which is prorated for shorter periods) is $6,750, to which is added $1,250 for each dependent who accompanies the recipient and is without other means of support. Junior fellows also receive: (a) furnished housing or housing allowance adjusted to need; (b) an expense account of $500 for the academic year for approved research expenses (such as typing, since secretarial and other support services are not provided); and (c) lunch in the Fellows Building on weekdays. Fellowships are not renewable, but initial application may be made for two successive years (two annual fellowships and an intervening summer fellowship, part of which may be spent away from Dumbarton Oaks). Applications from former fellows are accepted but reappointments are not normally made (except for fellows previously appointed for less than three months) before five years have elapsed since the tenure of the previous fellowship.

Application Information There is no application form. Application guidelines are available from the assistant director.

Deadline(s) Applications for all awards are due on or before November 15.

Subject Term(s) Fellowships; Doctoral Dissertation Support; Pre-Columbian Studies

80. Dumbarton Oaks Center for Byzantine Studies

1703 Thirty-second Street, NW
Washington, DC 20007
(202) 342-3232

Summer Fellowships

Program Description Dumbarton Oaks offers fellowships in the areas of Byzantine studies (including related aspects of late Roman, early Christian, western medieval, Slavic, and Near Eastern studies), Pre-Columbian studies, and the history of landscape architecture.

Sample Grants A summer fellowship in support of a study of Middle Horizon textiles, "Did Tiahuanacans wear Huari shirts?" (1983).

Eligibility/Limitations Scholars (on any level of advancement) who are not incumbent fellows or residents of the Washington area are eligible to apply.

Fiscal Information Summer fellowships are awarded for periods of four to ten weeks between June 15 and September 1. They include housing, lunch in the Fellows Building on weekdays, travel expenses between the fellow's home and Washington (if other support is unavailable) and an allowance of $100 a week. Accommodations for families are not available.

Application Information There is no application form. Application guidelines are available from the assistant director.

Deadline(s) The deadline for submission of applications for all awards is November 15.

Subject Term(s) Fellowships; Pre-Columbian Studies

81. Explorers Club

46 East 70th Street
New York, NY 10021
(212) 628-8383

The Exploration Fund

Program Description The Exploration Fund of the Explorers Club grants funds for various amounts in support of exploration. Grants from the fund may be made to anyone considered qualified by the Exploration Fund Committee. Expeditions aided will be for scientific purposes, in accordance with the club's stated objective, "to increase knowledge of the world."

Eligibility/Limitations The fund assists post-graduate students and independent researchers. Recipients of grants from the fund are expected to provide a report for the *Explorers Journal* of the results of their expedition within a reasonable period of time after completion of the expedition. Mere travel to remote areas or big game hunting is not scientific exploration. The club's name or flag must not be used for any commercial purpose.

Fiscal Information Grants have been made in various amounts, but typically not more than $1,000.

Application Information Application forms are available from the club.

Deadline(s) Applicants should send in applications no later than January 31.

Subject Term(s) Individuals, Eligibility of; Field Research, Support of

82. Exxon Education Foundation

111 West 49th Street
New York, NY 10020-1198
(212) 333-6327

Program Description The mission of the Exxon Education Foundation is to support improvements in the quality of education. Proposals for funding may be submitted under the foundation's Curriculum & Teaching program (higher education portion) and their Management in Higher Education program. Curriculum & Teaching grants support efforts that will lead to improvement in instructional methodology and content as well as the evaluation and dissemination of such efforts. The foundation is especially interested in projects that cross traditional lines between disciplines, professions, and institutions, and in projects that promote interaction between humanists and social scientists and representatives of scientific, technical, and professional fields. Priority is given to projects involving re-examination of basic educational purposes, programs, and requirements and to efforts to introduce consideration of values issues into professional and graduate training. Preference is given also to projects that reflect a concern for the international dimension of education and the need for heightened awareness of global issues. Under the Management of Higher Education program, the foundation is interested in projects that will foster improved allocation and use of resources among and within educational institutions and systems, improved understanding of the economic forces affecting educational services and institutions, and improved institutional response to economic change.

Sample Grants For research on comparison of recent and ancient carbonate sediments of Florida and the Caribbean, $16,500 to the University of Miami, Florida (1985). For their Institute of Latin American Studies, $5,000 to the University of Texas, Austin (1985). For public information and policy research, $7,000 to the Bermuda Biological Station, Bermuda (1985).

Eligibility/Limitations Educational institutions or organizations that are located in the United States, its territories or possessions, and that are qualified as eligible charitable donees by the Internal Revenue Service are eligible for grants. The foundation makes no grants to individuals. Grants are not ordinarily made to: (1) support the adoption of established educational or administrative methods or materials; (2) provide funds for capital purposes (equipment, buildings, or endowment); (3) support institutional scholarship funds; or (4) fund those standard course or curriculum development activities normally covered by institutional budgets. (This does not include special course or curriculum development efforts that would involve unusual expenditures for the institution.) The foundation is less likely to respond to requests for operating funds for an existing college or university program.

Fiscal Information In 1985 Exxon organizations made contributions of $60.5 million in the U.S. and $12.2 million in countries outside the U.S. Contributions in Latin America and the Caribbean totaled over $2.3 million.

Application Information An institution or organization wishing to submit a project for consideration should send the foundation a proposal outline. Guidelines for the proposal outline are available from the foundation.

Deadline(s) There are no specific closing dates for submission of the proposal outline; each will be reviewed as it is received.

Subject Term(s) Education; Social Sciences; Humanities

83. The Film Fund

80 East 11th Street
New York, NY 10003
(212) 475-3720

Grantmaking Program

Program Description These grants support the production and distribution of films, videotapes, and slide shows addressing social issues and social change. The fund is interested in films that reach a broad audience, are widely distributed, respect the intelligence of viewers, and combine intellectual clarity with creative and imaginative filmmaking. Highest priority is given to films on issues around which there are local or national organizing efforts and to films on subjects about which there are few or no films giving coverage.

Eligibility/Limitations The Film Fund supports the work of independent filmmakers. The filmmaker may apply through a tax-exempt organization if the project is affiliated to one. If not, the filmmaker may apply as an individual providing the project has a primarily tax-exempt purpose that is "artistic, educational, or charitable." The Film Fund is particularly interested in receiving proposals from Black, Latin, Asian, Native American, women, and gay and lesbian producers.

Fiscal Information In the fund's last grantmaking cycle, $115,000 was awarded and grant sizes ranged from $1,000 to $10,000.

Application Information Application information and guidelines are available on request.

Deadline(s) Deadline for receipt of applications is February 7.

Subject Term(s) Individuals, Eligibility of; Filmmaking; Social Issues

84. Fogarty International Center

Senior International Fellowship Program
National Institutes of Health, Building 38A, Room 615
Bethesda, MD 20892
(301) 496-6688

Senior International Fellowship Program

CFDA Program Number 13.989

Program Description The Senior International Fellowship Program of the Fogarty International Center provides opportunities for study or research in a foreign institution by biomedical, behavioral, or health scientists who have established themselves in their chosen career in the United States and whose professional stature is well recognized by their peers and nominating institution. The fellowship is intended to enhance the exchange of ideas and information about the latest advances in the health sciences, both basic and clinical; permit U.S. scientists to participate abroad in ongoing study or research in the health sciences; and improve the research, educational, and clinical potential of the U.S. nominating institution. The Fogarty International Center will not accept any proposal that has as the major feature brief observational visits; attendance at scientific meetings; attendance in formal training courses; independent research projects within the host country; or full-time clinical, technical, or teaching services.

Eligibility/Limitations To be eligible an applicant must: hold a doctoral degree in one of the biomedical, behavioral, or health sciences; have five years or more postdoctoral experience; have professional experience in one of the health, biomedical, or behavioral sciences for at least two of the last four years; be nominated by the academic dean or appropriate U.S. institutional official; hold a full-time appointment on the staff of the U.S. nominating institution, which must be a non-federal public or private not-for-profit research, clinical, or educational institution; be invited by a not-for-profit foreign institution; be a citizen or permanent resident of the United States; not be a previous recipient of a Senior International Fellowship; and not be employed by the federal government.

Fiscal Information Senior International Fellowships are awarded for a period of three to twelve months. The fellowship provides: a maximum stipend of $15,000 per year, or $1,250 per month; a foreign living allowance of $15,000 per year or $1,250 per month; round-trip fare, economy class on a U.S. air carrier between the U.S. nominating and foreign host institutions; and, if appropriate, an institutional allowance of up to $2,000 for twelve months or a prorated amount for lesser periods.

Application Information Institution officials requesting application kits or prospective applicants requesting information should direct their inquiries to the program.

Deadline(s) The receipt dates for completed applications are January 10, May 10, and September 10. Applications received too late for one review will be considered for the next review cycle.

Additional Information The Fogarty International Center administers additional research fellowships, postdoctoral research fellowships, and programs for scientific collaboration in the biomedical, behavioral, and health sciences that are funded by foreign governments or foreign institutions. The center is currently inviting applications from U.S. institutions with interest in developing multidisciplinary postdoctoral fellowship programs in AIDS research for U.S. and foreign scientists. Contact the Fogarty International Center for specific program opportunities.

Subject Term(s) Fellowships Abroad; Faculty Support Abroad; Postdoctoral Support Abroad; Foreign Nationals, Eligibility of; Biomedical Sciences; Behavioral Sciences; Health Sciences

85. Folger Shakespeare Library

Fellowship Committee
201 East Capitol Street, SE
Washington, DC 20003
(202) 544-4600

NEH Senior Fellowships and Folger Senior Fellowships

Program Description A limited number of NEH Senior Resident Fellowships and Folger Senior Fellowships are available to senior scholars who are pursuing research projects appropriate to the collections of the Folger. The Folger Library houses one of the world's finest collections of Renaissance books and manuscripts. Its principal collections are in the following areas: Shakespeareana; English, American, and European literature and drama (1500-1800); English, American, and continental history (1500-1715); political, economic, and legal history (1500-1715); history of philosophy, art, music, religion, science and medicine, and *exploration* (1500-1715). Applications are welcome in all areas covered by the Folger collection for work on projects which draw significantly on Folger holdings.

Eligibility/Limitations Senior scholars who have made substantial contributions in their fields of research and who are pursuing research projects appropriate to the collections of the Folger are eligible to apply.

Fiscal Information Fellowships are for a period of six to nine months and carry stipends of $13,750 to $20,625.

Application Information Applicants should submit five copies of both a five hundred-word description of the research project and a curriculum vitae including a list of publications. Applicants should also have three letters of reference sent directly to the fellowship committee.

Deadline(s) The deadline for application is November 1.

Additional Information Short-term postdoctoral fellowships with stipends of up to $1,500 per month for a term of one to three months are available. A completed application will consist of three copies of the applicant's curriculum vitae and three copies of a five hundred-word description of the research project plus three letters of recommendation submitted directly to the fellowship committee. The deadline for application is March 1.

Subject Term(s) Fellowships; Postdoctoral Support; Library Research; Humanities

86. The Ford Foundation

320 East 43rd Street
New York, NY 10017
(212) 573-5000

Program Description The Ford Foundation's domestic and international work is coordinated within six areas of general concern: urban poverty, rural poverty and resources, human rights and social justice, governance and public policy, education and culture, and international affairs. Program activities in individual countries are determined by local needs and priorities, within these subject areas. In much of its work, the foundation attempts to address the needs of people who suffer economic, social, and cultural deprivation. It is also concerned with the consequences of such deprivation for the larger society. Among the groups that receive aid are racial and ethnic minorities, poor women, deprived children, and refugees and migrants. The foundation is also deeply involved in work on a range of domestic and international issues, including the efficacy of government, the quality of education, the vitality of cultural pursuits, world peace and interdependency, and the rights of individuals in free and closed societies.

Sample Grants For a study of the effects of government development programs on indigenous communities in Mexico, $46,900 to Anthropological Center for Documentation of Latin America, Mexico (1986). For publication of human rights conditions in Latin America and analysis of the domestic and international contexts in which abuses occur, a $213,000 two-year supplement to the Washington Office on Latin America (1986). For a program addressing the development-related problems of indigenous peoples in Latin America, Africa, and Southeast Asia, a $300,000 three-year supplement to Cultural Survival, Cambridge, Massachusetts (1986). For a multidisciplinary, comparative study of the African diaspora in Latin America and the Caribbean, $315,000 over three years to Michigan State University (1986). For training of mid-career U.S. and Mexican journalists on the reporting of U.S.-Latin American relations, $80,000 to the University of Southern California (1986).

Eligibility/Limitations Activities supported by foundation grants must be charitable, educational, or scientific as defined under the appropriate provisions of the U.S. Internal Revenue Code and Treasury Regulations.

Fiscal Information The grants budget for the biennium 1984-85 was $258 million. As before, approximately 35% of the foundation's program budget is allocated for work in developing countries. Grants are not normally made for routine operating costs of institutions; programs for which substantial support from government or other sources is readily available; religious activities as such; or, except in rare cases, the construction or maintenance of buildings. Nor does the foundation conduct programs of undergraduate scholarship or make grants for purely personal or local needs. Support for graduate fellowships is generally funneled through grants to universities and other organizations, which are responsible for the selection of recipients.

Application Information Before any detailed formal application is made, a brief letter of inquiry is advisable in order to determine whether the foundation's present interests and funds permit consideration of the proposal.

Deadline(s) Applications are considered throughout the year.

Additional Information Most of the foundation's grant funds are given to organizations. Although the foundation also makes grants to individuals, such grants are few in number relative to demand and limited to research, training, and other activities related to the foundation's program interests.

Subject Term(s) Individuals, Eligibility of; Cultural Affairs, Support of; Poverty; Rural Poverty; Education; International Affairs; Government; International Security; Peace; Child Development; Refugees; Migrants; Social Justice; Human Rights

87. Foreign Policy Research Institute

3508 Market Street, Suite 350
Philadelphia, PA 19104
(215) 382-0685

Fellowship Program

Program Description The institute is an independent, nonprofit organization devoted to the study of the political, economic, social, and military dimensions of contemporary international developments. The institute's major activities include a broad-based research program on critical issues affecting U.S. interests abroad; an internationally renowned publications program; seminars, conferences, and workshops for business, government, and academic leaders; and a fellowship program designed to provide training in foreign policy analysis to promising scholars. The FPRI takes special pride in its fellowship program, which provides training in policy analysis to aspiring scholars and often serves as a springboard to active participation in the policymaking process itself. The training program relates academic skills to the theoretical and operational aspects of U.S. foreign policy and offers exposure to divers disciplines.

Fiscal Information FPRI offers stipends to its fellows, normally to defray tuition costs and dissertation fees and to enable the fellows to conduct research in cooperation with resident staff.

Application Information Application information is available upon request.

Deadline(s) Contact the institute for deadlines.

Additional Information The staff of the institute encompasses a variety of geographic areas of specialization, including Central America.

Subject Term(s) Fellowships; Doctoral Dissertation Support; Seminars and Conferences; International Studies; Foreign Policy Studies; Central America

88. Foreign Policy Research Institute

3508 Market Street, Suite 350
Philadelphia, PA 19104
(215) 382-0685

Thornton D. Hooper Fellowship in International Security Affairs

Program Description The Thornton D. Hooper Fellowship Competition seeks to promote original research on issues affecting U.S. national security. It is designed to attract the participation of international relations specialists, political scientists, economists, historians, and members of related disciplines.

Eligibility/Limitations Fellows must have received or be about to receive a doctoral degree or have equivalent experience.

Fiscal Information The applicant who is selected will spend a year in residence at the Foreign Policy Research Institute and will receive a stipend commensurate with his or her experience.

Application Information Applicants should submit copies of three publications (or publications-in-progress), a curriculum vitae, three letters of recommendation and a ten-page, double-spaced research proposal on some aspect of international security affairs.

Deadline(s) Application deadline is February 16.

Subject Term(s) Fellowships; International Security; Security Studies

89. Foundation for Field Research

787 South Grade Road
Alpine, CA 92001-0380
(619) 445-9264

Grants

Program Description The Foundation for Field Research supports basic research that can be appropriately funded and assisted by amateur teams in the field. Proposals will be considered for projects in the natural sciences, social sciences, and other recognized academic disciplines.

Sample Grants 1987 projects supported include: marine biology research on sea lions in Bahia de Los Angeles, Mexico; a study of primate behavior in the jungle area of the Nicoya Peninsula, Costa Rica; collecting moths and recording the Carnival on Trinidad in the Caribbean; conducting an inventory of Belize birds; an inventory of all animals and plants in a special preserve in southeastern Mexico.

Eligibility/Limitations Ongoing projects are welcomed, although it should be recognized that due to the limitations imposed by using volunteer assistants, only a portion of a major research project can generally be supported. The foundation will accept proposals for research anywhere in the United States or world, as long as the location is not a war zone or a danger area for travelers.

Fiscal Information The foundation will fund: travel for the researcher; food and lodging during the expedition; transportation as needed during the expedition; capital equipment; expendable field supplies; field labor (the contributing volunteer); and applicable grants-in-aid. The foundation will not fund: overhead to any individual or institution; payment of salaries; use of hotels; costs to publish expedition results; or projects that are unable to use volunteers.

Application Information Submission of an application according to the "Guidelines for Field Research Funding" is required to obtain foundation support. Foundation staff are always willing to work with researchers in planning and submitting their applications. Feel free to call or write for assistance.

Deadline(s) All project details must be received at the office by February 15, May 15, August 15, or November 15 for projects to enter the field by March 1, June 1, September 1, or December 1 of the following year.

Additional Information High school or university students or teachers who have demonstrated an active interest in one of the disciplines the foundation supports may apply for a limited number of scholarships available to support expedition participation. Contact the foundation for a scholarship form.

Subject Term(s) Field Research, Support of; Natural Sciences; Social Sciences; Graduate Support

90. General Service Foundation

P.O. Box 4012
Boulder, CO 80306
(303) 447-9541

Program Description The foundation has selected as its areas of concern education, international peace, population, and resources. Because the foundation's areas of concern are broad, the board has determined guidelines within each area. All applicants are urged to submit only applications coming within the following guidelines. The foundation supports education programs in both public and private universities for increasing research and teaching on the interrelationship of population, resources, and environment, particularly as applied in developing countries. The foundation is interested in making contributions only in the non-military aspects of international peace, particularly as follows: research and education on U.S. international relations that would contribute to international peace; international working groups concerned with increasing understanding and cooperation; policy and program analysis leading to development of alternatives to war; and research and education on the relationships between economic, environmental, and political development and international peace. In the area of population, the primary interest is in making contributions to organizations, tax-exempt under U.S. laws, for population work overseas, preferably in Latin America. Preferred applications include: models for better distribution of family planning information and services, particularly in rural and urban areas; models for introduction of additional services, particularly abortion and sterilization; models for maternal and child health, family planning, and food and economic development; and social research leading to policy and program formation. Other population interests in the U.S. include issues relating to teenage pregnancy, sexuality education, abortion, contraceptive development, and policy and program analysis. In the area of resources, the foundation is interested in improving the use, management, and quality of water in the United States, particularly west of the Mississippi River, and developing food, water, fuel, forage, forests, and/or fertilization on a sustainable basis in developing countries, and particularly tied in with family planning education and services.

Sample Grants In support of a degree program in development, interdisciplinary seminars on development, and an internship for students with an emphasis on organization in one of the following countries, Colombia, Jamaica, Senegal, Kenya, India, and an Arabic country, $35,000 to Minnesota Studies in International Development, University of Minnesota (1985). In support of a program seeking to inform the American public about covert operations and war in Nicaragua, $22,000 to the Center for National Security Studies, a joint program of the ACLU and The Fund for Peace (1985). In support of the initiation of adolescent services in family planning through the training of family nurses in the Republic of Belize, $19,000 to Planned Parenthood of New York City, Inc. and the Margaret Sanger Center (1985). For a project to bring reforestation technology to Latin American villages, $16,500 to the Institute of Cultural Affairs (1985). For the preparation of a master plan for the Pacaya-Samiria National Reserve of Peru, $22,000 to the World Wildlife Fund-U.S. (1985).

Eligibility/Limitations Contributions are made to organizations tax-exempt under U.S. laws. The foundation prefers projects and/or programs which give promise of significant contribution and which are new, innovative, demonstrational, and/or research in nature.

Fiscal Information In general, contributions are not made to operating budgets, nor to annual campaigns of established organizations. Nor does the foundation ordinarily contribute to capital (physical plant, equipment, endowment), to individuals, nor for relief.

Application Information Contribution policies, guidelines, and application procedures are available from the foundation upon request. There are no specific application forms. Prospective applicants may wish to discuss their particular proposal if they are uncertain as to whether it comes within approved contribution policy and guidelines. If so, please call the foundation.

Deadline(s) Contact the foundation for deadlines.

Additional Information The foundation will make occasional contributions to exceptional proposals in the four areas but not coming strictly within the approved guidelines; and, in addition, to specifically approved projects or programs proposed by directors from time to time.

Subject Term(s) Education; Peace; Population Control; International Relations; Family Planning; Health, Mothers and Children; Developing Countries; Natural Resources; Environment; Population

91. The Geological Society of America

P.O. Box 9140
Boulder, CO 80301
(303) 447-2020

Research Grants

Program Description The primary role of the research grant program is to provide partial support of master's or doctoral thesis research for graduate students at universities in the United States, Canada, Mexico, and Central America. Grants are intended as an aid in a research project, not to sustain the entire cost.

Eligibility/Limitations Members and nonmembers of the society are eligible. Grants are awarded only to individuals. Institutions, societies, universities, and so on are not eligible for grants. Only under the most unusual circumstances will postdoctoral and faculty research be supported. Undergraduate students are not eligible. Candidates for advanced degrees must present their projects under their own names.

Fiscal Information The GSA awarded $146,000 in grants in 1984. The awards went to 168 students doing research for advanced degrees. The average amount awarded was $871. The largest award was $1,500, but there is no predetermined maximum amount. There is no policy favoring projects to be completed in one year over those that may extend for several years. The committee will usually deny grants to cover one year of research if the applicants imply in any way that grants for continuing research will be expected. It will seriously consider such projects, however, if the applicants present their own comprehensive plans showing schedules of their time and budgetary requirements for each year of a two- or three-year extension of the program. The applicant should be prepared to reapply for a grant for research that extends beyond one year and must furnish evidence of progress accomplished during the first year.

Application Information Confidential evaluations from two faculty members are required from master's and doctoral candidates and must accompany applications submitted. Applications and appraisal forms are available from the society.

Deadline(s) Applications must be postmarked by February 15.

Subject Term(s) Graduate Support; Doctoral Dissertation Support; Foreign Nationals, Eligibility of; Geology

92. The Getty Center for the History of Art and the Humanities

401 Wilshire Boulevard, Suite 400
Santa Monica, CA 90401-1455
(213) 458-9811

Dissertation Residencies

Program Description The Getty Center for the History of Art and the Humanities is an institution dedicated to research in the history of art broadly conceived as an integral part of human history and society. It brings together art historians and scholars in the social sciences and the humanities to foster critical reexamination of the meaning of art in cultures past and present. Students are chosen according to qualifications and current departmental and scholarly projects. Students spend the residency at the Getty Center, pursuing their own research on topics in which the center's resources are particularly strong.

Eligibility/Limitations Eligible applicants are Ph.D. candidates in the humanities or social sciences working on dissertations in the arts or cultural history of Western Europe, or recent recipients rewriting their dissertations for publication.

Fiscal Information The residency amounts to $15,000 for a full-year period that may begin between July 1 and September 1. Residencies are not renewable.

Application Information Applications must include: a description of the topic of research, including a timetable for thesis completion, a synopsis, and a sample chapter; an official statement that course work is completed and the qualifying exams have been passed; a copy of a current transcript; a resume, including description of related studies, projects, languages, work experience, and travel; and the names of three references (one of whom is to be outside the area of academic specialization).

Deadline(s) Applications must be postmarked no later than February 15.

Subject Term(s) Doctoral Dissertation Support; Doctoral Dissertation Revision, Support of; Art History; Social Sciences; Humanities

93. The Getty Center for the History of Art and the Humanities

401 Wilshire Boulevard, Suite 400
Santa Monica, CA 90401-1455
(213) 458-9811

Internships: MA Students

Program Description The Getty Center for the History of Art and the Humanities is an institution dedicated to research in the history of art broadly conceived as an integral part of human history and society. It brings together art historians and scholars in the social sciences and the humanities to foster critical reexamination of the meaning of art in cultures past and present. Students are chosen according to qualifications and current departmental and scholarly projects. The purpose of the internship program is to provide training and educational experiences for persons planning a career of scholarship or administration in the arts or humanities. Interns will be assigned to one of the center's departments: the Library Photo Archive, the Archives, the History of Art and Administration, or Visiting Scholars.

Eligibility/Limitations Applicants must be MA candidates currently enrolled in a university program.

Fiscal Information Internships are for nine months, starting in September, and carry a stipend of $23,000. They are not renewable.

Application Information Applications should include a letter stating reasons for interest in the program; a copy of a current transcript; a resume including a description of applicable course work, languages, work experience, and travel; and the names of three references (one of whom is to be outside the area of academic specialization).

Deadline(s) Applications must be postmarked no later than February 15.

Subject Term(s) Graduate Support; Internships; Art History; Social Sciences; Humanities

94. The J. Paul Getty Trust

1875 Century Park East, Suite 2300
Los Angeles, CA 90067
(213) 277-9188

Conservation: Conservation of Major Works of Art

Program Description The J. Paul Getty Trust is a private operating foundation with programs in the visual arts and related areas of the humanities. The purpose of the grant program is to make possible work of vital importance to the visual arts and related areas of the humanities for which resources are limited. It supports projects throughout the world involving research in the history of art and the humanities and advancement of the understanding of art, and conservation. In order to increase the level and quality of art conservation around the world, the trust supports the treatment of major works of art. Proposals will be evaluated on the basis of the aesthetic significance of the works of art, the appropriateness of the conservation plan, the qualifications of the conservator, and the institution's long-range plans for the conservation of its collection.

Eligibility/Limitations Any institution with an ongoing exhibition program, open to the public on a regular basis, may apply for a matching grant for conservation of works of art in the permanent collection. Proposals are accepted from institutions but not from individuals.

Fiscal Information While grants may vary based on the requirements of the particular project, they do not usually exceed $50,000. These grants, which require a one-to-one match, are available for up to three years in order to bring outside conservation experts in-house or to fund work by regional laboratories or by qualified conservators.

Application Information Before any proposal is developed, a preliminary letter (not more than two pages) describing the project and an outline of its general financial requirements should be submitted. The trust will respond with an initial determination as to whether or not a full proposal should be submitted.

Deadline(s) There are no specific deadlines.

Additional Information Treatment reports and photographic documentation submitted with the final report on the project will become part of the Getty Conservation Institute's Documentation Program Archive.

Subject Term(s) Art History; Humanities; Art Conservation; Museums

95. The J. Paul Getty Trust

1875 Century Park East, Suite 2300
Los Angeles, CA 90067
(213) 277-9188

Conservation: Libraries

Program Description The J. Paul Getty Trust is a private operating foundation with programs in the visual arts and related areas of the humanities. The purpose of the grant program is to make possible work of vital importance to the visual arts and related areas of the humanities for which resources are limited. It supports projects throughout the world involving research in the history of art and the humanities and advancement of the understanding of art, and conservation. In order to increase the level and quality of art conservation around the world, the trust supports specialized conservation libraries. Grants may support library acquisitions and related staff and services and projects to organize and make accessible existing conservation archives.

Eligibility/Limitations Only an institution engaged in training activity, which has an existing conservation library systematically collected and organized to provide a research service to conservators, is eligible for support.

Fiscal Information While grants may vary based on the requirements of the particular project, they do not usually exceed $50,000.

Application Information Before any proposal is developed, a preliminary letter (not more than two pages) describing the project and an outline of its general financial requirements should be submitted. The trust will respond with an initial determination as to whether or not a full proposal should be submitted.

Deadline(s) There are no specific deadlines.

Subject Term(s) Art Conservation; Library Support; Humanities; Art History

96. The J. Paul Getty Trust

1875 Century Park East, Suite 2300
Los Angeles, CA 90067
(213) 277-9188

Conservation: Publications

Program Description The J. Paul Getty Trust is a private operating foundation with programs in the visual arts and related areas of the humanities. The purpose of the grant program is to make possible work of vital importance to the visual arts and related areas of the humanities for which resources are limited. It supports projects throughout the world involving research in the history of art and the humanities and advancement of the understanding of art, and conservation. In order to increase the level and quality of art conservation activities around the world, the trust supports the publication of manuscripts valuable to the conservation profession.

Eligibility/Limitations Support is available for publications that further knowledge of conservation science and practice. Eligible projects include: book-length manuscripts, collected papers from symposia, special issues of journals, and enhancements of journal articles. Only completed manuscripts already accepted for publication will be considered. Exceptions to this policy are special issues of journals, which need not be completed prior to submission.

Application Information Further details about publication grants are explained in special guidelines available from the trust. For an application form and specific guidelines, contact the Publication Grants Program of the trust.

Deadline(s) There are no specific deadlines.

Subject Term(s) Art Conservation; Publication Support; Humanities; Art History

97. The J. Paul Getty Trust

1875 Century Park East, Suite 2300
Los Angeles, CA 90067
(213) 277-9188

Conservation: Surveys of the Conservation Needs of Art Museums

Program Description The J. Paul Getty Trust is a private operating foundation with programs in the visual arts and related areas of the humanities. The purpose of the grant program is to make possible work of vital importance to the visual arts and related areas of the humanities for which resources are limited. It supports projects throughout the world involving research in the history of art and the humanities and advancement of the understanding of art, and conservation. In order to increase the level and quality of art conservation activities around the world, the trust supports surveys to determine the conservation needs of art museum collections. Support is available for surveys to analyze the conservation requirements of art collections in a single institution or group of institutions.

Eligibility/Limitations Single institutions or groups of institutions are eligible to apply.

Fiscal Information While grants vary based on the requirements, they do not usually exceed $50,000. They may extend over multi-year periods.

Application Information Applications must include the qualifications of the conservator who will undertake the survey, a description of the collection, and a plan for future implementation of the survey results. Before any proposal is developed, a preliminary letter (not more than two pages) describing the project and an outline of its general financial requirements should be submitted. The trust will respond with an initial determination as to whether or not a full proposal should be submitted.

Deadline(s) There are no specific deadlines.

Subject Term(s) Art Conservation; Museums; Humanities; Art History

98. The J. Paul Getty Trust

1875 Century Park East, Suite 2300
Los Angeles, CA 90067
(213) 277-9188

Conservation: Training

Program Description The J. Paul Getty Trust is a private operating foundation with programs in the visual arts and related areas of the humanities. The purpose of the grant program is to make possible work of vital importance to the visual arts and related areas of the humanities for which resources are limited. It supports projects throughout the world involving research in the history of art and the humanities and advancement of the understanding of art, and conservation. In order to increase the level and quality of art conservation activities around the world, the trust supports the training of young conservators.

Eligibility/Limitations Training programs that integrate art history, science, and conservation practice are eligible for consideration. Museums and regional conservation centers are also eligible to apply for support of internships. Applications for support of a specific individual may be submitted only by a sponsoring institution.

Fiscal Information While grants vary based on the requirements of the particular project, they do not usually exceed $50,000 a year. Proposals may include support for visiting faculty, acquisition of resource materials, and first- and second-year internships.

Application Information Before any proposal is developed, a preliminary letter (not more than two pages) describing the project and an outline of its general financial requirements should be submitted. The trust will respond with an initial determination as to whether or not a full proposal should be submitted.

Deadline(s) There are no specific deadlines.

Subject Term(s) Art Conservation; Humanities; Conservation Training, Museums; Internships, Art Conservation; Art History; Museums

99. The J. Paul Getty Trust

1875 Century Park East, Suite 2300
Los Angeles, CA 90067
(213) 277-9188

Documentation and Interpretation of Art Museum Collections: Cataloguing Projects

Program Description The J. Paul Getty Trust is a private operating foundation with programs in the visual arts and related areas of the humanities. The purpose of the grant program is to make possible work of vital importance to the visual arts and related areas of the humanities for which resources are limited. It supports projects throughout the world involving research in the history of art and the humanities and advancement of the understanding of art, and conservation. In order to assist museums to develop their collections as both scholarly and educational resources, the trust supports research projects to catalogue works of art in permanent collections. Proposals will be evaluated on the basis of the significance of the collection, the qualifications of the scholars/curators involved, a realistic plan for the implementation of the project, and the way in which the results of the research will be made available to the broader scholarly community. The institution's demonstrated commitment to the cataloguing of its collection will also be a consideration.

Eligibility/Limitations Cataloguing projects that result in full documentation of an art collection are eligible for consideration. Inventories, checklists, or summary catalogues are not eligible.

Fiscal Information While grants vary based on the requirements of the particular project, they do not usually exceed $50,000 a year. Awards may be made for up to two years for support for a visiting scholar/curator to work on a particular aspect of a museum's collection and funds for a substitute position so that staff members may undertake catalogue research. Related costs may be included in the grant request. Cataloguing grants are not intended to include publication of the results. However, a finished manuscript may be eligible for support under the publication grant category of the trust's grant programs.

Application Information Before any proposal is developed, a preliminary letter (not more than two pages) describing the project and an outline of its general financial requirements should be submitted. The trust will respond with an initial determination as to whether or not a full proposal should be submitted.

Deadline(s) There are no specific deadlines.

Subject Term(s) Museums; Collections, Cataloguing; Humanities

100. The J. Paul Getty Trust

1875 Century Park East, Suite 2300
Los Angeles, CA 90067
(213) 277-9188

Documentation and Interpretation of Art Museum Collections: Education Programs

Program Description The J. Paul Getty Trust is a private operating foundation with programs in the visual arts and related areas of the humanities. The purpose of the grant program is to make possible work of vital importance to the visual arts and related areas of the humanities for which resources are limited. It supports projects throughout the world involving research in the history of art and the humanities and advancement of the understanding of art, and conservation. In order to assist museums to develop their collections as both scholarly and educational resources, the trust supports education projects that make art works more understandable to the general public. Examples of eligible projects are explanatory labels, self-guides, handbooks, on-site audio-visual programs, and other projects that create a permanent resource for the institution. Proposals will be evaluated on the basis of the content of the program, the plan for its implementation, its potential as a model for other institutions, and the institution's long-term financial commitment to sustain a serious level of educational activity.

Eligibility/Limitations The trust will consider support for programs that enhance the general public's appreciation and understanding of permanent collections. Projects should involve curators as well as educators. Outside experts may be brought in for extended periods of time.

Fiscal Information While grants vary based on the requirements of the particular project, they do not usually exceed $50,000 a year. Awards may be made for up to three years. Lectures, symposia, and workshops are not eligible for support.

Application Information Before any proposal is developed, a preliminary letter (not more than two pages) describing the project and an outline of its general financial requirements should be submitted. The trust will respond with an initial determination as to whether or not a full proposal should be submitted.

Deadline(s) There are no specific deadlines.

Subject Term(s) Museums, Education; Museums; Humanities; Art History

101. The J. Paul Getty Trust

1875 Century Park East, Suite 2300
Los Angeles, CA 90067
(213) 277-9188

Scholarship in the History of Art and the Humanities: Archival Projects

Program Description The J. Paul Getty Trust is a private operating foundation with programs in the visual arts and related areas of the humanities. The purpose of the grant program is to make possible work of vital importance to the visual arts and related areas of the humanities for which resources are limited. It supports projects throughout the world involving research in the history of art and the humanities and advancement of the understanding of art, and conservation. In order to develop the relationship between art history and other disciplines of the humanities, and to further the vitality of advanced research in these areas, the trust supports projects to organize selected archival holdings of major importance to the field of art history. Proposals will be evaluated on the basis of the importance of the materials, the arrangement and catalogue procedures proposed, the qualifications of the project staff, and the commitment of the institution to maintain the collection and make it readily accessible to the scholarly community.

Eligibility/Limitations Only a nonprofit repository that owns the materials may apply. Also eligible for consideration are cooperative proposals from institutions or associations for projects designed to prepare and make accessible registers or archival holdings in a number of repositories.

Fiscal Information While grants vary based on the requirements of the particular project, they do not usually exceed $50,000 a year. Grants may be made for a maximum of three years and are nonrenewable. Requests may include support for a project archivist or archivists, for specialized scholarly consultants to analyze and describe the materials, and for other related project expenses. The institution seeking the grant will be expected to provide facilities and support services as required.

Application Information Before any proposal is developed, a preliminary letter (not more than two pages) describing the project and an outline of its general financial requirements should be submitted. The trust will respond with an initial determination as to whether or not a full proposal should be submitted.

Deadline(s) There are no specific deadlines.

Subject Term(s) Art History; Archival Support; Humanities

102. The J. Paul Getty Trust

1875 Century Park East, Suite 2300
Los Angeles, CA 90067
(213) 277-9188

Scholarship in the History of Art and the Humanities: Corpora and Other Art Historical Reference Tools

Program Description The J. Paul Getty Trust is a private operating foundation with programs in the visual arts and related areas of the humanities. The purpose of the grant program is to make possible work of vital importance to the visual arts and related areas of the humanities for which resources are limited. It supports projects throughout the world involving research in the history of art and the humanities and advancement of the understanding of art, and conservation. In order to develop the relationship between art history and other disciplines of the humanities, and to further the vitality of advanced research in these areas, the trust supports international projects for the creation of research tools in the field of art history. Projects must be international multi-institutional research efforts that will result in the creation of a corpus of information or a major reference tool useful to a large segment of the art historical community. Proposals will be evaluated on the basis of the scope, feasibility, and organization of the project; its importance to the field in general; and the method proposed for dissemination of information.

Eligibility/Limitations Applications may be made by a sponsoring institution or an international committee if it has registered nonprofit status. Research projects concerned with a single artist, or projects undertaken by a single individual or institution, are not eligible.

Fiscal Information While grants vary based on the requirements of the particular project, they do not usually exceed $50,000 a year. They may extend over multi-year periods.

Application Information Before any proposal is developed, a preliminary letter (not more than two pages) describing the project and an outline of its general financial requirements should be submitted. The trust will respond with an initial determination as to whether or not a full proposal should be submitted.

Deadline(s) There are no specific deadlines.

Subject Term(s) Art History; Reference Materials, Production of; Humanities

103. The J. Paul Getty Trust

1875 Century Park East, Suite 2300
Los Angeles, CA 90067
(213) 277-9188

Scholarship in the History of Art and the Humanities: Library and Photo Archive Projects at Centers for Advanced Research in the History of Art

Program Description The J. Paul Getty Trust is a private operating foundation with programs in the visual arts and related areas of the humanities. The purpose of the grant program is to make possible work of vital importance to the visual arts and related areas of the humanities for which resources are limited. It supports projects throughout the world involving research in the history of art and the humanities and advancement of the understanding of art, and conservation. In order to develop the relationship between art history and other disciplines of the humanities, and to further the vitality of advanced research in these areas, the trust supports library and photo archive projects at centers for advanced research in the history of art and the humanities. Grants may be made for library acquisitions and related staff services and for projects to organize and make accessible existing significant photographic archives.

Eligibility/Limitations Only an independent research center, which has its own extensive library holdings in the history of art and architecture and which provides services for scholars internationally, is eligible for support. University and museum libraries do not qualify.

Fiscal Information While grants vary based on the requirements of the particular project, they do not usually exceed $50,000 a year. They may extend for up to four years.

Application Information Before any proposal is developed, a preliminary letter (not more than two pages) describing the project and an outline of its general financial requirements should be submitted. The trust will respond with an initial determination as to whether or not a full proposal should be submitted.

Deadline(s) There are no specific deadlines.

Subject Term(s) Art History; Reference Materials, Production of; Archival Support; Library Support; Humanities

104. The J. Paul Getty Trust

1875 Century Park East, Suite 2300
Los Angeles, CA 90067
(213) 277-9188

Scholarship in the History of Art and the Humanities: Postdoctoral Fellowships

Program Description The Getty Postdoctoral Fellowships are designed to strengthen the history of the visual arts of all periods and areas by supporting the work of outstanding young scholars in the field considered broadly to include other humanistic studies that draw substantially on the materials, methods, and/or findings of art history.

Sample Grants Fellowship award to support a study "The Photographer and the Indian: A Historical Analysis of Photographic Representation in the Andes" (1986). Fellowship award to support a study "The Nunnery Quadrangle at Uxmal" (1986).

Eligibility/Limitations Scholars who have received their doctorates within the six years prior to applying for a grant and who demonstrate an unusual potential to contribute to knowledge in the history of art and the humanities are eligible to apply. Candidates may apply for one fellowship each year.

Fiscal Information All awards normally will provide a $21,000 stipend for the fellow for twelve months and a subvention of up to $4,000 to be allocated to the institution or institutions at which the fellow is based during the year of the award.

Application Information Inquiries should be sent to Getty Postdoctoral Fellowships in the History of Art and the Humanities at the address listed above.

Deadline(s) The last date completed applications will be accepted is January 10.

Subject Term(s) Fellowships; Postdoctoral Support; Humanities; Art History; Individuals, Eligibility of

105. The J. Paul Getty Trust

1875 Century Park East, Suite 2300
Los Angeles, CA 90067
(213) 277-9188

Scholarship in the History of Art and the Humanities: Publications

Program Description The J. Paul Getty Trust is a private operating foundation with programs in the visual arts and related areas of the humanities. The purpose of the grant program is to make possible work of vital importance to the visual arts and related areas of the humanities for which resources are limited. It supports projects throughout the world involving research in the history of art and the humanities and advancement of the understanding of art, and conservation. In order to develop the relationship between art history and other disciplines of the humanities, and to further the vitality of advanced research in these areas, the trust supports scholarly publications that disseminate the results of art historical research. Support is available for the publication of a broad range of manuscripts that make an important contribution to research and scholarship in the history of art.

Eligibility/Limitations Eligible projects include the following: manuscripts already accepted for publication that could be substantially improved in quality or reduced in price for wider distribution; scholarly catalogues of major museum collections (support must be requested on a matching basis); special exhibition catalogues that contain new scholarly contributions; completed excavation reports; collected papers from symposia; special issues of journals; and enhancements of journal articles. In addition, support is available on a highly selective basis (and for no more than three years) for start-up costs for new scholarly journals where there is a demonstrated need that is not met by existing publications. Only completed manuscripts already accepted for publication will be considered. Exceptions to this policy are special exhibition catalogues and special issues of journals, which need not be completed prior to submission. Manuscripts from a foreign publisher and/or manuscripts written in a foreign language are eligible for consideration.

Fiscal Information While grants vary based on the requirements of the particular project, they do not usually exceed $50,000 a year. They may extend over multi-year periods.

Application Information Applications should normally be submitted by the publisher. Further details about publication grants are explained in special guidelines available from the trust.

Deadline(s) There are no specific deadlines.

Subject Term(s) Publication Support; Art History; Humanities

106. Global Perspectives in Education, Inc.

218 East 18th Street
New York, NY 10003
(212) 674-4167

Project Grants

Program Description Project grants are entitled Youth Exchange Community Network Grants. These grants provide seed money for projects which show cooperation among community groups and which serve a useful purpose in (1) stimulating local interest in and support for international youth exchange and programs, (2) promoting a more favorable climate for exchanges, and (3) increasing international awareness in the community. Eligible projects might include, but are not restricted to, the following: directories of local, state, or regional youth exchange programs; resource lists of international projects which can be used to enhance youth exchange programs; orientation programs for host families; re-entry programs for returned exchange students; traveling exhibits on international youth exchange; or projects that seek to strengthen support systems for youth exchange where programs are scarce or difficult to manage.

Eligibility/Limitations Grants will be awarded to develop cooperation at the local level among two or more of the following types of groups: exchange organizations, education and government agencies, schools, civic groups, and other community groups. A direct benefit to youth exchange must be shown in the project.

Fiscal Information Grants of up to $2,000 will be awarded. Grants will not fund international travel, scholarships, language training, purchase of equipment, overhead expenditures, or administrative costs in excess of $500.

Application Information Application forms and program guidelines are available upon request.

Deadline(s) The deadlines for receipt of applications are June 15 and October 15.

Additional Information Although youth is commonly understood to mean persons between the ages of fifteen and twenty-five, projects involving all other age groups will be considered.

Subject Term(s) Exchanges, Youth

107. Graham Foundation

4 West Burton Place
Chicago, IL 60610
(312) 787-4071

Program Description It is the general policy of the Graham Foundation to limit its activities to matters relating to contemporary architecture, planning, and the study of urban problems.

Sample Grants Publication support for *Two Brazilian Capitals: Architecture and Urbanism in Rio de Janeiro and Brazilia* (1985).

Eligibility/Limitations Individuals and institutions are eligible to apply. In the case of individuals, consideration is given to those demonstrating mature creative talents with specific project objectives.

Application Information The foundation does not require submittal of special application forms. Procedures for submittal are available upon request from the foundation.

Deadline(s) The foundation does not have a specific funding schedule.

Subject Term(s) Individuals, Eligibility of; Architecture

108. The Harry Frank Guggenheim Foundation

527 Madison Avenue
New York, NY 10022-4301
(212) 644-4909

The Harry Frank Guggenheim Career Development Awards

Program Description The Harry Frank Guggenheim Foundation sponsors a program of research to advance the understanding of human social problems related to dominance, aggression, and violence. The Career Development Awards are designed to recognize an outstanding young scientist or academic leader in studies pertinent to the foundation's interests.

Eligibility/Limitations Candidates may be from any country. They must be at least three years beyond receipt of the doctorate and not yet forty years of age by the date on which funding is scheduled to begin. Candidates should have demonstrated outstanding capability and exceptional promise for significant future achievement. In addition, candidates should be investigators with substantial potential to contribute to the foundation's long-term aim to improve the human social condition through a better understanding of the causes and consequences of dominance, aggression, and violence. Nomination for a Career Development Award does not preclude separate application by the candidate for a Harry Frank Guggenheim grant for research.

Fiscal Information The awards cover three years (but are subject to annual review): the recipients receive an award for salary and fringe benefits of $30,000 the first year, $32,500 the second, and $35,000 the third, and research expenses of up to $5,000 each year, for scientific research or academic study at the nonprofit institution of the recipient's choice, subject to the foundation's approval. Awards are paid to the recipient's institution with the understanding that suitable space and general facilities will be provided by the institution and that the total amount of the award will be made available to the investigator. The foundation does not contribute to institutional overhead costs. Any amount not required for salary may be allotted to research expenses; however funding awarded for research expenses may be used only for those purposes. The award may be supplemented by other grants or by the home institution with salary, resources, and personnel. Total salary during tenure of the award may not exceed the prevailing range at the particular institution for the rank and position of the grantee. The award may be transferred from the original institution to another, with prior approval by the foundation.

Application Information Consideration for a Harry Frank Guggenheim Career Development Award can be initiated only by nomination, ordinarily by the head of the department or section in which the proposed work will be done, or someone in an equivalent supervisory position, and the sponsor should be willing and able to provide advice and direction to the recipient during the three years of the award. Only one nomination will be accepted from any one department. Further information and instructions and forms for nominators and nominees are available from the foundation.

Deadline(s) Nominations and supporting materials must be submitted to the foundation by August 1.

Subject Term(s) Individuals, Eligibility of; Foreign Nationals, Eligibility of; Dominance; Violence; Aggression; Social Issues

109. The Harry Frank Guggenheim Foundation

527 Madison Avenue
New York, NY 10022-4301
(212) 644-4907

The Harry Frank Guggenheim Foundation Grants for Research

Program Description The Harry Frank Guggenheim Foundation sponsors an international program of scientific research and scholarly study concerning Man's Relation to Man. The long-term aim is to improve the human social condition through a better understanding of the causes and consequences of dominance, aggression, and violence. Awards will be made only for projects with well-defined aims clearly germane to the human case (but not necessarily restricted to studies of humans). The foundation will consider projects designed to reveal basic physiological mechanisms, to elucidate fundamental psychological processes, to analyze critical social interrelations, to formulate and test unifying theories of those mechanisms, processes, and interrelations, or otherwise advance knowledge from any discipline that will further the foundation's intellectual and practical objectives. Whatever the discipline and whatever the method, the principal criteria for support of a project proposed to the foundation are the same: excellence and relevance.

Sample Grants Support for research on witchcraft, magic and the sexes in Mexico (1985-86). Support for research on peaceful politics: intertribal relations in Brazil's upper Xingu (1984-85). Support for research on the evolution of warfare, slaving and cannibalism in Carib society: 1500-1820 (1985-86).

Eligibility/Limitations Grants are made to individuals for individual projects, not to institutions for institutional programs. Awards may be made either to an institution on behalf of an individual or directly to an individual. Applications must clearly specify whether the funds requested will be administered through an institution or accounted for by the individual grantee. Application for a research grant does not preclude concurrent nomination for a Harry Frank Guggenheim Career Development Award.

Fiscal Information The foundation expects to make most awards in the range of $15,000 to $25,000 a year for periods of one or two years. Applications for larger amounts and longer durations must be very strongly justified. All awards are for one-year terms initially. Requests will be considered for salaries, employee benefits, research assistantships, computer time, supplies and equipment, field work, essential secretarial and technical help, and other items necessary to the successful completion of a project. The foundation does not supply funds for overhead costs of institutions, travel to professional meetings, self-education, elaborate fixed equipment, or support while completing the requirements for advanced degrees (apart from that indirectly involved in research assistantships). The foundation will not accept applications for the support of meetings and conferences or travel costs for participants. Capital equipment purchased on a grant to a university or other publicly supported institution on behalf of an individual becomes the property of the institution. In the case of a grant directly to an individual, however, the resale value of equipment must be returned to the foundation at the termination of the grant period.

Application Information Application procedures are available upon request from the foundation.

Deadline(s) The biannual deadlines are August 1 and February 1.

Subject Term(s) Individuals, Eligibility of; Dominance; Aggression; Violence; Social Issues

110. John Simon Guggenheim Memorial Foundation

90 Park Avenue
New York, NY 10016
(212) 687-4470

Fellowships to Assist Research and Artistic Creation

Program Description In order to improve the quality of education and the practice of the arts and professions, to foster research, and to provide for the cause of better international understanding, the John Simon Guggenheim Memorial Foundation offers fellowships to further the development of scholars and artists by assisting them to engage in research in any field of knowledge and creation in any of the arts, under the freest possible conditions and irrespective of race, color, or creed.

Sample Grants 1985 John Simon Guggenheim Memorial Fellowships were awarded in support of: a study of the Nicaraguan revolution; study of professional militarism in Latin America; studies in the Cuban literary vernacular. 1986 fellowships were awarded in support of a study in support of: a study of sin and confession in Aztec Mexico; a study of population and society in Latin America.

Eligibility/Limitations Fellowships are awarded through two annual competitions: one open to citizens and permanent residents of the United States and Canada, and the other open to citizens and permanent residents of all the other American states, of the Caribbean, of the Philippines, and of the French, Dutch, and British possessions in the Western Hemisphere. Fellows are usually between thirty and forty-five years of age, but the committee of selection is empowered to nominate persons older than forty-five and younger than thirty. The fellowships are awarded to men and women of high intellectual and personal qualifications who have already demonstrated unusual capacity for productive scholarship or unusual creative ability in the arts. Fellowships in music are awarded only to composers of music or to scholars who propose research into the history or theory of music.

Fiscal Information Appointments are ordinarily made for one year, but in no instance for less than six consecutive months. The amount of each grant will be adjusted to the needs of the fellows, considering their other resources and the purpose and scope of their studies. Members of the teaching profession receiving sabbatical leave on full or part salary are eligible for appointment, as are holders of appointments under the Fulbright program, but Guggenheim Fellowships may not be held concurrently with other fellowships. In 1985 the foundation awarded 269 United States and Canadian fellowships for a total of $5,386,000. There were 3,548 applicants.

Application Information Application forms will be mailed on request.

Deadline(s) Applications for fellowships must be made in writing on or before October 1 by the applicants themselves in the form prescribed. Fellows of the foundation who seek further assistance must apply before October 15 of each year. It should be noted that the foundation does not grant immediate renewals of its fellowships.

Additional Information The foundation may subsidize the publication of important contributions to knowledge produced by holders of fellowships, but does not undertake to aid in publishing all works so produced.

Subject Term(s) Fellowships; Foreign Nationals, Eligibility of; Canadian Nationals, Eligibility of; Social Sciences; Humanities; Fine Arts

111. Harvard University

Andrew W. Mellon Faculty Fellowships
Lamont Library 202
Cambridge, MA 02138
(617) 495-2519

Andrew W. Mellon Faculty Fellowships in the Humanities

Program Description The Andrew W. Mellon Foundation has provided Harvard University with a grant for a fellowship program to support experienced but non-tenured junior faculty in the humanities. The program's primary purpose is to seek out promising humanists in different parts of the United States and to offer them time to develop current research and an opportunity to demonstrate scholarly potential at a critical point in their careers. Applicable fields of study include: Afro-American studies, American studies, classics, comparative literature, English, fine arts, folklore, history, history of science, languages and literature programs, linguistics, music, philosophy, religion, visual, and environmental studies. Applications are encouraged from scholars working on significant topics in interdisciplinary fields.

Eligibility/Limitations Applicants must have the Ph.D. and have completed, at the time of appointment, at least two years of postdoctoral teaching in the humanities at the college or university level—usually as assistant professors. Special consideration will be given to candidates who have not recently had access to the resources of a major research university.

Fiscal Information The fellowships carry an annual salary of $27,000. There are approximately fifteen one-year fellowships available. Fellows hold one-year appointments with departmental affiliation and have full access to libraries and other benefits of membership in the Harvard University community. Each fellow will have limited teaching duties.

Application Information Application forms and additional information are available from the program director.

Deadline(s) November 2 is the deadline for receipt of application.

Subject Term(s) Postdoctoral Support; Faculty Support; Humanities

112. The H. John Heinz III Charitable Trust

301 Fifth Avenue, Suite 1417
Pittsburgh, PA 15222-2494
(412) 391-5122

Grants for Archeological Field Research in Latin America

Program Description The H. John Heinz III Charitable Trust announces a program of small grants to support archeological field research in Latin America. Grants are awarded for the following kinds of research activity: projects which are designed as an integral, but discrete part of a larger research program; preliminary research which is expected to lead to future, large-scale projects funded by other sources; and small self-contained research projects.

Eligibility/Limitations Applicants should have the Ph.D. or equivalent experience and be affiliated with a scholarly institution. Grant applications for dissertation research will not be considered.

Fiscal Information The maximum amount per grant will be $8,000 regardless of the amount requested. University overhead charges will not be paid.

Application Information Proposal guidelines and additional information may be obtained from the special advisor to the trust at the above address.

Deadline(s) Proposals must be received by October 17.

Subject Term(s) Archeology; Field Research, Support of

113. Howard Heinz Endowment

301 Fifth Avenue, Suite 1417
Pittsburgh, PA 15222-2494
(412) 391-5122

Grants

Program Description The endowment supports research on current issues in Latin American economics, politics, foreign policy, or social development.

Sample Grants In support of a research project on the dilemmas of Brazilian political liberalization in the elections of November 1982 and the presidential succession, $5,200 to Elizabethtown College (1984). In support of a research project on the Chilean financial system: an analysis of recent trends and future policy options, $10,110 to the University of Pennsylvania (1984).

Eligibility/Limitations Grants will be paid only to the institution of the researcher. Applicants should have the Ph.D. or its equivalent.

Fiscal Information The maximum grant is $25,000.

Application Information To be considered for a grant, an organization should submit a proposal describing the purpose of the grant, the amount requested, the procedures to be employed, the personnel involved, and a complete financial statement. If the proposal is within the endowment's areas of interest, the applicant will be requested to fill out a brief application form relevant to the proposal.

Deadline(s) Five copies of the proposal should be received no later than November 20.

Subject Term(s) Economics; Foreign Policy; Development

114. The Herb Society of America

300 Massachusetts Avenue
Boston, MA 02115

Annual Grant Program

Program Description The purpose of this program is to further the knowledge and use of herbs and contribute the results of the study and research to the records of horticulture, science, literature, history, art, or economics. The study could involve such varied topics as: history, medicinal research and usage from a historical perspective, fragrance, flavor, crafts, horticulture, landscaping, economic importance, chemurgy, taxonomy, hardiness, political and social influence, symbolism in art or literature, or uses in religion. In fact, the possibilities are as limitless as the delightful plants themselves.

Eligibility/Limitations Persons with a proposed program of scientific or academic investigation of herbal plants are eligible to apply.

Fiscal Information The grant of up to $4,000 is for a period of study not to exceed one year.

Application Information Grant applications should be mailed to the Scholarship Chairman, 5759 S. Meadow Park Drive, Hales Corners, WI, 53130.

Deadline(s) Applications must be postmarked no later than January 15.

Subject Term(s) Individuals, Eligibility of; Herbs

115. The William R. and Flora L. Hewlett Foundation

525 Middlefield Road
Menlo Park, CA 94025
(415) 329-1070

Grants

Program Description The foundation's broad purpose, as stated in its articles of incorporation, is to promote the well-being of mankind by supporting selected activities of a charitable, religious, scientific, literary, or educational nature, as well as organizations or institutions engaged in such activities. More particularly, to date, the foundation has concentrated its resources on activities in the performing arts; education, particularly at the university and college level; population issues; environmental issues; and more recently, conflict resolution.

Sample Grants For general support of the Latin American Studies Education Resources (LASER) Program, $25,000 to the Center for Latin American Studies, San Diego State University, San Diego, California (1985). For the Program of Social Research on Population in Latin America, $6,998 to El Colegio de Mexico, Mexico City (1985). For the Center for Demographic and Urban Studies, $150,000 to El Colegio de Mexico, Mexico City (1985). For the Center of Regional Development and Planning, $150,000 to Universidade Federal de Minas Gerais Cedeplar, Minas Gerais, Brazil (1985). For general support of family planning work, $25,000 to Social Marketing International Association, Queretaro, Mexico (1985).

Eligibility/Limitations Normally, the foundation will not consider for support: grants or loans to individuals, grants for basic research, capital construction funds, grants in the medical or health-related fields, or general fundraising drives. It will not make grants intended directly or indirectly to support candidates for political office or to influence legislation. Although the Hewlett Foundation is a national foundation, with no geographic limit stipulated in its charter, a modest proportion of disbursable funds has been earmarked for projects in the San Francisco Bay Area.

Fiscal Information There is no fixed minimum or maximum with respect to the size of grants.

Application Information The most efficient means of initial contact with the Hewlett Foundation is a letter of inquiry, addressed to the president. The letter should contain a brief statement of the applicant's need for funds and enough factual information to enable the staff to determine whether or not the application falls within the foundation's areas of preferred interests or warrants consideration as a special project. Applicants who receive a favorable response to their initial inquiry will be invited to submit a formal proposal.

Deadline(s) Grants must be approved by the board of directors, which meets quarterly. Meeting dates are available upon request, but applicants should realize that even proposals which are recommended for board approval cannot in every case be reviewed at the first meeting following their receipt. All inquiries and proposals are reported to the board, including both those that lie clearly outside the foundation's declared interests and those declined at the staff level.

Subject Term(s) Education; Arts, Support of; Population; Environment; Conflict Resolution

116. Hewlett-Packard Company Foundation

3000 Hanover Street
Palo Alto, CA 94304

Philanthropic Grants

Program Description Hewlett-Packard, since its founding in 1939, has sought to be an economic, intellectual, cultural, and social asset for each area—technical and geographical—within which it functions. One important means to this end is a wide array of carefully developed equipment and cash grants programs. These philanthropic programs can be grouped generally into four main categories: (1) community grants; (2) national grants in causes related to science, engineering, technology, and medicine; (3) employee-driven grants; and (4) international grants in those countries where direct contributions of cash and equipment are permitted and encouraged.

Eligibility/Limitations Hewlett-Packard does not make philanthropic grants to: organizations which are not tax-exempt; individuals; sectarian or denominational groups; agencies which practice or promote discriminatory or partisan policies; political activities; causes which offer specific direct benefits to grantors; university-industry associates programs; individual's research projects; or conferences, seminars, or meetings.

Application Information Application procedures are available upon request.

Deadline(s) Deadlines vary depending upon the backlog of prior cases, and upon the monthly, quarterly, or annual cycle of the program category involved. Contact Hewlett-Packard for specific information.

Additional Information Hewlett-Packard Company designs and manufactures computers and computer peripherals, test and measurement instruments, handheld calculators, electronic components, medical electronic equipment, and instrumentation for chemical analysis.

Subject Term(s) Equipment Grants, Computers; Equipment Acquisition

117. Hoover Institution on War, Revolution and Peace

National Fellows Program
Stanford University
Stanford, CA 94305
(415) 497-0163

National Fellows Program

Program Description The National Fellows Program allows particularly gifted younger scholars to spend one full year on unrestricted, creative research and writing at the Hoover Institution. During this period fellows are free from all other academic responsibilities. Accordingly, the fellowships afford scholars a unique opportunity to advance their professional careers by completing an original and significant research project. Research projects deal with both current and historical policy issues in domestic and foreign affairs. Special emphasis is placed on those proposals that consider important policy issues facing the United States today. A fellow may concentrate research and writing in one or more fields of study such as political science, economics, modern history, international relations, law, and sociology. Fellowships are awarded with the clear expectation that the fellows will take advantage of this opportunity to complete a publishable manuscript while in residence at the Hoover Institution.

Sample Grants A national fellowship was awarded to support a study of Soviet and Eastern Bloc penetration of Latin America, to a Ph.D. in government at Harvard University (1983-84).

Eligibility/Limitations Candidate qualifications should include a Ph.D. degree or its equivalent, approximately three or four years' experience beyond the doctorate, clear indications of intellectual competence, and promise as a productive scholar.

Fiscal Information Approximately fourteen to sixteen fellowships are awarded each year, twelve national and peace fellows, and four public affairs fellows.

Application Information Admission to the program is based primarily on nomination and recommendation of leading scholars throughout the United States, as well as on submission of a carefully prepared research proposal.

Deadline(s) Applications should be submitted to the executive secretary prior to January 15 of the year for which the fellowship is desired.

Subject Term(s) Fellowships; Postdoctoral Support; Foreign Affairs; Foreign Policy; Social Sciences

118. The George A. and Eliza Gardner Howard Foundation

Brown University
42 Charlesfield Street, Box 1867
Providence, RI 02912
(401) 863-2640

Program Description The Howard Foundation seeks to aid the personal development of promising individuals at the crucial middle stages of their careers. Fellowships are offered to support persons engaged in independent projects in the following fields: literary criticism, comparative literature, and language and literature.

Eligibility/Limitations Candidates should be in the "middle stages of their careers," and free of all professional responsibilities during the fellowship years. No grants are made to or through organizations, nor for institutional or programmatic support, but only to individuals. No fellowships are awarded for work leading to any academic degree or for coursework or training of any sort. Awards are made for projects requiring essentially full-time work over an extended period of time. Fellows must therefore, be eligible for sabbatical or other leave, or make arrangements with the institution involved for time released from normal duties.

Fiscal Information Stipends of $18,000 will be given for a period of one year beginning July 1 and ending June 30. No grants are made for summer research or other short-term projects. Awards are made for projects requiring essentially full-time work over an extended period of time.

Application Information The Howard Foundation does not accept direct application. Application forms are forwarded to candidates only upon the foundation's acceptance of a suitable nomination, submitted according to the following guidelines: (1) for all individuals associated with a college or university, a nomination should be submitted by the president of the institution, or a designated representative; and (2) independent scholars and others without academic institutional connections may be nominated by an editor of a professional journal, a museum director, or a person of equivalent professional standing in the relevant field.

Deadline(s) Nominations will be accepted between September 1 and November 1 for the fellowship year beginning on July 1 and ending on June 30.

Subject Term(s) Fellowships; Individuals, Eligibility of; Literary Criticism; Literature; Language; Comparative Literature

119. The Hudson Institute

Herman Kahn Center
5395 Emerson Way, P.O. Box 26-919
Indianapolis, IN 46226

Herman Kahn Resident Fellowship Program

Program Description The Hudson Institute announces Herman Kahn Resident Fellowships in support of Ph.D. candidates in the following fellowship areas. Fellowships in education are designed to support policy-relevant research in education. Fellowships in domestic political economy support research intended to enhance the policy analytic framework for assessing national and regional economic issues. Fellowships in international political economy support policy-oriented research in the area of international political economy; several areas are of special interest, including East-West commercial relations, economic development of both advanced and developing countries, macroeconomics policies in an interdependent world economy, the role of multinational enterprises, and the interactions of political, social, and economic dynamics in communist countries. Fellowships in national security studies are designed to support policy-oriented research on national security and defense issues; topics of particular interest include Third World security issues and the use of economic instruments and sanctions to further political and strategic objectives.

Eligibility/Limitations Ph.D. candidates who have completed their course work and have only their dissertation remaining are eligible to apply. Applicants must have completed their course work within the last five years and provide evidence that they have been formally admitted to candidacy for the Ph.D.

Fiscal Information An $18,000 stipend will be paid for the academic year, as well as one-way economy airfare to Indianapolis or Washington, DC, or reimbursement for travel by automobile for selected fellows and immediate family members.

Application Information Additional information is available on request. Applications should include a curriculum vitae, three letters of recommendation (two academic and one non-academic), recent university publications and transcripts, and graduate school transcripts. Selected candidates will be interviewed with travel costs being paid by the institute.

Deadline(s) Applications should be submitted no later than April 20.

Subject Term(s) Doctoral Dissertation Support; Economics; International Economics; Security Studies; Fellowships

120. Institute for Development Anthropology

99 Collier Street, Suite 302, P.O. Box 2207
Binghamton, NY 13902
(607) 772-6244

Research Associates/Assistants and Internships

Program Description The Institute for Development Anthropology (IDA) is an independent, nonpartisan, and nonprofit scientific research and educational organization.

IDA seeks to enhance the ability of low-income populations around the world to defend their human rights through programs and projects designed to promote growth and a more equitable distribution of the world's resources. IDA believes that genuine economic growth is facilitated by equality, and that freedom is necessary for all people. Thus, the institute seeks to participate in development actions that expand the economic opportunities of the poor, and that increase their ability to make meaningful decisions about the directions of their own lives. IDA was organized by a group of anthropologists with extensive experience in development who believe that the social sciences have much to contribute to the improvement of social and economic conditions of the world's poor, and who advocate actions that provide for maximum participation by beneficiary populations. IDA has initiated research, participated in project design and evaluation, and organized seminars, training sessions, and workshops dealing with development issues. From time to time opportunities develop for full- and part-time research associates/assistants and internships at IDA's Binghamton offices. These openings are advertised in the *Anthropology Newsletter* and IDA's Development Anthropology Network. Interested individuals can write to IDA or call IDA at (607) 772-9311.

Additional Information IDA maintains a computerized, carefully evaluated roster of associates, from developed and Third World countries, who make their expertise available as institute consultants and intermittent employees. IDA welcomes letters of interest and curriculum vitae from qualified applicants for the roster of associates.

Subject Term(s) Internships; Anthropology; Developing Countries; Economic Development

121. Institute for Intercultural Studies, Inc.

145 East 74th Street, Suite 1C
New York, NY 10021
(212) 737-1011

Research Grants

Program Description The institute is concerned with advancing knowledge of the behavior, customs, psychology, and social organization of the various peoples and nations of the world, with special attention to those peoples and those aspects of their life which are likely to affect intercultural and international relations. In determining priority areas of support, the institute is influenced by its history, especially its establishment in 1944 by Margaret Mead, its close association with Gregory Bateson, its previous grant commitments, and the responsible completion and preservation of on-going projects.

Eligibility/Limitations Applicants may propose doctoral level research, field research projects that build on the work of the institute's founders, or, occasionally, support for conferences, publications, and organizations with themes and purposes closely related to the interests of the institute.

Fiscal Information Grants for doctoral level research are normally made in amounts of $2,000 for field work and research. Grants of up to $5,000 are made for field research that builds on the work of the institute's founders. Occasional grants up to $10,000 are made to support conferences, publications, and organizations with themes and purposes closely related to the interests of the institute.

Application Information Official application forms and guidelines are available upon request.

Deadline(s) Completed applications must be on file by February 15.

Subject Term(s) Individuals, Eligibility of; Predoctoral Support; Anthropology; Field Research, Support of

122. Institute of Current World Affairs—The Crane-Rogers Foundation

Wheelock House, 4 West Wheelock Street
Hanover, NH 03755
(603) 643-5548

Fellowship Program

Program Description The purpose of the institute is to create a corps of international specialists and generalists well-versed in world affairs through a process of immersion in them. With this end in view the institute awards fellowships to men and women of divers academic and professional backgrounds to study and write about areas or issues of the world in need of in-depth understanding. Fellowship areas of interest vary from year to year. The most recent areas of interest include: peasant societies of Andean South America; the impact of arms aid on recipient nations, and environmental policy in Kalimantan.

Eligibility/Limitations Applicants are usually in their twenties or early thirties.

Fiscal Information Fellowships provide full support for periods ranging from two to four years. Fellowships are not awarded to support work toward academic degrees, nor to underwrite specific studies or programs of research as such.

Application Information The institute has no application forms for fellowships. Instead, candidates are invited to write to the executive director, explaining briefly the personal background and professional experience that would qualify them for the fellowship.

Deadline(s) Applications may be submitted at any time.

Additional Information A separately-funded program, known as Forest & Man Fellowships, offers people with graduate degrees in forestry-related specialties an opportunity to gain an understanding of forest-resource problems from the point of view of humans, including policy-makers, environmentalists, peasants, religious leaders, scientists, planners, and forest-product industrialists.

Subject Term(s) Fellowships; Individuals, Eligibility of; International Affairs; Forestry; International Studies

123. Institute of International Education

809 United Nations Plaza
New York, NY 10017

Fulbright Fixed Sum Grants

Program Description The Institute of International Education (IIE) is under contract to the U.S. Information Agency to organize publicly, receive and process applications, and, through its National Screening Committee, make recommendations to the Board of Foreign Scholarships for graduate study grants under the Fulbright Program. Under agreements with foreign governments, universities, and private donors, the institute performs the same functions with regard to grants sponsored by them. Fulbright Fixed Sum Grants provide a fixed-sum payment in U.S. dollars for predoctoral study or research abroad. Fulbright grants which are fixed sum are tenable in the American Republics, including Bolivia, Costa Rica, Guyana, Mexico, Panama, Paraguay, Venezuela, and others.

Eligibility/Limitations Applicants must be United States citizens and have received the majority of their high school and undergraduate college education at educational institutions in the United States. Applicants must hold a B.A. degree or the equivalent before the beginning date of the grant. Applicants may not hold a doctoral degree at the time of application. Applicants must have sufficient proficiency in the written and spoken language of the host country to communicate with the people and to carry out the proposed study. Such proficiency is especially important to students wishing to undertake projects in the social sciences and humanities. Although the majority of these grants are reserved for graduate students who, in most cases, will be engaged in research for the doctoral dissertation, it is the policy of the Board of Foreign Scholarships that awards also be available to other graduate students, graduating seniors, and candidates who wish to further their careers in the creative and performing arts.

Fiscal Information Most grants will be awarded for programs of study or research that will require an academic year. Grant amounts vary from country to country. In certain countries, grantees who, upon arrival, can submit proof that they have been admitted to doctoral candidacy and have completed all requirements except the writing of their dissertations may receive higher stipends.

Application Information Application forms and additional information are available from IIE. Before filling out an application, a prospective candidate should confirm that there will be awards in the country in which he or she is interested. Applicants who are enrolled in U.S. colleges and universities should contact their Fulbright program advisors for the latest information. Others should write to IIE.

Deadline(s) Deadlines vary from year to year and from country to country. Contact IIE for up-to-date information.

Subject Term(s) Doctoral Dissertation Support Abroad; Graduate Support Abroad; Predoctoral Support Abroad; Individuals, Eligibility of; Bolivia; Costa Rica; Guyana; Mexico; Panama; Paraguay; Venezuela; American Republics

124. Institute of International Education

809 United Nations Plaza
New York, NY 10017

Fulbright Full Grants

Program Description The Institute of International Education (IIE) is under contract to the U.S. Information Agency to organize publicly, receive and process applications, and, through its National Screening Committee, make recommendations to the Board of Foreign Scholarships for graduate study grants under the Fulbright Program. Under agreements with foreign governments, universities, and private donors, the institute performs the same functions with regard to grants sponsored by them. Fulbright Full Grants are tenable in most of the American Republics, except Bolivia, Costa Rica, Guyana, Mexico, Panama, Paraguay, and Venezuela.

Eligibility/Limitations Applicants must be United States citizens and have received the majority of their high school and undergraduate college education at educational institutions in the United States. Applicants must hold a B.A. degree or the equivalent before the beginning date of the grant. Applicants may not hold a doctoral degree at the time of application. Applicants must have sufficient proficiency in the written and spoken language of the host country to communicate with the people and to carry out the proposed study. Such proficiency is especially important to students wishing to undertake projects in the social sciences and humanities. Although the majority of these grants are reserved for graduate students who, in most cases, will be engaged in research for the doctoral dissertation, it is the policy of the Board of Foreign Scholarships that awards also be available to other graduate students, graduating seniors, and candidates who wish to further their careers in the creative and performing arts.

Fiscal Information Most grants will be awarded for programs of study or research that will require an academic year. Full Grants provide round-trip transportation, language or orientation courses (where appropriate), tuition, books, maintenance for one academic year in only one country, and health and accident insurance. Most of these benefits are payable in local currency. The maintenance allowance is based on living costs in the host country and is sufficient to meet the normal expenses of a single person.

Application Information Application forms and additional information are available from IIE. Before filling out an application, a prospective candidate should confirm that there will be awards in the country in which he or she is interested. Applicants who are enrolled in U.S. colleges and universities should contact their Fulbright program advisors for the latest information. Others should write to IIE.

Deadline(s) Deadlines vary from year to year and from country to country. Contact IIE for up-to-date information.

Subject Term(s) Doctoral Dissertation Support Abroad; Graduate Support Abroad; Predoctoral Support Abroad; Individuals, Eligibility of; American Republics

125. Institute of International Education

809 United Nations Plaza
New York, NY 10017

Fulbright Travel Grants

Program Description The Institute of International Education (IIE) is under contract to the U.S. Information Agency to organize publicly, receive and process applications, and, through its National Screening Committee, make recommendations to the Board of Foreign Scholarships for graduate study grants under the Fulbright Program. Under agreements with foreign governments, universities, and private donors, the institute performs the same functions with regard to grants sponsored by them. In general, Fulbright Travel Grants are tied to specific maintenance and tuition scholarships and may not be used to supplement awards other than these.

Eligibility/Limitations In general, applicants must be candidates for Fulbright maintenance and tuition scholarships.

Fiscal Information Travel Grants provide round-trip transportation to the country where the student will pursue studies for an academic year, health and accident insurance, and the cost of an orientation course abroad, if applicable.

Application Information Application forms and additional information are available from IIE. Before filling out an application, a prospective candidate should confirm that there will be awards in the country in which he or she is interested. Applicants who are enrolled in U.S. colleges and universities should contact their Fulbright program advisors for the latest information. Others should write to IIE.

Deadline(s) Deadlines vary from year to year and from country to country. Contact IIE for up-to-date information.

Subject Term(s) Travel Support Abroad

126. Institute of International Education

809 United Nations Plaza
New York, NY 10017

ITT International Fellowships

Program Description These fellowships are made possible solely by a contribution from the ITT Corporation to the Institute of International Education (IIE) and are awarded separately from Fulbright grants. Applications will be considered from well-qualified students in all fields, regardless of field limitations specified for other IIE grants. ITT fellowships are available for Argentina, Brazil, Chile, and Mexico.

Sample Grants For study in Argentina, an ITT fellowship was awarded to a graduate student in social psychology, Swarthmore College (1986).

Eligibility/Limitations Preference will be given to single graduating seniors. Applicants must be citizens and permanent residents of the United States, and must be resident in the United States at the time of application. Applicants should have completed more than half of their secondary and undergraduate educations in the United States, and must indicate their intention to return to the United States on completion of the period of award. Proficiency in the language of the country of study, sufficient to carry out the study, is required.

Fiscal Information Most grants will be awarded for programs of study or research that will require an academic year, two semesters from mid-September to late January and from mid-February to early July. Students must arrive between September 1 and September 10. The fellowships carry: a maintenance allowance based on the cost of living, tuition and books, an allowance for international travel, and health and accident insurance. No financial allowances are provided for dependents.

Application Information Application forms and additional information are available from the ITT program manager at IIE. Applicants who are enrolled in U.S. colleges and universities should contact their Fulbright program advisors for the latest information. Others should write to IIE.

Deadline(s) Deadlines vary from year to year. Contact IIE for up-to-date information.

Subject Term(s) Graduate Support Abroad; Fellowships; Argentina; Brazil; Chile; Mexico

127. Institute of International Education

International Human Rights Internship Program
1400 K Street, NW, Suite 650
Washington, DC 20005
(202) 898-0600

International Human Rights Internships Program

Program Description The goals of this program are: to provide individuals with practical training in international human rights implementation, to support the efforts of international human rights organizations, and to strengthen the international network of individuals trained in human rights work. The program arranges one-year fellowship placements with organizations in the U.S., Europe, Africa, Asia, and Latin America. A very small number of short-term placements of two to three months may be considered on a case-by-case basis for individuals and organizations in Africa, Asia, and Latin America.

Eligibility/Limitations Qualified individuals of all nationalities are eligible to apply.

Fiscal Information A fellowship grant covers international travel, a basic living stipend, and health insurance for a fellow. It does not provide support for spouses or families. Grants vary depending on the location of the fellowship, ranging normally from $5,000 to $15,000 for a one-year fellowship.

Application Information For information and an application form write to the program director at the address listed above.

Deadline(s) Annual application deadline for organizations is July 31. Annual application deadline for individuals is August 31.

Subject Term(s) Individuals, Eligibility of; Fellowships; Human Rights; Internships; Foreign Nationals, Eligibility of

128. Institute of International Education

U.S. Students Programs Division
809 United Nations Plaza
New York, NY 10017
(212) 984-5326

Fulbright Collaborative Research Grants

Program Description The Institute of International Education (IIE) is under contract to the U.S. Information Agency to organize publicly, receive and process applications, and, through its National Screening Committee, make recommendations to the Board of Foreign Scholarships for graduate study grants under the Fulbright Program. Under agreements with foreign governments, universities, and private donors, the institute performs the same functions with regard to grants sponsored by them. The Board of Foreign Scholarships has approved the introduction of a new project under the Fulbright program which will fund proposals for joint research abroad by teams of *two or three* U.S. graduate students or recent post-graduate researchers. The program is available for research in all countries of the world where conditions permit, except for most countries in Eastern Europe, the U.S.S.R., and Indochina. It is expected that all members of a team involved in a joint grant will carry out their research in one country abroad in the same academic year, although research does not need to be carried out simultaneously and the duration of the grant need not be the same in all cases. However, individual team members are required to carry out research within the host country for a minimum of six months. Application must include evidence of affiliation with a host-country institution or ongoing project that will oversee the collaborative research. The program does not impose restrictions as to fields of research.

Eligibility/Limitations Applicants must be United States citizens at the time of application. They must hold a B.A. degree or its equivalent before the beginning date of the grant. Those with a Ph.D. at the time of application may have obtained the degree no earlier than June 1984. Researchers in the creative arts need not hold a degree, but must have at least four years of relevant training and/or experience. Applicants in medicine must have an M.D. degree or the equivalent (e.g., O.D., D.D.S.) at the time of application. Applicants must have received the majority of their high school and undergraduate college educations at educational institutions in the United States. Applicants must have sufficient proficiency in the written and spoken language of the host country to communicate with the people and to carry out the proposed study. Such proficiency is especially important to those wishing to undertake projects in the social sciences and the humanities. Applicants must be in good health. There are no restrictions as to age, sex, race, or religion. Full-time permanent employees of the U.S. Information Agency are ineligible for grants for a period of one year following the termination of their employment. This limitation applies to members of their immediate families. Employees of any agency involved in administering the educational and cultural exchange programs of the U.S. Information Agency, and members of their immediate families, should check with IIE on their eligibility.

Fiscal Information The Fulbright Collaborative Research Grants will provide equal monthly fixed-sum payments to each member of the research team, based on the cost of living in the host country. These payments are intended to cover the normal travel and living expenses of a grantee for the tenure of the award, normally six to ten months. No extra funds for research expenses, translators, or other resource persons will be included. There is no allowance for dependent support, nor is it recommended that dependents accompany grantees abroad. Grantees will also receive basic health and accident insurance coverage as part of the award. Renewals or extensions of the grants will not be made.

Application Information Application forms and additional information are available from IIE. Before filling out an application, a prospective candidate should confirm that there will be awards in the country in which he or she is interested. Applicants who are enrolled in U.S. colleges and universities should contact their Fulbright program advisors for the latest information. Others should write to IIE.

Deadline(s) Completed applications for each team must reach IIE by January 16.

Subject Term(s) Doctoral Dissertation Support Abroad; Graduate Support Abroad; Predoctoral Support Abroad; Postdoctoral Support Abroad

129. Inter-American Foundation

1515 Wilson Boulevard
Rosslyn, VA 22209
(703) 841-3864

Doctoral Fellowship Program

Program Description The Inter-American Foundation awards fellowships for doctoral dissertation research in Latin America and the Caribbean. Through this program of support for field research, the foundation is seeking to encourage increased scholarly and professional attention to development issues affecting poor and disadvantaged groups in the region. Preference is given to candidates whose background and research are multidisciplinary, and to those with prior experience in development work.

Sample Grants 1983-84 fellowships were awarded for: a study of Aymara farming system transformations under differing responses to agrarian reform laws in two former hacienda communities in Bolivia; a study of the determinants of health and effects of disease in a native Amazonian population—the Pakaas Novas of Rondonia, Brazil; a study of industrialization and basic needs in Chile; support of the Sierra Juarez Ethnobiological Project, Mexico; a study of the expansion in Mexican handicraft production—its impact on women, men, and households.

Eligibility/Limitations The program is open to doctoral candidates at U.S. universities with an interest in Latin America and the Caribbean. Applicants may be from the social sciences, physical sciences, and the professions. Candidates must have fulfilled all degree requirements other than the dissertation before they travel overseas. Applicants are required to write and speak the language of the Latin American or Caribbean area in which they intend to study. Fellowships carry no restrictions regarding citizenship, sex, or age. Each fellow must establish a formal affiliation with a Latin American or Caribbean institution which shares his or her research interests. These arrangements are normally handled by the fellow, although occasionally the Inter-American Foundation does provide some assistance.

Fiscal Information Fellowship stipends average about $600 per month, but vary with the cost of living from country to country. Awards are initially made for a one-year period, and can be extended an additional year. Other allowances are made for legal dependents, transportation, and health and accident insurance. Fellowships also include a limited amount for research expenses.

Application Information Application forms may be obtained by writing to the Doctoral Fellowship Program of the Inter-American Foundation.

Deadline(s) Applications are due by December 5.

Subject Term(s) Fellowships Abroad; Doctoral Dissertation Support Abroad; Social Sciences; Physical Sciences; Field Research, Support of; Developing Countries; Economic Development; Development

130. Inter-American Foundation

1515 Wilson Boulevard
Rosslyn, VA 22209
(703) 841-3864

Latin America and Caribbean Program

Program Description The foundation awards fellowships to Latin American and Caribbean practitioners and researchers whose work in grass-roots development would benefit from advanced academic experience in the United States. Candidates must have demonstrated interest in the problems of poverty and development.

Eligibility/Limitations Fellowships are awarded primarily to candidates for master's and doctoral degrees, and occasionally to persons pursuing a non-degree program of supervised research. Candidates must make their own arrangements for admission to a U.S. university.

Fiscal Information Fellowships are awarded for a maximum of two years.

Application Information Candidates should submit an application form, available from the fellowship office, and two letters of recommendation, grade transcripts, and two samples of their writing. Candidates must be nominated by their home institutions and are expected to return to them.

Deadline(s) The application deadline is January 15.

Subject Term(s) Foreign Nationals, Eligibility of; Development; Graduate Support; Predoctoral Support; Poverty

131. Inter-American Foundation

1515 Wilson Boulevard
Rosslyn, VA 22209
(703) 841-3864

Master's Fellowship Program

Program Description The Inter-American Foundation awards fellowships to master's-level students to conduct three to six months of field research in Latin America and the Caribbean. Through this and other fellowship programs, the foundation is seeking to encourage increased scholarly and professional attention to development issues affecting poor and disadvantaged groups in the region. Preference is given to candidates whose background and proposed research are multidisciplinary.

Sample Grants 1983-84 fellowships were awarded in support of: a study of the demand in wheat products among highland peasants in Peru; a study of traditional pastoral patterns, Bolivia; a study of scavenging at a landfill in Mexico City; a study of foreign debt and development strategy in Argentina; a study of the influence of maternal nutritional status on birthweight, Chile.

Eligibility/Limitations The fellowship program is open to master's degree students or to doctoral candidates who are still completing their coursework. Applicants must be enrolled in professional schools or academic programs at U.S. universities, and are required to write and speak the language of the country in which they intend to do their research. Fellowships carry no restrictions regarding citizenship, sex, or age. Each fellow must establish a formal affiliation with a Latin American or Caribbean institution which shares his or her research interests. The arrangements are normally made directly by the fellow, although occasionally the Inter-American Foundation can provide assistance.

Fiscal Information Fellowship stipends average about $450 per month, but vary with the cost of living from country to country. Awards are normally made for a three-month period, but can be approved for up to six months. The foundation also provides round-trip airfare and health and accident insurance for the fellow. Fellowship recipients are expected to begin the field work no later than six months after their selection.

Application Information Application forms, help in contacting campus screening committees, and further information about selection procedures can be obtained by writing the Master's Fellowship Program of the Inter-American Foundation.

Deadline(s) Applications are due at the foundation by November 1 for the fall competition and by March 1 for the spring competition.

Subject Term(s) Fellowships Abroad; Graduate Support Abroad; Field Research, Support of; Developing Countries; Economic Development; Development

132. Interamerican Press Association

Scholarship Fund
2911 Northwest 39th Street
Miami, FL 33142
(305) 634-2465

Journalism Scholarships

Program Description The Interamerican Press Association (IAPA) was established in 1942 to defend and promote the right of the peoples of the Americas to be fully and freely informed through an independent press. At the same time the IAPA recognized that an independent press, fundamental as it is, could not be the sole objective of the association. Needed also was perceptive reporting that would contribute to better understanding among the countries of the Western Hemisphere. It was for this reason that in 1954 the IAPA established a scholarship fund for young journalists and journalism school graduates. Under the program U.S. or Canadians spend a school year studying and reporting in Latin America, and Latin Americans or West Indians spend a year at a U.S. or Canadian journalism school.

Eligibility/Limitations Journalists or journalism school graduates between twenty-one and thirty-five years of age with a good command of the language they are to use are eligible. Where experience is a prime consideration, three years of professional journalism are required; where professional experience is minimal, a journalism degree is required. Language ability must be attested to by a recognized authority in Spanish or Portuguese. Latin American applicants must take a TOEFL test.

Fiscal Information Awards are in the amount of $5,000. The award supports Latin Americans and West Indians for one year in a U.S. or Canadian university and U.S. or Canadian journalists or journalism school graduates for a year of study and reporting in Latin America.

Application Information Applications may be requested by writing to the IAPA Scholarship Fund at the address listed above.

Deadline(s) The deadline for applications is August 1.

Subject Term(s) Journalism; Foreign Nationals, Eligibility of; Individuals, Eligibility of

133. International Center for Reseach on Women

1717 Massachusetts Avenue, NW, Suite 501
Washington, DC 20036
(202) 797-0007

Fellowship Program for Latin America and the Caribbean

Program Description The International Center for Research on Women (ICRW) announces a fellowship program for young professionals and graduate students. The objective of the program is to train promising professionals from Latin America and the Caribbean in the use of social science research for the development of effective policies and programs to increase the economic participation of poor women in developing countries.

Eligibility/Limitations Applications will be accepted from individuals with formal backgrounds in the social sciences, economics, education, urban planning, and public health. Candidates must be actively affiliated with an institution to which they will return upon completion of the program. Students writing dissertations or theses are encouraged to apply. Candidates must be citizens of Latin American and Caribbean countries and the commonwealth of Puerto Rico who are studying in North America. Proficiency in the English language is required.

Fiscal Information Fellows receive transportation to and from Washington, DC, and a basic stipend to cover living expenses.

Application Information Application forms and additional information are available on request.

Deadline(s) Applications must be received by March 1.

Subject Term(s) Women, Eligibility of; Doctoral Dissertation Support; Economic Development; Women in Development; Developing Countries; Foreign Nationals, Eligibility of; Development; Fellowships

134. Inter-University Program for Latino Research

University of Texas at Austin, Center for Mexican American Studies
Student Services Building 4.120
Austin, TX 78712
(512) 471-4557

Grants for Public Policy Research on Contemporary Hispanic Issues

Program Description The purpose of these grants is to encourage research that will both have value to the Hispanic community and demonstrate the use of social science research in public policy formation; to benefit the field of Hispanic studies by increasing the number and quality of trained social researchers; and to advance an understanding of contemporary Hispanic life in the United States. The research program places high value on studies which distinguish Hispanics in terms of their country of origin, which compare differences and similarities across Hispanic groups, and which take into account gender differences. Priority will be given to research relevant to one or more of the following public policy related issues as they affect the Hispanic community: the impact of Hispanic immigration and Puerto Rican migration; the relationship of ethnicity, political participation, and civic involvement; issues affecting employment security for Hispanics; issues affecting income security for Hispanics; and the characteristics of effective schools for Hispanic students and the role of community, institution, and student characteristics in explaining elevated dropout rates.

Eligibility/Limitations Grants will be awarded to individuals and institutions. The competition is open to scholars who are citizens or residents of the United States. Primary consideration will be given to researchers with an established interest in Hispanic-related research and to those whose proposals will directly advance the professional development of Hispanic scholars.

Fiscal Information Grants will vary from small, individual awards to support for major collaborative research projects. They offer the possibility of one, two, or three years of research support. Although most of the award funds will support individual research, provision has been made for the possibility of a small number of major institutional grants of up to $150,000 each.

Application Information Application materials are available upon request from the Social Science Research Council, 605 Third Avenue, New York, NY, 10158, (212) 661-0280.

Deadline(s) The application deadline is July 15.

Additional Information This competition is administered jointly by the Inter-University Program for Latino Research and the Social Science Research Council. Funds for this purpose have been provided by a grant from the Ford Foundation.

Subject Term(s) Individuals, Eligibility of; Foreign Nationals, Eligibility of; Social Sciences; Hispanic Studies; Immigration

135. The Johns Hopkins University

Department of the History of Art
The Johns Hopkins University
Baltimore, MD 21218

The Program in History of Art and Anthropology

Program Description This graduate program leads to a Ph.D. in either history of art or anthropology and focuses on the interdisciplinary study of history of art and anthropology. The aim of the program is to bring together these fields in the formulation of novel approaches and in the development of theories which are capable of bridging institutional boundaries.

Eligibility/Limitations Applicants must have an MA in either history of art or anthropology (or equivalent coursework), but other forms of preparation may be taken into consideration.

Fiscal Information The program provides a fellowship for the first three years of study as well as funding for summer fieldwork and curatorial internships to be undertaken during the first and second year.

Application Information Additional information and application materials are available on request.

Deadline(s) The deadline for application is February 15.

Subject Term(s) Art History; Graduate Support; Anthropology; Fellowships

136. The Johns Hopkins University

Program in Atlantic History, Culture, and Society
3400 North Charles Street
Baltimore, MD 21218
(301) 338-7597

Rockefeller Foundation Fellowships in the Humanities

Program Description These fellowships are designed to support interdisciplinary research in anthropology, history, and other disciplines of the humanities and social sciences. They are intended to support scholarly research leading to publication. Of special interest is research on the history and culture of North America, Latin America, the Caribbean, Europe, and Africa; for the reconstruction of slavery and other settings of domination; and for the habilitation of the voices and activities of the inarticulate past.

Eligibility/Limitations Scholars in the above disciplines are invited to apply. Awards are not made for graduate study, advanced training, or for the writing of fiction or poetry.

Fiscal Information The fellowships carry stipends up to a maximum of $30,000. The program will make a contribution of up to $3,000 toward travel, benefits, and relocation expenses.

Application Information For application packet and detailed instructions, write to: Fellowships in the Humanities, The Rockefeller Foundation, Arts and Humanities Division, 1133 Avenue of the Americas, New York, NY, 10036; or, for further information, write to Selection Committee, Program in Atlantic History, Culture, and Society at the address above.

Deadline(s) Applications must be received no later than January 30.

Subject Term(s) Fellowships; Individuals, Eligibility of; Humanities; Social Sciences; History; Anthropology

137. W. Alton Jones Foundation

433 Park Street
Charlottesville, VA 22901
(804) 295-2134

Sustainable Society Program

Program Description The Sustainable Society Program seeks to keep the earth suitable for long-term habitation by preserving the natural resource base. The program supports proposals for projects which address the conservation of biological diversity worldwide. The goal of this program is to preserve the diversity of the earth's plants, animals, natural communities, and ecosystems, and to preserve the ecosystem services required to maintain a livable biosphere.

Sample Grants In support of the purchase of the "Zona Protectora," $250,000 to National Parks Fundation of Costa Rica (1984). Augmentation of Iguana Management Project, $100,000 to the Smithsonian Tropical Research Institute (1984). For the fourth year of a five-year "Alternatives to Destruction Project," $138,930 (total project support $1,029,200) to the Smithsonian Tropical Research Institute (1984). In support of a wildlife program for Latin America which develops model projects demonstrating rational use and conservation of wildlife and wildlands in the tropics, and building the region's professional expertise in natural resource management, $333,333 (third year of a three-year $1,000,000 grant) to World Wildlife Fund—U.S. (1984).

Eligibility/Limitations The foundation does not support scholarship funds or make direct awards to individuals. The foundation has in the past supported projects which educate the public and the government; monitor the government; foster conservation through land purchases, easements, parks and preserves; include basic and applied research; initiate policy development, litigation, and mediation; and train resource specialists or develop indigenous organizations, especially in the tropics and other species-rich areas.

Fiscal Information Grant awards range from $4,000 to over $300,000. The foundation ordinarily will not consider proposals for capital purposes, endowment funds, or deficit operations.

Application Information A preliminary inquiry prior to the submission of a detailed proposal is advisable. A grant request should be initiated by a letter describing the proposed project, its expected impact, the qualifications of the staff, a detailed expense budget, the time frames, and other funding sources, as well as copies of the applicant organization's tax-exempt rulings stating that it is described in Section 501(c)(3) of the Internal Revenue Code and is not a private foundation.

Deadline(s) The commitment of grant funds is the responsibility of the board of trustees. The board meets in March, June, September, and December. Proposals should be submitted to the foundation's executive director prior to January 15, April 15, July 15, and October 15 to allow adequate time for review before the quarterly meetings.

Subject Term(s) Conservation; Natural Resources

138. The Helen Kellogg Institute for International Studies

University of Notre Dame
Notre Dame, IN 46556
(219) 239-6580

Kellogg Institute Residential Fellowships

Program Description The Helen Kellogg Institute for International Studies aims to advance understanding of Third World development, particularly in Latin America, through research, education, and outreach. The Kellogg Institute does advanced academic research which is consciously value-oriented. Its research is directed toward four principal themes: (1) alternative policies of economic development and their social consequences; (2) responses of those excluded from effective participation in political and economic life, including new patterns of association and changes in popular culture; (3) the social roles of religion and the Catholic Church; and (4) the processes and possibilities of democratization, including the effects of economic policy on democracy and the relationships between political and social democracy. The institute is primarily focused on Latin America, but is also interested in comparative perspectives on these themes.

Eligibility/Limitations The institute seeks fellows of high scholarly accomplishment and promise, both at senior and junior levels, whose work and presence will contribute creatively to its major research themes. It welcomes applications from candidates holding a Ph.D. or equivalent degree in any discipline of the social sciences or history. Candidates may be from any country. Candidates will be evaluated individually, but joint projects will be considered.

Fiscal Information Stipends to fellows vary with seniority and are based on comparable North American academic salaries (American Association of University Professors, Midwest Region). Fellowships may include one direct round-trip economy airfare. The institute requests that all fellows from abroad apply for travel grants to aid with transportation expenses to the United States.

Application Information For application forms and more information contact the associate academic director of the institute.

Deadline(s) The deadline for receipt of applications is December 1.

Subject Term(s) Foreign Nationals, Eligibility of; Fellowships; Values; Religion; Social Sciences; International Studies; Catholicism; Democracy

139. W. K. Kellogg Foundation

400 North Avenue
Battle Creek, MI 49017-3398
(616) 968-1611

Program Description The W. K. Kellogg Foundation is concerned with the application of knowledge to solving the problems of people. Such problems are numerous and complex. Foundation financial resources are limited. Therefore, the foundation has established programming priorities which focus its efforts to achieve maximum effect. The foundation concentrates its grantmaking in the following programming areas: adult continuing education; betterment of health (health promotion/disease prevention/public health); communitywide, coordinated, cost-effective health services; a wholesome food supply; and broadening leadership capacity of individuals. The foundation's current areas of activity are limited to the broad fields of agriculture, education, and health. The foundation also assists educational and service projects of potential national or international importance that emphasize the application of new knowledge in addressing significant human problems.

Sample Grants To seek solutions to problems faced by family medicine programs in Argentina, Brazil, and Chile by supporting the first regional meeting of general/family medicine in Argentina, $27,500 to the Society of Teachers of Family Medicine Foundation, Kansas City, Missouri (1984). To increase understanding about child health care needs in Third World countries by publishing a book on the lessons learned in projects in northeast Brazil, $8,000 to the University of Virginia, Charlottesville (1985). To improve the health and nutritional self-sufficiency of poor rural people through conservation, training, reforestation, and agricultural improvement, $‘ to Plan Sierra, Santiago, Dominican Republic (1985).

Eligibility/Limitations To be eligible for support, organizations and institutions must qualify under the regulations of the United States Internal Revenue Service. Grantees must have the financial potential to sustain the project on a continuing basis after foundation funding is ended.

Fiscal Information During the 1984-85 fiscal year, foundation expenditures exceeded $69 million. Program expenditures in Latin America exceeded $6.9 million. The foundation does not make loans and does not provide grants for: operational phases of established programs; capital facilities, equipment, conferences, publications, films, or television or radio programs, unless they are an integral phase of a project already funded; endowments or developmental campaigns; basic research; planning and studies; religious purposes; or individuals—except for fellowships in specific areas of foundation programming.

Application Information The foundation does not have grant application forms. To be considered for foundation aid, an institution or organization should write a proposal letter or memorandum briefly describing the basic problem and the plan for its solution. The plan should include project objectives, operational procedures, time schedule, and personnel and financial resources available and needed. Proposal letters are carefully evaluated by the foundation. If the proposal is within the foundation's guidelines and interests, and if foundation priorities and resources permit consideration of the requested aid, conferences and staff investigation may follow. The organization may be asked to develop a more detailed proposal which includes a plan for evaluation of the project's effect. Proposal letters should be addressed to the chief programming officer of the foundation.

Subject Term(s) Education; Agriculture; Health

140. W. K. Kellogg Foundation

400 North Avenue
Battle Creek, MI 49017-3398
(616) 968-1611

Kellogg National Fellowship Program

Program Description The Kellogg National Fellowship Program offers outstanding young American professionals an opportunity to broaden their social and intellectual sensitivity, awareness, and leadership potential. The foundation created the program because it recognized that, while social and technical problems increase in complexity, much of the professional and disciplinary training people receive becomes extremely narrow and specialized. A basic aim of the program is to assist future leaders in developing skills and competencies which transcend traditional disciplinary and professional methods of addressing problems. To this end, the program provides experiences which equip participants to address social issues in creative ways. Of particular interest to the foundation are those pursuits involving broad issues in agriculture, education, and health. Fellows may be drawn from business, education, human service agencies, and private practice.

Eligibility/Limitations To be eligible, an applicant must: be nominated by the applicant's employing organization or institution, or one of the approved national associations involved in the foundation's programming interests; be a citizen of the United States; be in the early years of professional activity; have the endorsement of the applicant's immediate supervisor and the chief executive officer, or the president, of the institution, agency, or business for which the applicant works (not applicable for candidates in private practice); accept responsibility during the three-year fellowship period to participate in all activities related to the Kellogg National Fellowship Program; and not be, during the three-year period, or become, a "government official" as defined in the Internal Revenue Code.

Fiscal Information Awards of up to $30,000 for the three-year program, plus 12.5% of the fellow's annual salary (not to exceed an aggregate for the three years of $12,000), will be made in behalf of as many as fifty individuals. During the program, fellows maintain their present employment while pursuing fellowship-related activities. During the program, fellows should spend approximately 25% of their time on fellowship-related activities, including a self-designed learning plan for personal and professional development as well as group seminars. Awards will not be made for basic research or the acquisition of new knowledge or skills within the applicant's principal discipline or profession. Rather, the experience is intended to provide opportunities to develop new and broadened abilities.

Application Information Applicants are asked to complete an application, including a statement of personal and professional goals, and provide an outline of their proposed fellowship activities related to such goals. The applicant is required to submit recommendations from his or her immediate supervisor and from two other persons, using forms provided. Application forms are currently available in the offices of the presidents of eligible institutions, agencies, and associations. They are also available from the foundation. Based upon applications and letters of reference, candidates may be asked to appear for a personal interview at the Kellogg Foundation's expense.

Deadline(s) Completed applications and all institutional endorsements and reference forms (which may be mailed separately) must be postmarked by December 31.

Subject Term(s) Fellowships; Agriculture; Education; Health; Individuals, Eligibility of

141. Samuel H. Kress Foundation

221 West 57th Street
New York, NY 10019
(212) 586-4450

Fellowships in Art Conservation

Program Description Advanced students in the conservation of works of art may compete for funds to support their studies.

Eligibility/Limitations Applicants must be citizens of the United States, and must be already accepted into a training program.

Application Information Further information is available on written request to the foundation.

Deadline(s) Application deadline is January 31.

Subject Term(s) Fellowships; Art Conservation; Graduate Support

142. Samuel H. Kress Foundation

221 West 57th Street
New York, NY 10019
(212) 586-4450

Grants

Program Description Continuing its traditional concerns, the Kress Foundation concentrates its funding in the history and preservation of art. Present program areas of interest include: (1) fellowships for predoctoral research in art history, (2) training and research in conservation of works of art, (3) development of scholarly resources in the fields of art history and conservation, (4) conservation and restoration of monuments and works of art, (5) archeological fieldwork emphasizing art history, and (6) occasional related projects.

Sample Grants A dissertation grant was awarded for the study of Ntra. Sr. de Ocotlan and the group of "Memposteria" facade churches in the Tlaxcala area (1982-83).

Eligibility/Limitations The foundation does not consider grants for living artists, films, art history programs below the predoctoral level, or the purchase of works of art.

Fiscal Information Grants awarded in 1984 ranged in amount from $1,500 to $261,500.

Application Information The foundation does not have formal application forms. A simple letter describing the project and the funds to be requested will insure consideration.

Deadline(s) Proposals for projects within the program areas listed above may be submitted to the foundation at any time.

Subject Term(s) Fellowships; Predoctoral Support; Art History; Art Conservation; Archeology

143. Samuel H. Kress Foundation

221 West 57th Street
New York, NY 10019
(212) 586-4450

Research Fellowships in Art History

Program Description Travel grants to enable predoctoral candidates in the history of art to pursue essential research are available annually through a program administered by the foundation.

Eligibility/Limitations Applicants must be citizens of the United States, and must anticipate the completion of all requirements for the Ph.D. degree except the dissertation at the time the grant will be received.

Application Information Further information is available on written request to the foundation.

Deadline(s) Application deadline is November 30.

Subject Term(s) Fellowships; Doctoral Dissertation Support; Travel Support; Art History

144. L.S.B. Leakey Foundation

Foundation Center 1-7
Pasadena, CA 91125
(818) 449-0507, 449-0508

Fellowship for the Study of Foraging Peoples

Program Description The board of the foundation awards, from time to time, a fellowship in support of research among contemporary foraging peoples. The foundation is especially interested in proposals for urgent research that might not ordinarily be funded by other funding agencies.

Eligibility/Limitations Individuals proposing field research among contemporary foraging peoples are eligible to apply.

Fiscal Information A fellowship of up to $20,000 for one to two years of field expenses is available.

Application Information Additional information is available on request.

Deadline(s) The deadline for initial application is May 1.

Subject Term(s) Field Research, Support of; Anthropology; Fellowships

145. L. S. B. Leakey Foundation

Foundation Center 1-7
Pasadena, CA 91125
(818) 449-0507

Grants

Program Description The L.S.B. Leakey Foundation was formed to further research into human origins, behavior, and survival. Its sphere of interest lies in the support of research related to human evolution. In recent years this has meant that priority has been given to research into the ecology, archeology, and human paleontology of the Miocene, Pliocene, and Pleistocene; into the behavior of great apes and other Old World primate species; and into the ecology and adaptations of living hunter-gatherer peoples. The foundation recognizes that not all research related to human evolution falls into these categories and other areas of study have been funded occasionally. Priority is normally given to the exploratory phase of promising new projects and to enabling researchers to exploit novel opportunities in establishing programs.

Eligibility/Limitations Grants are normally made to scientists with professional qualifications and demonstrated capability. Applications from graduate students working for an advanced degree will be considered if supported by their faculty advisor. Undergraduates are not eligible to apply to the foundation directly. However, they may be supported as part of a principal investigator's project.

Fiscal Information The majority of the foundation's grants have been of $3,000 or less. The foundation is prepared to raise funds by special appeal to its membership to support special requests in addition to those projects approved for general funds. If grants are likely to be required in future years for long-term projects, some estimate of future requirements should be made in the initial application. In addition, applicants should be aware that publication subvention is generally given low priority.

Application Information Applicants should first complete the Petition for Grant Application form available from the foundation upon request. If the research plan described in the petition is considered for funding by the board of trustees, a formal application giving full particulars will be requested.

Deadline(s) Application deadlines are March 1, June 1, September 1, and December 1.

Additional Information Please note that the grant application process is initiated by submission of the *Petition for Grant Application.* Other material will not substitute for this form nor will it be accommodated as part of the review process for this petition.

Subject Term(s) Anthropology; Graduate Support

146. The Charles A. Lindbergh Fund, Inc.

Grants Office
Box O
Summit, NJ 07901
(201) 522-1392

The Lindbergh Grants Program

Program Description This program offers grants to individuals working for a balance between technological progress and the preservation of our natural and human environment to achieve a better quality of life for all. The board of directors of the fund is interested in increasing representation in the following areas: aeronautics/astronautics/aviation, agriculture, biomedical research, conservation of natural resources, health and population sciences, intercultural communication, oceanography and water resources, waste disposal management, and wildlife preservation.

Eligibility/Limitations The Lindbergh Grants Program is international in scope. Citizens of all countries are eligible. The fund welcomes candidates who are affiliated with an academic or non-profit institution. Grants are awarded to individuals, not to affiliated institutions for institutional programs.

Fiscal Information Grants of up to $10,580 will be awarded annually. In 1986 the average grant size was $8,625.

Application Information Copies of the Lindbergh Grants Announcement and application guidelines can be obtained by writing the fund.

Deadline(s) Complete applications should be received by the fund before October 15.

Additional Information The Lindbergh-Guggenheim Grants in Anthropology are provided by the Harry Frank Guggenheim Foundation for the study of the impact of technology on people and the quality of life. The recipient of the first (1985) grant was the Assistant Curator at the New York Botanical Garden for a project entitled "The Panare Indians and their forest: An ethnological inventory in Venezuelan Guayana."

Subject Term(s) Foreign Nationals, Eligibility of; Individuals, Eligibility of; Science and Technology; Environment; Conservation; Agriculture; Biomedical Sciences; Population Studies; Intercultural Studies; Wildlife Conservation; Oceanography; Natural Resources, Water; Anthropology

147. London School of Hygiene and Tropical Medicine

University of London
Keppel Street
London WC1E 7HT England
01-636 8636

Nestle Nutrition Research Grant Program

Program Description This program supports research whose objective is to improve the nutrition, growth, and development of children and the lactation and welfare of the mother. Within this general field the grants committee has identified certain areas in which it considers that more research is particularly needed: interactions between maternal nutrition, lactation, fertility, and infant survival and well-being; causes and functional significance of retarded fetal and postnatal growth; and child-rearing practices and their effects on mother and child. Although priority is given to proposals falling within these areas, applications are invited which relate to any aspect of the overall program.

Eligibility/Limitations The program is open to applications from investigators in any country. However, the grant committee considers that there is a special need to encourage research in developing countries and to promote the research capacity of younger people.

Fiscal Information The program does not provide scholarships or fellowships or grants to attend scientific meetings.

Application Information Additional information and application guidelines are available on request.

Subject Term(s) Child Development; Mothers and Children; Nutrition; Foreign Nationals, Eligibility of; Fertility

148. J. Roderick MacArthur Foundation

9333 North Milwaukee Avenue
Niles, IL 60648
(312) 966-0143

Program Description The primary aims of the J. Roderick MacArthur Foundation in fulfilling its charitable, scientific, literary, and educational purposes are to aid those who are inequitably or unjustly treated by established institutions. The foundation seeks to foster discussion about and needed changes in these institutions by protecting and encouraging freedom of expression, human rights, civil liberties, and social justice; and by eliminating political, economic, social, religious, and cultural oppression. The foundation supports efforts and projects, including litigation, throughout the world to: (1) eliminate censorship and protect freedom of expression, including the freedom to hold and express opinions in all media of communications, both within and between nations; (2) foster human rights, including political, social, economic, and cultural rights; (3) protect and foster civil liberties in the United States (including all Constitutional rights) and to encourage their eventual observance in the rest of the world; and (4) foster social justice and the elimination of political, economic, social, religious, and cultural oppression.

Sample Grants To support the Human Rights Commission of the El Salvador Project, $10,000 to the National Council of Churches of Christ in the U.S.A., Human Rights and Latin America and Caribbean Offices (1985). To send a team of forensic scientists to assist in the identification of human remains of the "disappeared" and to send a geneticist to assist in determination of grandpaternity of living children who "disappeared" with their parents (and whose parents were subsequently killed), $19,000 to the American Association for the Advancement of Science (1985).

Eligibility/Limitations Only nonprofit, tax-exempt organizations as defined under Section 501(c)(3) of the United States Internal Revenue Code are eligible for funding. Capital projects, endowments, loan requests, ordinary social services of an ongoing nature, programs that are the routine responsibilities of government, and religious/church-based activities ordinarily will not be considered. The foundation will not consider the purchase of blocks of tickets, support for benefits, solicitations from regular development campaigns, and annual contribution drives. Also generally excluded are requests for conference expenses, projects to erect statues, memorials, or the like, and organizations already supported by tax revenues.

Fiscal Information Grant awards are usually not more than $20,000.

Application Information Rather than submit a formal application with supporting materials, potential grantees may wish first to send a preliminary letter of inquiry to determine foundation interest in their request. This letter should describe succinctly the background, programs, personnel, and purposes of the organization and should briefly, but thoroughly, outline the proposal and its cost. When submitting a formal application, provide specific and detailed information. Include the legal name, address, and telephone number of the organization, and the name of a representative who can be contacted by telephone. Submit the organization's most recent budget, audited financial statements (if available), annual reports, and past and current funding information (grantors and the amounts contributed by each). Also include the most recent copies of IRS tax-exempt determination letters indicating status under Sections 501(c)(3) and 509(a) of the Internal Revenue Code, along with a brief history of the organization, its general goals, and purposes. Submit a specific statement detailing the objectives of the proposed grant, an itemized budget broken down to show specific costs related to the proposed project, and the names and backgrounds of any individuals involved in carrying it out. Point out any unique facts of the request and what differentiates it from other projects of the same nature. Specify the expected duration of the project and any details regarding other potential funding sources. Include a synopsis of the plans to evaluate the results of the project and any past evaluations done by the organization on similar programs or efforts.

Deadline(s) No deadlines are announced.

Subject Term(s) Human Rights; Civil Liberty; Social Justice

149. The John D. and Catherine MacArthur Foundation

140 South Dearborn Street
Chicago, IL 60603
(312) 726-8000

Grants Programs

Program Description The John D. and Catherine T. MacArthur Foundation is a private, independent, grant-making foundation created in 1978 for charitable and public service purposes. It has developed a limited number of innovative programs in areas within which it can act as a catalyst for useful change. There are currently specific areas of sustained foundation emphasis: (1) health, devoted primarily to research on mental health and on the biology of parasitic disease; (2) international security, which seeks to expand and strengthen the field of international security studies to increase public understanding of complex security issues; (3) world environment and resources, consisting principally of the development and initial sustaining support of the World Resources Institute, Washington, DC; (4) general grants, a locus for foundation interests in education, governance and public affairs, criminal and civil justice, and mass communications; and (5) special grants, supporting cultural and community activities in the Chicago area.

Sample Grants In support of the acquisition of the La Selva Protection Zone, a 19,000 acre property on the Atlantic slope of Costa Rica, on a dollar-for-dollar challenge basis, with the property ultimately to be turned over to the Costa Rican Park Service for management for scientific research, education and conservation, $1,000,000 to The Nature Conservancy, Arlington, Virginia (1983).

Eligibility/Limitations The foundation does not make awards to individuals, except by way of the MacArthur Fellows Program. Increasingly, grants are made in support of foundation-generated initiatives rather than in response to grant requests.

Application Information Detailed information on programs and policies is available from the foundation.

Subject Term(s) Health; International Security; Environment; Natural Resources

150. The John D. and Catherine MacArthur Foundation

140 South Dearborn Street
Chicago, IL 60603
(312) 726-8000

MacArthur Fellows Program

Program Description The MacArthur Fellows Program provides unique, unrestricted fellowships to exceptionally talented and promising individuals who have given evidence of originality, dedication to creative pursuits, and a capacity for self-direction. MacArthur fellowships are intended to enhance the ability of recipients to pursue their work in accordance with their own inclinations. Fellows are free to focus on more than one area through interdisciplinary work, to change fields if they wish, or even to alter the direction of their careers.

Sample Grants In 1984 fellowships were awarded to scholars in Mesoamerican archeology and in Mayan archeology and epigraphy.

Eligibility/Limitations Only an individual whose name is submitted to the foundation by a designated nominator is eligible for the MacArthur Fellows Program. The fellowships are intended to support individuals, not projects. Fellows may be writers, scientists, artists, social scientists, humanists, activists, or workers in any other field or fields, with or without institutional affiliations. Candidates for fellowships must be either residents or citizens of the United States, but otherwise there are no restrictions placed on nominators regarding their nominations.

Fiscal Information Fellows receive an income in monthly installments over five years so that they may have the time and freedom to fulfill their promise by devoting themselves to their own endeavors at their own pace. Fellows are paid amounts from $24,000 to $60,000 annually, determined by the age of the recipients, regardless of their professional fields. Fellows are provided with comprehensive health insurance, and if a fellow elects to work at a university or other eligible institution, that institution may receive a separate award of $15,000 annually. All fellows are invited, but not required, to attend an annual informal gathering, to meet each other and exchange ideas.

Application Information The MacArthur Fellows Program depends for its candidates on more than one hundred nominators across the country in many academic and professional fields. Nominators are invited to serve for one year, and are asked to propose extraordinarily creative and promising individuals at points in their careers when such an opportunity could make a marked difference. Applications and informal nominations are not accepted. Only an individual whose name is submitted by a designated nominator is eligible, and nominees are not contacted. Every nominee is considered by a selection committee which makes its recommendations to the board of directors of the foundation. Nominators and selectors serve anonymously.

Deadline(s) There are no times set for announcements or yearly quotas of MacArthur Fellows.

Additional Information The program also honors a very small number of MacArthur Fellows as Laureates. These individuals are at retirement age or older. The support for their continued creative work differs from that of the other fellows only in that Laureates are each guaranteed $60,000 annually for life.

Subject Term(s) Awards and Prizes; Fellowships

151. The Andrew W. Mellon Foundation

140 East 62nd Street
New York, NY 10021
(212) 838-8400

Grants

Program Description The purpose of the foundation is to "aid and promote such religious, charitable, scientific, literary, and educational purposes as may be in the furtherance of the public welfare or to tend to promote the well-doing or well-being of mankind." Within this broad charter the foundation currently makes grants on a selective basis to institutions of higher education; in cultural affairs and the performing arts; in medical, public health, and population education and research; and in certain areas of conservation, natural resources, the environment, and public affairs.

Sample Grants For the SAIS Central American and Caribbean program, $225,000 to Johns Hopkins University (1985). A matching endowment for advanced research and training on Latin America, $150,000 to the University of Chicago (1985). A matching endowment for advanced research and training on Latin America, $250,000 to the University of Florida, Gainesville (1985).

Eligibility/Limitations The foundation does not award fellowships or other grants to individuals or make grants to primarily local organizations.

Fiscal Information Grants awarded in fiscal 1985 totaled approximately $63 million.

Application Information No special application forms are required. Ordinarily a simple letter setting forth the need, the nature, and the amount of the request and the justification for it, together with evidence of suitable classification by the Internal Revenue Service and any supplementary exhibits an applicant may wish to submit, will suffice to assure consideration.

Deadline(s) Applications are considered throughout the year.

Subject Term(s) Cultural Affairs, Support of; Arts, Support of; Education; Health; Population Studies; Conservation; Natural Resources; Environment; Public Affairs

152. The Metropolitan Museum of Art

Fifth Avenue and 82nd Street
New York, NY 10028
(212) 879-5500

Andrew W. Mellon Fellowships

Program Description These fellowships are provided by the Andrew W. Mellon Fund for promising young scholars with commendable research projects related to the museum's collections, as well as for distinguished visiting scholars from this country and abroad who can serve as teachers and advisors and make their expertise available to catalogue and refine the collections.

Eligibility/Limitations Applicants should have received the doctorate or have completed substantial work toward it.

Fiscal Information The stipend amount varies with particular circumstances. Usually a fellowship will be given for a maximum of one year, most of which should be spent at the Metropolitan Museum.

Application Information There are no application forms. Applicants must submit a typed application including the following (in triplicate): name, home and present address, and telephone number; full resume of education (including official undergraduate and graduate transcripts) and employment; a two-part statement, not to exceed two thousand words, specifying what the applicant wishes to accomplish during the fellowship period, and detailing how the Metropolitan Museum's resources can be utilized to accomplish the applicant's goals; and tentative schedule of work to be accomplished and travel required during the fellowship period. Three recommendations (at least one academic and one professional) should be sent directly to the grants committee at the museum.

Deadline(s) Applications for fellowships must be made by letter and must be submitted by December 14 to the secretary of the grants committee.

Additional Information For all fellowships offered by the museum, it is the responsibility of the applicant, in connection with any project that may reasonably be expected to require assistance from a particular museum department, to discuss the project with the department concerned and to obtain that department's approval before submitting the application. Such departmental approval should not, however, be construed as assurance that a fellowship will be awarded by the grants committee. Fellowships generally cannot be given for projects proposing that an exhibition be organized and presented within the fellowship period.

Subject Term(s) Fellowships; Foreign Nationals, Eligibility of; Predoctoral Support; Collections Study, Museums; Cataloguing, Museum Collections; Art

153. The Metropolitan Museum of Art

Fifth Avenue and 82nd Street
New York, NY 10028
(212) 879-5500

Andrew W. Mellon Fellowships

Program Description The Andrew W. Mellon Foundation has made it possible for The Metropolitan Museum of Art to award annual conservation fellowships for training in one or more of the following departments of the museum: paintings conservation, objects conservation (including such materials and objects as metal, arms and armor, stone, wood, musical instruments, glass and ceramics), paper conservation, textile conservation, and the Costume Institute.

Eligibility/Limitations Whenever possible, fellowship applicants should already have reached an advanced level of experience or training.

Fiscal Information Fellowship recipients will receive stipends appropriate to their level of training or experience. Additional funds may be available for travel, books, photographs, and other reasonable or necessary expenses incident to the fellowship. Fellowships will typically be one year in duration with the possibility of renewal for up to two additional years. Fellowship recipients are expected to spend the fellowship in residence in the department with which they are affiliated.

Application Information There are no application forms. Applicants must submit a typed application including the following: name, home and present address, and telephone number; full resume of education and professional experience; a statement, not to exceed one thousand words, describing what the applicant expects to accomplish during the fellowship period, and detailing how the Metropolitan Museum's resources can be utilized to accomplish the applicant's goals; tentative schedule of work to be accomplished and travel required during the fellowship period; and three recommendations (at least one academic and one professional).

Deadline(s) Applications for fellowships must be submitted by January 16 to: The Mellon Fellowships in Conservation, Office of Academic Affairs.

Additional Information For all fellowships offered by the museum, it is the responsibility of the applicant, in connection with any project that may reasonably be expected to require assistance from a particular museum department, to discuss the project with the department concerned and to obtain that department's approval before submitting the application. Such departmental approval should not, however, be construed as assurance that a fellowship will be awarded by the grants committee.

Subject Term(s) Fellowships; Art Conservation; Museums; Conservation; Art

154. The Metropolitan Museum of Art

Fifth Avenue and 82nd Street
New York, NY 10028
(212) 879-5500

J. Clawson Mills Scholarships

Program Description Scholars interested in pursuing research projects in any branch of the fine arts related to the Metropolitan Museum's collections are eligible for J. Clawson Mills Scholarships.

Eligibility/Limitations The scholarships are generally reserved for mature scholars of demonstrated ability.

Fiscal Information The scholarships provide for study or research at the museum for one year with the possibility of renewal for a second year.

Application Information There are no application forms. Applicants must submit a typed application including the following (in triplicate): name, home and present address, and telephone number; full resume of education (including official undergraduate and graduate transcripts) and employment; a two-part statement, not to exceed two thousand words, specifying what the applicant wishes to accomplish during the fellowship period, and detailing how the Metropolitan Museum's resources can be utilized to accomplish the applicant's goals; and tentative schedule of work to be accomplished and travel required during the fellowship period. Three recommendations (at least one academic and one professional) should be sent directly to the grants committee at the museum.

Deadline(s) Applications for fellowships must be made by letter and must be submitted by November 22 to the Fellowship Program, Office of Academic Affairs.

Additional Information For all fellowships offered by the museum, it is the responsibility of the applicant, in connection with any project that may reasonably be expected to require assistance from a particular museum department, to discuss the project with the department concerned and to obtain that department's approval before submitting the application. Such departmental approval should not, however, be construed as assurance that a fellowship will be awarded by the grants committee. Fellowships generally cannot be given for projects proposing that an exhibition be organized and presented within the fellowship period.

Subject Term(s) Individuals, Eligibility of; Collections Study, Museums; Museums; Fine Arts; Fellowships; Art

155. National Association for Foreign Student Affairs

1860 Nineteenth Street, NW
Washington, DC 20009
(202) 462-4811

Cooperative Grants Program

Program Description The Cooperative Grants Program (COOP) supports the development of innovative programming for foreign college or university students in the U.S. and U.S. post-secondary students involved in study-abroad programs. Projects should focus on the direct involvement of foreign students and/or U.S. study-abroad students in enrichment activities which will make the host culture more accessible to the student, assist the student to understand the culture, and facilitate interaction between the student and the host community. Projects should complement the institutions' ongoing activities in international education and will be considered in one of the following areas: (1) innovative campus or community-based projects, presenting an idea not previously funded by COOP; (2) implementation projects which adapt ideas previously funded by COOP to a different setting; and (3) city and area-wide projects which incorporate/coordinate the resources available to foreign students in a broad geographic area.

Eligibility/Limitations Project proposals are accepted from any institution or group working with non-sponsored foreign students in the U.S. and U.S. study-abroad students at the post-secondary school level.

Fiscal Information Awards of up to $5,000 for one-year projects are available.

Application Information A "COOP Information Packet" which includes criteria, guidelines, and proposal forms and a "Model International Student Involvement Programs" brochure which lists the programs funded by COOP in the last ten years are available on request.

Deadline(s) For deadline information contact COOP program staff.

Subject Term(s) International Education; Education; Foreign Nationals, Eligibility of

156. National Association for Foreign Student Affairs

1860 Nineteenth Street, NW
Washington, DC 20009
(202) 462-4811

Field Service

Program Description Field Service funding is available to support the professional development of persons working in the field of international educational exchange and to strengthen services provided for foreign students and scholars at U.S. colleges and universities and for U.S. college and university students abroad. Field Service offers funding, on a cost-sharing basis, in order to: (1) introduce new personnel to professional standards, activities, and resources; (2) foster the improvement of campus and community services to foreign students and U.S. students abroad; and (3) assist institutions in fulfilling the responsibilities they incur in engaging in international educational exchange. Current program priorities include: (1) increasing the sophistication and effectiveness of intercultural programming conducted for students; (2) encouraging data collection, needs assessment, and research, the direct practice and application of which will affect the delivery of services to students and scholars; and (3) improving the intercultural re-entry process. The Field Service is particularly interested in encouraging efforts that are planned on a long-range basis, reach a high-level audience, involve faculty as well as international educational exchange professionals, involve more than one of the National Association for Foreign Student Affairs' (NAFSA) professional sections and/or other educational associations, and make use of new technologies available.

Eligibility/Limitations Individuals, institutions, and community organizations are eligible to apply. Field Service grants support a variety of activities, including: professional development projects from senior international educators, in-service training projects, workshops, and travel to NAFSA conferences or workshops.

Fiscal Information Awards vary according to project.

Application Information Additional information and application guidelines are available on request.

Deadline(s) Deadlines are available from NAFSA.

Subject Term(s) International Education; Education; Individuals, Eligibility of

157. National Association for Foreign Student Affairs

1860 Nineteenth Street, NW
Washington, DC 20009
(202) 462-4811

Grants for Research in Education for International Development

Program Description The Education for International Development (EID) Committee of the National Association for Foreign Student Affairs (NAFSA) announces the availability of grants to support research in the field of education for international development. The EID program exists to improve and support the educational services available to students from the developing world. Each year the members of the EID steering committee determine several areas in which they perceive a need for substantive research. Three areas are of current interest: (1) the professional integration of foreign students returning to the developing world; (2) technology transfer through international education; and (3) the foreign student as an educational, cultural, and/or economic resource.

Eligibility/Limitations Grants may be awarded only to institutions and organizations, not to individuals. The committee will fund only projects displaying innovation and earning financial support from other institutional or community sources. In addition, EID-supported research must be conducted within the United States.

Fiscal Information The maximum grant is $3,500. EID grants may not be used to fund the following: institutional overhead expenses, entertainment, international travel, refreshments, and nonexpendable items such as furniture or office equipment.

Application Information For further information on the grant application procedure, contact the EID program staff.

Deadline(s) The preliminary application deadline is in September; final application deadline is in December. Contact the program staff for more information.

Additional Information These grants are made possible through funding from the Office of International Training, U.S. Agency for International Development.

Subject Term(s) International Development; Education; Developing Countries; International Education; Foreign Nationals, Eligibility of

158. National Cancer Institute

Division of Cancer Etiology
Bethesda, MD 20205
(301) 496-6618

Cancer Cause and Prevention Research

CFDA Program Number 13.393

Program Description Cancer Cause and Prevention Research is concerned with identification of those factors which cause cancer in man and with the development of mechanisms for preventing cancer in man. The following research programs are included: epidemiology, chemical and physical carcinogenesis, biological carcinogenesis, nutrition, immunology, field studies and statistics, and organ site.

Eligibility/Limitations The awardee will be a university, college, hospital, public agency, nonprofit research institution, or for-profit organization that submits an application and receives a grant or cooperative agreement for support of research by a named principal investigator.

Fiscal Information Grants and cooperative agreements may be made to eligible institutions for the support of cancer research projects. The grants and cooperative agreements may be used for personnel, consultant costs, equipment, supplies, travel, patient costs, animals, alterations and renovations, miscellaneous items, and indirect costs. Grants and cooperative agreements average three to four years, with a maximum duration of five years. Renewals may be awarded for additional periods up to five years based on competitive peer review. Grants range from $2,000 to $3.5 million, with an average award of $161,000.

Application Information The standard application forms as furnished by DHHS and required by OMB Circular No. A-102 must be used for this program. Application form PHS-398 is the standard form which can be obtained from the Division of Research Grants, NIH, Bethesda, MD 20205 and submitted to the same address.

Deadline(s) New Grants and Cooperative Agreements applications should be submitted by February 1, June 1, and October 1. Renewal and supplement applications should be submitted by March 1, July 1, and November 1.

Subject Term(s) Cancer Research

159. National Cancer Institute

Division of Cancer Etiology
Bethesda, MD 20205
(301) 496-6618

Cancer Control

CFDA Program Number 13.399

Program Description The Cancer Control Program seeks to reduce cancer incidence, morbidity, and mortality through an orderly sequence from research on interventions and their impact in defined populations to the broad, systematic application of research results. Primary emphasis is on the inclusion of a cancer control intervention in any proposed study. Cancer control research studies are classified into one of five phases which represent the orderly progression noted in the definition: (1) hypothesis development; (2) methods development and testing; (3) controlled intervention trials to establish cause-and-effect relationships; (4) research in defined populations; and (5) demonstration and implementation studies. Primary interest is in research on cancer control interventions in phases two through five, with emphasis on studies in defined populations (phase four). There is no interest in studies which address only phase one. Cancer control programs include those in the following areas: (1) chemoprevention; (2) diet and nutrition; (3) occupational cancer control; (4) screening and early detection; (5) community oncology—management and continuing care and rehabilitation; (6) health promotion sciences; (7) public health applications; (8) evaluation and cancer control operations research; and (9) smoking, tobacco, and cancer.

Eligibility/Limitations The awardee will be a university, college, hospital, public agency, nonprofit research institution, or for-profit organization which submits an application and receives a grant or cooperative agreement for support of research by a principal investigator.

Fiscal Information Grants and cooperative agreements may be made to eligible institutions for the support of cancer research projects. The grants and cooperative agreements may be used for personnel, consultant costs, equipment, supplies, travel, patient costs, animals, alterations and renovations, miscellaneous items, and indirect costs. Restrictions are imposed against the use of funds for entertainment, foreign travel (unless specifically authorized), office equipment, and other items not normally necessary for the effective prosecution of such research. Grants and cooperative agreements average from three to four years, up to a maximum of five years. Renewals may be awarded for additional periods of up to five years based on competitive peer review.

Application Information The standard application forms, as furnished by DHHS and required by OMB Circular No. A-102 for state and local governments, must be used for this program. Application form PHS-398 is the standard form which can be obtained from the Division of Research Grants, NIH, Bethesda, MD 20205.

Deadline(s) Applications for new programs should be received by February 1, June 1, and October 1. Applications for renewal and supplements are due by March 1, July 1, and November 1.

Subject Term(s) Cancer Research

160. National Endowment for Democracy

1156 Fifteenth Street, NW, Suite 304
Washington, DC 20005
(202) 293-9072

Program Description The National Endowment for Democracy is a new U.S. initiative to strengthen democratic institutions throughout the world through private, nongovernmental efforts. Through its worldwide grant program, the endowment assists those abroad who are working for democratic goals. In this effort, it seeks to enlist the energies and talents of private citizens and groups in the United States to work in partnership with democrats abroad. The endowment is currently funding programs in five substantive areas: (1) Pluralism—the endowment encourages the development of strong, independent, private-sector organizations, especially trade unions and business associations. (2) Democratic Governance and Political Processes—the endowment seeks to promote strong, stable political parties committed to the democratic process. (3) Education, Culture and Communications—the endowment funds programs that nourish a strong democratic civic culture, including support for publications and other communications media and training programs for journalists; the production and dissemination of books and other materials to strengthen popular understanding and intellectual advocacy of democracy; and programs of democratic education. (4) Research—a modest portion of endowment resources is reserved for research, including studies of particular regions or countries where the endowment has special interest, and evaluations of previous or existing efforts to promote democracy. (5) International Cooperation—the endowment seeks to encourage regional and international cooperation in promoting democracy, including programs that strengthen cohesion among democracies and enhance coordination among democratic forces.

Sample Grants To organize and conduct a workshop in the Dominican Republic designed to improve Latin American employers' organizations use of modern communications equipment, $53,515 to International Organization of Employers, Geneva,

Switzerland (1985). To continue advocacy on behalf of the informal business sector within the Peruvian economy through efforts to effect institutional change and deregulation in Peru, $240,000 to Instituto Libertad y Democracia, Lima, Peru (1985). To produce an audiovisual presentation that explores means of promoting the integration of the informal business sector in Latin America into the formal economies of the region, $30,740 to Accion International, Washington, DC (1985).

Eligibility/Limitations Funding decisions are made by the board of directors on the basis of established selection criteria. In addition to evaluating how a program fits within the endowment's overall priorities, the board considers factors such as the urgency of a program, its relevance to specific needs and conditions in a particular country, and the democratic commitment and experience of the applicant. The endowment is especially interested in proposals that originate with indigenous democratic groups.

Fiscal Information Grant awards vary according to project.

Application Information Endowment staff is happy to discuss proposal ideas and welcomes preliminary letters of inquiry prior to submission of a formal proposal. Additional information and application guidelines are available from the director of public affairs of the endowment.

Deadline(s) Contact the endowment for current deadline information.

Subject Term(s) Business; Governance; Law; Communications; Area Studies; Democracy; International Affairs

161. National Endowment for the Arts

Expansion Arts Program
1100 Pennsylvania Avenue, NW
Washington, DC 20506
(202) 682-5443

Expansion Arts Organizations

CFDA Program Number 45.010

Program Description The Expansion Arts Program supports professionally-directed arts organizations of high artistic quality which are deeply rooted in and reflective of the culture of a minority, inner city, rural, or tribal community. These organizations must have a fundamental relationship to their community, and the provision of art to their community must be the organization's primary programmatic activity. Organizations that fit these criteria are referred to by the endowment as "expansion arts organizations." These characteristics distinguish expansion arts organizations from mainstream institutions that offer outreach programs at the communities described as an aspect of their overall activities. The program encourages original and promising works of art; performances of the classic repertoire of a particular culture; exhibitions of new artists or of important artists within a community; and provision of access to quality art of all types. The program also promotes the career development of artists from minority, inner city, rural, or tribal communities through support of professional training of serious and talented individuals.

Sample Grants For the production of four plays, including two original works by a Cuban playwright and a contemporary Latin American writer, $30,000 to the Bilingual Foundation of the Arts, Los Angeles, California (1984). For a filmmaking promotion program and professional training workshops expressive of Puerto Rican culture, $6,850 to Bondo, Santurce, Puerto Rico (1984). For a professional dance training program, including master classes, Caribbean music instruction, and performances, $5,000 to the Buffalo Inner City Ballet Company, Buffalo, New York (1984). For administrative costs and a scholarship program for advanced classes in classical and popular Chinese/Latin styles, $30,000 to the Community Music Center, San Francisco, California (1984). For film, video, and slide presentations by independent artists from Latin and North America, concerts of folk music, a film editing workshop, and exhibits of works by Central American artists at the Taller Art Gallery, $25,000 to Latin American Workshop, New York (1984). For the Theatre Training Unit, a professional training program for Hispanic youth, and the season of the Puerto Rican

Traveling Theatre, $60,000 to the Puerto Rican Traveling Theatre Company, New York (1984). For a career training program in folkloric dance and a performance schedule for rural communities throughout Puerto Rico, $9,000 to Compania Folklorica Puertorriquena, Inc., San Juan, Puerto Rico (1985). For workshops in traditional Mexican music of Veracruz and Jalisco by master artists and a workshop in traditional dance of the Huasteca, $10,400 to Centro Cultural de la Raza, San Diego, California (1985). To cover post-production editing costs of the folk arts section of the NEH-funded film, *Drums Across the Sea: The Roots of Latin Music*, documenting the Afro-Cuban musical heritage of the United States, $20,000 to Cultural Research and Communication, Inc., Los Angeles, California (1985). For a series of workshops in the construction and performance of the traditional Puerto Rican *guiro*, a gourd rasp, $17,300 to the Institute of Puerto Rican Culture, San Juan, Puerto Rico (1985).

Eligibility/Limitations Expansion arts organizations may apply in *one* of the following subcategories: performing arts, including dance, theater, music, or a combination; visual, media, or design arts, including visual arts, media arts (film, video, television, radio), design arts, or a combination; literary arts; or interdisciplinary arts. Applicant organizations usually must meet all of the following requirements: be a tax-exempt arts organization; comply with applicable federal regulations; employ professional artists; and have been in existence for at least three years. In addition, former grantees must have submitted a final report for the most recently completed Expansion Arts Program grant with an ending date more than ninety days before the application deadline of October 14.

Fiscal Information Grants generally range from $5,000 to $30,000 and generally will not exceed 20% of an organization's annual total fiscal activity. Grants must be matched on at least a one-to-one basis.

Application Information Application guidelines, instructions, and additional information are available from the Expansion Arts Program.

Deadline(s) Application postmark deadline is October 14.

Subject Term(s) Performing Arts; Visual Arts; Literary Arts; Arts, Support of; Media; Design Arts

162. National Endowment for the Arts

Expansion Arts Program
1100 Pennsylvania Avenue, NW
Washington, DC 20506
(202) 682-5443

Services to the Field

CFDA Program Number 45.010

Program Description This program aids organizations of regional or national scope whose primary function is to offer technical assistance and services to expansion arts organizations. There will be very few grants awarded in this category. Only organizations of exceptional quality with an established national or regional orientation and ongoing working relationships with expansion arts organizations should apply. This program funds regional or national service activities, such as: preparation of arts directories, newsletters, workshop programs leading to economic development of artists and arts organizations, loans of equipment, public relations, audience development, and management assistance.

Sample Grants For administrative costs, development of a fundraising guide, workshops, conferences, the publication of *Tenaz Talks Teatro*, a newsletter on developments in Latin theater, $6,392 to Teatros Nacionales de Aztlan, Santa Barbara, California (1985).

Eligibility/Limitations Applicant organizations usually must meet all of the following requirements: be tax-exempt; comply with applicable federal regulations; have as their primary function service to expansion arts organizations; employ professional administrators; and have an established regional or national service program which has been functioning for at least two years. In addition, former grantees must have submitted a final report for the most recently completed Expansion Arts Program grant with an ending date more than ninety days before the application deadline of December 2.

Fiscal Information Grants generally range from $5,000 to $30,000. Grants must be matched on at least a dollar-for-dollar basis and generally will not exceed 20% of an organization's total annual fiscal activity. The program generally does not fund local, state, or regional arts agencies.

Application Information Application guidelines, instructions, and additional information are available from the Expansion Arts Program.

Deadline(s) Application postmark deadline is December 2.

Subject Term(s) Performing Arts; Visual Arts; Literary Arts; Arts, Support of; Media; Design Arts

163. National Endowment for the Arts

Folk Arts Program
1100 Pennsylvania Avenue, NW
Washington, DC 20506
(202) 682-5449

Folk Arts Grants to Organizations: Media Preservation and Presentation of Traditional Arts

CFDA Program Number 45.015

Program Description It is the purpose of the Folk Arts Program to honor and make visible the stylistic and cultural variety that has made life in the United States an exciting challenge and an adventure in human understanding. Within this purpose, the special responsibility of the Folk Arts Program is to encourage those community and family-based arts that have endured through several generations, that carry with them a sense of community aesthetic, and that demonstrate the highest degree of artistic excellence. The objectives of the program are positive: to identify, assist, and honor those local men and women who demonstrate the highest traditional artistic knowledge and skills; to support the cultural activities of traditional communities in which such artists flourish; and to make the sophistication, vivacity, and significance of our multicultural artistic heritage more available to the wider public. The skills, repertoires, and performance styles of many folk artists may often reach a wider public and be preserved for future generations through carefully conceived and well executed media documentation. Matching grants are available to organizations for radio or television programs or series, recordings, small publications such as tune books, still photographs, and films that preserve or present traditional arts.

Eligibility/Limitations Applicant organizations must be tax exempt and must comply with applicable federal regulations.

Fiscal Information Amounts requested should reflect a realistic budget for the particular project. Funding will depend upon the significance of the proposed project and the availability of money. Ordinarily, organizational grants will range between $2,500 and $30,000 and will be made on a dollar-for-dollar matching basis. The program encourages cash contributions from other sources, but also allows in-kind contributions as part of the match. The program does not fund general operating expenses; start-up costs for institutes, regional centers, or service agencies; research, except as a necessary part of a presentation or documentation project; foreign travel; construction or major repair of buildings or other facilities; the purchase of major equipment; book publishing; historical presentations; theater or dance companies that dramatize or re-create the traditional folk dance and music of many lands; and contemporary studio crafts.

Application Information Application guidelines and additional information are available from the program.

Deadline(s) Application deadlines are October 1 and January 5.

Additional Information Additional programs within the division are Services to the Field, the State Apprenticeship Program, and National Heritage Fellowships.

Subject Term(s) Cultural Affairs, Support of; Arts, Support of; Media; Folk Art

164. National Endowment for the Arts

Folk Arts Program
1100 Pennsylvania Avenue, NW
Washington, DC 20506
(202) 682-5449

Folk Arts Grants to Organizations: Presentation of Traditional Arts and Artists

CFDA Program Number 45.015

Program Description It is the purpose of the Folk Arts Program to honor and make visible the stylistic and cultural variety that has made life in the United States an exciting challenge and an adventure in human understanding. Within this purpose, the special responsibility of the Folk Arts Program is to encourage those community and family-based arts that have endured through several generations, that carry with them a sense of community aesthetic, and that demonstrate the highest degree of artistic excellence. The objectives of the program are positive: to identify, assist, and honor those local men and women who demonstrate the highest traditional artistic knowledge and skills; to support the cultural activities of traditional communities in which such artists flourish; and to make the sophistication, vivacity, and significance of our multicultural artistic heritage more available to the wider public. Matching grants are available for local or regional celebrations, exhibits, workshops, concerts, residencies, and tours that present traditional arts and artists of the highest excellence.

Sample Grants For a series of concert demonstrations of traditional Afro-Cuban music and dance and two workshop series in Afro-Cuban music and dance conducted by a master artist, $17,900 to Boys Harbor, New York (1984). For two series of workshops in traditional Puerto Rica crafts, including *santo de palo* carving and the making of traditional masks and carnival headdresses by master artists, $6,000 to Grupo Morivivi, New York (1984). For a concert of Afro-Puerto Rican music and dance, an exhibit of related crafts accompanying the performance, and a one-day workshop with local Hispanic performing artists, $20,000 to Hispanic Institute for the Performing Arts, Washington, DC (1984). For a series of fifteen workshops in traditional arts of the Caribbean carnival, concentrating especially on the arts of wire-bending, traditional costume design, and mask-making, $15,000 to the West Indian American Day Carnival Association, New York (1984).

Eligibility/Limitations Applicant organizations must be tax exempt and must comply with applicable federal regulations.

Fiscal Information Amounts requested should reflect a realistic budget for the particular project. Funding will depend upon the significance of the proposed project and the availability of money. Ordinarily, organizational grants will range between $2,500 and $30,000 and will be made on a dollar-for-dollar matching basis. The program encourages cash contributions from other sources, but also allows in-kind contributions as part of the match. The program does not fund general operating expenses; start-up costs for institutes, regional centers, or service agencies; research, except as a necessary part of a presentation or documentation project; foreign travel; construction or major repair of buildings or other facilities; the purchase of major equipment; book publishing; historical presentations; theater or dance companies that dramatize or re-create the traditional folk dance and music of many lands; and contemporary studio crafts.

Application Information Application guidelines and additional information are available from the program.

Deadline(s) Application deadlines are October 1 and January 5.

Subject Term(s) Cultural Affairs, Support of; Arts, Support of; Folk Art

165. National Endowment for the Arts

Literature Program
1100 Pennsylvania Avenue, NW
Washington, DC 20506
(202) 682-5451

Audience Development Projects

CFDA Program Number 45.004

Program Description These grants are designed to promote and develop audiences for contemporary creative writing of the highest quality. A few grants are awarded for a variety of projects, including: cooperative literary promotion projects; regional small press bookfairs; traveling exhibits of literary works; permanent exhibits of literary works; projects which distribute review materials; and other innovative projects, in print or other media, which promote literature or literary publishing.

Sample Grants To support the Latin American Book Fair, which features books and journals that touch upon the Hispanic experience in the U.S., $11,100 to Coordinating Council of Literary Magazines, New York (1985). For Revista Chicano-Riqvena to sponsor a series of eleven mini-book fairs in small cities and towns of Texas that are Mexican-American population centers, $15,825 to the University of Houston (1985).

Eligibility/Limitations Applicant organizations must be tax exempt and must comply with applicable federal regulations.

Fiscal Information In general, grants will range between $2,000 and $20,000. No grant will exceed half of the cash costs of the project. Applicants are encouraged to match grants with cash and to include in their budgets cash salaries for key personnel. In addition, in-kind contributions may be designated as part of the match. However, no grant may be matched entirely with in-kind contributions.

Application Information Application forms, guidelines, and additional information are available from the Literature Program.

Deadline(s) Application postmark deadline is January 16.

Subject Term(s) Literature

166. National Endowment for the Arts

Literature Program
1100 Pennsylvania Avenue, NW
Washington, DC 20506
(202) 682-5451

Audience Development: Residencies for Writers

CFDA Program Number 45.004

Program Description These grants are designed to promote and develop audiences for contemporary creative writing of the highest quality. Through its support of residencies, the program aims to: introduce creative writers to varied communities in many areas of the country; develop new audiences for contemporary writers in their own communities; and assist writers, particularly those just achieving recognition, in establishing new sources of income. Grants support residencies for published writers of poetry, fiction, creative essays and belles lettres, performance poets, and translators.

Eligibility/Limitations Applicant organizations must be tax exempt and must comply with applicable federal regulations. State arts agencies, colleges, universities, libraries, museums, art centers, radio and television stations, and other professional and community organizations which meet these legal requirements are eligible to apply. Elementary and secondary schools are not eligible. Grants are available only on an *every-other-year basis*: organizations that were awarded Residencies for Writers grants in calendar year 1986 are not eligible to apply in 1988. To be eligible, former grantees must have submitted required final reports for all completed Literature Program grants since (and including) Fiscal Year 1983.

Fiscal Information Organizations may request up to $10,000. In most cases, grants will be for less. Residency grants usually are given in the amount requested or not at all.

Application Information Application forms, guidelines, and additional information are available from the Literature Program.

Deadline(s) Application postmark deadline is December 3.

Subject Term(s) Literature

167. National Endowment for the Arts

Literature Program
1100 Pennsylvania Avenue, NW
Washington, DC 20506
(202) 682-5451

Fellowships for Translators

CFDA Program Number 45.004

Program Description The Literature Program of the National Endowment for the Arts assists individual creative writers of excellence or promise, encourages wider audiences for contemporary literature, and helps support nonprofit organizations that foster literature as a professional pursuit. Fellowships are available to published translators of creative literature to enable them to set aside time for specific translation projects from other languages into English. Translations should be of the highest quality. The endowment seeks to encourage translations of writers insufficiently represented in English translation.

Sample Grants To translate from Portuguese the prose and poetry of Adelia Prado, a contemporary Brazilian writer whose work has not yet been translated into English, $16,000 (1984). For the translation from Spanish of an anthology of 150 contemporary Mexican poets, *Asamblea de poetas jovenes de Mexico*, published in 1980, $10,000 (1985). For the translation of the novel *LARVA: Babel de una noche de San Juan* by Julian Rios, $20,000 (1985).

Eligibility/Limitations Fellowships are awarded only to United States citizens or permanent residents of the U.S. Applicants are eligible if, since January 1, 1972, they have published: a translation of a novel or of a volume of fifty or more pages of fiction or poetry, or a book-length translation of a work of literary merit, *or* a total of fifty pages of translations of creative literature in literary magazines, anthologies, or books. Applications are accepted from individuals only. Projects should be for translations of published literary material *from any language into English only.*

Fiscal Information Fellowships for translators are for $10,000 or $20,000, depending upon the length and scope of the project. Applicants should specify one of these two amounts on the application form.

Application Information Application forms, guidelines, and additional information are available from the Literature Program.

Deadline(s) The application deadline is January 9.

Additional Information Translators must be able to obtain permission to translate the work specified. Applicants recommended for fellowships will not receive monies until the program receives verification of rights.

Subject Term(s) Fellowships; Individuals, Eligibility of; Translation Support; Literature

168. National Endowment for the Arts

Literature Program
1100 Pennsylvania Avenue, NW
Washington, DC 20506
(202) 682-5451

Literary Publishing: Assistance to Literary Magazines

CFDA Program Number 45.004

Program Description The Literature Program of the National Endowment for the Arts assists individual creative writers of excellence or promise, encourages wider audiences for contemporary literature, and helps support nonprofit organizations that foster literature as a professional pursuit. Grants in this category provide assistance to the nation's noncommercial literary journals and are awarded for publication projects. Examples include: payments to authors and contributors for their work; production, design, and related costs of issues; efforts to improve distribution and to increase readership; purchase of technical assistance; and development of local and private sources of financial support.

Sample Grants For authors' payments and production costs for two issues of *Review*, $10,000 to the Center for Inter-American Relations, New York (1985). For authors' payments and production costs for one special issue of *New England Review/Bread Loaf Quarterly* devoted to Caribbean literature in translation, $6,854 to Kenyon Hill Publications, Inc., Hanover, New Hampshire (1985).

Eligibility/Limitations Applicant organizations must be tax exempt and must comply with applicable federal regulations. Literary magazines which meet these legal requirements and have published at least three issues in the two years prior to the application deadline may apply. State arts agencies may apply on behalf of literary magazines in their states (one application per magazine). Also, individual literary magazine editors may apply for matching fellowships. Review journals which include as a substantial portion of their regular format reviews and discussion of contemporary literature and literary publications are eligible. Magazines dedicated to special viewpoints or directed toward special audiences are eligible only if they publish substantial amounts of contemporary creative writing or literary reviewing. To be eligible, former grantees must have submitted required final reports for all completed Literature Program grants since (and including) Fiscal Year 1983. Magazines with time extensions on more than one grant are not eligible to apply.

Fiscal Information Grants will range between $2,000 and $10,000. Grants are awarded on the condition that at least 10% of grant funds received are earmarked for writers. Grants may be used to pay only such direct costs as royalties, printing, binding, paper, supplies, proofreading, editing, postage, distribution, and promotion. Applicants are encouraged to match grants with cash. While in-kind contributions may be used as match, no grant should be matched entirely with in-kind contributions. The program prefers that all grants over $5,000 be matched in cash on at least a dollar-for-dollar basis.

Application Information Application forms, guidelines, and additional information are available from the program.

Deadline(s) Application postmark deadline is August 11.

Subject Term(s) Publication Support; Literature

169. National Endowment for the Arts

Literature Program
1100 Pennsylvania Avenue, NW
Washington, DC 20506
(202) 682-5451

Literary Publishing: Small Press Assistance

CFDA Program Number 45.004

Program Description The Literature Program of the National Endowment for the Arts assists individual creative writers of excellence or promise, encourages wider audiences for contemporary literature, and helps support nonprofit organizations that foster literature as a professional pursuit. Grants in this category assist the nation's noncommercial literary small presses and university and college presses with a substantial history of publishing contemporary creative literature of the highest quality. Grants may be used to assist the publication, promotion, and distribution of books and anthologies of contemporary creative writing and translation, to implement organizational development plans, to purchase technical assistance, and to secure continuing local and private sources of financial support.

Sample Grants For Red Dust to publish a bilingual edition of selected poems by Peruvian poet Antonio Cisneros, the translation of a book of fiction by Robert Pinget, a long prose-poem by Emmanual Hocquard, a collection of poems by Agnes Stein, and the translation of the first novel of Mark Isingel, $16,000 (1984). For the publication of ten books by Chicano, Cuban-American, and Puerto Rican writers by Bilingual Review Press, $18,000 (1985).

Eligibility/Limitations Small presses, and university and college presses which have published at least four volumes (of twenty-four pages or more each) of fiction, poetry, plays, or other creative prose in the past three years may apply. Books of 40,000 or more words will count as the equivalent of two volumes. State arts agencies may apply on behalf of small presses in their states. Applicant organizations must be tax exempt and must comply with applicable federal regulations.

Fiscal Information Grants generally ranging from $2,000 to $12,000 are available to all presses which meet the eligibility requirements. Grants generally ranging from $12,000 to $25,000 are available only to small presses which published six or more volumes of forty-eight or more pages (books of 40,000 or more words will count as the equivalent of two volumes) in the year prior to application. Presses which apply to publish a volume of literary prose of 40,000 or more words in a press run of 2,500 or more are eligible for up to $5,000 for that volume. This amount may be in addition to the grant amounts specified above. Applicants are encouraged to match grants with cash, including anticipated sales. While in-kind contributions such as the services of the publishing staff, outside editorial assistance, use of facilities, and materials may be used as part of the match, no grant should be matched entirely with in-kind contributions. The program prefers that all grants over $7,500 be matched in cash on at least a dollar-for-dollar basis. State and local arts agencies may provide non-federal funds for a full or partial match.

Application Information Application forms, guidelines, and additional information are available from the program.

Deadline(s) Applications must be postmarked no later than September 11 for projects scheduled to begin after May 1. Late applications will be rejected.

Additional Information The program does not fund books to which the author is required to make a financial contribution toward publication cost. In addition the program does not fund reprints of titles supported under previous grants. Grants are awarded on the condition that the author(s) of an endowment-supported publication receive a minimum of 10% of the sales income in cash (or the equivalent in copies) as at least partial payment of royalties. Preference will be given to presses which pay cash advances or royalties.

Subject Term(s) Publication Support; Literature

170. National Endowment for the Arts

Media Arts: Film/Radio/Television Program
1100 Pennsylvania Avenue, NW
Washington, DC 20506
(202) 682-5452

Film/Video Production Grants

CFDA Program Number 45.006

Program Description The Media Arts: Film/Radio/Television Program of the National Endowment for the Arts recognizes the central role the individual artist plays in the distinctive and innovative use of media. The media arts include documentary, experimental, and narrative works, as well as electronic manipulations, animated film, and audio art. Film/Video Production grants are designed to encourage and support artworks in film and video of the the highest quality. Irrespective of subject or genre, productions must emphasize creative use of media, fulfilling, and, on occasion, extending their artistic possibilities. Grants are generally made for single film and video productions which exemplify the use of these media as art forms.

Sample Grants For a film on the Chilean-American artist, Matta, who influenced the Abstract Expressionists as their ideas were forming in the 1940s, $20,000 to a project in New York (1984). For a documentary film exploring the music culture of the youth of Puerto Rico, $30,000 to the Film Fund, New York (1984).

Eligibility/Limitations Applicant organizations must be tax exempt and must comply with applicable federal regulations. Applicant organizations must have existed at least one year. Individuals must have substantial professional experience and must be U.S. citizens or permanent residents of the United States. Former grantees must have submitted required final reports and interim reports in order to be eligible for subsequent funding.

Fiscal Information Matching grants for organizations generally range from $20,000 to $50,000. A limited number of nonmatching grants to individuals generally range from $10,000 to $25,000. Projects should be completed within two years of the starting date.

Application Information Application forms, guidelines, and special application requirement instructions are available from the program.

Deadline(s) Applications must be postmarked no later than November 13. Late applications will be rejected.

Subject Term(s) Individuals, Eligibility of; Film; Video; Filmmaking; Media

171. National Endowment for the Arts

Media Arts: Film/Radio/Television Program
1100 Pennsylvania Avenue, NW
Washington, DC 20506
(202) 682-5452

Media Arts Centers

CFDA Program Number 45.006

Program Description The Media Arts: Film/Radio/Television Program of the National Endowment for the Arts recognizes the central role the individual artist plays in the distinctive and innovative use of media. The media arts include documentary, experimental, and narrative works, as well as electronic manipulations, animated film, and audio art. The purpose of these grants is to advance the arts of film and video and to encourage their wider appreciation and practice. The Media Arts Program assists a limited number of Media Arts Centers of the highest quality and of national or regional importance.

Sample Grants For video and radio production, workshops, conferences, documentary production, and operation of a low-power television station, $3,900 to Caribbean Center for Understanding Media, St. Croix, Virgin Islands (1985).

Eligibility/Limitations A Media Arts Center may be an independent organization, or it may be affiliated with a university, museum, city or state arts agency, or other tax-exempt body. Each Media Arts Center must identify itself as *one* of the following: a multipurpose center which provides a variety of services, e.g., exhibitions, workshops, production facilities; an exhibition center which provides a variety of services, e.g., seminars, study collections, publications, with an emphasis on the ongoing exhibition of film and video art; or a production/post-production center which provides a number of services, e.g., workshops, distribution, with an emphasis on making available production and post-production facilities. In addition, applicant organizations must be tax exempt and must comply with applicable federal guidelines. Applicant organizations must have a record of demonstrated excellence in carrying out two or more of the eight following activities: (1) exhibition to wider audiences of high quality film and video art, with accompanying program notes and visiting filmmakers, videomakers, and critics; (2) making available production and post-production facilities for filmmakers and videomakers; (3) workshops and residency programs involving filmmakers, videomakers, and critics; (4) making available study materials, research facilities, and film or video collections; (5) collection and dissemination of information about media activities on a local, regional, and national basis; (6) distribution of high quality film and video art; (7) conducting seminars, symposia, and conferences; and (8) publication of catalogues, magazines, newsletters, and critical journals. In addition, former grantees must have submitted required final and interim reports in order to be eligible for subsequent funding.

Fiscal Information Matching grants generally range from $10,000 to $50,000.

Application Information Application forms, guidelines, and special application requirements are available from the program.

Deadline(s) Applications must be postmarked no later than April 24. Late applications will be rejected.

Subject Term(s) Media; Film; Video; Radio

172. National Endowment for the Arts

Media Arts: Film/Radio/Television Program
1100 Pennsylvania Avenue, NW
Washington, DC 20506
(202) 682-5452

Radio Production

CFDA Program Number 45.006

Program Description The Media Arts: Film/Radio/Television Program of the National Endowment for the Arts recognizes the central role the individual artist plays in the distinctive and innovative use of media. The Radio Section of the Media Arts Program supports outstanding single productions and series for radio broadcast. Radio production projects may include: documentaries, classic or experimental drama, audio art, children's programming, and the presentation of literature and music. Projects should emphasize the creative use of the radio medium.

Sample Grants For a series of four half-hour stereo portraits of the Island of Tortola in the British Virgin Islands, $8,000 to Montague Center, Massachusetts (1985). For "Music of the Americas," a series of concert, feature, and documentary programs based on a symphonic concert of North and South American compositions, $7,000 to Springbrook, Wisconsin (1985).

Eligibility/Limitations Applicant organizations must be tax exempt and must comply with applicable federal regulations. Applicant organizations must have existed at least one year. Individual radio producers must have substantial professional experience and must be U.S. citizens or permanent residents of the United States. Joint applications from individual producers are eligible; however, only one producer should sign, and accept legal responsibility for, the application. To be eligible for support, former grantees must have submitted required final reports for all completed Media Arts grants since (and including) Fiscal Year 1984. Only one application per project may be submitted.

Fiscal Information Matching grants for organizations generally range from $3,000 to $50,000. Nonmatching grants for individual radio producers generally range from $3,000 to $15,000.

Application Information Application forms, guidelines, special application requirements, and additional information are available from the Media Arts Program.

Deadline(s) Application postmark deadline is July 17.

Additional Information The Radio Workshops and Residencies Program funds organizations that invite nationally recognized radio producers for workshops and residencies of various lengths. Contact the Media Arts Program for additional information about this program.

Subject Term(s) Radio

173. National Endowment for the Arts

Museum Program
1100 Pennsylvania Avenue, NW
Washington, DC 20506
(202) 682-5442

Care of Collections: Collection Maintenance

CFDA Program Number 45.012

Program Description These awards are designed to help museums preserve collections primarily of artistic significance through solving problems in the areas of climate control, security, and storage. Grants are available for two types of projects: (1) *Surveys*: for surveys identifying problems and recommending solutions, including a specific renovation plan and cost estimates; and (2) *Implementation*: for renovation projects for which careful plans and cost estimates have been developed.

Sample Grants To purchase and install custom-made storage units for the Museum of International Folk Art's collection of Hispanic New Mexican folk art and the costume, textile, and basketry collections, $35,000 to the Museum of New Mexico, Santa Fe, New Mexico (1984). To provide proper storage for the museum's collection of Andean archeological textiles, $27,000 to the American Museum of Natural History, New York (1985).

Eligibility/Limitations While accreditation by the American Association of Museums (AAM) is not an eligibility requirement, the endowment generally uses the definition of museums developed by the AAM "...a nonprofit institution essentially educational or aesthetic in purpose with professional staff, which owns or utilizes tangible objects, cares for them, and exhibits them to the public on some regular schedule." In addition to museums, organizations that serve museums, organizations that perform museum functions, state arts agencies, and regional arts organizations are also eligible to apply. Applicant organizations must submit a copy of the Internal Revenue Service determination letter for tax-exempt status or the official document identifying the applicant as a unit of state or local government. In general, organizations should be in operation two years prior to submitting an application. Renovation of galleries may be supported only when directly related to climate control, security systems, or storage facilities. Museums applying for implementation grants must have fully developed plans and cost estimates at the time of application.

Fiscal Information Up to $15,000 is available for surveys; grant awards must be matched at least one-to-one and the minimum grant generally will not be less than $2,500. Up to $200,000 is available for implementation projects. Implementation project awards of $50,000 or less require at least a one-to-one match; grant awards between $50,000 and $100,000 require a two-to-one match; and grant awards of $100,000 or more require a three-to-one match. The minimum implementation grant generally will not be less than $5,000. A grant period of up to one year is allowed for survey projects. A grant period of up to two years is allowed for implementation projects. Grants in this category are not awarded for new construction or for collection maintenance projects in new facilities.

Application Information Application guidelines, application forms, special application requirements, and additional information are available from the Museum Program.

Deadline(s) Application postmark deadline is September 17.

Subject Term(s) Museums; Collections, Conservation; Museums, Collections Maintenance

174. National Endowment for the Arts

Museum Program
1100 Pennsylvania Avenue, NW
Washington, DC 20506
(202) 682-5442

Care of Collections: Conservation

CFDA Program Number 45.012

Program Description These awards are designed to help museums conserve collections primarily of artistic significance. Works undergoing conservation treatment must be wholly owned by the applicant institution. Grants are available for: (1) *Conservation Planning*: to help museums and other organizations plan conservation programs or plan specific treatment of collections; (2) *Conservation of Collections*: for treatment projects executed within a museum's own conservation facilities or by an outside facility and for the purchase of major equipment for a conservation laboratory at a museum or regional conservation center (each institution may submit no more than one application for treatment and one for equipment purchase under this deadline); and (3) *Conservation Training*: for student stipends at existing university-based training centers, for master-apprentice internship programs (generally of at least one-year duration), to support new or existing professional training programs for the conservation of ethnographic or archeological works of art, and for seminars and workshops to familiarize museum professionals with current methods used in the handling, packing, examination, conservation, and stabilization of works of art.

Sample Grants For the conservation of archeological metals from the Andean regions of South America for display in the new Hall of South American Peoples, $25,000 to the American Museum of Natural History, New York (1984).

Eligibility/Limitations While accreditation by the American Association of Museums (AAM) is not an eligibility requirement, the endowment generally uses the definition of museums developed by the AAM "...a nonprofit institution essentially educational or aesthetic in purpose with professional staff, which owns or utilizes tangible objects, cares for them, and exhibits them to the public on some regular schedule." In addition to museums, organizations that serve museums, organizations that perform museum functions, state arts agencies, and regional arts organizations are also eligible to apply. Applicant organizations must submit a copy of the Internal Revenue Service determination letter for tax-exempt status or the official document identifying the applicant as a unit of state or local government. In general, organizations should be in operation two years prior to submitting an application. Individuals are not eligible to apply.

Fiscal Information All grants must be matched at least one-to-one. Up to $10,000 is available for conservation planning. Up to $25,000 is available for conservation of collections; the minimum grant in this category generally will not be less than $2,500. Institutions may request: up to $100,000 for student stipends at existing university-based training centers; up to $40,000 for master-apprentice internship programs; up to $150,000 to support new or existing professional training programs for the conservation of ethnographic or archeological works or art; and up to $20,000 for seminars and workshops. A grant period of up to eighteen months is allowed, except for conservation internships (under Conservation Training) where a longer period of support is possible. Requests for equipment purchases should be submitted in a separate application from requests for treatment projects. Equipment costs are the only allowable expenses in equipment purchase applications.

Application Information Application guidelines, application forms, special application requirements, and additional information are available from the Museum Program.

Deadline(s) Applications should be received by September 17.

Subject Term(s) Museums; Conservation, Collections; Conservation Training, Museums; Collections, Conservation

175. National Endowment for the Arts

Museum Program
1100 Pennsylvania Avenue, NW
Washington, DC 20506
(202) 682-5442

Professional Development: Fellowships for Museum Professionals

CFDA Program Number 45.012

Program Description This award allows museum professionals to conduct arts-related independent study or to travel, write, engage in community projects, or otherwise improve their professional qualifications. This program is designed to encourage museums to develop and implement programs of regular leave for professional staff members.

Sample Grants A 1983-1984 fellowship was awarded for the study of South American ethnographic collections at east coast American and European museums.

Eligibility/Limitations Only currently employed professionals who have served on a museum staff for at least one year may apply. Applicants must be citizens or permanent residents of the United States. Organizations are not eligible. Fellowships are not awarded to cover study or research directed toward a graduate degree or expenses incurred in formal courses of study, workshops, seminars, or conferences. These fellowships are not intended to support research or development of projects eligible elsewhere in the museum program, but rather to encourage independent work.

Fiscal Information Fellowships will not exceed $25,000. Amounts will be based on travel requirements, salary support, and need for materials. Although the fellowships may extend for up to a full year, salary support may be included for only a period of up to three months. Fellowships need not be matched. The minimum grant generally will not be less than $2,500.

Application Information Application guidelines, application forms, and further information are available from the Museum Program.

Deadline(s) Applications should be received by February 17.

Subject Term(s) Fellowships; Museums; Museums, Professional Development

176. National Endowment for the Arts

Museum Program
1100 Pennsylvania Avenue, NW
Washington, DC 20506
(202) 682-5442

Professional Development: Museum Training

CFDA Program Number 45.012

Program Description These grants are awarded to support arts-related formal training programs, internships, and apprenticeships. Priority will be given to programs for minorities and to efforts to improve staff in geographic areas where there is a demonstrated need to improve professionalism. Grants are awarded for: (1) *Formal Training*: formal education programs, including workshops and seminars directed to mid-career professional training and development, and graduate-level programs in curatorial training, museum administration, exhibit preparation and design, or museum education, conducted jointly by museums and universities, in which courses in art history form an integral part of the program; (2) *Internships*: for internships provided by a museum—priority will be given to those at the graduate and postgraduate level; and (3) *Apprenticeships*: for apprenticeships to prepare students or staff for positions such as installer, preparator, framer, packer, or carpenter.

Eligibility/Limitations All grants go directly to institutions, not individuals. While accreditation by the American Association of Museums (AAM) is not an eligibility requirement, the endowment generally uses the definition of musuems developed by the AAM "...a nonprofit institution essentially educational or aesthetic in purpose with professional staff, which owns or utilizes tangible objects, cares for them, and exhibits them to the public on some regular schedule." In addition to museums, organizations that serve museums, organizations that perform museum functions, state arts agencies, and regional arts organizations are also eligible to apply. Applicant organizations must submit a copy of the Internal Revenue Service determination letter for tax-exempt status or the official document identifying the applicant as a unit of state or local government.

Fiscal Information Grant awards of up to $60,000 are available for formal training programs. The minimum grant generally will not be less than $5,000. Grant awards of up to $20,000 are available for support of internships and apprenticeships. Endowment funds may be used for stipend support and travel only. The minimum grant generally will not be less than $3,000. Grant awards of $30,000 or less require at least a one-to-one match; grant awards over $30,000 require at least a two-to-one match. A grant period of up to two years is allowed for training programs. A grant period of up to one year is allowed for other types of projects.

Application Information Application forms and additional information are available from the Museum Program.

Deadline(s) Applications should be received by February 17.

Subject Term(s) Museums; Museums, Training

177. National Endowment for the Arts

Museum Program
1100 Pennsylvania Avenue, NW
Washington, DC 20506
(202) 682-5442

Special Exhibitions

CFDA Program Number 45.012

Program Description These awards are designed to help museums and other organizations develop, tour, or participate in exhibitions of borrowed works primarily of artistic significance.

Sample Grants For an exhibition of more than two hundred and fifty Mayan art objects spanning the Formative, Classic, and Postclassic periods of that civilization, including sculpture, ceramics, jade carvings, gold work, and architectural embellishments, $90,000 to the Albuquerque Museum Foundation, Albuquerque, New Mexico (1984). For the showing in the United States of an exhibition of works by Uruguayan artist Joaquin Torres-Garcia (1874-1949), $40,000 to the American Federation of Arts, New York (1985). For an exhibition of colonial art from viceregal Bolivia and Peru, which illustrates two specific motifs: angels and virgins, $25,000 to the Center for Inter-American Relations, New York (1985). For an exhibition of photographs by Alfred Maudslay and Teobert Maler documenting Mayan sites in the Yucatan, $25,000 to the Center for Inter-American Relations, New York (1985). For the planning of an exhibition of colonial Baroque painting from South America, $4,270 to New York University, New York (1985).

Eligibility/Limitations Exhibitions of privately owned collections generally will not be funded. Nor will exhibitions that include works by the exhibition's curator, organizers, or applicant's staff, paid or unpaid. While accreditation by the American Association of Museums (AAM) is not an eligibility requirement, the endowment generally uses the definition of museums developed by the AAM "...a nonprofit institution essentially educational or aesthetic in purpose with professional staff, which owns or utilizes tangible objects, cares for them, and exhibits them to the public on some regular schedule." In addition to museums, organizations that serve museums, organizations that perform museum functions, state arts agencies, and regional arts organizations are also eligible to apply. Applicant organizations must submit a copy of the Internal Revenue Service determination letter for tax-exempt status or the official document identifying the applicant as a unit of state or local government.

Fiscal Information All grants go directly to institutions, not individuals. There is no grant maximum for organizing an exhibition. Grants of up to $20,000 are available to help institutions borrow exhibitions. Grants of $50,000 or less require a one-to-one match; grant awards between $50,000 and $100,000 require a two-to-one match; and grant awards of $100,000 or more require a three-to-one match. Grants may be used to pay for: planning and organizing an exhibition; services of an outside specialist; shipping, insurance, and related costs; installation; catalogues; documentation; related events such as education programs, performing arts activities, and film and lecture series; publicity; or regional touring of exhibitions by regional arts organizations and service organizations. Organizations requesting funds to borrow exhibitions may not include rental fees in their applications if the exhibition was initially funded by the endowment. Grants may not be used to pay for opening receptions. A grant period of more than one year is allowed. The period of support should span the amount of time necessary to plan, execute, and close out the project.

Application Information Application guidelines, application forms, special application requirements, and additional information are available from the Museum Program.

Deadline(s) Applications must be received by November 16.

Additional Information The arts endowment's Inter-Arts Program provides support to arts institutions to commission and produce interdisciplinary collaborations between visual artists and artists of other disciplines. Support is also available for multidisciplinary arts organizations which present series of national or regional significance on an ongoing annual basis. Museums with programs eligible under these guidelines are encouraged to contact the program at (202) 682-5444 or write for guidelines to: Inter-Arts Program, National Endowment for the Arts, 1100 Pennsylvania Avenue, NW, Washington, DC, 20506.

Subject Term(s) Museums; Museums, Exhibitions

178. National Endowment for the Arts

Museum Program
1100 Pennsylvania Avenue, NW
Washington, DC 20506
(202) 682-5442

Special Projects

CFDA Program Number 45.012

Program Description These awards are designed to respond to innovative and exemplary projects which will have a broad impact on the museum field and that are not eligible under other categories. Projects must be consistent with the policies of the Museum Program. Only a limited number of projects of national or regional significance will be supported.

Application Information Organizations interested in applying must contact the Museum Program before application.

Subject Term(s) Museums

179. National Endowment for the Arts

Museum Program
1100 Pennsylvania Avenue, NW
Washington, DC 20506
(202) 682-5442

Utilization of Museum Resources: Catalogue Program

CFDA Program Number 45.012

Program Description This program is designed to support the cataloguing of permanent collections primarily of artistic significance. Works to be catalogued must be wholly owned by the applicant institution. Grants are available for: (1) *Documentation*: for the documentation of uncatalogued or inadequately documented permanent collections, whether or not a publication will result; the services of an outside consultant may be included in the project, if appropriate. (2) *Preparation of Manuscript*: for research and preparation of catalogue copy for publication; the services of an outside consultant may be included. (3) *Publication*: for publication of catalogues, handbooks, or brochures related to permanent collections; applicants should indicate readiness of manuscript for publication.

Sample Grants To document and catalog the Helen Allen Textile Collection of approximately six hundred Latin American textiles, $20,000 to the University of Wisconsin (1984).

Eligibility/Limitations While accreditation by the American Association of Museums (AAM) is not an eligibility requirement, the endowment generally uses the definition of museums developed by the AAM "...a nonprofit institution essentially educational or aesthetic in purpose with professional staff, which owns or utilizes tangible objects, cares for them, and exhibits them to the public on some regular schedule." In addition to museums, organizations that serve museums, organizations that perform museum functions, state arts agencies, and regional arts organizations are also eligible to apply. Applicant organizations must submit a copy of the Internal Revenue Service determination letter for tax-exempt status or the official document identifying the applicant as a unit of state or local government. In general, applicant organizations should be in operation two years prior to submitting an application. Applicants seeking support for the production of a catalogue of the permanent collect should request aid for either research *or* publication, but not both. Applicants may apply for publication support in a subsequent year, whether or not funding was received for research. Generally, no more than one grant will be awarded for the research phase, and no more than one grant will be awarded for publication. Applicants seeking support under Presentation and Education should include costs of accompanying catalogues in those applications. Applicants seeking support for catalogues to accompany special exhibitions should apply under Special Exhibitions.

Fiscal Information Grant requests of up to $75,000 will be considered. Grant awards of $50,000 or less require at least a one-to-one match, and grant awards of more than $50,000 require at least a two-to-one match. The minimum grant generally will not be less than $5,000. A grant period of two years is allowed.

Application Information Application guidelines, application forms, and additional information are available from the Museum Program.

Deadline(s) Applications must be received by June 30.

Subject Term(s) Museums; Cataloguing, Museum Collections

180. National Endowment for the Arts

Museum Program
1100 Pennsylvania Avenue, NW
Washington, DC 20506
(202) 682-5442

Utilization of Museum Resources: Presentation and Education

CFDA Program Number 45.012

Program Description This award is designed to help organizations make greater use of museum collections and other resources primarily of artistic significance. Grants are available for: (1) *Presentation: Reinstallation* awards to help museums install works from their permanent collections in semi-permanent or long-term displays and prepare and publish exhibition catalogues directly related to these activities; *Exhibition* awards to mount temporary exhibitions from their permanent collections, generally for a period of at least three months, or mount a coherent sequence of exhibitions drawn from their permanent collections, to present temporary exhibitions from their permanent collections development in conjunction with loan exhibitions, or to develop related programs and events that enrich these presentations, including the preparation and publication of exhibition catalogues; and *Collection Sharing* awards to support extended loans to or from one or more museums or other organizations (planning as well as implementation grants are available), to support touring exhibitions of an organization's own permanent collection, and support for exhibition catalogues and educational programs directly related to these activities; and (2) *Education*: for innovative projects which interpret permanent collections of works of art and demonstrate effective collaboration between education and curatorial staff; for specific programs that make a museum's own permanent collection more widely available to the public, including museum education and outreach programs (this can include the use of video, film, television, and other media); and for outreach and education projects undertaken by exhibition spaces, museums, and other organizations without permanent collections (this can include the use of video, film television, and other media).

Sample Grants For a series of exhibitions drawn from the Taylor Museum's collections of Native American, Spanish Colonial, and Hispanic art, $50,000 to Colorado Springs Fine Arts Center, Colorado Springs, Colorado (1985).

Eligibility/Limitations All grants go directly to institutions, not individuals. While accreditation by the American Association of Museums (AAM) is not an eligibility requirement, the endowment generally uses the definition of museums developed by the AAM "...a nonprofit institution essentially educational or aesthetic in purpose with professional staff, which owns or utilizes tangible objects, cares for them, and exhibits them to the public on some regular schedule." In addition to museums, organizations that serve museums, organizations that perform museum functions, state arts agencies, and regional arts organizations are also eligible to apply. Applicant organizations must submit a copy of the Internal Revenue Service determination letter for tax-exempt status or the official document identifying the applicant as a unit of state or local government.

Fiscal Information Presentation grants for reinstallment are up to $75,000; the minimum grant generally will not be less than $7,500. Grants for exhibitions are up to $75,000; the minimum grant generally will not be less than $7,500. Grants for collection sharing are up to $75,000; the minimum grant generally will not be less than $10,000. Presentation grant awards of $50,000 or less require at least a one-to-one match, and grant awards of more than $50,000 require at least a two-to-one match. Education grants for innovative projects which interpret permanent collections of works of art are up to $50,000; the minimum grant generally will not be less than $20,000. Other education programs and projects awards are up to $25,000; the minimum grant generally will not be less than $2,500. All education grant awards must be matched at least one-to-one. Presentation and education grants may be used to purchase material needed for installation. They may not, however, be used to pay for major structural modifications of a building. A grant period of more than one year is allowed. The period of support should span the amount of time necessary to plan, execute, and close out the project.

Application Information Application guidelines, application forms, special application requirements, and additional information are available from the Museum Program.

Deadline(s) Applications should be received by June 30.

Subject Term(s) Museums; Museums, Education; Museums, Exhibitions; Museums, Collections Sharing; Cataloguing, Museum Collections

181. National Endowment for the Arts

Museum Program
1100 Pennsylvania Avenue, NW
Washington, DC 20506
(202) 682-5442

Utilization of Museum Resources: Special Artistic Initiatives

CFDA Program Number 45.012

Program Description These awards are designed to support special long-term initiatives by museums to define or redefine their mission and artistic direction through a carefully coordinated series of exhibitions, reinstallations, educational programs, publications, and interdisciplinary projects of the highest artistic level and of national or regional significance. These exhibitions and programs should be primarily concerned with the use and interpretation of the permanent collection. Grants may be used for: planning and organizing a series of special exhibitions, exhibitions primarily from the permanent collection, and/or reinstallations of the permanent collection, conceived within a larger contextual framework; publications, media productions, and education programs; and projects that involve more than one art form, particularly where performing arts and artists are integrated into the visual exhibitions.

Eligibility/Limitations While accreditation by the American Association of Museums (AAM) is not an eligibility requirement, the endowment generally uses the definition of museums developed by the AAM "...a nonprofit institution essentially educational or aesthetic in purpose with professional staff, which owns or utilizes tangible objects, cares for them, and exhibits them to the public on some regular schedule." In addition to museums, organizations that serve museums, organizations that perform museum functions, state arts agencies, and regional arts organizations are also eligible to apply. Applicant organizations must submit a copy of the Internal Revenue Service determination letter for tax-exempt status or the official document identifying the applicant as a unit of state or local government. Projects funded under this program are not eligible for funding under other categories in the Museum Program.

Fiscal Information Planning and implementation grants will be available. Planning grants will range from $15,000 to $25,000 and will require at least a one-to-one match. Implementation grants will range from $50,000 to $250,000. Implementation grants will require at least a two-to-one match. Applicants are expected to spend the first eight months of the grant period in planning and organization. The subsequent projects should be scheduled over a period of at least two years.

Application Information Museums interested in applying under this category should contact the Museum Program before applying. Application guidelines, application forms, and additional information are available from the Museum Program.

Deadline(s) The application postmark deadline is April 4.

Additional Information A *limited* number of grants are available in this category.

Subject Term(s) Museums; Museums, Education; Museums, Exhibitions

182. National Endowment for the Arts

Opera-Musical Theater Program
1100 Pennsylvania Avenue, NW
Washington, DC 20506
(202) 682-5447

Professional Companies

CFDA Program Number 45.014

Program Description The Opera-Musical Theater Program assists all forms of music theater involving voice—from experimental musical theater to operetta, from ethnic musical theater to classic musical comedy, from grand opera to still-developing forms. Grants to professional companies are intended to assist professional organizations that are producers of opera and/or musical theater work of high artistic quality and of national or regional significance.

Eligibility/Limitations Applicant organizations must be tax exempt and must comply with applicable federal regulations. In addition, applicant organizations, for the three preceding fiscal years, must have: employed professional artistic and managerial staff; used orchestra and chorus of professional quality appropriate to the work performed and to the performing environment; had an annual total operating budget of at least $100,000; produced a resident season of at least two performances each of at least two fully-staged productions of opera and/or musical theater; and, for all former grantees, submitted all required final or interim reports on previous Opera-Musical Theater grants. Companies which may not meet all of these criteria, but are current grantees of the arts endowment's Theater Program and demonstrate an ongoing commitment to the production of opera and/or musical theater, may apply under this category for specific opera and/or musical theater projects.

Fiscal Information Grants generally range from $5,000 to $300,000. Grants in this category rarely exceed 10% of a company's expenses for opera-musical theater activities. Grants are awarded on at least a one-to-one matching basis. Larger grants (over $20,000) will generally require a match of three nonfederal dollars for each federal dollar.

Application Information Application forms, guidelines, and additional information are available from the program.

Deadline(s) Applications must be postmarked no later than May 22. Late applications will be rejected.

Subject Term(s) Music; Opera; Theater; Arts, Support of; Cultural Affairs, Support of; Performing Arts

183. National Endowment for the Humanities

Division of Education Programs, Room 302
1100 Pennsylvania Avenue, NW
Washington, DC 20506
(202) 786-0377

Elementary and Secondary Education in the Humanities: Collaborative Projects

CFDA Program Number 45.127

Program Description Collaborative projects are designed to promote ongoing partnerships between schools and institutions of higher education. They bring scholars together with teachers, often for a two- to three-year period, to study materials central to their disciplines, to revise curricula, and to address problems in humanities education common to the schools of a given area. Collaborative projects should focus on specific curricular or educational issues, and they should address these issues in light of the best scholarship available. Collaborative projects may include seminars, colloquia, and other activities. They may also include conferences, meetings, or working groups to address issues in humanities education. They should involve school administrators, curriculum specialists, and other educational leaders responsible for educational policy in the subjects under consideration. Above all else, they should establish relationships that promise to continue after the conclusion of the activities supported by the grant.

Eligibility/Limitations Applicants may be individual schools, school systems, colleges, universities, or groups of institutions working in collaboration.

Fiscal Information The cost of a project will depend on a number of variables. Potential applicants should contact the program for additional information on budget preparation.

Application Information If you plan to seek a grant from the endowment, you should request guidelines and application forms for the program in which you are interested. Write or call the program. Guidelines and application forms are generally available two months in advance of an application deadline. One of the institutions involved in the project should be designated as the applicant organization with responsibility for administering the project.

Deadline(s) Application postmark deadlines are May 16 and January 8.

Additional Information A new NEH program supports planning grants. Some projects are of such scope and complexity that they require extensive planning. The endowment provides funds in modest amounts to support meetings, consultant services, and other planning activities. Endowment support may not be requested solely for the purpose of designing grant proposals. Planning grants must have intrinsic value independent of any subsequent requests for endowment support. The award of an NEH planning grant does not imply that the endowment will necessarily provide support for implementation of the full project.

Subject Term(s) Humanities; Education

184. National Endowment for the Humanities

Division of Education Programs, Room 302
1100 Pennsylvania Avenue, NW
Washington, DC 20506
(202) 786-0377

Elementary and Secondary Education in the Humanities: Conferences

CFDA Program Number 45.127

Program Description Conference grants are available for institutions and associations that wish to address important issues in humanities education. Conferences may be local, state, or national in scope. They may involve a single meeting or a series of meetings. Their participants may be teachers, professors, school administrators, or other educational leaders. They may be sponsored by colleges, school systems, professional associations, or other kinds of educational or cultural institutions. A proposal for a conference should be addressed to specific issues in humanities education and should reflect the highest standards of scholarship. The proposal should include a plan for disseminating the results of the conference.

Eligibility/Limitations Applicants must be individual schools, school systems, colleges, universities, museums, libraries, or groups of institutions working in collaboration.

Fiscal Information The cost of a conference will depend on a number of variables. Potential applicants should contact the program for additional information on budget preparation.

Application Information If you plan to seek a grant from the endowment, you should request guidelines and application forms for the program in which you are interested. Write or call the program. Guidelines and application forms are generally available two months in advance of an application deadline.

Deadline(s) Application postmark deadlines are May 16 and January 8.

Subject Term(s) Humanities; Education; Seminars and Conferences

185. National Endowment for the Humanities

Division of Education Programs, Room 302
1100 Pennsylvania Avenue, NW
Washington, DC 20506
(202) 786-0377

Elementary and Secondary Education in the Humanities: Institutes for Teachers and Administrators

CFDA Program Number 45.127

Program Description One of the most effective ways of improving humanities instruction is to provide opportunities for teachers and educational leaders to increase their knowledge and understanding of the disciplines they impart to their students. To achieve this goal, the endowment sponsors institutes for teachers and administrators. These institutes provide an opportunity for intensive summer residential study, promote collegial exchange, and foster the kind of intellectual renewal that leads to revitalized teaching. An institute should focus on important works, topics, and ideas in the humanities and on the most effective ways to teach them. It should provide a rigorous intellectual program that includes reading and writing about major works under the guidance of leading scholars. Its schedule should provide ample time for thorough treatment of the selected subject. And its plan should include follow-up activities to ensure that the summer's work is applied to the school setting.

Sample Grants To support a four-week institute and follow-up activities on the treatment of the child in literary texts from France, Spain, West Africa, the Caribbean, and Latin America, $140,851 to the District of Columbia Public Schools, Washington, DC (1985). To support a four-week institute and extensive follow-up activities on Latin American history and culture for sixty New York City area fifth-grade teachers, $130,248 to New York University, New York (1985).

Eligibility/Limitations Typically, an institute is organized by two or more faculty in higher education and one or more master teachers in elementary and secondary education. They plan the program together, secure commitments from other faculty and from visiting lecturers, and make arrangements for such details as meeting space and housing for participants. Usually an institute is conducted by a college or university, but school systems and cultural institutions are also encouraged to apply.

Fiscal Information The cost of an institute will depend on a number of variables. Potential applicants should contact the program for additional information on budget preparation.

Application Information If you plan to seek a grant from the endowment, you should request guidelines and application forms for the program in which you are interested. Write or call the program. Guidelines and application forms are generally available two months in advance of an application deadline.

Deadline(s) Application postmark deadlines are May 16 and January 8.

Subject Term(s) Humanities; Education; Seminars and Conferences

186. National Endowment for the Humanities

Division of Education Programs, Room 302
1100 Pennsylvania Avenue, NW
Washington, DC 20506
(202) 786-0377

Elementary and Secondary Education in the Humanities: Masterwork Study Grants

CFDA Program Number 45.127

Program Description Teachers from a particular school or school system may find it beneficial to meet for a period of time with scholars at nearby colleges or universities to study important texts, topics, and issues in the disciplines of the humanities. Such activities may be funded by masterwork study grants.

Eligibility/Limitations Elementary and secondary school teachers with appropriate credentials are eligible to apply.

Application Information If you plan to seek a grant from the endowment, you should request guidelines and application forms for the program in which you are interested. Write or call the program. Guidelines and application forms are generally available two months in advance of an application deadline.

Deadline(s) Application postmark deadlines are May 16 and January 8.

Subject Term(s) Humanities; Education

187. National Endowment for the Humanities

Division of Education Programs, Room 302
1100 Pennsylvania Avenue, NW
Washington, DC 20506
(202) 786-0373

Faculty Projects for Teachers at Historically Black Colleges and Universities

Program Description The endowment has established a special program of Faculty Projects for Teachers at Historically Black Colleges and Universities. This program is designed to respond to the specific needs of an institution by providing opportunities for faculty at that institution to engage in the substantive study of significant works, topics, and issues in the disciplines of the humanities. The most important component of a project is its focus on the study of significant works in the humanities. Projects must make provision for the participants to contribute actively through small-group discussions and oral presentations and must also provide opportunities for the writing of expository essays.

Eligibility/Limitations Projects that can be supported include summer workshops lasting three or four weeks, workshops series during the academic year, and combinations of the two. The director of each project should be a recognized scholar in the humanities; the staff of each project should include other accomplished scholars in the discipline and topic under study. Scholars from institutions other than the host institution may serve as project directors and be included as consultants for such projects.

Fiscal Information The cost of a faculty project will depend on a number of variables. The potential applicant should contact the program on budget preparation.

Application Information For additional information about these faculty projects, and for application forms specific to them, prospective applicants should call or write the division's Higher Education program.

Deadline(s) Application postmark deadline is March 15.

Subject Term(s) Humanities; Education; Minorities, Eligibility of

188. National Endowment for the Humanities

Division of Education Programs, Room 302
1100 Pennsylvania Avenue, NW
Washington, DC 20506
(202) 786-0380

Higher Education in the Humanities: Collaborative Projects

Program Description Two or more institutions may request support for collaborative activities that will benefit the teaching of the humanities. Such projects may be proposed by cultural institutions such as libraries and museums, by schools, by universities, or by any combination of institutions.

Eligibility/Limitations Proposals for collaborative projects may be submitted either by existing consortia or by institutions that come together for the purpose of a particular endeavor. A proposal should provide evidence that all of the participating institutions are fully involved in and committed to the project.

Fiscal Information The cost of a collaborative project will depend on a number of variables. Potential applicants should contact the program for additional information on budget preparation.

Application Information If you plan to seek a grant from the endowment, you should request guidelines and application forms for the program in which you are interested. Write or call the program. Guidelines and application forms are generally available two months in advance of an application deadline.

Deadline(s) Application postmark deadlines are October 1 and April 1.

Subject Term(s) Humanities; Education

189. National Endowment for the Humanities

Division of Education Programs, Room 302
1100 Pennsylvania Avenue, NW
Washington, DC 20506
(202) 786-0380

Higher Education in the Humanities: Conferences

Program Description The endowment provides support for conferences that have as their goal the improvement of teaching in the humanities in particular disciplines or in particular types of institutions. The goals of the conferences should be clear and specific, the materials under consideration should be substantial, and as many as possible of the participants should be identified.

Eligibility/Limitations The applicant for a conference may be an academic or cultural institution, an association, or a group of institutions.

Fiscal Information The cost of a conference will depend on a number of variables. Potential applicants should contact the program for additional information on budget preparation.

Application Information If you plan to seek a grant from the endowment, you should request guidelines and application forms for the program in which you are interested. Write or call the program. Guidelines and application forms are generally available two months in advance of an application deadline.

Deadline(s) Application postmark deadlines are October 1 and April 1.

Subject Term(s) Humanities; Education; Seminars and Conferences

190. National Endowment for the Humanities

Division of Education Programs, Room 302
1100 Pennsylvania Avenue, NW
Washington, DC 20506
(202) 786-0380

Higher Education in the Humanities: Humanities Projects in Individual Institutions

CFDA Program Number 45.150

Program Description Individual institutions may propose projects to strengthen their curricula or to improve their faculties' knowledge of the disciplines and materials they teach. Each proposal should be based on a coherent plan for the teaching of the humanities in the institution applying for support. It should emphasize the close examination of primary texts and sources. It should provide syllabi for any proposed courses and reading lists for any faculty development activities. It should identify all participants, including visiting scholars, and provide evidence of their commitment. And it should include brief resumes for key project personnel.

Eligibility/Limitations The endowment expects an institution to maintain a project developed under a grant after the grant period has ended. The proposal should include a letter from the chief academic officer of the institution documenting the institution's long-term commitment to the program and explaining how the improvements will be maintained financially after the grant period.

Fiscal Information Because the endowment does not fund regular operating costs, a proposal must be based on activities that go beyond the usual responsibilities of faculty for course revision and professional development and beyond the regular responsibility of the institution to its faculty and students. The endowment will provide released time or stipends for faculty to collaborate on curriculum change or to examine works outside their specialties with the help of visiting scholars. The endowment will also support related costs, such as library acquisitions, travel for visiting scholars, travel for faculty to visit model programs, and administrative costs specifically related to the project activities. Only rarely will the endowment support new positions or teaching costs.

Application Information If you plan to seek a grant from the endowment, you should request guidelines and application forms for the program in which you are interested. Write or call the program. Guidelines and application forms are generally available two months in advance of an application deadline.

Deadline(s) Application postmark deadlines are April 1 and October 1.

Additional Information Support for planning, implementation, and dissemination is available in this category. Contact the endowment for additional information.

Subject Term(s) Humanities; Education

191. National Endowment for the Humanities

Division of Education Programs, Room 302
1100 Pennsylvania Avenue, NW
Washington, DC 20506
(202) 786-0380

Higher Education in the Humanities: Institutes for College and University Faculty

Program Description An effective means for improving the quality of humanities instruction is to provide college and university faculty with opportunities for intensive study of important materials in the humanities under the guidance of leading scholars in a field. For this purpose, the endowment supports national and regional institutes in which college and university faculty come together to study texts related to a theme, issue, major figure, period, or cultural movement. The topic of an institute should be clearly focused, and it should be broadly applicable to subjects frequently taught at the undergraduate level.

Sample Grants To support an institute on Brazilian culture for twenty college and university Latin American specialists, including intensive instruction in the Portuguese language, $119,218 to the University of New Mexico, Albuquerque (1985).

Eligibility/Limitations An institute can be sponsored by a university or college, a research library, a museum, a professional association, or any other cultural institution with research facilities and collections appropriate to the institute topic. Institutes may vary in length, but each should allow sufficient time for a thorough examination of the topic. Typically, institutes involve twenty to thirty participants who come together for four to eight weeks during the summer or meet at regular intervals during an academic year. The distinguished scholars who serve as faculty for an institute may be drawn from throughout the country and, where appropriate, from abroad. An individual institution or group of institutions may also employ the institute format for internal use in preparing their own faculty to teach in an improved curriculum.

Fiscal Information The cost of an institute will depend on a number of variables. Potential applicants should contact the program for additional information on budget preparation.

Application Information If you plan to seek a grant from the endowment, you should request guidelines and application forms for the program in which you are interested. Write or call the program. Guidelines and application forms are generally available two months in advance of an application deadline.

Deadline(s) Application postmark deadlines are October 1 and April 1.

Subject Term(s) Humanities; Education; Seminars and Conferences

192. National Endowment for the Humanities

Division of Education Programs, Room 302
1100 Pennsylvania Avenue, NW
Washington, DC 20506
(202) 786-0377

Independent Study in the Humanities

Program Description Grants under this program support projects designed to increase the effectiveness with which the humanities are taught in our nation's elementary, middle, and secondary schools. The purpose of the program is to strengthen instruction principally through teacher training and in-service activities. The intent of this program is to provide an opportunity for teachers to improve their knowledge of the subjects they teach.

Eligibility/Limitations The endowment has awarded a grant to the Council of Basic Education to support this program of summer fellowships for high school teachers with at least five years of teaching experience.

Fiscal Information Fellowships of $3,000 are available for experienced teachers who wish to spend two months of independent study in one of the disciplines of the humanities.

Application Information For information about this program write to Independent Study in the Humanities, Council for Basic Education, 725 Fifteenth Street, NW, Washington, DC, 20005

Deadline(s) Contact the program for deadlines.

Subject Term(s) Humanities; Education; Fellowships

193. National Endowment for the Humanities

Division of Education Programs, Room 302
1100 Pennsylvania Avenue, NW
Washington, DC 20506
(202) 786-0373

Special Initiatives: The Columbian Quincentenary

Program Description In commemoration of the 500th anniversary of the voyages of Columbus, the Division of Education Programs invites proposals for projects that would enhance humanities education at any level on the historical, political, philosophical, and cultural ramifications of the voyages of Columbus and his contemporaries. The division will be especially receptive to proposals that bring scholars and teachers together to explore the larger contexts of the voyages: e.g., the medieval and Renaissance cultural assumptions that led to and conditioned the voyages of discovery, the "transatlantic encounters" that resulted from them, and the effects that the voyages have had on the world since the fifteenth century. Proposals may be submitted under any of the division's program headings.

Sample Grants Support for a comprehensive three-year program designed to improve teaching in a wide range of disciplines to be touched by the Columbian Quincentenary was awarded to the Newberry Library for a project "Transatlantic Encounters," to explore the reciprocal effects of cultural contact between Europe and America during the period 1400 to 1650 featuring two summer institutes for college and university faculty (1985).

Eligibility/Limitations Strengthening the teaching of the humanities in schools, colleges, and universities is the purpose of this division. Projects to improve the teaching of the history of precolonial America or to promote excellence in a Latin American studies curriculum are examples of proposals appropriate to this division under the Columbian Quincentenary initiative. An institute for college and university faculty members on the origins of the New World could be proposed, for example. The institute might focus on recent research from Spanish and Portuguese archives related to expeditions to the Americas. It could be devoted to improving the participants' understanding of particular developments during the colonial period in this hemisphere and to providing the participants with a broader understanding of the transatlantic world in the early modern period.

Application Information Applicants who are not certain where to direct an inquiry about this special initiative should call or write the director of the Division of Education Programs.

Subject Term(s) Columbian Quincentenary; Humanities; Education

194. National Endowment for the Humanities

Division of Fellowships and Seminars, Room 316
1100 Pennsylvania Avenue, NW
Washington, DC 20506
(202) 786-0466

Faculty Graduate Study Program for Historically Black Colleges and Universities

Program Description Grants provide support for faculty to undertake one year of full-time study leading to a doctoral degree in the humanities with preference given to those individuals who are at the dissertation stage of their work. This is the only NEH program that supports work leading to a graduate degree.

Eligibility/Limitations Teachers in historically black colleges and universities are eligible to apply. Grants are made through the applicant's institution.

Application Information For additional information write or call the program.

Deadline(s) The deadline for receipt of applications is March 15.

Subject Term(s) Minorities, Eligibility of; Humanities; Doctoral Dissertation Support; Predoctoral Support

195. National Endowment for the Humanities

Division of Fellowships and Seminars, Room 316
1100 Pennsylvania Avenue, NW,
Washington, DC 20506
(202) 786-0466

Fellowships for College Teachers and Independent Scholars

CFDA Program Number 45.143

Program Description These fellowships provide opportunities for individuals to pursue independent study and research that will enhance their capacities as teachers, scholars, or interpreters of the humanities and that will enable them to make significant contributions to thought and knowledge in the humanities. Fellowships enable people to devote extended periods of uninterrupted time to investigation, reflection, and often writing. The program is intended for a range of people, from those who have made significant contributions to the humanities to those who stand at the beginning of their careers. Projects, too, may cover a range of activities from general study to specialized research. Fellowships for College Teachers and Independent Scholars are for faculty members of two-year, four-year, and five-year colleges, faculty members of departments and programs in universities that do not grant the Ph.D., individuals affiliated with institutions other than colleges and universities, and scholars and writers working independently.

Sample Grants For research on "The Huancavelica Mercury Mines and the Spanish Imperial Economy, 1700-1824," $27,500 (1986). For a study "Before Brasilia: Settlement Patterns and Population Change in Goias, 1780-1890," $27,500 (1986).

Eligibility/Limitations The program of Fellowships for College Teachers and Independent Scholars, including special NEH initiatives within this program, is open to faculty members, either full-time or part-time, of two-year, four-year, and five-year colleges; faculty members of university departments, interdepartmental programs, and central graduate schools that do not grant the Ph.D.; individuals affiliated with institutions other than colleges and universities; and scholars and writers working independently. Individuals who have such positions on terminating contracts are eligible for this program as long as they do not take appointments in departments or programs that grant the Ph.D. before the January following the application deadline. Retired faculty members who had such positions are also eligible for this program. Although applicants need not have advanced degrees, those whose professional training includes a degree program must have received their degrees or completed all official requirements for them by June 1, the application deadline. If a prospective applicant has completed all of the official requirements for the degree and is awaiting only the formal award, certification that all requirements for the degree have been met by the application deadline must be submitted by the dean of the school awarding the degree. Persons seeking support for work leading to a degree are not eligible to apply, nor are active candidates for degrees, even if they expect to have finished all work for their degree by the time they would begin tenure of the fellowship and the work proposed is not related to the degree program. Persons who have recently held major fellowships or grants are not eligible to apply for an NEH fellowship; specifically, three years must have elapsed between the conclusion of tenure of the fellowship or grant and the proposed beginning date of tenure for an NEH fellowship. For the endowment, a "major fellowship or grant" is a postdoctoral award or its equivalent which provides a continuous period of released time covering at least one term of the academic year; which enables the recipient to pursue scholarly research, personal study, professional development, or writing; which provides a stipend of at least $6,000; and which comes from sources other than the recipient's employing institution. Thus, sabbaticals and grants from an individual's own institution are not considered major fellowships, nor are stipends and grants from other sources supporting study and research during the summer academic recess, such as NEH Summer Stipends and NEH Summer Seminar awards. An applicant for an NEH fellowship should be a U.S. citizen, a native resident of a U.S. territorial possession, or a foreign national who has been residing in the United States or its territories for at least the three years immediately preceding the application deadline.

Fiscal Information Fellowships normally support full-time work and are awarded for continuous periods of six to twelve full months of tenure. The stipend is intended primarily to replace salary lost through the taking of leave. The maximum amount of the NEH stipend for tenure periods of between nine and twelve months, which for teachers encompass the full academic year, is $27,500. The maximum for periods of between six and nine months is prorated by months or, for teachers, by academic year terms. Some assistance may be provided within the stipend limit to help defray the costs of necessary travel, but no allowance is given for any other expense. Fellows may supplement their awards with small grants from other sources but may not hold other major fellowships or grants during fellowship tenure, except sabbaticals and grants from their own institutions. Successful applicants who receive offers of fellowships from other foundations after June 1 must hold the NEH fellowship first.

Application Information Guidelines and application materials are available from the Division of Fellowships and Seminars.

Deadline(s) Applications must be postmarked by June 1.

Subject Term(s) Fellowships; Individuals, Eligibility of; Faculty Support; Humanities; Foreign Nationals, Eligibility of

196. National Endowment for the Humanities

Division of Fellowships and Seminars, Room 316
1100 Pennsylvania Avenue, NW,
Washington, DC 20506
(202) 786-0466

Fellowships for University Teachers

CFDA Program Number 45.142

Program Description These fellowships provide opportunities for individuals to pursue independent study and research that will enhance their capacities as teachers, scholars, or interpreters of the humanities and that will enable them to make significant contributions to thought and knowledge in the humanities. Fellowships enable people to devote extended periods of uninterrupted time to investigation, reflection, and often writing. The program is intended for a range of people, from those who have made significant contributions to the humanities to those who stand at the beginning of their careers. Projects, too, may cover a range of activities from general study to specialized research. Fellowships for University Teachers are for faculty members of departments and programs in universities that grant the Ph.D. and faculty members of post-graduate professional schools.

Sample Grants For research on "Agrarian Puerto Rico, 1765-1934: An Economic History," $27,500 (1986).

Eligibility/Limitations The program of fellowships for university faculty, including special NEH initiatives within this program, is open only to faculty members of departments in universities that grant the Ph.D., faculty members with appointments to interdepartmental programs and central graduate schools that grant the Ph.D., and faculty members of post-graduate professional schools. Individuals who have such appointments either part-time or full-time or on terminating contracts are eligible only for this program. Retired faculty members who had such positions are normally eligible for this program. Although applicants need not have advanced degrees, those whose professional training includes a degree program must have received their degrees or completed all official requirements for them by June 1, the application deadline. If a prospective applicant has completed all of the official requirements for the degree and is awaiting only the formal award, certification that all requirements for the degree have been met by the application deadline must be submitted by the dean of the school awarding the degree. Persons seeking support for work leading to a degree are not eligible to apply, nor are active candidates for degrees, even if they expect to have finished all work for their degree by the time they would begin tenure of the fellowship and the work proposed is not related to the degree program. Persons who have recently held major fellowships or grants are not eligible to apply for an NEH fellowship; specifically, three years must have elapsed between the conclusion of tenure of the fellowship or grant and the proposed beginning date of tenure for an NEH fellowship. For the endowment, a "major fellowship or grant" is a postdoctoral award or its equivalent which provides a continuous period of released time covering at least one term of the academic year; which enables the recipient to pursue scholarly research, personal study, professional development, or writing; which provides a stipend of at least $6,000; and which comes from sources other than the recipient's employing institution. Thus, sabbaticals and grants from an individual's own institution are not considered major fellowships, nor are stipends and grants from other sources supporting study and research during the summer academic recess, such as NEH Summer Stipends and NEH Summer Seminar awards. An applicant for an NEH fellowship should be a U.S. citizen, a native resident of a U.S. territorial possession, or a foreign national who has been residing in the United States or its territories for at least the three years immediately preceding the application deadline.

Fiscal Information Fellowships normally support full-time work and are awarded for continuous periods of six to twelve full months of tenure. The stipend is intended primarily to replace salary lost through the taking of leave. The maximum amount of the NEH stipend for tenure periods of between nine and twelve months, which for teachers encompass the full academic year, is $27,500. The maximum for periods of between six and nine months is prorated by months or, for teachers, by academic year terms. Some assistance may be provided within the stipend limit to help defray the costs of necessary travel, but no allowance is given for any other expense. Fellows may supplement their awards with small grants from other sources but may not hold other major fellowships or grants during fellowship tenure, except sabbaticals and grants from their own institutions. Successful applicants who receive offers of fellowships from other foundations after June 1 must hold the NEH fellowship first.

Application Information Guidelines and application materials are available from the Division of Fellowships and Seminars.

Deadline(s) Applications must be postmarked by June 1.

Subject Term(s) Fellowships; Faculty Support; Humanities; Foreign Nationals, Eligibility of

197. National Endowment for the Humanities

Division of Fellowships and Seminars, Room 316
1100 Pennsylvania Avenue, NW
Washington, DC 20506
(202) 786-0458

Special Initiatives: The Columbian Quincentenary

Program Description As part of the international observance of the 500th anniversary of Christopher Columbus's voyage of discovery to the New World, NEH invites proposals for original scholarship on related topics and for the dissemination of both new and existing scholarship. This division supports individual scholarship within the humanities and provides opportunities for the collegial study of topics and texts. All programs of the division welcome applications to conduct projects related to the Columbian Quincentenary.

Sample Grants Support for a summer seminar for secondary school teachers on "Origins of a Central American Ethos: The *Popul Vuh* and the Conquistadors" to Tufts University (1986).

Eligibility/Limitations A scholar wishing to explore a topic in early Latin American colonial history or a researcher describing the effect of the discovery of the New World upon a particular artistic or literary tradition might submit a proposal for a Fellowship for University Teachers, a Fellowship for College Teachers and Independent Scholars, or a Summer Stipend. A historian of Renaissance technology might wish to organize a Summer Seminar for College Teachers to examine the cultural and historical foundations underlying the Columbian adventure.

Application Information Applicants who are not certain where to direct an inquiry about this special initiative should call or write the director of the Division of Fellowships and Seminars.

Subject Term(s) Fellowships; Columbian Quincentenary; Humanities; Individuals, Eligibility of

198. National Endowment for the Humanities

Division of Fellowships and Seminars, Room 316
1100 Pennsylvania Avenue, NW
Washington, DC 20506
(202) 786-0463

Summer Seminars for College Teachers

CFDA Program Number 45.116

Program Description Summer seminars for college teachers are offered for teachers at undergraduate and two-year colleges who wish to deepen and enrich their knowledge of the subjects they teach. The purpose of the seminars is to provide college teachers with opportunities to work with distinguished scholars in their teaching or research fields; to work with other college teachers who share similar interests; and to undertake an individual project (e.g., intensive reading, scholarly research, or writing) of their own choosing at institutions with libraries suitable for advanced work. The seminars offered in the program deal with significant works and subject matter of central concern to the humanities. Proposals to direct summer seminars for college teachers are encouraged from professors who are not only recognized scholars in their fields but who are also well qualified by virtue of their interest and ability in undergraduate teaching or the pertinence of their work to the interests of undergraduate teachers.

Sample Grants To support a summer seminar for college teachers on "The U.S.-Mexico Borderland Perspective," $54,438 to the University of Texas, El Paso (1985). To support a summer seminar for college teachers on "The Concept of Culture and the Idea of Literature in Modern Latin America," $67,616 to Yale University, Connecticut (1985). To support a summer seminar for college teachers on "Modern Central America," $54,472 to Tulane University, Louisiana (1986).

Eligibility/Limitations College teachers wishing to participate in the seminars should be persons who are well qualified to do the work of the seminar, who are able and committed teachers, and who can make significant contributions to the seminar. The program is intended primarily for individuals teaching undergraduate courses, full- or part-time, at two-year, four-year, or five-year colleges and universities, but other persons who are qualified to do the work of the seminar and make a contribution are also eligible to apply. Preference will be given to those who have been teaching at least three years and who have not recently had the resources of a major library readily available to them. Faculty members of departments with doctoral programs in the humanities are not eligible as participants in this program.

Fiscal Information Participation in each seminar is limited to twelve college teachers, each of whom receives a stipend of $3,500 for the eight-week seminar. The selection of participants and the awarding of stipends is the responsibility of seminar directors, acting in consultation with their selection committees and within the guidelines established by the endowment. Funds are officially awarded to the institution hosting the NEH summer seminar (in most instances the institution with which the selected seminar director is affiliated). The grant will include stipends for the participants, salary for the seminar director, secretarial support, and direct and indirect costs to the host institution. General grant provisions, narrative and financial reporting requirements and forms, payment information, and applicable conditions and special provisions are provided within the award notification. Institutional fiscal personnel and the seminar director will be expected to comply with normal grant procedures.

Application Information After the decisions are made on the seminars to be offered, the complete list of seminars will be publicized by the endowment. College teachers wishing to participate in the seminars apply directly to the seminar director.

Deadline(s) The deadline for receipt of applications is March 1.

Subject Term(s) Faculty Support; Seminars and Conferences; Humanities

199. National Endowment for the Humanities

Division of Fellowships and Seminars, Room 316
1100 Pennsylvania Avenue, NW
Washington, DC 20506
(202) 786-0463

Summer Seminars for Secondary School Teachers

CFDA Program Number 45.151

Program Description At the core of the Summer Seminars for Secondary School Teachers program is the belief that the significant texts of civilization form the foundation of the intellectual life of the humanities. Knowledge of these texts constitutes both the starting point and the focus of educational inquiry. Summer Seminars for Secondary School Teachers are offered by the National Endowment for the Humanities in order to provide teachers of grades seven through twelve a unique opportunity for intense advanced study of significant texts. For four, five, or six weeks during the summer, depending on the seminar, the fifteen selected participants in each seminar will work under the direction of a distinguished teacher and active scholar, studying seminal works in the humanities in a systematic and thorough way. Through reading, writing, and reflection, and through frequent discussions—formal and informal—with the seminar director and with other teachers from across the country, seminar participants will deepen their knowledge and enhance their ability to impart an understanding of the humanities to their students. Proposals to direct summer seminars are encouraged from those with demonstrated excellence in teaching who are also active scholars in their fields. Because of the relatively short duration of the seminars, and because a principle value of each seminar for the secondary school teachers is the close association with the seminar director, it is preferable for a seminar to have a single director, except in those cases where the topic is such that joint directors can provide greater opportunities for the seminar participants than can a single director. Seminars are to be especially designed for this program and are not intended to duplicate courses normally offered by graduate departments. After the decisions have been made on the seminars to be offered, the complete list will be publicized widely by the endowment. Teachers wishing to participate in the seminars will apply directly to the seminar director.

Sample Grants To support a summer seminar for secondary school teachers on "Mexican Literature: Octavio Paz, Carlos Fuentes and Juan Rulfo," $57,878 to Arizona State University, Tempe (1985). To support a summer seminar for secondary school teachers on "Origins of A Central American Ethos: The *Popol Vuh* and the Conquistadors," $54,932 to Tufts University (1986).

Eligibility/Limitations To be eligible as a seminar participant, an individual must be a full-time or regular part-time teacher at a public, private, or parochial school, grades seven through twelve, or in exceptional cases, other school personnel, K-12. Preference will be given to those who have been teaching at least three years. An individual may apply to only one seminar in any one year; those found to have applied to more than one will be declared ineligible for a place in a seminar.

Fiscal Information The seminar director is expected to request compensation for the time required for conducting the seminar during the summer and for the time involved in the selection of participants. For a six-week seminar, the maximum amount allowable is 22.2% of the annual academic salary; for a five-week seminar, 19.4%; and for a four-week seminar, 16.6%. Two codirectors would each receive 60% of these amounts. An institution is allowed to charge fringe benefits on salary and wages according to its current negotiated rate and is eligible to claim indirect costs for this program if it has established a current indirect cost rate with an agency of the U.S. government. Each of the fifteen participants will receive a stipend of $2,000, $2,375, or $2,750 depending on the length of the seminar. The stipend is intended to cover travel expenses to and from the seminar location, books and other research expenses, and living expenses for the tenure of the seminar.

Application Information Proposal instructions and application forms are available from the Division of Fellowships and Seminars.

Deadline(s) The proposal deadline for participants is March 1; for directors, April 1.

Subject Term(s) Humanities; Seminars and Conferences; Education

200. National Endowment for the Humanities

Division of Fellowships and Seminars, Room 316
1100 Pennsylvania Avenue, NW
Washington, DC 20506
(202) 786-0466

Summer Stipends

CFDA Program Number 45.121

Program Description The Summer Stipends program provides support for faculty members in universities and in two-year and four-year colleges, and for others working in the humanities so that they can devote two consecutive months of full-time study and research to a project. The proposed project should be not only an immediate contribution to learning in a particular field, but also a contribution to the advancement of knowledge in the humanities more generally, and to the applicant's development as a scholar, teacher, and interpreter of the humanities. Each college and university in the United States and its territorial possessions may nominate three members of its faculty for the Summer Stipend competition. No more than two of the nominees may be in the early stages of their careers, i.e., junior nominees; no more than two may be at a more advanced stage, i.e., senior nominees.

Sample Grants Summer stipend for a study of "The Economic Role of the Jesuits in Portugal and its Empire, 1540-1808," $3,000 (1986). Summer stipend for a study of "The *Milonga* Poems of Jorge Luis Borges," $3,000 (1986). Summer stipend for a study of "The Beginnings of Civilization on the South Coast of Guatemala: The Archaeological Evidence," $3,000 (1986). Summer stipend for a study of "Afro-Antillean Literature and the Harlem Renaissance," $3,000 (1986). Summer stipend for a study of "Liberalism and the Debate for Indian Integration in Bolivia," $3,000 (1986).

Eligibility/Limitations An applicant for an endowment fellowship should be a U.S. citizen, a native resident of a U.S. territorial possession, or a foreign national who has been residing in the United States or its territories for at least the three years immediately preceding the application deadline. Although applicants need not have advanced degrees, those whose professional training includes a degree program must have received their degrees, or completed all official requirements for them by October 1. If a prospective applicant has completed all of the official requirements for the degree and is awaiting only the formal award, certification that all requirements have been met by the application deadline must be submitted by the dean of the school awarding the degree. Persons seeking support for work leading toward degrees are not eligible to apply, nor are active candidates for degrees, even if they expect to have finished all work for their degree by the time they would begin tenure of the summer stipend and the work proposed is not related to their degree program. Individuals who have recently received major fellowships or research grants are eligible to apply, and their applications will be accorded serious consideration. However, preference is given to persons who have not received major fellowships or other leave-providing grants, except sabbaticals or grants from their own institutions, within the last five years. The more recent the grant, the more heavily it weighs in the endowment's decision.

Fiscal Information Each summer stipend provides $3,500 for two consecutive months of full-time study or research. Recipients of summer stipends may not hold major fellowships or grants during the tenure of their awards, and they must devote full time to their projects for the two months of their tenure. Summer stipends normally support work carried out during the summer months.

Application Information Application forms and additional information and guidelines are available from the Division of Fellowships and Seminars.

Deadline(s) Applications must be postmarked by October 1.

Subject Term(s) Faculty Support; Humanities; Foreign Nationals, Eligibility of; Fellowships

201. National Endowment for the Humanities

Division of Fellowships and Seminars, Room 316
1100 Pennsylvania Avenue, NW
Washington, DC 20506
(202) 786-0463

Travel to Collections

CFDA Program Number 45.152

Program Description The purpose of the Travel to Collections program is to enable American scholars to travel to use the research collections of libraries, archives, museums, or other repositories to consult research materials of fundamental importance for the progress of their scholarly work. This grant program is intended to help scholars meet the costs associated with a research trip anywhere in the world. The research proposed must fall within the scope of the humanities. Projects in the social sciences which are historical or philosophical, or which attempt to cast light on questions of interpretation or criticism traditionally in the humanities, are eligible, as are historical or philosophical studies of the natural sciences. Projects that involve critical, historical, and theoretical studies of the arts are eligible for support. The program is designed for scholars whose research could not progress satisfactorily without consultation of materials at a specific location.

Sample Grants Travel to Collections grants have been awarded: to support research on technology and social change in the Puerto Rican sugar industry (1985); to support research on the history of Mexican mural painting (1985); to support research on a history of foreign oil companies in Mexico (1985); to support research on Quirigua artifacts in the Middle American Research Institute (1985); to support research on style as a measure of economic and political integration of the Central Lowland Maya (1986); to support reseach on the United States and Central America, 1952-1972 (1986); to support research on the Mexican Revolution in Puebla, 1905-1917 (1986); to support an analysis of Inca art in Peru (1986).

Eligibility/Limitations Applicants should be citizens of the United States, native residents of U.S. territorial possessions, or foreign nationals who have lived in the United States or its territories for three years immediately prior to submitting an application. Applicants need not have academic affiliations to be eligible. Although applicants need not have advanced degrees, candidates for degrees and persons seeking support for work leading to degrees are not eligible. Applications that are focused on pedagogical theory, research in educational methods, tests, and measurements, or cognitive psychology, are not eligible.

Fiscal Information Applicants recommended for awards will receive an award of $750 in one payment. The award is to be used exclusively to help defray the scholar's expenses in undertaking the specific research trip, including travel costs, subsistence and lodging, reproduction and photoduplication costs, and other associated research expenses. Applications for research travel to locations easily accessible to the applicant on a regular basis will not be competitive. Applicants are expected to undertake the research travel during the period proposed in the application. The expenditures proposed may not include salary support or replacement or support for released time from the applicant's regular employment.

Application Information Application forms and additional information and guidelines are available from the Division of Fellowships and Seminars.

Deadline(s) To be eligible for consideration an application must be postmarked no later than July 15 or January 15.

Subject Term(s) Travel Support; Individuals, Eligibility of; Humanities; Foreign Nationals, Eligibility of; Travel Support Abroad

202. National Endowment for the Humanities

Division of Fellowships and Seminars, Room 316
1100 Pennsylvania Avenue, NW
Washington, DC 20506
(202) 786-0463

Younger Scholars Program

CFDA Program Number 45.115

Program Description Awards for younger scholars provide the nation's students with opportunities to conduct noncredit independent research and writing projects during the summer months. Under the close supervision of advisers who are humanities scholars, individuals pursue their own humanities projects during a concentrated period of time not normally available during the school year. This program enables grantees to enhance their intellectual development by producing research papers on a specific humanities topic. In both subject matter and methodology, projects must be firmly grounded in one of the disciplines of the humanities. Applicants are expected to discuss the way in which their projects engage one or more of the following areas of emphasis: the interpretation of cultural works; the study of historical ideas, figures, and events; and understanding the disciplines of the humanities.

Sample Grants To support research on "The Role of Women in the Mexican Revolution," $2,200 (1986). To support "A Study of Gesture in Classic Maya Art," $2,200 (1986). To support a study of "The U.S. Constitution as a Precedent in Latin America," $1,800 (1986).

Eligibility/Limitations Applicants must be twenty-one years of age or under throughout the entire calendar year in which the application is submitted; or, if they are over twenty-one, they must be full-time college students pursuing an undergraduate degree at the time of application. Applicants must be either U.S. citizens or foreign nationals who have lived in the United States for at least three consecutive years at the time of application. Proposed projects require a project adviser with knowledge and qualifications in an appropriate humanities discipline and must result in a substantial research paper. Individuals who will have received or expect to receive a bachelor's degree by October 1 are not eligible to apply. No project activities may take place outside the United States during the grant period. Joint projects by two or more individuals may not be submitted.

Fiscal Information College students (or high-school graduates at the time of application) may apply for $2,200, of which $400 is allotted to the adviser. High-school students (at the time of application) may apply for $1,800, of which $400 is allotted to the adviser. All grants involve nine weeks of full-time work by an individual on a specific humanities project during the summer months. Grantees may not be enrolled in a credit course during the grant period, and projects may not be used for academic credit.

Application Information Application forms and additional information are available from the Division of Fellowships and Seminars.

Deadline(s) Applications should be received by November 1.

Subject Term(s) Undergraduate Support; Humanities; Foreign Nationals, Eligibility of

203. National Endowment for the Humanities

Division of General Programs
1100 Pennsylvania Avenue, NW, Room 420
Washington, DC 20506
(202) 786-0271

Humanities Projects in Libraries

CFDA Program Number 45.137

Program Description Through Humanities Projects in Libraries the endowment supports programs that are designed to increase public understanding of the humanities through the discovery, interpretation, and greater appreciation of books and other resources in library collections. Projects should involve the active collaboration of scholars from the appropriate disciplines of the humanities and the professional staff of libraries during both the planning and implementation of programs. The Humanities Projects in Libraries program encourages public, academic, or special libraries to plan and present programs in the humanities. The program also encourages the development of cooperative projects between public, academic, or special libraries, as well as between libraries, museums, historical societies, and other cultural institutions. Programs may also take place at locations other than a library, but the primary objective of using the resources of libraries to enhance the understanding and appreciation of the humanities must be evident in the design of any project. Applicants for these grants are expected to address the manner in which their projects deal with one or more of the following areas: the appreciation and interpretation of cultural works; the illumination of historical ideas, figures, and events; and an understanding of the disciplines of the humanities.

Sample Grants To support the development and circulation of a program package about European historical and cultural dominance in the New World and American cultural traditions, $125,340 to Texas Humanities Resource Center, Inc., Austin (1986).

Eligibility/Limitations Eligible applicants include nonprofit public, academic, special, or institutional libraries; local, state-wide or regional library systems; and state, regional, or national library associations. The following types of projects are not eligible for support: projects to create musical composition, dance, painting, sculpture, poetry, short stories or novels, and projects providing for performance or training in these arts; projects from profit-making organizations or institutions, or from individuals without an organizational or institutional base; projects whose primary function is to mount exhibitions from the collections of museums or historical societies; projects that have as their primary focus a media production; projects for renovation, restoration, rehabilitation, construction, establishment of historic markers and plaques or historic preservation; projects that have as their primary focus organizing, cataloguing, indexing, microfilming, or preserving collections; projects that consist primarily of research activities; individual fellowships and stipends, support for graduate education, or projects that require participants to register for academic credit; projects for training of personnel or individual requests for travel to professional meetings; the publication or editorial costs of articles or monographs for scholarly audiences; and projects directed at persuading an audience to a particular political, philosophical, religious, or ideological point of view or that advocate a particular program of social action or change.

Fiscal Information Humanities Projects in Libraries offers planning and implementation grants. Planning grants are awarded to support the collaborative efforts of scholars and an institution's administrative staff to design programs. Planning grants generally last no longer than six months and usually range from $5,000 to $15,000. Support may occasionally exceed $15,000 if such activities are regional or national in scope or involve more than one type of institution. Requests for funds in excess of $15,000 should be discussed with the program's staff before an application is made. Implementation grants support the presentation of fully developed public programs in the humanities. Such grants are normally funded for periods of one to three years. These grants usually range from $15,000 to $200,000. Requests for funds in excess of $200,000 should be discussed with the program's staff before an application is submitted. Cost sharing of at least 20% of a project's total budget is recommended for an implementation grant.

Application Information Application forms and additional information are available from the Division of General Programs.

Deadline(s) Applications must be received by March 20 or September 18.

Subject Term(s) Humanities; Library Support; Education

204. National Endowment for the Humanities

Division of General Programs, Room 420
1100 Pennsylvania Avenue, NW
Washington, DC 20506
(202) 786-0278

Humanities Projects in Media

CFDA Program Number 45.104

Program Description The Media Program seeks to transmit work in scholarship and learning in the humanities, to convey the best in thought and culture, and to engage the public in critical analysis and interpretation through quality television, film, and radio programming. The program expects high standards, not only of technical quality but also of intellectual depth and rigor. Other public and private agencies support media projects, but the endowment funds only those that centrally involve the disciplines of the humanities. This is accomplished by collaboration between scholars in the humanities and media professionals. Humanities scholars are expected to participate in each project at every stage: planning, script preparation, and production. Proposals must reflect the knowledge of scholars and teachers as well as the expertise and talent of producers, directors, and writers. Scholars ensure that the programs reflect the critical and reflective work of the humanities in content and approach and that the information presented in the programs is conceptually sound and factually accurate. Producers, directors, and writers help the scholars translate materials from their research into effective and interesting programs. Constructive collaboration is the basis and the key to high quality programs that are aesthetically and intellectually stimulating. The Media Program encourages applicants to select the media format and the program length best suited for the material—dramatization, documentary, talk show, animation, or other. In order to reach the largest number of adults and children, all television projects supported through the program should be designed for broadcast to national audiences or, if cable is selected, have demonstrable value for a national audience. Radio projects may be designed for local, regional, or national distribution and broadcast on public and commercial stations or distributed on cable audio systems. Applicants are expected to discuss the manner in which their projects embody one or more of the division's three categories of special concern: the appreciation and interpretation of cultural works; the illumination of historical ideas, figures, and events; and an understanding of the disciplines of the humanities.

Sample Grants To support production of a thirty-minute animated film on *Popol Vuh*, the Mayan creation myth, $25,330 to the Film Arts Foundation, San Francisco, California (1986). To support revision of a script for a sixty-minute film synthesizing for the general public the knowledge contained in the written literature of the Classic Maya civilization, $15,000 to InterCultural, Inc., Fort Worth, Texas (1986). To support the planning of a series of five radio documentaries on the life and work of Brazilian composer Heitor Villa-Lobos, to commemerate the 100th anniversary of his birth, $20,000 to National Public Radio, Washington, DC (1986).

Eligibility/Limitations Any private, nonprofit organization, college or university, or branch of state or local government may apply for a Media Program grant. In addition, any group of scholars or professionals with experience in media and the humanities may form their own nonprofit group to apply for funding. Applicants are not required to be incorporated or to have 501(c)(3) status with the Internal Revenue Service although obtaining such status is recommended, especially for larger projects. In any case, applicants must have the ability to administer the project in compliance with federal regulations as well as generally accepted accounting principles. The Media Program does not provide support for the following projects: projects to create musical composition, dance, painting, sculpture, poetry, short stories, novels, or projects providing for performance or training in these arts; projects directed at persuading an audience to a particular political, philosophical, religious, or ideological point of view or that advocate a particular program of social action or change; projects that are designed exclusively to preserve information for deposit in archives; projects that require the permanent acquisition of facilities or equipment or the establishment of training programs in film, radio, or television productions; projects aimed at technological experimentation in the development of electronic media; and instructional projects primarily designed for classroom use.

Fiscal Information The endowment provides three types of funding for projects: matching grants, outright grants, and a combination of the two.

Application Information Early contact with Media Program staff can be helpful and is strongly recommended. Either a letter describing the project or a draft proposal may be submitted (no later than six weeks before the deadline to allow time for a response). A staff member will be able to determine if the basic idea fits within the general guidelines of the program and, if time permits, can help anticipate some questions that reviewers and panelists may later raise. In preparing the application, applicants should remember that it will be read by both authorities in the subject area and professionals in the broadcast industry. The more precise an applicant can be about a proposal's concept, its importance in the humanities, the way it will be developed, how the medium will be used to enhance it, and the roles of key participants, the more likely it is that evaluators will have confidence in the quality of the project, in the applicant's control of it and ability to carry it out.

Deadline(s) Applications should be received by March 18 and September 18.

Additional Information The Media Program has three funding categories—planning, scripting, and production—which are designed to help applicants produce high quality programs, following appropriate stages and steps. However, the applicant may apply in any category depending on the status and needs of the project in question.

Subject Term(s) Humanities; Media; Education

205. National Endowment for the Humanities

Division of General Programs, Room 420
1100 Pennsylvania Avenue, NW
Washington, DC 20506
(202) 786-0284

Humanities Projects in Museums and Historical Organizations

CFDA Program Number 45.125

Program Description The goal of this program is to help make possible exhibitions that "speak" to people today, exhibitions that give visitors an understanding and appreciation of an object itself and also of its relationship to ideas, events, and aesthetics. The endowment seeks to facilitate the groundwork of research and collections management that are the foundation for any intellectually substantial public exhibition, and it seeks to help in the planning and implementation of the exhibitions themselves. The spectrum of endowment support extends from an inventory of permanent collections, to the preparation of catalogues, to the sharing of collections among several museums. The endowment supports projects designed especially for children as well as those designed for adults. It supports the preparation of publications related to permanent collections and to both temporary and permanent exhibitions. In addition, the endowment can assist in the conservation of objects used in an exhibition or, under some circumstances, objects that are part of the permanent collection.

Sample Grants To create an exhibition and educational programs presenting the culture of the Huichol Indians of western Mexico, $107,627 to the San Diego Museum of Man, San Diego, California (1986). To plan a major exhibition on Mexican masquerade emphasizing the history of masking and costume from the Spanish conquest to the present day, $40,000 to the International Folk Art Museum, Santa Fe, New Mexcio (1987). To support the conservation of artifacts and the installation of a permanent exhibit hall interpreting the prehistoric cultures of the Andes and the ethnology of the cultures of Amazonia, $250,000 to the American Museum of Natural History, New York (1986).

Eligibility/Limitations Eligible applicants include museums, historical societies, and other nonprofit organizations and institutions.

Fiscal Information Project costs can be supported by (1) endowment funds and (2) cash and noncash contributions, such as donated services and goods, which are contributed to the project by the applicant and nonfederal third parties. Contributions from the applicant and third parties constitute the applicant organization's "cost sharing." While the program for museums and historical organizations does not have established requirements on levels of cost sharing, all applicants are encouraged to participate in the support of the expenses related to carrying out a project, especially for large projects. More specific information on cost sharing is available from the program. The endowment provides three types of funding for projects: matching grants, outright grants, and a combination of the two. The program for museums and historical organizations does not provide support for the following activities: projects in the creative or performing arts; establishment of a new institution; general operating expenses; architectural preservation; acquisition of artifacts, works of art, or documents; purchase of permanent equipment for general operation purposes (filing cabinets, office equipment, or furniture); capital improvements of buildings; attendance at professional meetings; and projects that focus on current affairs or events for the purpose of eliciting a specific public response or advocating a particular program of social action or change.

Application Information Additional information and specific guidelines are available from the program.

Deadline(s) Applications should be received by June 12 and December 9.

Subject Term(s) Humanities; Museums; Museums, Exhibitions; Education

206. National Endowment for the Humanities

Division of General Programs, Room 426
1100 Pennsylvania Avenue, NW
Washington, DC 20506
(202) 786-0271

Public Humanities Projects

CFDA Program Number 45.113

Program Description This program offers support to a wide variety of projects designed to increase public understanding of the humanities. Through this program the endowment recognizes exemplary public programs and promotes model projects that may have national significance. The program is especially interested in identifying new opportunities for calling the public's attention to the work of humanities scholars. This program does not restrict its grant-making to any one type of project, and applicants may make use of a number of formats—including public symposia, community forums, debates, interpretive pamphlets, or audio-visual materials—to reach segments of the general public with humanities scholarship.

Eligibility/Limitations Eligible applicants include colleges and universities, professional organizations or associations, cultural and community organizations, agencies of state and local governments, and various non-profit community groups. In many cases, an applicant will be a consortium of such groups or an ad-hoc group formed to mount special, one-time events such as the commemoration of an anniversary. As a general rule, priority is given to applications which promise to reach a national and regional audience, but well-conceived local projects are frequently competitive. All projects should feature the participation of scholars from one or more disciplines of the humanities.

Fiscal Information The program offers both planning grants and implementation awards. Normally, planning grants range from $5,000 to $20,000 and last no longer than six months. Cost sharing is not required for planning grants. Implementation grants may range from $15,000 to $150,000 and are funded for periods of one to three years. Normally, the endowment will support no more than 80% of the total costs of an implementation project.

Application Information Applicants should submit a preliminary proposal six to eight weeks before a deadline, and this draft should include a tentative budget to enable the program staff to determine eligibility and competitiveness. Contact the program for guidelines and application forms.

Deadline(s) The program runs two competitions each year; deadlines are March 18 and September 18.

Subject Term(s) Humanities; Education

207. National Endowment for the Humanities

Division of General Programs, Room 426
1100 Pennsylvania Avenue, NW
Washington, DC 20506
(202) 786-0267

Special Initiatives: The Columbian Quincentenary

Program Description As part of the international observance of the 500th anniversary of Christopher Columbus's voyage of discovery to the New World, NEH invites proposals for original scholarship on related topics and for the dissemination of both new and existing scholarship. Topics may include the expansion of European civilization through the efforts of the Spanish and Portuguese crowns; the establishment of new societies and new forms of cultural expression through encounter among native American, European, and African peoples; and the ideas—political, religious, philosophical, scientific, technological, and aesthetic—that shaped the processes of exploration, settlement, and cultural conflict and transformation set into motion by Columbus's momentous voyage. Proposals related to this initiative are welcome in any of the grant categories of the Division of General Programs. Of particular interest are projects that will result in a deeper appreciation and understanding of important works of literature and the arts; a heightened understanding of significant historical figures, events, and ideas; and a greater comprehension of the disciplines or methodology of the humanities.

Sample Grants Support for an exhibition tracing the variety of interpretations of ancient Mayan culture offered by scholars in different centuries and different disciplines, using architectural drawings, maps, prints, and other materials to document the theories put forward by explorers, archeologists, and scholars (1986). Support for a sixty-minute television documentary that examines the destruction of the Inca empire by the conquistadors; as part of the *Odyssey* series, this documentary also surveys the current status of archeological research on this pre-Columbian civilization (1986). Support for a project at a university in Puerto Rico to involve local youth in archeological investigation as part of a year-long extracurricular study focusing on the history of the island during the period of Spanish settlement and colonization (1986).

Eligibility/Limitations The division supports projects intended to increase public understanding of the humanities. To achieve this end, the division makes grants for the planning and implementation of traveling and permanent exhibitions at museums, historical organizations, and libraries; for the planning, scripting, and production of humanities programming for television and radio; and for lectures, conferences, symposia, discussion groups, and related activities held at libraries, colleges, universities, and other institutions and organizations. All projects receiving awards must reflect an active collaboration among scholars in the humanities and professionals with knowledge of humanities programming for the general public.

Application Information For further information about the Columbian Quincentenary and for application guidelines, contact the Division of General Programs.

Subject Term(s) Columbian Quincentenary; Humanities; Education

208. National Endowment for the Humanities

Division of Research Programs, Room 318
1100 Pennsylvania Avenue, NW
Washington, DC 20506
(202) 786-0210

Interpretive Research: Humanities, Science, and Technology

CFDA Program Number 45.133

Program Description In this program the endowment supports research that employs the theories and methods of humanities disciplines to study science and technology as well as research that broadens and deepens understanding of the fundamental concerns that lie behind current issues about the conduct and applications of science and technology. The endowment encourages studies that promote the collaboration of scientists or engineers with humanities scholars as well as projects that promise to improve interdisciplinary research methods. Support is available for collaborative or coordinated research in many areas of inquiry that include, but are not limited to, the form, content, and purposes of scientific knowledge; the processes through which scientific knowledge is developed; the invention, innovation, and transfer of technology; the social, moral, and legal meaning of specific scientific and technological innovations; the interaction among sciences, technology, and other elements of culture; and the methods and concepts that the humanities use to study science and technology. The endowment supports projects that involve historical and philosophical approaches to the social sciences but does not support empirical social scientific research, specific policy studies, or technical impact assessments.

Eligibility/Limitations Institutions in the United States engaged in the humanities and individual United States citizens or foreign nationals who have been living in the United States or its territories for at least three years at the time of application are eligible to apply. Support may also be given to any individual or organization whose work promises significantly to advance knowledge and understanding of the humanities in the United States. Foreign nationals who do not meet the residence requirement may apply if they are formally affiliated with a United States educational institution and in these cases must apply through the institution. In exceptional circumstances, the endowment may also provide support to a foreign institution or foreign national not meeting the eligibility criteria mentioned above when a project promises to advance knowledge and understanding of the humanities in the United States to an unusually large extent. The endowment does not support research in pursuit of an academic degree.

Fiscal Information Awards can support full- or part-time activities, for up to three years. Although requests for grants may be of any size, each project budget should be appropriate to the scope and magnitude of the proposed activities. The average grant is $50,000 per year. Applicants proposing complex projects or projects that are likely to involve large budget requests should consult with a member of the program staff before final application is submitted. Normally, the endowment's contribution to a project will not exceed 80% of the project's total costs. For all types of projects, applicants are encouraged to consider seeking support through federal matching funds.

Application Information Program guidelines are available upon request. After reading these guidelines, the prospective applicant should draft a brief description (no more than five pages) of the proposed project. This description should be sent to the program officer. So that staff members have sufficient time to give the project thorough attention, this correspondence should begin at least two or three months prior to the formal application deadline. Applicants should not attempt to prepare a full proposal using only general guidelines. Upon receipt of the brief description, endowment staff will assess the eligibility and competitiveness of the project and will contact the applicant about the proposal. If the project is eligible, the endowment staff member will send application forms and instructions. If sufficient time before the deadline remains, the applicant may submit a draft of the proposal for further informal comment. After this additional consultation with the staff, the applicant should prepare a full application using the appropriate forms.

Deadline(s) Deadline for receipt of applications is October 1.

Subject Term(s) Individuals, Eligibility of; Foreign Nationals, Eligibility of; Humanities; Science and Technology; Social Sciences

209. National Endowment for the Humanities

Division of Research Programs, Room 318
1100 Pennsylvania Avenue, NW
Washington, DC 20506
(202) 786-0210

Interpretive Research: Projects

CFDA Program Number 45.140

Program Description Grants in this category are intended to support major collaborative or coordinated projects that will be influential in and important for humanities scholarship. The endowment encourages applications that are grounded in the individual disciplines of the humanities as well as those that cross disciplinary boundaries. Applicants must make a convincing case for the importance of the project as well as for the choice of the proposed methodology. Applicants must also demonstrate that the proposed personnel and institutional resources are available and appropriate to the project's goals. Projects supported in this program include biographies; historical and analytical studies in literature and the arts; research in history, philosophy, and other basic humanities disciplines; focused interdisciplinary studies; humanistic research in political science, sociology, and cultural anthropology; and other major collaborative or cooperative undertakings that promise to advance research methods or the means of interpretation in the humanities. In this category, the endowment also supports archeological projects that promise to strengthen scholarly knowledge and understanding of history and culture. Support is available for foreign and American archeology, including survey, excavation, materials analysis, laboratory research, artifact preservation, and preparation of archeological monographs.

Sample Grants To prepare a data base, the *Corpus Maya Hieroglyphic Inscriptions*, which will serve the needs of cultural and art historians, epigraphists, and archeologists, $135,000 to Harvard University (1986). To implement an archeological investigation of the formation of chiefdoms in northern South America through a regional examination of human settlement in the Alto Magdelena of Colombia, $30,000 to the University of Pittsburgh (1986). To support a study of the linquistic expression of spatial, temporal, and other relationships in a contemporary Mayan language, $90,940 to the University of Chicago (1986). To support renewal of an emergency grant made jointly by NEH and NEA for a newsletter, *Encuentro*, which provides information on arts and humanities events related to the Columbus Quincentenary, $30,548 to the University of New Mexico (1986).

Eligibility/Limitations Institutions in the United States engaged in the humanities and individual United States citizens or foreign nationals who have been living in the United States or its territories for at least three years at the time of application are eligible to apply. Support may also be given to any individual or organization whose work promises significantly to advance knowledge and understanding of the humanities in the United States. Foreign nationals who do not meet the residence requirement may apply if they are formally affiliated with a United States educational institution and in these cases must apply through the institution. In exceptional circumstances, the endowment may also provide support to a foreign institution or foreign national not meeting the eligibility criteria mentioned above when a project promises to advance knowledge and understanding of the humanities in the United States to an unusually large extent. The endowment does not support research in pursuit of an academic degree.

Fiscal Information Awards can support full-or part-time activities, for up to three years. Although requests for grants may be of any size, each project budget should be appropriate to the scope and magnitude of the proposed activities. The average grant is

$50,000 per year. Applicants proposing complex projects or projects that are likely to involve large budget requests should consult with a member of the program staff before final application is submitted. Normally, the endowment's contribution to a project will not exceed 80% of the project's total costs. For all types of projects, applicants are encouraged to consider seeking support through federal matching funds. Applicants who seek funding for major archeological expeditions should already have completed preliminary survey work. If a survey has not been made, the applicant may request an initial grant to fund a preparatory investigation. Support is available for materials analysis only if the analysis is an integral part of a larger project that focuses on problems of research and interpretation in the humanities.

Application Information Program guidelines are available upon request. After reading these guidelines, the prospective applicant should draft a brief description (no more than five pages) of the proposed project. This description should be sent to the program officer. So that staff members have sufficient time to give the project thorough attention, this correspondence should begin at least two or three months prior to the formal application deadline. Applicants should not attempt to prepare a full proposal using only general guidelines. Upon receipt of the brief description, endowment staff will assess the eligibility and competitiveness of the project and will contact the applicant about the proposal. If the project is eligible, the endowment staff member will send application forms and instructions. If sufficient time before the deadline remains, the applicant may submit a draft of the proposal for further informal comment. After this additional consultation with the staff, the applicant should prepare a full application using the appropriate forms.

Deadline(s) Deadline for receipt of applications is October 1.

Subject Term(s) Individuals, Eligibility of; Foreign Nationals, Eligibility of; Humanities; Archeology

210. National Endowment for the Humanities

Division of Research Programs, Room 318
1100 Pennsylvania Avenue, NW
Washington, DC 20506
(202) 786-0358

Reference Materials: Access

CFDA Program Number 45.124

Program Description In this category the endowment supports projects that promise to increase the availability of important research collections and other significant source material in all fields of the humanities. Support is provided for such activities as archival arrangement and description projects; bibliographies; records surveys; cataloguing projects involving print, graphic, film, sound, and artifact collections; indices; and other guides to humanities documentation. Under certain circumstances, oral histories are also eligible. In addition, support is provided for the development of national standards for access to different types of scholarly resources and for projects that promise to improve significantly the ways in which libraries, archives, and other repositories make research documentation available. Archival arrangement and description projects that involve the microfilming of unique materials are also eligible for support in the access category, as are projects to microfilm important collections in foreign repositories that are largely inaccessible to American scholars. An applicant must demonstrate that the level and form of description proposed is an appropriate and cost-effective means of gaining bibliographic control over the collection or collections involved. In standard archival arrangement and description projects, support is normally limited to the preparation of finding aids to the box and folder level. Applicants who propose to organize non-textual collections are urged to employ minimal level cataloguing.

Sample Grants An individual grant to support development of a guide to photographs, prints, and paintings in Mexican repositories documenting the cultural and social history of Mexico, $54,480 (1985). An individual grant to support the preparation of a bibliography of works printed in Nicaragua or written by Nicaraguans or about Nicaragua, 1900-1978, based on the holdings of the U.S., Nicaraguan, and other foreign collections, $68,116 (1985). To support the development of a computerized catalogue of photographic collections which will offer a means for subject access to a major photographic archive documenting native American history and culture in North and South America, $14,824 to the Museum of the American Indian, New York (1985). To support coversion to a data-base format of an existing index to articles on black history and culture found in serials and ephemeral publications issued in the U.S., Africa, Latin America, and the Caribbean from 1948-1985, $70,000 to the New York Public Library (1986).

Eligibility/Limitations Institutions in the United States engaged in the humanities and individual United States citizens or foreign nationals who have been living in the United States or its territories for at least three years at the time of application are eligible to apply. Support may also be given to any individual or organization whose work promises significantly to advance knowledge and understanding of the humanities in the United States. Foreign nationals who do not meet the residence requirement may apply if they are formally affiliated with a United States educational institution and in these cases must apply through the institution. In exceptional circumstances, the endowment may also provide support to a foreign institution or foreign national not meeting the eligibility criteria mentioned above when a project promises to advance knowledge and understanding of the humanities in the United States to an unusually large extent. The endowment does not support research in pursuit of an academic degree.

Fiscal Information Awards can provide up to three years of support and usually range from $20,000 to $150,000, depending upon the size and scope of the project. Applicants whose projects are complex in organization or are likely to involve large budget requests should consult with a member of the program staff before a final application is submitted. Normally, the endowment's contribution to projects that are focused chiefly on an applicant institution's own holdings will not exceed 60% of the project's total costs. Endowment support of projects that do not primarily benefit the applicant institution will usually not exceed 80% of the project's total costs. All applicants are encouraged to seek full or partial support through federal matching funds.

Application Information Program guidelines are available upon request. After reading these guidelines, the prospective applicant should draft a brief description (no more than five pages) of the proposed project. This description should be sent to the program officer. So that staff members have sufficient time to give the project thorough attention, this correspondence should begin at least two or three months prior to the formal application deadline. Applicants should not attempt to prepare a full proposal using only general guidelines. Upon receipt of the brief description, endowment staff will assess the eligibility and competitiveness of the project and will contact the applicant about the proposal. If the project is eligible, the endowment staff member will send application forms and instructions. If sufficient time before the deadline remains, the applicant may submit a draft of the proposal for further informal comment. After this additional consultation with the staff, the applicant should prepare a full application using the appropriate forms.

Deadline(s) Deadline for receipt of applications is November 1.

Subject Term(s) Individuals, Eligibility of; Foreign Nationals, Eligibility of; Humanities; Reference Materials; Archival Support

211. National Endowment for the Humanities

Division of Research Programs, Room 318
1100 Pennsylvania Avenue, NW
Washington, DC 20506
(202) 786-0358

Reference Materials: Tools

CFDA Program Number 45.145

Program Description Grants in this category support the creation of dictionaries, historical or linguistic atlases, encyclopedias, concordances, *catalogues raisonnes*, linguistic grammars, descriptive catalogues, data bases, and other materials that serve to codify information essential to research in the humanities. Applicants must make a convincing case for the project's editorial and administrative procedures and for the importance of the final product to scholars in several fields. In addition, applicants must demonstrate that the form chosen for the proposed research tool (printed volume, microform, on-line data base, etc.) represents the most effective means of disseminating the information.

Sample Grants To support preparation of a detailed analytical index and statistical analysis of the diaries, commonplace books, and family sketches written by Thomas Thistlewood, an Anglo-Jamaican plantation owner, from 1748 through 1786, $45,000 to the College of William and Mary, Williamsburg, Virginia (1985). To support preparation of a computerized index and related subject indices to the documents of the Provincias Internas Branch of the General Archive of Mexico, $155,155 to the University of Arizona (1986). To support a pilot project to develop a computerized database of the indigenous languages of South America, $60,000 to the University of California, Berkeley (1986). To support the preparation of a lexical database of Chol, a Mayan language, $75,000 to an individual scholar (1986).

Eligibility/Limitations Institutions in the United States engaged in the humanities and individual United States citizens or foreign nationals who have been living in the United States or its territories for at least three years at the time of application are eligible to apply. Support may also be given to any individual or organization whose work promises significantly to advance knowledge and understanding of the humanities in the United States. Foreign nationals who do not meet the residence requirement may apply if they are formally affiliated with a United States educational institution and in these cases must apply through the institution. In exceptional circumstances, the endowment may also provide support to a foreign institution or foreign national not meeting the eligibility criteria mentioned above when a project promises to advance knowledge and understanding of the humanities in the United States to an unusually large extent. The endowment does not support research in pursuit of an academic degree.

Fiscal Information Awards can be made for periods extending from one to three years, and typically range from less than $10,000 to more than $150,000, depending upon the scope of the project. Applicants whose projects are complex in organization or are likely to involve large budget requests should consult with a member of the program staff before final application is submitted. Normally, the endowment's contribution to a project will not exceed 80% of the project's total costs. All applicants are encouraged to seek full or partial support through federal matching funds.

Application Information Program guidelines are available upon request. After reading these guidelines, the prospective applicant should draft a brief description (no more than five pages) of the proposed project. This description should be sent to the program officer. So that staff members have sufficient time to give the project thorough attention, this correspondence should begin at least two or three months prior to the formal application deadline. Applicants should not attempt to prepare a full proposal using only general guidelines. Upon receipt of the brief description, endowment staff will assess the eligibility and competitiveness of the project and will contact the applicant about the proposal. If the project is eligible, the endowment staff member will send application forms and instructions. If sufficient time before the deadline remains, the applicant may submit a draft of the proposal for further informal comment. After this additional consultation with the staff, the applicant should prepare a full application using the appropriate forms.

Deadline(s) Deadline for receipt of applications is November 1.

Subject Term(s) Individuals, Eligibility of; Foreign Nationals, Eligibility of; Humanities; Reference Materials

212. National Endowment for the Humanities

Division of Research Programs, Room 318
1100 Pennsylvania Avenue, NW
Washington, DC 20506
(202) 786-0204

Regrants: Centers for Advanced Study

CFDA Program Number 45.122

Program Description Through grants in this category, the endowment supports coordinated research in well-defined subject areas at independent centers for advanced study, overseas research centers, independent research libraries, and research museums. In assessing an application from a center, the endowment emphasizes the intrinsic importance of the work to be undertaken at the center, the relation of this work to the center's collections and other facilities, and the degree to which arrangements at the center will promote collegial exchange. The regrants awarded by the centers enable individual scholars to pursue their own research for periods ranging from six to twelve months and to participate in the interchange of ideas among the center's scholars.

Eligibility/Limitations Awards are made to colleges and universities and to organizations such as learned societies, federations and committees of scholarly associations, and major independent research libraries and centers.

Application Information Centers, libraries, museums, or other appropriate institutions that wish to apply to this program should write to the endowment to request more detailed information and application instructions. Individuals interested in pursuing research at any of the centers receiving endowment support should apply directly to the centers themselves. A list of currently funded centers is available from the endowment on request.

Deadline(s) Applications should be received by December 1.

Subject Term(s) Humanities; Museums; Library Support

213. National Endowment for the Humanities

Division of Research Programs, Room 318
1100 Pennsylvania Avenue, NW
Washington, DC 20506
(202) 786-0204

Regrants: Conferences

CFDA Program Number 45.134

Program Description Grants in this category support conferences that enable both American and foreign scholars to advance the current state of research on topics of major importance in the humanities. These conferences should be designed to accomplish objectives that cannot be achieved by other means. Normally, presenters at the conference number from ten to twenty and include both junior and senior scholars. Other conference participants number from thirty to two hundred and should draw junior and senior faculty from a wide range of institutions and fields of specialty.

Sample Grants To support an international symposium on new iconographic and monumental evidence for the prehistoric Huari government in the central Andes, $9,945 to Harvard University (1986). To conduct an international conference on the role of books in the Americas, especially in the development of colonial Latin American society and culture, $10,000 to the John Carter Brown Library, Providence, Rhode Island (1986).

Eligibility/Limitations Awards are made to colleges and universities and to organizations such as learned societies, federations and committees of scholarly associations, and major independent research libraries and centers.

Fiscal Information In addition to the costs of organizing and publicizing the conference itself, endowment funds awarded to the sponsoring institution or organization support travel and other expenses for the presenters as well as stipends to participants for partial travel and per diem expenses. Support is also available for the publication of conference results, but such publication costs are frequently contributed by the applicant as cost sharing. Normally, the endowment's contribution to the total costs of a conference will range from $6,000 to $40,000, depending upon the number of participants. All applicants are encouraged to seek full or partial support through federal matching funds.

Application Information Centers, libraries, museums, or other appropriate institutions that wish to apply to this program should write to the endowment to request more detailed information and application instructions.

Deadline(s) Applications should be received by February 15 and July 1.

Subject Term(s) Humanities; Seminars and Conferences; Museums; Library Support

214. National Endowment for the Humanities

Division of Research Programs, Room 318
1100 Pennsylvania Avenue, NW
Washington, DC 20506
(202) 786-0204

Regrants: International Research

CFDA Program Number 45.148

Program Description Through this category, the endowment awards funds to national organizations and learned societies to enable American scholars to pursue research abroad, to attend or participate in international conferences, and to engage in collaborative work with foreign colleagues. The regranting organizations also sponsor international scholarly exchange and collaborative international research endeavors.

Eligibility/Limitations National organizations and learned societies are eligible to apply.

Application Information Organizations and societies that wish to apply to this program should write to the endowment to request more detailed information and application instructions. Individuals interested in applying for support should write directly to the funded organization or society; a list of currently funded organizations and societies is available from the endowment upon request.

Deadline(s) Applications should be received by February 15.

Subject Term(s) Seminars and Conferences; Exchanges; Humanities

215. National Endowment for the Humanities

Division of Research Programs, Room 318
1100 Pennsylvania Avenue, NW
Washington, DC 20506
(202) 786-0200

Special Initiatives: The Columbian Quincentenary

Program Description As part of the international observance of the 500th anniversary of Christopher Columbus's voyage of discovery to the New World, NEH invites proposals for original scholarship on related topics and for the dissemination of both new and existing scholarship. Topics may include the expansion of European civilization through the efforts of the Spanish and Portuguese crowns; the establishment of new societies and new forms of cultural expression through encounter among native American, European, and African peoples; and the ideas—political, religious, philosophical, scientific, technological, and aesthetic—that shaped the processes of exploration, settlement, and cultural conflict and transformation set into motion by Columbus's momentous voyage. Proposals related to this initiative are welcome in any of the grant categories of the Division of Research Programs.

Sample Grants Support for the production of a five-volume documentary history of the discovery and settlement of Latin America to the early seventeenth century; the work, *New Iberian World* (Times Books, 1984), consists mostly of translations of original documents, two-thirds of which have never before been published in English (1984). Support to the University of Florida to establish a research center at its Institute for Early Contact Period Studies, where historians, archeologists, and anthropologists conduct coordinated research on the settlements established by Columbus and other early explorers in the Florida and Caribbean region—an endowment grant supports four main projects at the center: a search for Columbus's first settlement in Haiti; an excavation and analysis of Puerto Real, Haiti, fourth oldest site in the New World; editing of documents related to Columbus's third voyage; and an international conference on early explorations (1984).

Application Information Applicants who are not certain where to direct an inquiry about this special initiative should call or write the director of the Division of Research Programs.

Subject Term(s) Columbian Quincentenary; Humanities

216. National Endowment for the Humanities

Division of Research Programs, Room 318
1100 Pennsylvania Avenue, NW
Washington, DC 20506
(202) 786-0207

Texts: Editions

CFDA Program Number 45.146

Program Description Grants in this category support various stages of the preparation of authoritative and annotated editions of sources of significant value to humanities scholars and general readers. Support is provided for projects that make available important texts and documents that have been either previously unavailable or accessible only in seriously flawed editions. All printed editions supported by the endowment are accompanied by critical introductions and annotations that provide essential information about the form, transmission, and historical and intellectual context of the texts and documents involved. Since complete editions in printed volumes are expensive to produce, endowment reviewers frequently recommend selected editions, microform editions, and editions that combine printed volumes and microform. Consequently, applicants must demonstrate that the form proposed for the edition represents the most effective means of disseminating the material involved. Applicants for microform editions must also demonstrate that the project will make available materials dispersed among a number of widely scattered repositories.

Eligibility/Limitations Institutions in the United States engaged in the humanities and individual United States citizens or foreign nationals who have been living in the United States or its territories for at least three years at the time of application are eligible to apply. Support may also be given to any individual or organization whose work promises significantly to advance knowledge and understanding of the humanities in the United States. Foreign nationals who do not meet the residence requirement may apply if they are formally affiliated with a United States educational institution and in these cases must apply through the institution. In exceptional circumstances, the endowment may also provide support to a foreign institution or foreign national not meeting the eligibility criteria mentioned above when a project promises to advance knowledge and understanding of the humanities in the United States to an unusually large extent.

Fiscal Information Awards in this category are made for up to three years and range from $25,000 to $100,000 per year, with the amount of the award dependent on the scope and importance of the project. Applicants whose projects are complex in organization or are likely to involve large budget requests should consult with a member of the program staff before a final application is submitted. Normally, the endowment's contribution to a project will not exceed 80% of the project's total costs. All applicants are encouraged to seek full or partial support through federal matching funds.

Application Information Program guidelines are available upon request. After reading these guidelines, the prospective applicant should draft a brief description (no more than five pages) of the proposed project. This description should be sent to the program officer. So that staff members have sufficient time to give the project thorough attention, this correspondence should begin at least two or three months prior to the formal application deadline. Applicants should not attempt to prepare a full proposal using only general guidelines. Upon receipt of the brief description, endowment staff will assess the eligibility and competitiveness of the project and will contact the applicant about the proposal. If the project is eligible, the endowment staff member will send application forms and instructions. If sufficient time before the deadline remains, the applicant may submit a draft of the proposal for further informal comment. After this additional consultation with the staff, the applicant should prepare a full application using the appropriate forms.

Deadline(s) Deadline for receipt of application is June 1.

Subject Term(s) Individuals, Eligibility of; Foreign Nationals, Eligibility of; Humanities; Publication Support

217. National Endowment for the Humanities

Division of Research Programs, Room 318
1100 Pennsylvania Avenue, NW
Washington, DC 20506
(202) 786-0207

Texts: Publication Subvention

CFDA Program Number 45.132

Program Description Grants in this category are intended to assist the publication and dissemination of distinguished scholarly works in all fields of the humanities. In all cases, the scholarly work for which an application is being made must have been formally accepted for publication by the appropriate editor or editorial board. All applications for subvention will be judged on the basis of the quality and scholarly importance of the work to be published as well as on the appropriateness of the budget and publishing plan. In this category, the endowment will also consider applications for projects designed to diminish the need for individual publication subventions by introducing cost-effective mechanisms, such as computerized typesetting machines, into the operation of a press.

Sample Grants To support the publication of a history of the labor force in four Latin American countries from the mid-19th century to the present, $4,865 to Stanford University (1986). To support the publication of a book that examines the roots of agrarian rebellion in Mexico to determine why a peasant-led revolution was successful in 1910 but unsuccessful a century earlier, $7,000 to Princeton University Press (1987). To support the publication of a literary analysis of an Andean chronicle written by a 17th-century Peruvian, Guaman Poma, for the Spanish King Philip III, $2,677 to the University of Texas, Austin (1986). To support the publication of the first translation into English of an early 17th-century account of life in Brazil, $2,000 to the University of New Mexico (1987).

Eligibility/Limitations Applicants must be established publishers or scholarly publishing entities; applications from individual scholars are not accepted.

Fiscal Information Awards in this category average $6,000 per volume; no award for a single volume will exceed $10,000 in outright funds. All applicants are encouraged to seek support through federal matching funds. In a federal fiscal year a single publisher may not receive more than $50,000 in outright and federal matching funds or support for more than five works, whichever is less.

Application Information Program guidelines are available upon request. After reading these guidelines, the prospective applicant should draft a brief description (no more than five pages) of the proposed project. This description should be sent to the program officer. So that staff members have sufficient time to give the project thorough attention, this correspondence should begin at least two or three months prior to the formal application deadline. Applicants should not attempt to prepare a full proposal using only general guidelines. Upon receipt of the brief description, endowment staff will assess the eligibility and competitiveness of the project and will contact the applicant about the proposal. If the project is eligible, the endowment staff member will send application forms and instructions. If sufficient time before the deadline remains, the applicant may submit a draft of the proposal for further informal comment. After this additional consultation with the staff, the applicant should prepare a full application using the appropriate forms.

Deadline(s) Deadlines for receipt of applications are April 1 and September 1.

Subject Term(s) Humanities; Publication Support

218. National Endowment for the Humanities

Division of Research Programs, Room 318
1100 Pennsylvania Avenue, NW
Washington, DC 20506
(202) 786-0207

Texts: Translations

CFDA Program Number 45.147

Program Description In this category the endowment supports the translation into English of works that will provide insight into the history, literature, philosophy, and artistic achievements of other cultures and that will make available the thought and learning of their civilizations. Applicants may propose to translate from any language, and the texts to be translated may be either primary sources or secondary works. Every applicant must make a convincing case for the importance of the translation to those scholars and general readers who do not command the language of the original text. All translations supported by the endowment provide critical introductions and explanatory annotations that clearly establish the historical and intellectual contexts of the work involved. Where an authoritative text in the original language does not exist, applicants may apply for support to establish one. Applicants proposing to retranslate works that already exist in English must provide a strong argument for a new version or for an emendation of the existing version.

Sample Grants To support the edition and translation of the *History of New Spain* (16th century) by the Dominican friar Diego Duran, a chronicle which is one of the most comprehensive early accounts of Aztec history and religion, $17,300, to an individual scholar, Mexico, DF (1985-1987). To support the translation of a critical study by Octavio Paz of the Mexican poetess and nun, Sister Juana Inez de la Cruz (d.1691), $10,000 to University of Missouri, Columbia (1985-1986). To support the translation of a 15th-century Mayan drama of human sacrifice called *Man of Rabinal* or *Dance of the Trumpet*, $35,000 to Boston University (1985-1987). To support a six-volume scholarly translation of the journals of Diego de Vargas, govenor and colonizer of Spanish New Mexico, 1680-1710, $100,000 to the University of New Mexico (1986).

Eligibility/Limitations Institutions in the United States engaged in the humanities and individual United States citizens or foreign nationals who have been living in the United States or its territories for at least three years at the time of application are eligible to apply. Support may also be given to any individual or organization whose work promises significantly to advance knowledge and understanding of the humanities in the United States. Foreign nationals who do not meet the residence requirement may apply if they are formally affiliated with a United States educational institution and in these cases must apply through the institution. In exceptional circumstances, the endowment may also provide support to a foreign institution or foreign national not meeting the eligibility criteria mentioned above when a project promises to advance knowledge and understanding of the humanities in the United States to an unusually large extent.

Fiscal Information Grant awards in this category usually range from $3,500 to $75,000, depending upon the scope and magnitude of the project. Applicants are encouraged to seek support from appropriate foreign governments and from foundations and are also encouraged to apply for federal matching funds.

Application Information Program guidelines are available upon request. After reading these guidelines, the prospective applicant should draft a brief description (no more than five pages) of the proposed project. This description should be sent to the program officer. So that staff members have sufficient time to give the project thorough attention, this correspondence should begin at least two or three months prior to the formal application deadline. Applicants should not attempt to prepare a full proposal using only general guidelines. Upon receipt of the brief description, endowment staff will assess the eligibility and competitiveness of the project and will contact the applicant about the proposal. If the project is eligible, the endowment staff member will send application forms and instructions. If sufficient time before the deadline remains, the applicant may submit a draft of the proposal for further informal comment. After this additional consultation with the staff, the applicant should prepare a full application using the appropriate forms. All translation applications must be accompanied by a seven-page sample of the translation to be undertaken during the course of the grant.

Deadline(s) Deadline for receipt of application is June 1.

Subject Term(s) Individuals, Eligibility of; Foreign Nationals, Eligibility of; Translation Support; Humanities

219. National Endowment for the Humanities

Division of State Programs, Room 411
1100 Pennsylvania Avenue, NW
Washington, DC 20506
(202) 786-0254

Special Initiatives: The Columbian Quincentenary

Program Description Humanities councils in each state, the District of Columbia, Puerto Rico, and the U.S. Virgin Islands make grants for humanities projects to engage the citizens of these states in the texts, disciplines, and methods of the humanities. The state councils are uniquely positioned to bring to localities the benefits of the latest humanities scholarship on the 1492 voyages and their global consequences. Since the beginning of the program in 1971, state councils have sponsored and funded scholarly symposia, museum exhibitions, book discussion projects, local media productions, and an array of other programming vehicles to present the humanities to general audiences. The Columbian Quincentenary is an initiative well-suited for projects that invite public consideration of the events of 1492. In recent years, many of the councils have supported projects designed to strengthen elementary and secondary education. This grant category has included workshops, institutes, and seminars for teachers in connection with the Quincentenary. A summer institute on the place of Italian maritime exploration in the development of European commerce would be as likely in this category as, for example, a project intended to produce a traveling exhibition for school libraries.

Sample Grants The Fundacion Puertorriquena de las Humanidades has set aside $25,000 annually for the period 1985-1993 for programs about the Columbian Quincentenary.

Eligibility/Limitations Nonprofit agencies, cultural and educational institutions, civic organizations, or groups may apply to the council in their states, the District of Columbia, Puerto Rico, or the Virgin Islands.

Application Information Each state council establishes its own grant guidelines and application deadlines. Contact the endowment for addresses of all councils.

Subject Term(s) Humanities; Columbian Quincentenary; Education

220. National Endowment for the Humanities

Office of Challenge Grants, Room 429
1100 Pennsylvania Avenue, NW
Washington, DC 20506
(202) 786-0361

Challenge Grants

CFDA Program Number 45.130

Program Description The endowment developed the Challenge Grants Program to join federal and major nonfederal support for the humanities and to improve financial stability and program quality within those institutions and organizations in which teaching, learning, and research in the humanities occur. Endowment challenge grants offer support for a variety of purposes so that institutions or organizations performing meritorious work within the context of their missions and resources may improve the quality of their work and achieve greater financial stability and an appropriate growth of their resources. Challenge grant applicants must demonstrate that the funds will sustain or develop a high quality of work which will contribute significantly to the promotion of the humanities.

Eligibility/Limitations With the exception of public and private elementary and secondary schools, any nonprofit institution or organization working wholly or in part within the humanities may apply for a challenge grant. Such institutions and organizations include junior and community colleges, four-year colleges, universities, museums, historical societies, research libraries, public libraries, advanced study centers, media organizations, university presses, professional societies, and educational, cultural, or community groups.

Fiscal Information Endowment challenge grants in the last three years have ranged from $5,000 to $1 million. These amounts are the federal portion of the total challenge grant. Because each challenge grant recipient must raise three times the amount of the offer in nonfederal funds from new or increased contributions, the federal portion is 25% of the total proposed fund-raising campaign goal. The amount requested for a challenge grant should be reasonable and yet sufficient to accomplish the applicant's proposed aims. Any endowment challenge offer exceeding $1 million is rare (less than one percent of all grants offered). Although there have been a few such offers in the history of the program, there has been none in recent years. Anyone intending to request funding in excess of $1 million should discuss the proposal with the staff of the Office of Challenge Grants.

Application Information Application information and guidelines are available upon request. The office encourages potential applicants to discuss an institution's or organization's proposal plans with the staff before submitting the formal application and also to submit a draft application for staff review. Draft applications should be sent to the office at least six weeks prior to the formal application deadline.

Deadline(s) The deadline for receipt of applications is May 1. There are no extensions or exceptions.

Subject Term(s) Humanities

221. National Endowment for the Humanities

Office of Challenge Grants, Room 429
1100 Pennsylvania Avenue, NW
Washington, DC 20506
(202) 786-0361

Special Initiatives: The Columbian Quincentenary

Program Description Challenge grants stimulate long-range institutional planning and financial development. A challenge grant is intended to improve the financial stability of a college, university, museum, historical organization, research or public library, public media station, or university press so that it may reach or sustain excellence in its humanities programs, collections, and research. Challenge grants may be used to develop long-term support for institutional needs in areas related to the Columbian Quincentenary.

Sample Grants An endowment for faculty chairs in disciplines related to the 1992 celebration—history, archeology, anthropology, the history of science, linguistics (1984). Renovation of buildings used to house Columbian Quincentenary exhibitions, collections, or archives (1984). The development of acquisition funds for books or other collections related to the period of discovery, to studies of the Americas, or to ethnocultural fields (1984). Endowments to support faculty and curriculum development in humanities disciplines relevant to the 500th anniversary of Columbus's discovery (1984).

Eligibility/Limitations Nonprofit educational and cultural institutions and organizations working in the humanities are eligible to apply.

Fiscal Information Recipients must raise three times the offered federal funds in the form of new or increased contributions from nonfederal sources.

Application Information Additional information is available from the office.

Subject Term(s) Columbian Quincentenary; Humanities

222. National Endowment for the Humanities

Office of Preservation, Room 802
1100 Pennsylvania Avenue, NW
Washington, DC 20506
(202) 786-0570

Special Initiatives: The Columbian Quincentenary

Program Description Projects funded through the Office of Preservation address the problem of the physical deterioration of humanities resources—books, photographs, drawings, film, audio and video tapes, recordings, pamphlets, maps, charts, and manuscripts. The office welcomes applications concerned with the preservation of scholarly materials relating to the Quincentenary.

Sample Grants Support to the Art Institute of Chicago for the production of a microfiche-use copy of the final report of the 1893 Chicago World's Columbian Exposition, issued by Burnham and Root, the architectural firm in charge of planning and construction for the exposition (1984).

Eligibility/Limitations Grants support projects that address national preservation needs of research documentation in the humanities.

Application Information Contact the office for additional information.

Subject Term(s) Humanities; Columbian Quincentenary; Collections, Conservation

223. National Eye Institute

National Institutes of Health
Bethesda, MD 20892
(301) 496-4903

Eye Diseases Research

CFDA Program Number 13.867-13.871

Program Description The mission of the National Eye Institute (NEI) is to reduce the prevalence of blindness, visual impairment, and eye diseases in the United States and worldwide through basic and applied research and training. The World Health Organization (WHO) estimates that about twenty-eight million of the world's people are blind, the majority of them living in the developing nations of Asia, Latin America, and Africa. At the current level of activity, the number of blind people is projected to double by the year 2000. This need not occur, however. Well-planned sight conservation programs that use current medical knowledge and resources could be used to avoid 50% to 80% of all blindness. What is needed is to increase public and governmental awareness worldwide of the problem of blindness, to mobilize available resources, to promote development of effective programs in countries that now lack them, and to increase the effectiveness of the programs already in existence. The specific objective of NEI international activities is to facilitate the development and application of appropriate effective programs by: evaluating available health technologies, promoting the most cost-effective intervention and prevention programs, and encouraging their availability to affected populations, especially in developing countries; conducting collaborative applied research studies aimed at developing preventive methods for dealing with specific eye diseases; conducting controlled clinical evaluations of research findings that appear to be effective; and exchanging information on recent scientific advances and their appropriate application to blindness and visual problems.

Eligibility/Limitations Universities, colleges, hospitals, laboratories, federal institutions, and other public or private nonprofit and for-profit domestic institutions are eligible to apply. Foreign institutions may apply for research grants. Predoctoral and postdoctoral research training may be supported in specific program areas.

Fiscal Information There is no precise limitation on the dollar value of research grants that may be awarded to any one investigator or institution. Research grants provide funds for salaries, equipment, supplies, travel, and other expenses, and afford the collateral benefits of enriching the training and experience of research workers. In 1986 grants ranged from $23,000 to $90,000.

Application Information The standard application form as furnished by PHS and required by OMB Circular No. A-102 for state and local governments must be used. Also, consultation is available from institute staff.

Deadline(s) The deadlines are February 1, June 1, and October 1 for all new research grant applications. Applications for competing renewal and supplements are due March 1, July 1, and November 1.

Subject Term(s) Eye Diseases Research; Biomedical Research

224. National Geographic Society

Committee for Research and Exploration
Seventeenth and M Streets, NW
Washington, DC 20036
(202) 857-7439

Research Grants

Program Description Grants-in-Aid support basic research in the sciences pertinent to geography. These sciences include but are not limited to projects in anthropology, archeology, astronomy, biology, botany, ecology, physical and human geography, geology, oceanography, paleontology, and zoology.

Sample Grants To support the Rio Azul archeological project, $45,283 to the Center for Archeological Research, University of Texas, San Antonio, Texas (1985). To support research on labor intensification and productivity in the Titicaca Basin (Peru), $21,231 to Shepherd College, Shepherdstown, West Virginia (1985). Continuation support for a study of Jurassic and Cretaceous terrestrial vertebrates (Patagonia), $10,800 to Museo Argentino de Ciencias Naturales, Buenos Aires, Argentina (1985). To support an ecological assessment of a rain forest herpetofauna (Peru), $6,124 to the University of Kansas, Lawrence, Kansas (1985).

Eligibility/Limitations Investigators who hold earned doctor's degrees and are associated with institutions of higher learning or other scientific and educational nonprofit organizations, such as museums, are eligible to apply. Occasionally, grants are awarded to exceptionally well-qualified graduate students or scientific workers who do not have research degrees or who are not associated with a university but who do have full qualifications for research on a scientific project of significance. Citizens of any country are eligible.

Fiscal Information Grants vary in amount, depending upon the need and nature of the projects. Recent awards ranged from $1,200 to $49,000. The society's annual budget for its research program is currently $3.9 million. Grants will be considered for up to three years when a project requires more than one year. Society policy does not permit the payment of overhead to any individual or institution. Except under most unusual circumstances, payment of salary to the principal investigator is not approved; it is also unusual to make a grant that involves the payment of salaries of research associates, especially those having faculty status or other similar institutional connections or who are candidates for the Ph.D. degree. The society does not provide fellowships or pay tuition at any level. The Committee for Research and Exploration is reluctant to provide funds for capital equipment. In cases where funds are made available for such purposes, it is always with the stipulation that the equipment or its salvage value shall be returned to the society when the project is complete. If still or motion picture film or equipment is necessary to the research, it should be included in the budget. The society does not provide funds for publication or for travel to scientific meetings.

Application Information Official application forms are available upon request. Applications will not be considered unless submitted on this standard form. It is suggested that the investigator in writing for application forms state the nature of the program briefly. This may help a candidate avoid loss of time required for completing an application for a grant that is outside the stated interests of the society.

Deadline(s) Applications may be submitted at any time. The society's Committee for Research and Exploration usually meets every month.

Additional Information Grants are normally made only for field research. Museum or archival research may occasionally qualify as field research. Laboratory work is supported only to the extent that it may be a necessary follow-up to field research.

Subject Term(s) Foreign Nationals, Eligibility of; Individuals, Eligibility of; Graduate Support; Geography; Anthropology; Archeology; Biology; Ecology; Geology; Paleontology; Zoology; Field Research, Support of; Botany; Oceanography

225. National Heart, Lung, and Blood Institute

National Institutes of Health
7550 Wisconsin Avenue
Bethesda, MD 20892
(301) 496-4869

Blood Diseases and Resources Programs

CFDA Program Number 13.839

Program Description The National Heart, Lung, and Blood Institute (NHLBI) plans, conducts, and supports research, clinical trials, and demonstrations relating to the causes, prevention, diagnosis, and treatment of heart, blood vessel, lung, and blood diseases and blood resources. The objectives of the Blood Diseases and Resources Programs are to further the development of blood resources and coordinate national and regional activities of blood centers and to promote research on blood diseases and develop new scientists for such research.

Eligibility/Limitations Any nonprofit organization engaged in biomedical research and institutions or companies organized for profit may apply for grants.

Fiscal Information Grants awarded in 1986 ranged from $10,000 to $2,312,442 with an average award of $187,585. Grants may support salaries, equipment, supplies, travel, and patient hospitalization as required to perform the research effort. Restrictions or limitations are imposed against the use of funds for entertainment, foreign travel, general-purpose equipment, alterations and renovations, and other items not regularly required for the performance of research.

Application Information Applications are submitted on designated forms to the Division of Research Grants, NIH, Bethesda, MD, 20892. For some special grant programs, applicants may be advised to submit directly to the Review Branch, Division of Extramural Affairs, National Heart, Lung, and Blood Institute, Bethesda, MD 20892. This program is subject to the provisions of OMB Circular No. A-110.

Deadline(s) All new research grant applications, unless specified differently in a program announcement or request for applications, all career development awards and conference grant applications, all new and competing and continuation program project and center applications must be received by February 1, June 1, or October 1; all competing continuation and supplemental research grant applications must be received by March 1, July 1, or November 1.

Subject Term(s) Blood Diseases Research; Biomedical Research

226. National Heart, Lung, and Blood Institute

National Institutes of Health
7550 Wisconsin Avenue
Bethesda, MD 20892
(301) 496-5656

Heart and Vascular Diseases Programs

CFDA Program Number 13.837

Program Description The National Heart, Lung, and Blood Institute (NHLBI) plans, conducts, and supports research, clinical trials, and demonstrations relating to the causes, prevention, diagnosis, and treatment of heart, blood vessel, lung, and blood diseases and blood resources. Heart and Vascular Diseases Programs support basic animal and clinical research into the etiology, pathogenesis and treatment of arteriosclerosis, hypertension, and lipid metabolic disorders. Related hospital-based clinical trials are also supported. Most of the work is funded through the grant mechanism which includes regular grants, program project grants and specialized centers of research; in addition, collaborative research or resources funded through the contract mechanism may be appropriate.

Eligibility/Limitations Any nonprofit organization engaged in biomedical research and institutions or companies organized for profit may apply for grants.

Fiscal Information Grants awarded in 1986 ranged from $3,674 to $4,948,862 with an average award of $188,187. Grants may support salaries, equipment, supplies, travel, and patient hospitalization as required to perform the research effort. Restrictions or limitations are imposed against the use of funds for entertainment, foreign travel, general-purpose equipment, alterations and renovations, and other items not regularly required for the performance of research.

Application Information Applications are submitted on designated forms to the Division of Research Grants, NIH, Bethesda, MD, 20892. For some special grant programs, applicants may be advised to submit directly to the Review Branch, Division of Extramural Affairs, National Heart, Lung, and Blood Institute, Bethesda, MD 20892. This program is subject to the provisions of OMB Circular No. A-110.

Deadline(s) All new research grant applications, unless specified differently in a program announcement or request for applications, all career development awards and conference grant applications, all new and competing and continuation program project and center applications must be received by February 1, June 1, or October 1; all competing continuation and supplemental research grant applications must be received by March 1, July 1, or November 1.

Subject Term(s) Cardiovascular Research; Vascular Diseases Research; Biomedical Research

227. National Heart, Lung, and Blood Institute

National Institutes of Health
5333 Westbard Avenue
Bethesda, MD 20892
(301) 496-7208

Lung Diseases Programs

CFDA Program Number 13.838

Program Description The National Heart, Lung, and Blood Institute (NHLBI) plans, conducts, and supports research, clinical trials, and demonstrations relating to the causes, prevention, diagnosis, and treatment of heart, blood vessel, lung, and blood diseases and blood resources. The objectives of the Lung Diseases Programs are to use available knowledge and technology to solve specific disease problems of the lungs; to promote further studies on the structure and function of the lung; and to achieve improvement in prevention and treatment of lung diseases.

Eligibility/Limitations Any nonprofit organization engaged in biomedical research and institutions or companies organized for profit may apply for grants.

Fiscal Information Grants awarded in 1986 ranged from $6,606 to $2,063,329 with an average average award of $165,700. Grants may support salaries, equipment, supplies, travel, and patient hospitalization as required to perform the research effort. Restrictions or limitations are imposed against the use of funds for entertainment, foreign travel, general-purpose equipment, alterations and renovations, and other items not regularly required for the performance of research.

Application Information Applications are submitted on designated forms to the Division of Research Grants, NIH, Bethesda, MD, 20892. For some special grant programs, applicants may be advised to submit directly to the Review Branch, Division of Extramural Affairs, National Heart, Lung, and Blood Institute, Bethesda, MD 20892. This program is subject to the provisions of OMB Circular No. A-110.

Deadline(s) All new research grant applications, unless specified differently in a program announcement or request for applications, all career development awards and conference grant applications, all new and competing and continuation program project and center applications must be received by February 1, June 1, or October 1; all competing continuation and supplemental research grant applications must be received by March 1, July 1, or November 1.

Subject Term(s) Lung Disease Research; Biomedical Research

228. National Humanities Center

7 Alexander Drive
Research Triangle Park, NC 27709
(919) 549-0661

Fellowships

Program Description The National Humanities Center supports advanced study in history, philosophy, literature, and other fields of the humanities. The center admits thirty-five to forty fellows annually who pursue research and writing in residence at the center. In addition to scholars from fields normally associated with the humanities, representatives of the natural and social sciences, the arts, the professions, and public life are welcome.

Sample Grants Recent fellows (1985, 1986) have studied: the U.S. and Latin America, 1815-1836; historical discourse in Haitian culture, 1804; Spanish-American Creole society in Cuba, 1750-1840.

Eligibility/Limitations Senior scholars and young scholars several years beyond the doctorate are eligible to apply. Fellows are expected to remain in residence during the period of fellowship.

Fiscal Information The amount of fellowship stipend is based on a scholar's usual academic salary. Many fellows have partial funding in the form of sabbatical salaries or grants from other sources and receive from the center the difference between that funding and their usual salaries. All fellows are given travel expenses to and from the center for themselves and their families. Most fellowships at the center are awarded for the full academic year. The center does not cover fringe benefits.

Application Information For information and application material write to the assistant director.

Deadline(s) Applications and letters of recommendation must be postmarked no later that October 15.

Subject Term(s) Humanities; History; Philosophy; Literature; Foreign Nationals, Eligibility of; Individuals, Eligibility of; Fellowships; Social Sciences

229. National Institute of Allergy and Infectious Diseases

National Institutes of Health
Extramural Activities Program, Westwood Building, Room 703
Bethesda, MD 20892
(301) 496-7291

Immunology, Allergic and Immunologic Diseases Program

CFDA Program Number 13.855

Program Description The National Institute of Allergy and Infectious Diseases (NIAID) conducts and supports research contributing to a better understanding of the causes of allergic, immunologic, and infectious diseases and to the development of better means of preventing, diagnosing, and treating these illnesses. The Immunology, Allergic and Immunologic Diseases Program concerns the immune system as it functions in the maintenance of health and as it malfunctions in the production of disease. Basic research support is aimed at providing the information necessary for understanding immune system structure and function and at the histo-compatibility antigens and their role in graft rejection, autoimmunity, immune responsiveness, and a variety of diseases. Clinical research is supported in: (1) the area of asthma and allergic diseases focusing on determining the cause and improving the diagnosis, prevention and treatment of a variety of common allergic diseases and (2) studies in the area of immunologic diseases including disorders of the human immune system.

Sample Grants Support for research on acquired immunodeficiency disease in Haitian children, University of Miami School of Medicine (1985). Support for a study of HTLV retrovirus infections in Haitians with AIDS, University of Miami School of Medicine (1985).

Eligibility/Limitations Universities, colleges, hospitals, laboratories, and other public or private nonprofit and for-profit domestic institutions, including state and local governments, and individuals are eligible to make application for grant support of research by a named principal investigator or a research career development candidate.

Fiscal Information No precise limitation exists on the dollar value of research grants that may be awarded to any one investigator or institution. Research grants provide funds for salaries, equipment, supplies, and travel. They also afford the collateral benefits of enriching the training and experience of research workers. Grant awards in 1986 ranged from $1,000 to $1,414,505 with an average award of $168,529.

Application Information The standard application forms, as furnished by DHHS and required by OMB Circular No. A-102, must be used for the research grant programs by those applicants which are state or local units of government. Application forms and information are available from the program.

Deadline(s) All new research grant applications, unless specified differently in a program announcement or request for applications, all career development awards and conference grant applications, all new and competing and continuation program project and center applications must be received by February 1, June 1, or October 1; all competing continuation and supplemental research grant applications must be received by March 1, July 1, or November 1.

Subject Term(s) Immunology

230. National Institute of Allergy and Infectious Diseases

National Institutes of Health
Westwood Building, Room 703
Bethesda, MD 20892
(301) 496-7291

Microbiology and Infectious Diseases Program

CFDA Program Number 13.856

Program Description The National Institute of Allergy and Infectious Diseases (NIAID) conducts and supports research contributing to a better understanding of the causes of allergic, immunologic, and infectious diseases and to the development of better means of preventing, diagnosing, and treating these illnesses. The Microbiology and Infectious Diseases Program supports research with the broad aim of improving health by controlling diseases caused by infectious or parasitic agents. Projects range from studies of microbial physiology and antigenic structure to collaborative trials of experimental drugs and vaccines. The program also supports studies on the mechanisms of resistance to antibiotics as well as research dealing with epidemiologic observations in hospitalized patients or community populations. Research focuses on all aspects of microbiology, with particular emphasis on human pathogens, including basic research in molecular microbiology, bacteriology and mycology, virology, and parasitology.

Sample Grants Support for research in Brazil (Bahia University) on cutaneous and visceral leishmaniasis and Chagas' disease with a focus on epidemiology, genetics, and immunopathology, Cornell University (1985). Support for research in Colombia (COLCIENCIAS) and Haiti (Institute Francais) on Chagas' disease, filariasis, onchocerciasis (Colombia), and filariasis (Haiti), Tulane University (1985). Support for research in Peru (Universidad Peruana) on bacterial diarrheal disease, Johns Hopkins University (1985). Support for research in Venezuela (National Institute of Dermatology) on leprosy with a focus on immunology, Albert Einstein College, Yeshiva University (1985).

Eligibility/Limitations Universities, colleges, hospitals, laboratories, and other public or private nonprofit and for-profit domestic institutions, including state and local governments, and individuals are eligible to make application for grant support of research by a named principal investigator or a research career development candidate.

Fiscal Information No precise limitation exists on the dollar value of research grants that may be awarded to any one investigator or institution. Research grants provide funds for salaries, equipment, supplies, and travel. They also afford the collateral benefits of enriching the training and experience of research workers. Grant awards in 1986 ranged from $1,000 to $514,550 with an average award of $128,206.

Application Information The standard application forms, as furnished by DHHS and required by OMB Circular No. A-102, must be used for the research grant programs by those applicants which are state or local units of government. Application forms and information are available from the program.

Deadline(s) All new research grant applications, unless specified differently in a program announcement or request for applications, all career development awards and conference grant applications, all new and competing and continuation program project and center applications must be received by February 1, June 1, or October 1; all competing continuation and supplemental research grant applications must be received by March 1, July 1, or November 1.

Subject Term(s) Microbiology; Infectious Diseases Research

231. National Institute of Arthritis, Musculoskeletal and Skin Diseases

National Institutes of Health
Building 31, 9000 Rockville Pike
Bethesda, MD 20892
(301) 496-4353

Arthritis, Musculoskeletal and Skin Diseases Research

CFDA Program Number 13.846

Program Description The primary objective of the National Institute of Arthritis, Musculoskeletal and Skin Diseases is development of measures for prevention, treatment, and therapy of these diseases. To reach this objective, the institute supports clinical studies on mechanisms for the development of those diseases and studies on basic biological processes, as well as clinical studies of persons suffering from these disorders. The institute supports basic laboratory research and clinical investigations extramurally and provides postdoctoral biomedical research training for individuals interested in careers in health sciences and fields related to these programs.

Eligibility/Limitations Individuals and public and private institutions, both nonprofit and for-profit, who propose to establish, expand, and improve research activities in health sciences and related fields are eligible to apply for research grants.

Fiscal Information Research grant awards in 1986 ranged from $28,900 to $478,000 with an average award of $134,100. Research grants provide funds for salaries, equipment, supplies, travel, and other expenses associated with scientific investigation relevant to program objectives.

Application Information The standard application forms as furnished by DHHS and required by OMB Circular No. A-102 must be used for this program by those applicants which are state or local units of government. For research grants, PHS Form 398 (with current instructions) is available from the Division of Research Grants, NIH, Bethesda, MD 20892, and completed forms should be submitted to the same address.

Deadline(s) All new research grant applications, unless specified differently in a program announcement or request for applications, all career development awards and conference grant applications, all new and competing and continuation program project and center applications must be received by February 1, June 1, or October 1; all competing continuation and supplemental research grant applications must be received by March 1, July 1, or November 1.

Subject Term(s) Biomedical Sciences; Health Sciences; Arthritis; Musculoskeletal Diseases Research; Skin Diseases Research; Individuals, Eligibility of

232. National Institute of Child Health and Human Development

National Institutes of Health, Center for Research for Mothers and Children
9000 Rockville Pike
Bethesda, MD 20892
(301) 496-5001

Research for Mothers and Children

CFDA Program Number 13.865

Program Description Program objectives are to stimulate, coordinate, and support fundamental and clinical, biomedical and behavioral research and research training associated with normal development from conception to maturity and those factors or special health problems which may delay or interfere with normal development. The Center for Research for Mothers and Children (CRMC) supports research for mothers, children, and families, and is designed to: (1) advance knowledge about fetal development, pregnancy, and birth; (2) identify the prerequisites of optimal growth and development through infancy, childhood, and adolescence; and (3) contribute to the prevention and treatment of mental retardation, developmental disabilities, and other childhood and adolescent problems.

Sample Grants Support for a comparative study of household structure in Latin America, University of Wisconsin, Madison (1985). Support for a study of the formation process of Haitian ethnic organizations, Columbia University (1985). Support for a study of marital instability among Hispanics, University of Texas, Austin (1985).

Eligibility/Limitations Eligible applicants include universities, colleges, medical, dental, and nursing schools, schools of public health, laboratories, hospitals, state and local health departments, other for-profit public institutions, and individuals.

Fiscal Information Research project grants in 1986 ranged from $1,178 to $935,408 with an average award of $139,435. Awards are usually made annually with no project period to exceed five years in length.

Application Information The standard application forms as furnished by DHHS and OMB Circular No. A-102 must be used for this program.

Deadline(s) All new research grant applications, unless specified differently in a program announcement or request for applications, all career development awards and conference grant applications, all new and competing and continuation program project and center applications must be received by February 1, June 1, or October 1; all competing continuation and supplemental research grant applications must be received by March 1, July 1, or November 1.

Subject Term(s) Children; Child Development; Family; Genetics; Nutrition; Individuals, Eligibility of

233. National Institute of Child Health and Human Development

National Institutes of Health, Office of Grants and Contracts
Bethesda, MD 20205
(301) 496-5001

Population Research: Project Grants

CFDA Program Number 13.864

Program Description Program objectives are: to seek solutions to the fundamental problems of the reproductive processes; to strive to develop and evaluate safer and more effective contraceptives; and to understand how population structure and change affect the health and well-being of individuals and society.

Eligibility/Limitations Eligible applicants include universities, colleges, medical, dental, and nursing schools, schools of public health, laboratories, hospitals, state and local health departments, other for-profit public institutions, and individuals.

Fiscal Information Research project grants in 1986 ranged from $1,200 to $1,295,894 with an average award of $116,297. Awards are usually made annually with no project period to exceed five years in length.

Application Information The standard application forms as furnished by DHHS and OMB Circular No. A-102 must be used for this program. Contact the program for additional information and application instructions.

Deadline(s) Applications deadlines for new research grants are February 1, June 1, and October 1. Continuation and supplemental research grant applications must be received by March 1, July 1, or November 1.

Subject Term(s) Individuals, Eligibility of; Population; Population Studies; Reproduction; Contraception

234. National Institute of Dental Research

National Institutes of Health
Westwood Building, 5333 Westbard Avenue
Bethesda, MD 20892
(301) 496-7884

Diseases of the Teeth and Supporting Tissues

CFDA Program Number 13.121

Program Description The objectives of this program are to obtain improved information on the etiology and prevention of dental caries; develop improved restorative materials and devices including dental implants, for the repair of damaged oral structures; develop new knowledge on the cause, pathology, diagnosis, treatment, and prevention of periodontal and oral soft tissue diseases of the tooth pulp; develop new knowledge of relationships between nutritional factors and oral health; and improve the understanding of the role of salivary secretions in the prevention of oral disease.

Eligibility/Limitations Research grants are awarded to universities, colleges, medical and dental schools, hospitals, and other nonprofit and for-profit institutions. National Research Service Awards (NRSAs) are made directly to individuals for research training in specified areas. In addition, grants may be made to institutions to enable them to accept individuals for research training in specified areas.

Fiscal Information In 1986 grants ranged from $15,000 to $672,000.

Application Information Application forms and additional information are available from the Division of Research Grants, National Institutes of Health.

Deadline(s) Deadlines for application of new research grants are February 1, June 1, and October 1; for renewal research grants and supplementals, March 1, July 1, and November 1. NRSA applications must be received by January 10, May 10, and September 10.

Subject Term(s) Dental Research; Individuals, Eligibility of

235. National Institute of Dental Research

National Institutes of Health
Westwood Building, 5333 Westbard Avenue
Bethesda, MD 20892
(301) 496-7807

Disorders of Craniofacial Structure and Function, and Behavioral Aspects of Dentistry

CFDA Program Number 13.122

Program Description The objectives of this program are to conduct research on the cause, prevention, and treatment of cleft lip/palate, other craniofacial birth defects, malocclusion of the teeth and jaws, and disfigurements acquired through accidents and surgery to reduce their impact; to increase the understanding of dental and orofacial pain to develop more effective methods of prevention, diagnosis, and treatment; and to determine how behavioral and social factors influence disease risk, prevention, diagnosis, and treatment.

Eligibility/Limitations Any nonprofit or for-profit organization, company or institution engaged in biomedical research is eligible to apply for support.

Fiscal Information 1986 grants ranged from $15,500 to $390,000 with an average award of $114,000, for projects not to exceed five years.

Application Information Application forms and additional information are available from the Division of Research Grants, National Institutes of Health.

Deadline(s) Deadlines for application of new research grants are February 1, June 1, and October 1; for renewal research grants and supplementals, March 1, July 1, and November 1. NRSA applications must be received by January 10, May 10, and September 10.

Subject Term(s) Dental Research

236. National Institute of Diabetes and Digestive and Kidney Diseases

National Institutes of Health
Westwood Building, 5333 Westbard Avenue
Bethesda, MD 20892
(301) 496-7348

Diabetes, Endocrinology, and Metabolic Diseases

CFDA Program Number 13.847

Program Description The institute conducts and supports research focused on a number of diseases that are characterized by chronicity and long-term disabling effects rather than mortality. Areas of interest include diabetes and other inherited errors of metabolism, including cystic fibrosis. The diabetes research program provides grant support for a wide range of fundamental and clinical studies relating to the etiology, pathogenesis, prevention, diagnosis, treatment, and cure of diabetes mellitus and its complications. The endocrinology program supports basic and clinical studies of the normal and abnormal function of the pituitary, thyroid, parathyroid, adrenal, pineal, and thymus glands. The program encourages research in the mode of action of hormones, their biosynthesis, secretion, and metabolism, as well as their binding to protein carriers, subsequent release, and the kinetics of binding. The metabolic diseases program provides support for investigator-initiated research into enzymatic mechanisms and their regulation, biological transport, and membrane structure.

Eligibility/Limitations Individuals and public and private institutions, both nonprofit and for-profit, who propose to establish, expand, and improve research activities in health sciences and related fields are eligible to apply for research grants.

Fiscal Information Research grants awarded in 1986 ranged from $16,600 to $2,044,000 with an average award of $150,700.

Application Information The standard application forms as furnished by DHHS and required by OMB Circular No. A-102 must be used for this program by those applicants which are state or local units of government. For research grants, PHS Form 398 (with current instructions) is available from the Division of Research Grants, NIH, Bethesda, MD 20892, and completed forms should be submitted to the same address.

Deadline(s) All new research grant applications, unless specified differently in a program announcement or request for applications, all career development awards and conference grant applications, all new and competing and continuation program project and center applications must be received by February 1, June 1, or October 1; all competing continuation and supplemental research grant applications must be received by March 1, July 1, or November 1.

Subject Term(s) Medical Sciences; Diabetes; Endocrinology; Metabolism Research; Individuals, Eligibility of

237. National Institute of Diabetes and Digestive and Kidney Diseases

National Institutes of Health
Westwood Building, 5333 Westbard Avenue
Bethesda, MD 20892
(301) 496-1333

Digestive Diseases and Nutrition Research

CFDA Program Number 13.848

Program Description The institute conducts and supports research focused on a number of diseases that are characterized by chronicity and long-term disabling effects rather than mortality. Research is supported in the study of: esophageal, gastric, and colonic diseases; intestinal and pancreatic diseases; liver and biliary tract diseases; anorectal diseases and disorders; and basic, clinical, and behavioral research in nutrition directed to the improvement of human health.

Eligibility/Limitations Individuals and public and private institutions, both nonprofit and for-profit, who propose to establish, expand, and improve research activities in health sciences and related fields are eligible to apply for research grants.

Fiscal Information Research grants awarded in 1986 ranged from $8,700 to $2,238,000 with an average award of $231,000.

Application Information The standard application forms as furnished by DHHS and required by OMB Circular No. A-102 must be used for this program by those applicants which are state or local units of government. For research grants, PHS Form 398 (with current instructions) is available from the Division of Research Grants, NIH, Bethesda, MD 20892, and completed forms should be submitted to the same address.

Deadline(s) All new research grant applications, unless specified differently in a program announcement or request for applications, all career development awards and conference grant applications, all new and competing and continuation program project and center applications must be received by February 1, June 1, or October 1; all competing continuation and supplemental research grant applications must be received by March 1, July 1, or November 1.

Subject Term(s) Medical Sciences; Digestive Diseases Research; Nutrition; Individuals, Eligibility of

238. National Institute of Diabetes and Digestive and Kidney Diseases

National Institutes of Health
Westwood Building, 5333 Westbard Avenue
Bethesda, MD 20892
(301) 496-6325

Kidney, Urologic and Hematologic Diseases

CFDA Program Number 13.849

Program Description The institute conducts and supports research focused on a number of diseases that are characterized by chronicity and long-term disabling effects rather than mortality. These programs provide support for research in the basic mechanisms underlying biologic processes and diseases with nephrologic, urologic, and hematologic systems.

Eligibility/Limitations Individuals and public and private institutions, both nonprofit and for-profit, who propose to establish, expand, and improve research activities in health sciences and related fields are eligible to apply for research grants.

Fiscal Information Research grants awarded in 1986 ranged from $30,500 to $2,017,000 with an average award of $141,600.

Application Information The standard application forms as furnished by DHHS and required by OMB Circular No. A-102 must be used for this program by those applicants which are state or local units of government. For research grants, PHS Form 398 (with current instructions) is available from the Division of Research Grants, NIH, Bethesda, MD 20892, and completed forms should be submitted to the same address.

Deadline(s) All new research grant applications, unless specified differently in a program announcement or request for applications, all career development awards and conference grant applications, all new and competing and continuation program project and center applications must be received by February 1, June 1, or October 1;

all competing continuation and supplemental research grant applications must be received by March 1, July 1, or November 1.

Subject Term(s) Medical Sciences; Kidney Diseases Research; Hematologic Diseases Research; Urologic Diseases Research; Individuals, Eligibility of

239. National Institute of Environmental Health Sciences

National Institutes of Health
P.O. Box 12233
Research Triangle Park, NC 27709
(919) 541-7723

Environmental Health Research

CFDA Program Number 13.112-13.115

Program Description The rapid growth in the scope and nature of the chemical environment in recent decades has generated an equivalent increase in public concern about the hazards of chemicals. Concerns for health-related environmental problems are likely to increase in both the developed and developing countries as the world's population expands, as urbanization, industrialization, and agricultural production increase, and as understanding of the potential health hazards of environmental agents improves. The National Institute of Environmental Health Sciences (NIEHS) serves as the principal federal agency for biomedical research on the effects of chemical and physical environmental agents on human health. NIEHS research aims: to identify and investigate environmental factors that may have deleterious effects on human health (e.g., mutations, cancer, lung disease, birth defects); to quantify these effects; to understand the mechanisms of action of toxic agents on biologic systems; and to develop test methods for predicting the toxicity of chemicals. Through these efforts, NIEHS research provides the information necessary to establish disease prevention programs. Such efforts transcend national boundaries, and NIEHS plays a leading role in the organization and development of international research into environmental health problems.

Eligibility/Limitations Any nonprofit or for-profit organization, company, or institution engaged in biomedical research is eligible to apply. Individuals may apply for career development awards and individual physician scientist or clinical investigator awards.

Fiscal Information In 1986 project awards ranged from $4,000 to $2,300,000.

Application Information Application forms and instructions for their submission are available from the Division of Research Grants, National Institutes of Health.

Deadline(s) The deadlines for new grant applications are February 1, June 1, and October 1. Supplemental applications and all renewal applications are due by March 1, July 1, and November 1.

Subject Term(s) Biomedical Research; Environmental Health; Individuals, Eligibility of

240. National Institute of General Medical Sciences

National Institutes of Health
9000 Rockville Pike
Bethesda, MD 20892
(301) 496-7463

Biophysics and Physiological Sciences Program

CFDA Program Number 13.821

Program Description The National Institute of General Medical Sciences supports research and research training in the basic medical sciences and related natural and behavioral sciences which have significance for two or more institutes, or which are outside the general area of responsibility of any institute. The major objectives of the Biophysics and Physiological Sciences Program are to foster the application of physical, chemical, physiological, and engineering sciences to the solution of significant biomedical problems; to encourage the development of new and improved instruments and techniques for research at the molecular, cellular, and organismic levels; and to broaden and strengthen the scientific base in those areas of clinical and physiological research, including trauma and burn injury, for which the institute is responsible. Research supported by the program ranges from studies on the structure of proteins to clinical investigations, and includes certain aspects of the behavioral sciences.

Eligibility/Limitations Universities, colleges, hospitals, laboratories, and other public or private nonprofit and for-profit domestic institutions, including state and local governments, and individuals are eligible to make application for grant support of research by a named principal investigator.

Fiscal Information Funds may be used for salaries and wages, equipment, supplies, travel, and other costs directly required to carry out the research project. Grant awards in 1986 ranged from $18,996 to $930,994 with an average award of $163,755.

Application Information The standard application forms, as furnished by DHHS and required by OMB Circular No. A-102, must be used for the research grant program by those applicants which are state or local units of government. Application forms and information are available from the program.

Deadline(s) All new research grant applications, unless specified differently in a program announcement or request for applications, all career development awards and conference grant applications, all new and competing and continuation program project and center applications must be received by February 1, June 1, or October 1; all competing continuation and supplemental research grant applications must be received by March 1, July 1, or November 1.

Subject Term(s) Biophysics; Physiology; Individuals, Eligibility of

241. National Institute of General Medical Sciences

National Institutes of Health
9000 Rockville Pike
Bethesda, MD 20892
(301) 496-7021

Cellular and Molecular Basis of Disease Program

CFDA Program Number 13.863

Program Description The National Institute of General Medical Sciences supports research and research training in the basic medical sciences and related natural and behavioral sciences which have significance for two or more institutes, or which are outside the general area of responsibility of any institute. The Cellular and Molecular Basis of Disease Program is devoted to a greater understanding of the function of living cells in terms of ultrastructure, on the premise that many forms of human disease are the direct result of disturbed or abnormal function of cells. Investigations receiving support are concerned with the biophysical and biochemical description and analysis of molecular events in normal and diseased cells, and the structure and function of cell organelles and membrane processes at molecular and sublevels.

Eligibility/Limitations Universities, colleges, hospitals, laboratories, and other public or private nonprofit and for-profit domestic institutions, including state and local governments, and individuals are eligible to make application for grant support of research by a named principal investigator.

Fiscal Information Funds may be used for salaries and wages, equipment, supplies, travel, and other costs directly required to carry out the research project. Grant awards in 1986 ranged from $18,996 to $826,000 with an average award of $129,536.

Application Information The standard application forms, as furnished by DHHS and required by OMB Circular No. A-102, must be used for the research grant program by those applicants which are state or local units of government. Application forms and information are available from the program.

Deadline(s) All new research grant applications, unless specified differently in a program announcement or request for applications, all career development awards and conference grant applications, all new and competing and continuation program project and center applications must be received by February 1, June 1, or October 1; all competing continuation and supplemental research grant applications must be received by March 1, July 1, or November 1.

Subject Term(s) Medical Sciences; Individuals, Eligibility of

242. National Institute of General Medical Sciences

National Institutes of Health
9000 Rockville Pike
Bethesda, MD 20892
(301) 496-7087

Genetics Program

CFDA Program Number 13.862

Program Description The National Institute of General Medical Sciences supports research and research training in the basic medical sciences and related natural and behavioral sciences which have significance for two or more institutes, or which are outside the general area of responsibility of any institute. The Genetics Program is directed toward better understanding of the processes and mechanisms of inheritance in health and disease. Its ultimate objectives are the prevention and improved treatment of human genetic ills, including diseases with a strong hereditary factor, such as diabetes, atherosclerosis, hypertension, and schizophrenia. Topics of supported research include the mechanism of transmission and expression of genetic information, genetic control mechanisms, and the dynamics of genes in populations of organisms.

Eligibility/Limitations Universities, colleges, hospitals, laboratories, and other public or private nonprofit and for-profit domestic institutions, including state and local governments, and individuals are eligible to make application for grant support of research by a named principal investigator.

Fiscal Information Funds may be used for salaries and wages, equipment, supplies, travel, and other costs directly required to carry out the research project. Grant awards in 1986 ranged from $18,966 to $844,000 with an average award of $131,918.

Application Information The standard application forms, as furnished by DHHS and required by OMB Circular No. A-102, must be used for the research grant program by those applicants which are state or local units of government. Application forms and information are available from the program.

Deadline(s) All new research grant applications, unless specified differently in a program announcement or request for applications, all career development awards and conference grant applications, all new and competing and continuation program project and center applications must be received by February 1, June 1, or October 1; all competing continuation and supplemental research grant applications must be received by March 1, July 1, or November 1.

Subject Term(s) Genetics; Individuals, Eligibility of

243. National Institute of General Medical Sciences

National Institutes of Health
9000 Rockville Pike
Bethesda, MD 20892
(301) 496-7707

Pharmacological Sciences Program

CFDA Program Number 13.859

Program Description The National Institute of General Medical Sciences supports research and research training in the basic medical sciences and related natural and behavioral sciences which have significance for two or more institutes, or which are outside the general area of responsibility of any institute. The Pharmacological Sciences Program supports a wide spectrum of research aimed at providing an understanding of the biological and chemical processes involved in the action of therapeutic drugs and anesthetics, from the synthesis of new drugs to basic studies on the molecular and cellular mechanisms of drug action and controlled clinical studies in man. Support is provided for research on the absorption, metabolism, distribution, and excretion of drugs in man; the human, genetic, and environmental variables influencing drug response; the interactions of drugs with cell receptors; the design and control of new methods of drug delivery; and the mechanisms of adverse reactions and toxicity of therapeutic drugs. Anesthesiology research, biorelated chemistry research, and clinical pharmacology are also supported.

Eligibility/Limitations Universities, colleges, hospitals, laboratories, and other public or private nonprofit and for-profit domestic institutions, including state and local governments, and individuals are eligible to make application for grant support of research by a named principal investigator.

Fiscal Information Funds may be used for salaries and wages, equipment, supplies, travel, and other costs directly required to carry out the research project. Grant awards in 1986 ranged from $18,996 to $687,006 with an average award of $118,306.

Application Information The standard application forms, as furnished by DHHS and required by OMB Circular No. A-102, must be used for the research grant program by those applicants which are state or local units of government. Application forms and information are available from the program.

Deadline(s) All new research grant applications, unless specified differently in a program announcement or request for applications, all career development awards and conference grant applications, all new and competing and continuation program project and center applications must be received by February 1, June 1, or October 1; all competing continuation and supplemental research grant applications must be received by March 1, July 1, or November 1.

Subject Term(s) Pharmacology; Individuals, Eligibility of

244. National Institute of Mental Health

5600 Fishers Lane
Rockville, MD 20857
(301) 443-3683

Mental Health Research Grants

CFDA Program Number 13.242

Program Description These grants are awarded to increase knowledge and improve research methods on mental and behavioral disorders; to generate information regarding basic biological and behavioral disorders; to generate information regarding basic biological and behavioral processes underlying these disorders and the maintenance of mental health; and to improve mental health services. Research supported by the institute may employ theoretical, laboratory, clinical, methodological, and field studies, any of which may involve clinical, subclinical, and normal subjects and populations of all age ranges, as well as animal models appropriate to the system being investigated and the state of the field. Areas eligible for support include the neurosciences, behavioral sciences, epidemiology, clinical assessment and etiological studies, treatment, prevention, and services research. Four types of projects are funded: (1) research project grants provide support for clearly defined projects or a small group of related research activities, and when appropriate, support research conferences; (2) program project and center grants support large-scale, broad-based programs of research, usually interdisciplinary, consisting of several projects with a common focus; (3) small grants support small-scale exploratory and pilot-studies or exploration of an unusual research opportunity; and (4) investigator awards support physicians, clinician-scientists, and specialists in prevention research in order to develop and encourage their interest in research careers in mental health areas.

Eligibility/Limitations Public, private, profit, or nonprofit agencies (including state and local government agencies), eligible federal agencies, universities, colleges, hospitals, academic or research institutions, and small business organizations may apply for research grants. Small grants are primarily intended for the newer, less experienced investigator, and others who do not have regular research support or resources available from their institution.

Fiscal Information Awards range in amount from $15,000 to $590,000, with an average award of $132,552. The length and time phasing of assistance varies, but a project period is generally limited to five years or less. Small grants are limited to $15,000 direct costs for a period of one year or less.

Application Information Preapplication consultation with NIMH is not mandatory, but is encouraged. The standard application forms as furnished by DHHS and required by OMB Circular No. A-102 (PHS 5161-1) must be used for applicants that are state and local governments. Application kits containing the necessary form PHS 398 and instructions, if not available at applicant institutions, may be obtained from the Grants Management Branch, NIMH.

Deadline(s) The deadlines for receipt of applications are February 1, June 1, and October 1. Small grants may be submitted at any time, however, applications for summer support must be received by February 1 for July and August starting dates.

Subject Term(s) Mental Health Research

245. National Institute of Neurological and Communicative Disorders and Stroke

National Institutes of Health
Building 31, 9000 Rockville Pike
Bethesda, MD 20892
(301) 496-9248

Biological Basis Research in the Neurosciences and Communicative Sciences

CFDA Program Number 13.854

Program Description Programs of the National Institute of Neurological and Communicative Disorders and Stroke (NINCDS) focus on the identification, encouragement, and support of research aimed at improved diagnosis, treatment, and prevention of disorders of the nervous system, the neuromuscular apparatus of the ear, human communication, and the special senses of taste, smell, touch, and pain. The biological basis research program includes: (1) neurological and communicative science basic research which explores the fundamental structure and function of the brain and the nervous system; (2) research to understand the causes and origins of pathological conditions of the nervous system and hearing with the goal of prevention of these disorders; (3) research on the natural course of neurological and communicative disorders; (4) research training in the basic communicative sciences and basic neurological sciences; and (5) mechanisms associated with stroke and other cerebrovascular disorders, effects of trauma to the nervous system, neuroplasticity and regeneration, and tumors of neural and sensory tissues.

Eligibility/Limitations Any public, private or non-profit or for profit institution is eligible to apply for research grants.

Fiscal Information Research grants awarded in 1986 ranged from $12,000 to $830,187 with an average award of $150,000.

Application Information The standard application forms as furnished by DHHS and required by OMB Circular No. A-102 must be used for this program by those applicants which are state or local units of government. For research grants, PHS Form 398 (with current instructions) is available from the Division of Research Grants, NIH, Bethesda, MD 20892, and completed forms should be submitted to the same address.

Deadline(s) All new research grant applications, unless specified differently in a program announcement or request for applications, all career development awards and conference grant applications, all new and competing and continuation program project and center applications must be received by February 1, June 1, or October 1; all competing continuation and supplemental research grant applications must be received by March 1, July 1, or November 1.

Subject Term(s) Neurological Disorders Research; Communicative Disorders Research

246. National Institute on Aging

National Institutes of Health
Building 31, 9000 Rockville Pike
Bethesda, MD 20892
(301) 496-1752

Aging Research

CFDA Program Number 13.866

Program Description The National Institute on Aging (NIA) is responsible for biomedical, behavioral, and epidemiological research, and research training directed toward greater understanding of the aging process, and the diseases, special problems, and needs of the elderly. Programs have been established to pursue these goals. The biomedical research and clinical medicine program emphasizes the twin goals of understanding aging as a process and of improving the abilities of health care practitioners to respond to the diseases and other clinical problems of the aged. The behavioral sciences program supports research which will lead to greater understanding of the social, cultural, economic, and psychological factors that affect both the process of growing old and the place of older people in society. The epidemiology program supports research on the epidemiology of health and disease, as well as the interaction of demographic, social, and economic factors as they affect the health of the elderly.

Eligibility/Limitations Eligible applicants include universities, colleges, medical, dental, and nursing schools, schools of public health, laboratories, hospitals, state and local health departments, other public or private institutions (both for-profit and nonprofit), and individuals.

Fiscal Information Research grants are intended to support the direct costs of a project in accordance with an approved budget, plus an appropriate amount for indirect costs. Awards in 1986 ranged in amount from $15,800 to $1,275,047 with an average award of $170,280. Grant awards are usually made annually with no project periods to exceed five years in length.

Application Information The standard application forms as furnished by DHHS and required by OMB Circular No. A-102, must be used for this program by those applicants which are state or local units of government. An application form, PHS-398, may be requested from the Division of Research Grants, NIH. NIA support for research and research training is primarily provided through the award of grants. Research contract awards are generally reserved for the development and support of research resources, including animal and cellular resources as well as community populations of the elderly. NIA encourages the submission of applications and proposals for such support by means of program announcements and requests for applications (for grants) and requests for proposals (for contracts) as well as through individual contact. Applicants are encouraged to discuss questions about the NIA mission or the format or procedure for making applications with institute staff.

Deadline(s) All new research grant applications, unless specified differently in a program announcement or request for applications, all career development awards and conference grant applications, all new and competing and continuation program project and center applications must be received by February 1, June 1, or October 1; all competing continuation and supplemental research grant applications must be received by March 1, July 1, or November 1.

Additional Information A plan for scientific collaboration between the NIH and the Center for Research and Advanced Studies of the National Polytechnic Institute in Mexico was prepared for official signing in 1985. Promising areas of collaboration include neurosciences, endrocrinology, and molecular aging.

Subject Term(s) Aging; Individuals, Eligibility of

247. National Institute on Alcohol Abuse and Alcoholism

Division of Extramural Research
5600 Fishers Lane
Rockville, MD 20857
(301) 443-2530

Alcohol Research Programs

CFDA Program Number 13.273

Program Description The objective of these awards is to develop a sound fundamental knowledge base which can be applied to the development of improved methods of treatment and more effective strategies for preventing alcoholism and alcohol-related problems. The National Institute on Alcohol Abuse and Alcoholism (NIAAA) supports research in a broad range of discipline and subject areas related to biomedical and genetic factors, psychological and environmental factors, and alcohol-related problems and medical disorders. Four types of projects are funded: (1) research project grants provide support for clearly defined projects or a small group of related research activities, and when appropriate, support research conferences; (2) program project and center grants support large-scale, broad-based programs of research, usually interdisciplinary, consisting of several projects with a common focus; (3) small grants support small-scale exploratory and pilot-studies or exploration of an unusual research opportunity; and (4) investigator awards support physicians, clinician-scientists, and specialists in prevention research in order to develop and encourage their interest in research careers in alcoholism areas.

Sample Grants Support for a study of adolescent drinking patterns in Puerto Ricans, Hispanic Health Council, Hartford, Connecticut (1985).

Eligibility/Limitations Public or private profit and nonprofit agencies, including state, local, or regional government agencies, universities, colleges, hospitals, and academic or research institutions may apply for research grants. Small grants are primarily intended for the newer, less experienced investigator and others who do not have regular research support or resources available from their institution.

Fiscal Information Grant awards range in amount from $16,000 to $366,000 with an average award of $110,000. Project support varies in duration, but a project period is generally limited to five years or less. Small grants are limited to $15,000 direct costs for a period of one year or less.

Application Information Preapplication consultation with NIAAA is not mandatory but is encouraged. The standard application forms as furnished by DHHS and required by OMB Circular No. A-102 must be used for grant applicants that are state and local governments. Research grant applications are unsolicited. Application kits containing the necessary forms and instructions, if not available at applicant institutions, may be obtained from NIAAA. The amount of the award and the period of support are determined on the basis of the merit of the project.

Deadline(s) Deadlines for receipt of applications are February 1, June 1, and October 1. Small grant applications may be submitted at any time, however, applications for July and August starting dates must be received by February 1.

Subject Term(s) Alcoholism

248. National Institute on Drug Abuse

Division of Preclinical Research
5600 Fishers Lane
Rockville, MD 20857
(301) 443-1887

Drug Abuse Research

CFDA Program Number 13.279

Program Description The objective of these awards is to develop new knowledge and approaches to the epidemiology, etiology, diagnosis, treatment, control, and prevention of narcotic addiction and drug abuse through basic, clinical, and applied research, investigations, experiments, and studies. Four types of projects are funded: (1) research project grants provide support for clearly defined projects or a small group of related research activities, and when appropriate, support research conferences; (2) program project and center grants support large-scale, broad-based programs of research, usually interdisciplinary, consisting of several projects with a common focus; (3) small grants support small-scale exploratory and pilot-studies or exploration of an unusual research opportunity; and (4) investigator awards support physicians, clinician-scientists, and specialists in prevention research in order to develop and encourage their interest in research careers in drug abuse areas.

Eligibility/Limitations Public or private profit and nonprofit agencies, including state, local, or regional government agencies, universities, colleges, hospitals, academic, or research institutions may apply for research grants. Small grants are primarily intended for the newer, less experienced investigator, and others who do not have regular research support or resources available from their institution.

Fiscal Information Awards range from $16,000 to $292,000 with an average award of $120,000. Length of assistance varies, but a project period is generally limited to five years or less. Small grants are limited to $15,000 direct costs for a period of one year or less.

Application Information Preapplication coordination is not mandatory, but is encouraged by NIDA. The standard forms as furnished by DHHS and required by OMB Circular No. A-102 for state and local governments must be used. Research grant applications are unsolicited. Application kits containing the necessary forms and instructions, if not available at the applicant institution, may be obtained from NIDA.

Deadline(s) The deadlines for receipt of applications are February 1, June 1, and October 1. Small grants may be submitted at any time, however, small grant applications for summer support must be received by February 1 for July and August starting dates.

Subject Term(s) Drug Abuse

249. National Research Council

2101 Constitution Avenue, NW
Washington, DC 20418
(202) 334-2860

Ford Foundation Doctoral Fellowships for Minorities

Program Description The National Research Council will administer the Ford Foundation Doctoral Fellowships for Minorities program which will offer forty three-year predoctoral fellowships and ten one-year dissertation fellowships to American Indians or Alaskan Natives (Eskimo or Aleut), Black Americans, Mexican Americans/Chicanos, and Puerto Ricans. Designed to increase the presence of underrepresented minorities on the nation's college and university faculties, these fellowships will provide higher education opportunities for members of these four minority groups that are most severely underrepresented in the nation's Ph.D. population, the pool from which colleges and universities draw their faculties. Fellowships will be awarded in the behavioral and social sciences, humanities, engineering, mathematics, physical sciences, and biological sciences and for interdisciplinary programs comprised of two or more eligible disciplines. Awards will not be made in such areas as business administration and management, communications, health sciences, journalism, library science, educational administration, curriculum development and supervision, teacher training, or personnel and guidance. In addition, awards will not be made for work leading to terminal master's degrees, Doctor of Education (Ed.D.) degrees, Doctor of Fine Arts (D.F.A.) degrees, or practice-oriented professional degrees in areas such as medicine, law, or social work.

Eligibility/Limitations Citizens of the United States who are members of one of the designated minority groups, who are beginning graduate students or who are within one year of completing the dissertation, and who expect to work toward the Ph.D. or Sc.D. degree may apply for a fellowship award.

Fiscal Information Fellowships will be tenable at any accredited nonprofit United States institution of higher learning offering the Ph.D. or Sc.D. in the fields eligible for support in this program. Each predoctoral fellowship will include an annual stipend of $10,000 to the fellow, and an annual institutional grant of $6,000 to the fellowship institution in lieu of tuition and fees. Dissertation Fellows will receive a stipend of $18,000 for the twelve-month tenure with no institutional grant.

Application Information All inquiries concerning application materials and program administration should be addressed to the Fellowship Office, National Research Council.

Deadline(s) The deadline for entering the fellowship competition is November 15.

Subject Term(s) Fellowships; Minorities, Eligibility of; Predoctoral Support; Doctoral Dissertation Support; Behavioral Sciences; Social Sciences; Humanities; Engineering; Mathematics; Physical Sciences; Biological Sciences

250. National Research Council

2101 Constitution Avenue, NW
Washington, DC 20418
(202) 334-2860

Ford Foundation Postdoctoral Fellowships for Minorities

Program Description The National Research Council plans to award approximately thirty-five Ford Foundation Postdoctoral Fellowships for Minorities in a program designed to provide opportunities for continued education and experience in research for American Indians and Alaskan Natives (Eskimo and Aleut), Black Americans, Mexican Americans/Chicanos, and Puerto Ricans. Fellows will be selected from among scientists, engineers, and scholars in the humanities who show promise of future achievement in academic research and scholarship in higher education. Awards will be made in the behavioral and social sciences, humanities, engineering, mathematics, physical sciences, and biological sciences, and for interdisciplinary programs comprised of two or more eligible disciplines. Awards will not be made in professions such as medicine, law, social work, library science, and such areas as business administration and management, educational administration, curriculum development and supervision, teacher training, and personnel and guidance.

Sample Grants Recent fellows (1986) have studied: Caribbean literature; Latin American and Caribbean history; and Mexican-American literature.

Eligibility/Limitations Citizens of the United States who are members of one of the designated minority groups, who are preparing for or are already engaged in college or university teaching, and who hold doctoral or other terminal degrees may apply for a fellowship of one year's duration. Fellowships are awarded for research at an appropriate not-for-profit institution of higher education or research, primarily in the United States. Appropriate institutions include universities, museums, libraries, government or national laboratories, privately sponsored not-for-profit institutes, government chartered not-for-profit research organizations, and centers for advanced study.

Fiscal Information The stipend for fellows at the regular postdoctoral level is $20,000 per year, and that for fellows at the senior postdoctoral level is $26,000 per year. Stipends for tenures of less than twelve months will be prorated. No dependency allowance is available. In addition to the stipend, the fellow will receive a travel and relocation allowance up to a maximum of $2,000. Each fellow's employing institution will be provided a $2,500 grant-in-aid for the fellow's use once the fellowship tenure is completed. The employing institution will be asked to match the grant. These funds are designated to be used for the fellow's research expenditures. Fellowship recipients are required to choose for affiliation an institution other than that from which they apply.

Application Information Application materials and information are available from the Fellowship Office, National Research Council.

Deadline(s) All application materials must be received by the Fellowship Office by January 16.

Subject Term(s) Fellowships; Postdoctoral Support; Minorities, Eligibility of; Behavioral Sciences; Social Sciences; Humanities; Engineering; Mathematics; Physical Sciences; Biological Sciences

251. National Science Foundation

1800 G Street, NW
Washington, DC 20550
(202) 357-7806

Doctoral Dissertation Research Improvement

Program Description The foundation awards grants to improve the scientific quality of doctoral dissertation research. Awards are made to allow doctoral candidates opportunities for greater creativity in the gathering and analysis of data than would otherwise be possible. Dissertation improvement awards are available only in certain disciplines. These include the social and behavioral sciences and certain of the biological, earth, atmospheric, and ocean sciences. No dissertation improvement awards are made in the mathematical and physical sciences, engineering, cellular and molecular biology, or physiology.

Sample Grants For dissertation research in systematic biology on the phylogeny and evolution of South American Quaternary Tayassuidae (Mamalia), $5,500 to a student from the University of Massachusetts, Amherst (1986). For dissertation research in anthropology on fetal growth and neonatal mortality, $9,930 to a student from Cornell, for foreign travel and activity (1986). For dissertation research in anthropology on the functions of myth-telling in Shavante society, $9,795 to a student from the University of Texas, Austin (1986). For dissertation research in population biology and physiology on a comparative study of social wasp prey foraging, $3,700 to a student from Cornell University for foreign travel and activity (1986).

Eligibility/Limitations Doctoral students in appropriate disciplines are eligible to apply.

Fiscal Information Grants generally do not exceed $10,000 and are intended to cover research-related expenses. These include expenses for field equipment and supplies and for travel to and from research sites. These awards are not fellowships and no stipend is included. However, the student may concurrently receive support from other sources.

Application Information Each NSF division that administers grants treats applications in a different way. Doctoral students who wish to apply for a dissertation improvement grant should write directly to the appropriate research division(s).

Subject Term(s) Doctoral Dissertation Support

252. National Science Foundation

Directorate for Biological, Behavioral, and Social Sciences, Division of Behavioral and Neural Sciences
1800 G Street, NW
Washington, DC 20550
(202) 357-7804

Anthropology Program

CFDA Program Number 47.051

Program Description The Division of Behavioral and Neural Sciences is responsible for the support of research on nervous systems and human and animal behavior. The division's goals are to advance understanding of the biological, environmental, and cultural factors that underlie the behavior of humans and animals, with explicit emphasis on nervous system structure and function. The Anthropology Program supports research in cultural and social anthropology, archeology, and physical anthropology. It provides support for scientific research on all topics, techniques, and geographic areas. Support is also provided for preserving and increasing research accessibility of systematic anthropological collections, and for archeometric research and laboratories.

Sample Grants For collaborative research on the social effects of mortality and divorce on the Yanomamo nuclear family, $40,727 to the University of California, Santa Barbara and $18,144 to the University of Nebraska, Lincoln (1986). For study of early anthropoid development in South America, $61,781 to SUNY Stony Brook (1986). For a study of eastern Caribbean fertility transition, $18,000 to Humboldt State

University (1986). For a study of the technology and organization of agricultural production in the Tiwanadua state, $52,000 to the University of Illinois, Chicago (1986). For archeological research on Marajo Island, Brazil, $10,370 to the Museum of the American Indian (1986). For a study of intertribal relations (peaceful politics) in Brazil's Upper Xingu, $19,640 to Vanderbilt University (1986). For a study of land tenure and historical knowledge in highland Colombia, $24,802 to University of Maryland, Baltimore (1986). For a study of the toxicity of manioc in the northwest Amazon, $47,864 to the University of Colorado, Boulder (1986). For a study of settlement patterns, regional demography, and prehispanic chiefdoms in the Valle de la Plata, Colombia, $54,369 to the University of Pittsburgh (1986).

Eligibility/Limitations The most frequent recipients of support for research are academic institutions and nonprofit research groups. In special circumstances, grants are also awarded to other types of institutions and to individuals. In these cases, preliminary inquiry should be made to the appropriate program officer before a proposal is submitted. Support may be provided for projects involving a single scientist or a number of scientists. Awards are made for projects confined to a single disciplinary area and for those that cross or merge disciplinary interests.

Fiscal Information Level of support varies from project to project. Grant awards range from $700 to $1,574,000 with an average award of $61,458. Although most grants are for much shorter periods, up to five years of support may be requested. Grant funds may be used for paying direct and indirect costs necessary to conduct research or studies. Institutions are required to share in the cost of each research project. This may be accomplished by a contribution to any cost element, direct or indirect.

Application Information Address inquiries to the program director. Guidelines are contained in the publication "Grants for Research and Education in Science and Engineering."

Deadline(s) The target dates for the submission of senior research proposals in archeology, social/cultural, and physical anthropology are July 1 and December 1. Proposals received by July 1 may receive support as early as January 1, while December 1 submissions may receive funding as early as June 1. The target date for archeometry is October 31 and for Systematic Anthropological Collections proposals the target date is January 1. Proposals for doctoral dissertation support may be submitted at any time during the year.

Additional Information The Division of Behavioral and Neural Sciences also provides funds for doctoral dissertation research, research conferences, publication costs, acquisition of specialized research equipment and materials, construction of specialized research facilities, and special projects such as data banks and preservation of anthropological collections. Special funds are also available for small-college personnel whose research is related to ongoing NSF-supported projects.

Subject Term(s) Individuals, Eligibility of; Doctoral Dissertation Support; Publication Support; Seminars and Conferences; Anthropology; Archeology; Archeometry; Equipment Acquisition

253. National Science Foundation

Directorate for Biological, Behavioral, and Social Sciences, Division of Behavioral and Neural Sciences
1800 G Street, NW
Washington, DC 20550
(202) 357-7696

Linguistics Program

CFDA Program Number 47.051

Program Description The Division of Behavioral and Neural Sciences is responsible for the support of research on nervous systems and human and animal behavior. The division's goals are to advance understanding of the biological, environmental, and cultural factors that underlie the behavior of humans and animals, with explicit emphasis on nervous system structure and function. The Linguistics Program supports research into the syntactic, semantic, phonological, and phonetic properties of individual languages and of language in general. Research into the acquisition of language by children, the psychological processes in the production and perception of speech, the biological foundations of language, the social influences on and effects of language and dialect variation, and the formal and mathematical properties of language models is also supported.

Sample Grants For support of the production of a Chol (Mayan) dictionary database, $39,999 (1986). For support of linguistic analysis, texts, and a dictionary of Parare, $70,927 to the University of Oregon, Eugene (1986).

Eligibility/Limitations The most frequent recipients of support for research are academic institutions and nonprofit research groups. In special circumstances, grants are also awarded to other types of institutions and to individuals. In these cases, preliminary inquiry should be made to the appropriate program officer before a proposal is submitted. Support may be provided for projects involving a single scientist or a number of scientists. Awards are made for projects confined to a single disciplinary area and for those that cross or merge disciplinary interests.

Fiscal Information Level of support varies from project to project. Grant awards range from $700 to $1,574,000 with an average award of $61,458. Although most grants are for much shorter periods, up to five years of support may be requested. Grant funds may be used for paying direct and indirect costs necessary to conduct research or studies. Institutions are required to share in the cost of each research project. This may be accomplished by a contribution to any cost element, direct or indirect.

Application Information Address inquiries to the program director. Guidelines are contained in the publication "Grants for Research and Education in Science and Engineering."

Deadline(s) Proposals may be submitted at any time. Allow six months for review. Proposals to be funded in a particular fiscal year (ending September 30) normally should be received no later than January of that year. Target dates are published in the NSF *Bulletin.*

Additional Information The Division of Behavioral and Neural Sciences also provides funds for doctoral dissertation research, research conferences, publication costs, acquisition of specialized research equipment and materials, construction of specialized research facilities, and special projects. Special funds are also available for small-college personnel whose research is related to ongoing NSF-supported projects.

Subject Term(s) Individuals, Eligibility of; Doctoral Dissertation Support; Publication Support; Seminars and Conferences; Linguistics; Language; Equipment Acquisition

254. National Science Foundation

Directorate for Biological, Behavioral, and Social Sciences, Division of Behavioral and Neural Sciences
1800 G Street, NW
Washington, DC 20550
(202) 357-7471

Molecular and Cellular Neurobiology

CFDA Program Number 47.051

Program Description The Division of Behavioral and Neural Sciences is responsible for the support of research on nervous systems and human and animal behavior. The division's goals are to advance understanding of the biological, environmental, and cultural factors that underlie the behavior of humans and animals, with explicit emphasis on nervous system structure and function. The Molecular and Cellular Neurobiology Program supports research on: the biochemical and biophysical properties of neurons and glia which determine their special functions; molecular events related to the regulation of transmitter and receptor synthesis; generation and transmission of electrical impulses by the neuron; metabolic events that respond to changes in neuronal activity; and approaches using gene-splicing and monoclonal antibodies in the study of neural mechanisms.

Sample Grants For support of research by an Argentinian scientist of ligand interactions with the Na PUMP, Ca PUMP and Na-Ca exchange mechanisms in squid axons, $32,000 to the Marine Biological Laboratory (1986).

Eligibility/Limitations The most frequent recipients of support for research are academic institutions and nonprofit research groups. In special circumstances, grants are also awarded to other types of institutions and to individuals. In these cases, preliminary inquiry should be made to the appropriate program officer before a proposal is submitted. Support may be provided for projects involving a single scientist or a number of scientists. Awards are made for projects confined to a single disciplinary area and for those that cross or merge disciplinary interests.

Fiscal Information Level of support varies from project to project. Although most grants are for much shorter periods, up to five years of support may be requested. Grant funds may be used for paying direct and indirect costs necessary to conduct research or studies. Institutions are required to share in the cost of each research project. This may be accomplished by a contribution to any cost element, direct or indirect.

Application Information Address inquiries to the program director. Guidelines are contained in the publication "Grants for Research and Education in Science and Engineering."

Deadline(s) Proposals may be submitted at any time. Allow six months for review. Proposals to be funded in a particular fiscal year (ending September 30) normally should be received no later than January of that year. Target dates are published in the NSF *Bulletin.*

Additional Information The Division of Behavioral and Neural Sciences also provides funds for doctoral dissertation research, research conferences, publication costs, acquisition of specialized research equipment and materials, construction of specialized research facilities, and special projects. Special funds are also available for small-college personnel whose research is related to ongoing NSF-supported projects.

Subject Term(s) Individuals, Eligibility of; Doctoral Dissertation Support; Publication Support; Seminars and Conferences; Neurobiology; Equipment Acquisition

255. National Science Foundation

Directorate for Biological, Behavioral, and Social Sciences, Division of Behavioral and Neural Sciences
1800 G Street, NW
Washington, DC 20550
(202) 357-7949

Psychobiology

CFDA Program Number 47.051

Program Description The Division of Behavioral and Neural Sciences is responsible for the support of research on nervous systems and human and animal behavior. The division's goals are to advance understanding of the biological, environmental, and cultural factors that underlie the behavior of humans and animals, with explicit emphasis on nervous system structure and function. The Psychobiology Program supports: field and laboratory studies of behavior and its genetic, environmental, hormonal, neural, and motivational determinants, using a wide range of observational, experimental, theoretical, comparative, and quantitative approaches; animal learning and memory, conditioning and stimulus control, preferences and aversions, foraging and ingestion, migration and homing, and communication; and the social and reproductive behaviors of animals.

Sample Grants Foreign travel and activity support for a study of secondary reproductive strategies, $43,000 to the University of Minnesota (1986). Foreign travel and activity support for a study of orientation/navigation abilities of open-ocean sharks, $77,371 to the University of California, San Diego (1986). Foreign travel support for a study of sperm whale identification sounds, $108,384 to Woods Hole Oceanographic Institute (1986).

Eligibility/Limitations The most frequent recipients of support for research are academic institutions and nonprofit research groups. In special circumstances, grants are also awarded to other types of institutions and to individuals. In these cases, preliminary inquiry should be made to the appropriate program officer before a proposal is submitted. Support may be provided for projects involving a single scientist or a number of scientists. Awards are made for projects confined to a single disciplinary area and for those that cross or merge disciplinary interests.

Fiscal Information Level of support varies from project to project. Although most grants are for much shorter periods, up to five years of support may be requested. Grant funds may be used for paying direct and indirect costs necessary to conduct research or studies. Institutions are required to share in the cost of each research project. This may be accomplished by a contribution to any cost element, direct or indirect.

Application Information Address inquiries to the program director. Guidelines are contained in the publication "Grants for Research and Education in Science and Engineering."

Deadline(s) Proposals may be submitted at any time. Allow six months for review. Proposals to be funded in a particular fiscal year (ending September 30) normally should be received no later than January of that year. Target dates are published in the NSF *Bulletin.*

Additional Information The Division of Behavioral and Neural Sciences also provides funds for doctoral dissertation research, research conferences, publication costs, acquisition of specialized research equipment and materials, construction of specialized research facilities, and special projects. Special funds are also available for small-college personnel whose research is related to ongoing NSF-supported projects.

Subject Term(s) Individuals, Eligibility of; Doctoral Dissertation Support; Publication Support; Seminars and Conferences; Psychobiology; Equipment Acquisition

256. National Science Foundation

Directorate for Biological, Behavioral, and Social Sciences, Division of Behavioral and Neural Sciences
1800 G Street, NW
Washington, DC 20550
(202) 357-7428

Sensory Physiology and Perception

CFDA Program Number 47.051

Program Description The Division of Behavioral and Neural Sciences is responsible for the support of research on nervous systems and human and animal behavior. The division's goals are to advance understanding of the biological, environmental, and cultural factors that underlie the behavior of humans and animals, with explicit emphasis on nervous system structure and function. The Sensory Physiology and Perception Program supports study of: sensory mechanisms and processes at the molecular, cellular, physiological, and behavioral levels involved in transduction, neural coding, and information processing; and neurobiological and psychophysical correlates of sensory and perceptual phenomena.

Sample Grants Foreign travel support for a study of frequency tuning and its plasticity in the electroreceptors of an electric fish, $55,000 to the University of Texas, Austin (1986).

Eligibility/Limitations The most frequent recipients of support for research are academic institutions and nonprofit research groups. In special circumstances, grants are also awarded to other types of institutions and to individuals. In these cases, preliminary inquiry should be made to the appropriate program officer before a proposal is submitted. Support may be provided for projects involving a single scientist or a number of scientists. Awards are made for projects confined to a single disciplinary area and for those that cross or merge disciplinary interests.

Fiscal Information Level of support varies from project to project. Although most grants are for much shorter periods, up to five years of support may be requested.

Grant funds may be used for paying direct and indirect costs necessary to conduct research or studies. Institutions are required to share in the cost of each research project. This may be accomplished by a contribution to any cost element, direct or indirect.

Application Information Address inquiries to the program director. Guidelines are contained in the publication "Grants for Research and Education in Science and Engineering."

Deadline(s) Proposals may be submitted at any time. Allow six months for review. Proposals to be funded in a particular fiscal year (ending September 30) normally should be received no later than January of that year. Target dates are published in the NSF *Bulletin*.

Additional Information The Division of Behavioral and Neural Sciences also provides funds for doctoral dissertation research, research conferences, publication costs, acquisition of specialized research equipment and materials, construction of specialized research facilities, and special projects. Special funds are also available for small-college personnel whose research is related to ongoing NSF-supported projects.

Subject Term(s) Individuals, Eligibility of; Doctoral Dissertation Support; Equipment Acquisition; Seminars and Conferences; Sensory Physiology; Perception

257. National Science Foundation

Directorate for Biological, Behavioral, and Social Sciences, Division of Biotic Systems and Resources
1800 G Street, NW
Washington, DC 20550
(202) 357-9734

Biological Research Resources

CFDA Program Number 47.051

Program Description The Biological Research Resources Program provides operational and refurbishment support for biological research resources—including living-organism stock centers, biological field-research facilities, and systematic research collections—to enhance the use of these resources by U.S. scientists.

Sample Grants Foreign travel and activity support of a study of the biogeography and evolution of the lomas formations of Peru and Chile, $46,703 to the Field Museum of Natural History (1986). Foreign travel and activity support of the administration, maintenance and development of La Selva Biological Station, Puerto Viejo de Sarapiqui, Costa Rica, $255,000 to Duke University (1986). Foreign travel and activity support of a study of the caddisfly (Trichoptera) fauna of Costa Rica, $39,200 to Clemson University (1986). Foreign travel and activity support of a survey of the Cuban shorefish fauna, $29,000 to the University of Colorado, Denver (1986).

Eligibility/Limitations The most frequent recipients of support for research are academic institutions and nonprofit research groups. In special circumstances, grants are also awarded to other types of institutions and to individuals. In these cases, preliminary inquiry should be made to the appropriate program officer before a proposal is submitted. Support may be provided for projects involving a single scientist or a number of scientists. Awards are made for projects confined to a single disciplinary area and for those that cross or merge disciplinary interests.

Fiscal Information Level of support varies from project to project. Although most grants are for much shorter periods, up to five years of support may be requested. Grant funds may be used for paying direct and indirect costs necessary to conduct research or studies. Institutions are required to share in the cost of each research project. This may be accomplished by a contribution to any cost element, direct or indirect.

Application Information Address inquiries to the program director. Guidelines are contained in the publication "Grants for Research and Education in Science and Engineering."

Deadline(s) Deadlines and target dates for receipt of proposals are published in the NSF *Bulletin.*

Subject Term(s) Biology

258. National Science Foundation

Directorate for Biological, Behavioral, and Social Sciences, Division of Biotic Systems and Resources
1800 G Street, NW
Washington, DC 20550
(202) 357-9734

Ecology Program

CFDA Program Number 47.051

Program Description The Ecology Program provides support for research on relationships within and between communities of animals and plants in terrestrial and inland aquatic habitats. These include studies of plant-animal, predator-prey interactions and symbioses, as well as studies of the effects of key species on communities. The program also supports research on microbial ecology of soils and sediments, and paleoecology. Emphasis is placed on multi-species interactions at the community level.

Sample Grants Foreign travel and activity support of a study of the environmental hardships for rainforest trees in abandoned Amazon pastures, $82,647 to Penn State University Central Office (1986). Foreign travel and activity support of a study of the role of fine roots and Mycorrhizae in the cycling of P in Brazilian tropical forest and agroecosystems, $186,239 to Colorado State University (1986). Foreign travel and activity support of a study of group foraging in spiders, $125,000 to Miami University Hamilton Campus (1986). Foreign travel and activity support of collaborative research on the role of interspecific aggression in structuring Amazonian bird communities, $62,746 to Princeton University and $29,889 to the University of Illinois at Urbana (1986). Foreign travel support for a study of Amazon fires in an ancient and current-day context, $16,044 to Penn State University Central Office (1986).

Eligibility/Limitations The most frequent recipients of support for research are academic institutions and nonprofit research groups. In special circumstances, grants are also awarded to other types of institutions and to individuals. In these cases, preliminary inquiry should be made to the appropriate program officer before a proposal is submitted. Support may be provided for projects involving a single scientist or a number of scientists. Awards are made for projects confined to a single disciplinary area and for those that cross or merge disciplinary interests.

Fiscal Information Level of support varies from project to project. Although most grants are for much shorter periods, up to five years of support may be requested. Grant funds may be used for paying direct and indirect costs necessary to conduct research or studies. Institutions are required to share in the cost of each research project. This may be accomplished by a contribution to any cost element, direct or indirect.

Application Information Address inquiries to the program director. Guidelines are contained in the publication "Grants for Research and Education in Science and Engineering."

Deadline(s) Deadlines and target dates for receipt of proposals are published in the NSF *Bulletin.*

Additional Information Proposals for specialized research equipment, doctoral dissertation research, and research conferences and workshops will also be considered.

Subject Term(s) Doctoral Dissertation Support; Individuals, Eligibility of; Seminars and Conferences; Publication Support; Ecology; Equipment Acquisition

259. National Science Foundation

Directorate for Biological, Behavioral, and Social Sciences, Division of Biotic Systems and Resources
1800 G Street, NW
Washington, DC 20550
(202) 357-9596

Ecosystem Studies

CFDA Program Number 47.051

Program Description The Ecosystem Studies Program supports mainly multidisciplinary studies of the structure and function of complex biotic-abiotic associations. Processes, mechanisms, and system behavior are major research foci, as is the study of energy and nutrient transfer through ecosystems. The development of new elements and syntheses of ecology theory is emphasized, and mathematical modeling of ecosystems for analysis and integration is encouraged. Both short-term and long-term research are supported, with foci ranging from the behavior of individual processes to large ecosystem response to environmental changes.

Sample Grants Foreign travel and activity support for research on the spatial and temporal variability of the biogeochemistry of the Amazon River, $400,000 to the University of Washington (1986). Foreign travel and activity support for research on the biological control of soil charge properties and nutrient retention in variable charge soils of the humid tropics, $225,000 to Duke University (1986). Foreign travel and activity support for data analysis and modeling of ecosystem metabolism and mass balance for the Orinoco River and its major tributaries, $150,000 to the University of Colorado, Boulder (1986).

Eligibility/Limitations The most frequent recipients of support for research are academic institutions and nonprofit research groups. In special circumstances, grants are also awarded to other types of institutions and to individuals. In these cases, preliminary inquiry should be made to the appropriate program officer before a proposal is submitted. Support may be provided for projects involving a single scientist or a number of scientists. Awards are made for projects confined to a single disciplinary area and for those that cross or merge disciplinary interests.

Fiscal Information Level of support varies from project to project. Although most grants are for much shorter periods, up to five years of support may be requested. Grant funds may be used for paying direct and indirect costs necessary to conduct research or studies. Institutions are required to share in the cost of each research project. This may be accomplished by a contribution to any cost element, direct or indirect.

Application Information Address inquiries to the program director. Guidelines are contained in the publication "Grants for Research and Education in Science and Engineering."

Deadline(s) Deadlines and target dates for receipt of proposals are published in the NSF *Bulletin.*

Additional Information Proposals for specialized research equipment, doctoral dissertation research, and research conferences and workshops will also be considered.

Subject Term(s) Doctoral Dissertation Support; Individuals, Eligibility of; Seminars and Conferences; Ecology; Ecosystem Studies; Equipment Acquisition

260. National Science Foundation

Directorate for Biological, Behavioral, and Social Sciences, Division of Biotic Systems and Resources
1800 G Street, NW
Washington, DC 20550
(202) 357-7332

Fellowship Opportunities for New Ph.D.s

Program Description To promote particularly innovative and creative efforts in any of the areas included in the normal purview of its programs, the Division of Biotic Systems and Resources makes available these fellowships. The annual competition serves to foster enhancement of breadth and depth in technical proficiency, association with novel intellectual environments and institutions, prolonged tenure at field sites and/or in foreign countries, and development of scientific personnel in underdeveloped disciplinary subfields.

Eligibility/Limitations These fellowships will be offered only to persons who (1) at the time of application are nationals of the United States, (2) have the doctoral degree, and (3) have not previously been an investigator or coinvestigator on an NSF conventional research or fellowship award (Doctoral Dissertation Improvement awards are not included in this restriction).

Fiscal Information Each fellowship provides a stipend, a special allowance, and an institutional allowance. The stipend will be paid directly to the fellow at the rate of $1,600 per month ($19,200 per full year). A special allowance of $400 per month is expendable at the fellow's discretion and is intended to be used for scientific supplies, travel, publication expenses, and other research-related costs. An institutional allowance of $200 per month of tenure is for partial reimbursement of expenses incurred in support of the fellow and will be paid directly to the host institution. Awards will be made for either twelve or twenty-four months, depending on the time requested, the research design, and proposal evaluation. No allowance for dependents is available.

Application Information To be eligible for consideration, a completed application must be received by the submission date. Application forms and additional information are available from the division. Reproductions of any required forms are acceptable.

Deadline(s) All application materials should be submitted by October 1.

Subject Term(s) Fellowships; Postdoctoral Support; Biology

261. National Science Foundation

Directorate for Biological, Behavioral, and Social Sciences, Division of Biotic Systems and Resources
1800 G Street, NW
Washington, DC 20550
(202) 357-9720

Population Biology and Physiological Ecology Program

CFDA Program Number 47.051

Program Description The Population Biology and Physiological Ecology Program provides support for research which seeks to identify the most important ecological and evolutionary factors responsible for shaping the adaptive responses of organisms to their environment, and how these adaptations at the individual level translate into interactions at the population and species levels. The focus is on research using theoretical, experimental, laboratory, and field approaches to the understanding of populations of single species with regard to genetic relationships, population dynamics, and behavioral and physiological adaptations to specific environments.

Sample Grants Foreign travel and activity support for a study of the population biology and virulence of malarial parasites, $100,000 to the University of Vermont (1986). Foreign travel and activity support of a study of the demography and ecophysiology of regeneration of tropical rain forest trees, $122,292 to Duke University (1986). Foreign travel and activity support of a study of the ecology and behavior of Darwin's Finches on the Galapagos Islands, $120,002 to Princeton University (1986).

Eligibility/Limitations The most frequent recipients of support for research are academic institutions and nonprofit research groups. In special circumstances, grants are also awarded to other types of institutions and to individuals. In these cases, preliminary inquiry should be made to the appropriate program officer before a proposal is submitted. Support may be provided for projects involving a single scientist or a number of scientists. Awards are made for projects confined to a single disciplinary area and for those that cross or merge disciplinary interests.

Fiscal Information Level of support varies from project to project. Although most grants are for much shorter periods, up to five years of support may be requested. Grant funds may be used for paying direct and indirect costs necessary to conduct research or studies. Institutions are required to share in the cost of each research project. This may be accomplished by a contribution to any cost element, direct or indirect.

Application Information Address inquiries to the program director. Guidelines are contained in the publication "Grants for Research and Education in Science and Engineering."

Deadline(s) Deadlines and target dates for receipt of proposals are published in the NSF *Bulletin.*

Additional Information Proposals for specialized research equipment, doctoral dissertation research, and research conferences and workshops will also be considered.

Subject Term(s) Doctoral Dissertation Support; Individuals, Eligibility of; Seminars and Conferences; Biology; Population Biology; Ecology

262. National Science Foundation

Directorate for Biological, Behavioral, and Social Sciences, Division of Biotic Systems and Resources
1800 G Street, NW
Washington, DC 20550
(202) 357-9588

Systematic Biology Program

CFDA Program Number 47.051

Program Description The Systematic Biology Program supports comparative and experimental research on the characterization, affinities, adaptations, and evolutionary histories of all groups of organisms. Emphasis is on description and analysis of biotic diversity using modern methods of comparative morphology-physiology, biochemical and numerical systematics, experimental hybridization, biogeography, floristics, and faunistics; elements of paleobiology, except studies that deal with humans or that are primarily ecological or stratigraphic, are also pertinent. Practical and theoretical aspects of classification at all taxonomic levels are included in the scope of the program.

Sample Grants For support of "Projecto Flora Amazonica—Phase IV," $164,132 to the New York Botanical Garden (1986). Foreign travel in support of systematic investigations of Delesseriaceae (Rhodophyta), $16,000 to the University of Michigan, Ann Arbor (1986). Foreign travel and activity support of systematic investigations on Philodendron Sect. Pteromischum (Araceae), $54,583 to Missouri Botanical Garden (1986). Foreign travel and activity support for research on population cytogenetics of selected chromosome races of Sceloporus Grammicus (Sauria: Iguanidae) in Central Mexico, $58,807 to Brigham Young University (1986). Foreign travel and activity support for a systematic study of Viguiera section Chloracra, $90,006 to the University of Tennessee, Knoxville (1986). Foreign travel support for research on the systematics and phylogeny of Late Tertiary horses in North America, $92,078 to the University of Florida (1986). Foreign travel and activity support for a study of the ethnobotany of Amazonian Jivaro: medical flora and folk taxonomy, $37,818 to Washington University (1986).

Eligibility/Limitations The most frequent recipients of support for research are academic institutions and nonprofit research groups. In special circumstances, grants are also awarded to other types of institutions and to individuals. In these cases, preliminary inquiry should be made to the appropriate program officer before a proposal is submitted. Support may be provided for projects involving a single scientist or a number of scientists. Awards are made for projects confined to a single disciplinary area and for those that cross or merge disciplinary interests.

Fiscal Information Level of support varies from project to project. Although most grants are for much shorter periods, up to five years of support may be requested. Grant funds may be used for paying direct and indirect costs necessary to conduct research or studies. Institutions are required to share in the cost of each research project. This may be accomplished by a contribution to any cost element, direct or indirect.

Application Information Address inquiries to the program director. Guidelines are contained in the publication "Grants for Research and Education in Science and Engineering."

Deadline(s) Deadlines and target dates for receipt of proposals are published in the NSF *Bulletin.*

Additional Information Proposals for specialized research equipment, doctoral dissertation support, and research conferences and workshops will also be considered.

Subject Term(s) Doctoral Dissertation Support; Individuals, Eligibility of; Seminars and Conferences; Biology; Systematic Biology; Equipment Acquisition

263. National Science Foundation

Directorate for Biological, Behavioral, and Social Sciences, Division of Cellular Biosciences
1800 G Street, NW
Washington, DC 20550
(202) 357-0112

Eukaryotic Genetics

CFDA Program Number 47.051

Program Description The Eukaryotic Genetics Program supports research on the organization, characterization, regulation of expression, recombination, function, transmission, and evolution of heritable information (both nuclear and extranuclear) in all eukaryotic organisms—from yeast to plants and animals. Host-parasite interactions at the genetic level, when both are eukaryotic, are also of interest.

Sample Grants Foreign travel support to attend a workshop on Drosophila Alpha-Amylases, $2,000 to Arizona State University (1986).

Eligibility/Limitations The most frequent recipients of support for research are academic institutions and nonprofit research groups. In special circumstances, grants are also awarded to other types of institutions and to individuals. In these cases, preliminary inquiry should be made to the appropriate program officer before a proposal is submitted. Support may be provided for projects involving a single scientist or a number of scientists. Awards are made for projects confined to a single disciplinary area and for those that cross or merge disciplinary interests.

Application Information For additional information contact the Division of Cellular Biosciences.

Deadline(s) Proposals may be submitted at any time; allow about six months for review. Proposals to be funded in a particular fiscal year (ending September 30) normally should be received no later than January of that year. Target dates are published in the NSF *Bulletin.*

Subject Term(s) Genetics; Individuals, Eligibility of

264. National Science Foundation

Directorate for Biological, Behavioral, and Social Sciences, Division of Molecular Biosciences
1800 G Street, NW
Washington, DC 20550
(202) 357-7954

Biochemistry

CFDA Program Number 47.051

Program Description The Biochemistry Program supports study of the structure and function of proteins, carbohydrates, and nucleic acids, and the identification of the molecular parameters that determine their functions; the mechanism and regulation of the biosynthesis of DNA, RNA, proteins, carbohydrates, and lipids; enzyme structure and function; the biogenesis, topography, and assembly of membranes and macromolecular complexes; and, virus structure, assembly, replication, and expression.

Sample Grants Foreign travel support for study of biochemistry of hemoglobins and oxygen transport, $50,000 to University of Texas, Austin (1986). Support for a study of the metabolic action of bioregulators in the induction of cis-polyisoprene (rubber) in Guayule plants, $3,500 to Texas A&M Research Foundation (1986).

Eligibility/Limitations The most frequent recipients of support for research are academic institutions and nonprofit research groups. In special circumstances, grants are also awarded to other types of institutions and to individuals. In these cases, preliminary inquiry should be made to the appropriate program officer before a proposal is submitted. Support may be provided for projects involving a single scientist or a number of scientists. Awards are made for projects confined to a single disciplinary area and for those that cross or merge disciplinary interests.

Application Information For additional information contact the Division of Molecular Biosciences.

Deadline(s) Proposals may be submitted at any time; allow about six months for review. Proposals to be funded in a particular fiscal year (ending September 30) normally should be received no later than January of that year. Target dates are published in the NSF *Bulletin.*

Subject Term(s) Individuals, Eligibility of; Biochemistry

265. National Science Foundation

Directorate for Biological, Behavioral, and Social Sciences, Division of Molecular Biosciences
1800 G Street, NW
Washington, DC 20550
(202) 357-7987

Metabolic Biology

CFDA Program Number 47.051

Program Description The Metabolic Biology Program supports research on the mechanisms of regulation and characterization of biochemical pathways by which plant, microbial, and animal systems assimilate and transform metabolites, provide energy for vital processes, and respond to environmental changes. The program does not generally support research in biochemical pharmacology, metabolism of xenobiotics, or the metabolic basis of disease.

Sample Grants Foreign travel support for study of the transport, post-translational modification and sorting of proteins in developing legume cotyledons, $89,000 to University of California, San Diego (1986).

Eligibility/Limitations The most frequent recipients of support for research are academic institutions and nonprofit research groups. In special circumstances, grants are also awarded to other types of institutions and to individuals. In these cases, preliminary inquiry should be made to the appropriate program officer before a proposal is submitted. Support may be provided for projects involving a single scientist or a number of scientists. Awards are made for projects confined to a single disciplinary area and for those that cross or merge disciplinary interests.

Application Information For additional information contact the Division of Molecular Biosciences.

Deadline(s) Proposals may be submitted at any time; allow about six months for review. Proposals to be funded in a particular fiscal year (ending September 30) normally should be received no later than January of that year. Target dates are published in the NSF *Bulletin.*

Subject Term(s) Individuals, Eligibility of; Metabolic Biology

266. National Science Foundation

Directorate for Biological, Behavioral, and Social Sciences, Division of Social and Economic Science
1800 G Street, NW
Washington, DC 20550
(202) 357-7326

Geography and Regional Science Program

CFDA Program Number 47.051

Program Description The Geography and Regional Science Program supports basic research on location and its effects. The program promotes a deeper understanding of the causes and consequences of geographical differences in economic, social, cultural, and physical phenomena; of the ramifications of location; of the interconnections and interactions among places and regions; and of the interrelations between man and environment. Research on a rich diversity of specific topics may qualify for support if it enlarges geographical theory and its applications.

Sample Grants Foreign travel and activity support for research on ecological space and resource perceptions among the Gorotire Kayapo Indians of the Brazilian Amazon, $55,816 to the University of Maryland, Baltimore (1986).

Eligibility/Limitations The most frequent recipients of support for research are academic institutions and nonprofit research groups. In special circumstances, grants are also awarded to other types of institutions and to individuals. In these cases, preliminary inquiry should be made to the appropriate program officer before a proposal is submitted. Support may be provided for projects involving a single scientist or a number of scientists. Awards are made for projects confined to a single disciplinary area and for those that cross or merge disciplinary interests.

Fiscal Information Level of support varies from project to project. Although most grants are for much shorter periods, up to five years of support may be requested. Grant funds may be used for paying direct and indirect costs necessary to conduct research or studies. Institutions are required to share in the cost of each research project. This may be accomplished by a contribution to any cost element, direct or indirect.

Application Information Address inquiries to the program director. Guidelines are contained in the publication "Grants for Research and Education in Science and Engineering."

Deadline(s) Proposals for research support may be submitted at any time. Submission target dates/deadlines are published in the *Bulletin*, available free from Public Affairs and Publications, NSF. To allow time for adequate planning, the following schedule is offered as a guide: proposals should arrive at the Data Support Services Station of the foundation no later than January 1 for funds needed on or after July-August; August 15 for funds needed on or after January-February.

Additional Information Proposals for doctoral dissertation support, research conferences, the acquisition of specialized research and computation equipment, group international travel, and data resource development will be considered.

Subject Term(s) Doctoral Dissertation Support; Individuals, Eligibility of; Seminars and Conferences; Travel Support Abroad; Geography; Equipment Acquisition

267. National Science Foundation

Directorate for Biological, Behavioral, and Social Sciences, Division of Social and Economic Science
1800 G Street, NW
Washington, DC 20550
(202) 357-9677

History and Philosophy of Science Program

CFDA Program Number 47.051

Program Description The History and Philosophy of Science Program supports research having clear and direct relevance to the understanding of science (including the physical, biological, and social sciences), scientific change, and technological development. This includes studies of the nature and development of scientific theories and methodology, the interactions between science and technology, and social and intellectual factors that affect scientific development. (The history of medicine is normally supported by NIH.)

Sample Grants Foreign travel support for a study of Latin America and the world eugenics movement, $30,000 to Columbia University (1986). Foreign travel support for a study of scientists, engineers, and urban technology in Mexico, $7,624 to an individual scholar (1986).

Eligibility/Limitations The most frequent recipients of support for research are academic institutions and nonprofit research groups. In special circumstances, grants are also awarded to other types of institutions and to individuals. In these cases, preliminary inquiry should be made to the appropriate program officer before a proposal is submitted. Support may be provided for projects involving a single scientist or a number of scientists. Awards are made for projects confined to a single disciplinary area and for those that cross or merge disciplinary interests.

Fiscal Information Level of support varies from project to project. Although most grants are for much shorter periods, up to five years of support may be requested. Grant funds may be used for paying direct and indirect costs necessary to conduct research or studies. Institutions are required to share in the cost of each research project. This may be accomplished by a contribution to any cost element, direct or indirect.

Application Information Address inquiries to the program director. Guidelines are contained in the publication "Grants for Research and Education in Science and Engineering."

Deadline(s) Proposals for research support may be submitted at any time. Submission target dates/deadlines are published in the *Bulletin*, available free from Public Affairs and Publications, NSF. To allow time for adequate planning, the following schedule is offered as a guide: proposals should arrive at the Data Support Services Station of the foundation no later than January 1 for funds needed on or after July-August; August 15 for funds needed on or after January-February.

Additional Information Proposals for doctoral dissertation support, research conferences, the acquisition of specialized research and computation equipment, group international travel, and data resource development will be considered.

Subject Term(s) Doctoral Dissertation Support; Individuals, Eligibility of; Seminars and Conferences; Travel Support Abroad; History of Science; Science and Technology; Equipment Acquisition

268. National Science Foundation

Directorate for Biological, Behavioral, and Social Sciences, Division of Social and Economic Science
1800 G Street, NW
Washington, DC 20550
(202) 357-9567

Law and Social Sciences Program

CFDA Program Number 47.051

Program Description The Law and Social Sciences Program supports social scientific research on law and law-like systems of rules. Included are studies of the processes that enhance or diminish the impact of law; causes and consequences of variations and changes in legal institutions; personal, social, and cultural factors affecting the use of law; dynamics and effects of dispute processing and alternative means of dispute resolution; determinants of decision making in legal forums and contexts; and conditions and processes that create transformations between formal legal rules and law in action.

Eligibility/Limitations The most frequent recipients of support for research are academic institutions and nonprofit research groups. In special circumstances, grants are also awarded to other types of institutions and to individuals. In these cases, preliminary inquiry should be made to the appropriate program officer before a proposal is submitted. Support may be provided for projects involving a single scientist or a number of scientists. Awards are made for projects confined to a single disciplinary area and for those that cross or merge disciplinary interests.

Fiscal Information Level of support varies from project to project. Although most grants are for much shorter periods, up to five years of support may be requested. Grant funds may be used for paying direct and indirect costs necessary to conduct research or studies. Institutions are required to share in the cost of each research project. This may be accomplished by a contribution to any cost element, direct or indirect.

Application Information Address inquiries to the program director. Guidelines are contained in the publication "Grants for Research and Education in Science and Engineering."

Deadline(s) Proposals for research support may be submitted at any time. Submission target dates/deadlines are published in the *Bulletin*, available free from Public Affairs and Publications, NSF. To allow time for adequate planning, the following schedule is offered as a guide: proposals should arrive at the Data Support Services Station of the foundation no later than January 1 for funds needed on or after July-August; August 15 for funds needed on or after January-February.

Additional Information Proposals for doctoral dissertation support, research conferences, the acquisition of specialized research and computation equipment, group international travel, and data resource development will be considered.

Subject Term(s) Doctoral Dissertation Support; Individuals, Eligibility of; Seminars and Conferences; Travel Support Abroad; Law; Social Sciences; Equipment Acquisition

269. National Science Foundation

Directorate for Biological, Behavioral, and Social Sciences, Division of Social and Economic Science
1800 G Street, NW
Washington, DC 20550
(202) 357-9406

Political Science

CFDA Program Number 47.051

Program Description The Political Science Program supports research on the political forms and processes by which societies coordinate their activities through governments, including studies of governmental institutions and their effects on social life, the effects of structural factors on political participation, conflict and political instability, and how political processes are modified in response to social and economic change.

Sample Grants Foreign travel and activity support of a study of inequality, violence, and regime stability in Costa Rica, $49,997 to the University of Arizona (1986).

Eligibility/Limitations The most frequent recipients of support for research are academic institutions and nonprofit research groups. In special circumstances, grants are also awarded to other types of institutions and to individuals. In these cases, preliminary inquiry should be made to the appropriate program officer before a proposal is submitted. Support may be provided for projects involving a single scientist or a number of scientists. Awards are made for projects confined to a single disciplinary area and for those that cross or merge disciplinary interests.

Fiscal Information Level of support varies from project to project. Although most grants are for much shorter periods, up to five years of support may be requested. Grant funds may be used for paying direct and indirect costs necessary to conduct research or studies. Institutions are required to share in the cost of each research project. This may be accomplished by a contribution to any cost element, direct or indirect.

Application Information Address inquiries to the program director. Guidelines are contained in the publication "Grants for Research and Education in Science and Engineering."

Deadline(s) Proposals for research support may be submitted at any time. Submission target dates/deadlines are published in the *Bulletin*, available free from Public Affairs and Publications, NSF. To allow time for adequate planning, the following schedule is offered as a guide: proposals should arrive at the Data Support Services Station of the foundation no later than January 1 for funds needed on or after July-August; August 15 for funds needed on or after January-February.

Additional Information Proposals for doctoral dissertation support, research conferences, the acquisition of specialized research and computation equipment, group international travel, and data resource development will be considered.

Subject Term(s) Doctoral Dissertation Support; Individuals, Eligibility of; Travel Support Abroad; Seminars and Conferences; Political Science; Government; Equipment Acquisition

270. National Science Foundation

Directorate for Biological, Behavioral, and Social Sciences, Division of Social and Economic Science
1800 G Street, NW
Washington, DC 20550
(202) 357-7802

Sociology Program

CFDA Program Number 47.051

Program Description The Sociology Program supports research on problems of human social organization, demography, and the processes of individual and institutional change. The program encourages theoretically focused empirical investigations aimed at improving the explanation of fundamental social processes. Included is research on decision making, organizational change, social movements, urbanization, labor force processes, resource allocation, reward distribution, social networks, socialization, and the sociology of science.

Eligibility/Limitations The most frequent recipients of support for research are academic institutions and nonprofit research groups. In special circumstances, grants are also awarded to other types of institutions and to individuals. In these cases, preliminary inquiry should be made to the appropriate program officer before a proposal is submitted. Support may be provided for projects involving a single scientist or a number of scientists. Awards are made for projects confined to a single disciplinary area and for those that cross or merge disciplinary interests.

Fiscal Information Level of support varies from project to project. Although most grants are for much shorter periods, up to five years of support may be requested. Grant funds may be used for paying direct and indirect costs necessary to conduct research or studies. Institutions are required to share in the cost of each research project. This may be accomplished by a contribution to any cost element, direct or indirect.

Application Information Address inquiries to the program director. Guidelines are contained in the publication "Grants for Research and Education in Science and Engineering."

Deadline(s) Proposals for research support may be submitted at any time. Submission target dates/deadlines are published in the *Bulletin*, available free from Public Affairs and Publications, NSF. To allow time for adequate planning, the following schedule is offered as a guide: proposals should arrive at the Data Support Services Station of the foundation no later than January 1 for funds needed on or after July-August; August 15 for funds needed on or after January-February.

Additional Information Proposals for doctoral dissertation support, research conferences, the acquisition of specialized research and computation equipment, group international travel, and data resource development will be considered.

Subject Term(s) Doctoral Dissertation Support; Individuals, Eligibility of; Seminars and Conferences; Travel Support Abroad; Sociology; Equipment Acquisition

271. National Science Foundation

Directorate for Biological, Behavioral, and Social Sciences, Divisions of Cellular and Molecular Biosciences
1800 G Street, NW
Washington, DC 20550
(202) 357-9782 (Molecular) or (202) 357-0127 (Cellular)

Postdoctoral Research Fellowships in Plant Biology

CFDA Program Number 47.051

Program Description Supported by both Cellular Biosciences and Molecular Biosciences, this initiative is designed to encourage a wide range of biological and physical scientists to pursue research careers in the plant sciences, and to let recipients choose research environments that will be most beneficial to their future scientific development. Applicants should present a research plan that contributes to a basic understanding of plant biology at the molecular, cellular, or whole plant level, preferably in a discipline or subfield other than that of their doctoral training. Fellowships are awarded for scientific research at any appropriate nonprofit United States institution or nonprofit foreign institution.

Eligibility/Limitations Applicants must be nationals of the United States; have earned the doctoral degree in a biological science, physical science, or engineering; have made prior arrangements for research and training in plant biology with a scientific advisor at the institution where the fellowship is to be held; and have interests in plant research that fall within the program areas of the Divisions of Molecular Biosciences and Cellular Biosciences.

Fiscal Information The fellowship is initially awarded for two years. Under special circumstances, during the second year, a fellow may apply for extension of the fellowship for an additional year. The fellowship provides a stipend, an institutional allowance, and a special allowance to aid in defraying costs associated with research. The stipend is paid at the rate of $1,800 per month; there is no dependency allowance. The institutional allowance of $200 per month of tenure is for partial reimbursement of expenses incurred in support of research and will be paid directly to the institution. The special allowance of $200 per month is expendable at the fellow's discretion and is intended to be used for scientific supplies, special travel, publication expenses, and other research-related costs.

Application Information Application forms and instructions are available upon request. Local reproductions of all forms are acceptable. Completed applications and supporting materials are to be sent to NSF Postdoctoral Research Fellowships in Plant Biology, DMB and DCB Room 325, NSF.

Deadline(s) All application materials must be received by January 12.

Subject Term(s) Biology; Fellowships; Postdoctoral Support; Botany

272. National Science Foundation

Directorate for Engineering, Division of Fundamental Research in Emerging and Critical Engineering Systems
1800 G Street, NW
Washington, DC 20550
(202) 357-9545

Earthquake Hazards Mitigation

CFDA Program Number 47.041

Program Description Research on mitigating earthquake hazards is conducted in four categories: siting and geotechnical systems, structural systems, architectural and mechanical systems, and earthquake systems integration. Basic science research in earthquake hazard mitigation is supported in the Earth Sciences Division of NSF's Directorate for Geosciences.

Sample Grants Support for evaluation of design and analysis techniques for masonry structures based on performance in the Chilean earthquake of March 3, 1985, $99,828 to Computech (1986). Support for study of strong motion array along the Mexican subduction thrust, $235,932 to the University of California, San Diego (1986). Support for investigation of two buildings shaken during the September 19, 1985 Mexico earthquake, $169,967 to the University of Illinois, Urbana (1986). Support for experimental and analytical studies of promising techniques for the repair and retrofitting of buildings, $289,992 to the University of California, Berkeley (1986).

Eligibility/Limitations The most frequent recipients of support for research are academic institutions, although awards are occasionally made to profit-making organizations, individuals, and government agencies at all levels. Cooperative projects between industry and university groups, especially those advocating a systems approach, are encouraged.

Application Information Application information and guidelines are available from the program.

Deadline(s) Research proposals may be submitted at any time. Those received too late for review in a particular fiscal year (ending September 30) are considered in the following year if the program is continued. If a specific start date is important, explain the circumstances and allow at least six months lead time for review and processing.

Subject Term(s) Individuals, Eligibility of; Engineering; Earthquake Mitigation

273. National Science Foundation

Directorate for Engineering, Division of Fundamental Research in Emerging and Critical Engineering Systems
1800 G Street, NW
Washington, DC 20550
(202) 357-9545

Environmental Engineering

CFDA Program Number 47.041

Program Description Environmental engineering research activities deal with the impact of human activities that adversely affect water, air, and land. The problems of environmental quality and water-borne pollutants are addressed by research activities in the hydrodynamics of mixing, diffusion, dispersion, and sedimentation; the chemical reactions in water, on land, and in the air; and the biological activity of plants and animals on land and in water. Other research activities are directed toward investigating alternative chemical manufacturing processes that would produce less hazardous wastes; converting hazardous wastes into useful by-products; and using recombinant DNA techniques to produce organisms for enhancing the treatment of hazardous wastes.

Sample Grants Foreign travel support to attend the fourth River Basin Management Conference, Sao Paulo, Brazil, $1,107 (1986). Foreign travel support to attend the 13th Biennial International Conference-International Association on Water Pollution Research and Control, in Sao Paulo and Rio de Janiero, Brazil, $1,200 (1986).

Eligibility/Limitations The most frequent recipients of support for research are academic institutions, although awards are occasionally made to profit-making organizations, individuals, and government agencies at all levels. Cooperative projects between industry and university groups, especially those advocating a systems approach, are encouraged.

Application Information Application information and guidelines are available from the program.

Deadline(s) Research proposals may be submitted at any time. Those received too late for review in a particular fiscal year (ending September 30) are considered in the following year if the program is continued. If a specific start date is important, explain the circumstances and allow at least six months lead time for review and processing.

Subject Term(s) Individuals, Eligibility of; Engineering; Environmental Engineering

274. National Science Foundation

Directorate for Geosciences, Division of Atmospheric Sciences
1800 G Street, NW
Washington, DC 20550
(202) 357-9874

Aeronomy Program

Program Description The overall objective of the Directorate for Geosciences is to increase scientific knowledge of the natural environment on earth and in space and of the various effects of human activity that interacts with this environment. The purpose of the Division of Atmospheric Sciences is to continue to build a base of fundamental knowledge on the atmospheres of the earth, other planets, and the sun. The Aeronomy Program supports research in: upper and middle atmosphere phenomena of ionization, recombination, chemical reaction, photoemission, and transport; the transport of energy, momentum, and mass in the mesosphere-thermosphere-ionosphere system (includes the processes involved and the coupling of this global system to the stratosphere below and magnetosphere above); and the plasma physics of phenomena manifested in the upper atmosphere-ionosphere system, including magnetospheric coupling efforts.

Sample Grants Support for studies of global electrodynamics and high latitude irregularities, $80,000 to Cornell University (1986). Support for experimental and theoretical investigations in aeronomy, $125,000 to the University of Michigan, Ann Arbor (1986). Support for airglow and auroral studies of the earth's ionosphere, $115,000 to the University of Pittsburgh (1986). Support for multiexperimental studies of the wind and wave patterns in the upper atmosphere and ionosphere, $105,000 to Cornell University (1986). Support for radar studies of the equatorial ionosphere, $105,000 to the University of Illinois, Urbana (1986).

Eligibility/Limitations Proposals may be submitted by academic institutions, non-academic and nonprofit research organizations, profitmaking and private research organizations, and individuals.

Application Information For more information contact the Division of Atmospheric Sciences.

Deadline(s) Proposals may be submitted at any time during the year for all research. Allow about six to nine months for review and processing of proposals.

Subject Term(s) Individuals, Eligibility of; Atmospheric Sciences; Aeronomy

275. National Science Foundation

Directorate for Geosciences, Division of Atmospheric Sciences
1800 G Street, NW
Washington, DC 20550
(202) 357-9874

Atmospheric Chemistry

Program Description The overall objective of the Directorate for Geosciences is to increase scientific knowledge of the natural environment on earth and in space and of the various effects of human activity that interacts with this environment. The purpose of the Division of Atmospheric Sciences is to continue to build a base of fundamental knowledge on the atmospheres of the earth, other planets, and the sun. The Atmospheric Chemistry Program supports the measurement and modeling of concentration and distribution of gases and aerosols in the lower and middle atmosphere; chemical reactions among atmospheric species; sources and sinks of important trace gases and aerosols; aqueous phase atmospheric chemistry; transport of gases and aerosols between the troposphere and stratosphere; and improved methods for measuring the concentrations of trace species and their flow through the atmosphere.

Sample Grants Foreign travel and activity support for a study of mass transformations in tropical forest burning, $110,000 to the University of California, Santa Barbara (1986).

Eligibility/Limitations Proposals may be submitted by academic institutions, nonacademic and nonprofit research organizations, profitmaking and private research organizations, and individuals.

Application Information For more information contact the Division of Atmospheric Sciences.

Deadline(s) Proposals may be submitted at any time during the year for all research. Allow about six to nine months for review and processing of proposals.

Subject Term(s) Individuals, Eligibility of; Atmospheric Sciences; Atmospheric Chemistry

276. National Science Foundation

Directorate for Geosciences, Division of Atmospheric Sciences
1800 G Street, NW
Washington, DC 20550
(202) 357-9874

Centers and Facilities

Program Description NSF supports four large incoherent-scatter radar facilities located along a longitudinal chain from Greenland to Peru. Upper atmospheric facilities (UAF) located in Latin America and the Caribbean are the Arecibo Observatory at Arecibo, Puerto Rico and the Jicamarca Radio Observatory, at the magnetic equator in Jicamarca, Peru. The major goal of the UAF program is to promote basic research on the structure and dynamics of the earth's upper atmosphere by (1) supporting the operation and scientific research of the incoherent-scatter radars which comprise the longitudinal chain and (2) ensuring that these radars are maintained as state-of-the-art research tools available to all interested and qualified scientists.

Sample Grants Foreign travel and activity support for a cooperative agreement to support aeronomical and meterological research at the Jicamarca Radio Observatory, $500,000 to Cornell University (1986).

Eligibility/Limitations UAF facilities are available on a competitive basis to all qualified scientists. Use is based on scientific merit of the proposed research, capabilities of the radars to carry out the proposed observations, and availability of the requested time.

Application Information For more information contact the Director, NAIC (for Arecibo Observatory), Cornell University, Ithaca, New York, 14853 or Jicamarca Radio Observatory Project, Department of Electrical Engineering, Cornell University, Ithaca, New York, 14853.

Deadline(s) Contact the division for deadline information.

Subject Term(s) Individuals, Eligibility of; Atmospheric Sciences

277. National Science Foundation

Directorate for Geosciences, Division of Earth Sciences
1800 G Street, NW
Washington, DC 20550
(202) 357-7721

Continental Lithosphere Program

CFDA Program Number 47.050

Program Description The objective of the Division of Earth Sciences (EAR) is to achieve a greater understanding about the physical structure and chemical composition of the earth and the geological processes that have led to its evolution. The focus is primarily on the constitution of the earth's lithosphere, which includes the upper mantle, crust, continents, and plates. Emphasis is on the application of plate tectonics to the study of the origin and evolution of the continents. The Continental Lithosphere Program supports multidiscipline, consortia-type research that focuses on a better understanding of the structure, composition, and evolution of the continental lithosphere. Topics proposed must have the endorsement of a major segment of the earth science community.

Sample Grants Foreign activity support for an electromagnetic study of the lithosphere and asthenosphere beneath the Juan de Fuca Plate and the adjacent continent-magnetotelluric profiling phase, $120,000 to San Diego State University (1986). Support for Benioff zone mapping and deep seismic profiles in Mexico (DSPM), $17,753 to the University of California, Santa Cruz (1986).

Eligibility/Limitations Proposals may be submitted by academic institutions, non-academic and nonprofit research organizations, and individuals.

Application Information For more information contact the Division of Earth Sciences.

Deadline(s) The program deadline dates for submission of proposals will be August 15 and January 15.

Subject Term(s) Earth Sciences; Individuals, Eligibility of

278. National Science Foundation

Directorate for Geosciences, Division of Earth Sciences
1800 G Street, NW
Washington, DC 20550
(202) 357-7915

Crustal Structure and Tectonics

CFDA Program Number 47.050

Program Description The objective of the Division of Earth Sciences (EAR) is to achieve a greater understanding about the physical structure and chemical composition of the earth and the geological processes that have led to its evolution. The focus is primarily on the constitution of the earth's lithosphere, which includes the upper mantle, crust, continents, and plates. Emphasis is on the application of plate tectonics to the study of the origin and evolution of the continents. The Crustal Structure and Tectonics Program supports investigation of rock deformation and deformation mechanics by field, laboratory, and theoretical techniques. Investigation includes reconstruction of past crustal plate configurations, and use of techniques from structural geology, mapping, seismology, geochronology, and paleomagnetic dating.

Sample Grants Foreign travel and activity support for paleomagnetic studies in the southern Andean Orogen, $31,789 to Western Washington University (1986). Foreign travel and activity support for a study of the origin and evolution of disrupted Blueschist-facies and lower pressure metamorphic rocks on Cedros Island, Central Baja California, $90,074 to Stanford University (1986). Foreign travel and activity support for a study of plateau uplift and kinematics over the transition from steep to flat subduction in the southern Puna, northwest Argentina, $94,558 to Cornell University (1986).

Eligibility/Limitations Proposals may be submitted by academic institutions, non-academic and nonprofit research organizations, and individuals.

Application Information For more information contact the Division of Earth Sciences.

Deadline(s) The program deadline dates for submission of proposals will be August 15 and January 15.

Subject Term(s) Earth Sciences; Individuals, Eligibility of

279. National Science Foundation

Directorate for Geosciences, Division of Earth Sciences
1800 G Street, NW
Washington, DC 20550
(202) 357-7355

Experimental and Theoretical Geophysics

CFDA Program Number 47.050

Program Description The objective of the Division of Earth Sciences (EAR) is to achieve a greater understanding about the physical structure and chemical composition of the earth and the geological processes that have led to its evolution. The focus is primarily on the constitution of the earth's lithosphere, which includes the upper mantle, crust, continents, and plates. Emphasis is on the application of plate tectonics to the study of the origin and evolution of the continents. The Experimental and Theoretical Geophysics Program supports research on the physical properties of the solid earth. Areas of interest include studies in geodesy, electromagnetism, paleomagnetism, convection, heat flow, and gravity, as well as theoretical and laboratory modeling of geophysical processes.

Sample Grants Foreign travel and activity support for a comparative three-dimensional magnetotelluric characterization of the Salton Sea Scientific Drilling Project (SSSDP) and Cerro Prieto, Mexico, $94,323 to San Diego State University (1986).

Eligibility/Limitations Proposals may be submitted by academic institutions, non-academic and nonprofit research organizations, and individuals.

Application Information For more information contact the Division of Earth Sciences.

Deadline(s) The program deadline dates for submission of proposals will be August 15 and January 15.

Subject Term(s) Earth Sciences; Individuals, Eligibility of; Geophysics

280. National Science Foundation

Directorate for Geosciences, Division of Earth Sciences
1800 G Street, NW
Washington, DC 20550
(202) 357-7911

Petrogenesis and Mineral Resources

CFDA Program Number 47.050

Program Description The objective of the Division of Earth Sciences (EAR) is to achieve a greater understanding about the physical structure and chemical composition of the earth and the geological processes that have led to its evolution. The focus is primarily on the constitution of the earth's lithosphere, which includes the upper mantle, crust, continents, and plates. Emphasis is on the application of plate tectonics to the study of the origin and evolution of the continents. The Petrogenesis and Mineral Resources Program supports integration of laboratory, field, and experimental data to infer conditions and process that formed crustal rocks, minerals, and ores. Studies involve igneous and metamorphic petrology, rock-water interactions, economic geology, and studies of active and fossil magma-hydrothermal systems.

Sample Grants Support for petrologic studies in northwestern Mexico and adjacent west Texas (collaborative research), $55,635 to the University of California, Santa Cruz (1986). Support for collaborative petrological, geochemical and isotopic investigation of Late Cenozoic volcanism in the Andes of Chile, $62,100 to Southern Methodist University (1986).

Eligibility/Limitations Proposals may be submitted by academic institutions, non-academic and nonprofit research organizations, and individuals.

Application Information For more information contact the Division of Earth Sciences, NSF.

Deadline(s) The program deadline dates for submission of proposals will be August 15 and January 15.

Subject Term(s) Earth Sciences; Individuals, Eligibility of; Petrogenesis

281. National Science Foundation

Directorate for Geosciences, Division of Earth Sciences
1800 G Street, NW
Washington, DC 20550
(202) 357-7356

Seismology

CFDA Program Number 47.050

Program Description The objective of the Division of Earth Sciences (EAR) is to achieve a greater understanding about the physical structure and chemical composition of the earth and the geological processes that have led to its evolution. The focus is primarily on the constitution of the earth's lithosphere, which includes the upper mantle, crust, continents, and plates. Emphasis is on the application of plate tectonics to the study of the origin and evolution of the continents. The Seismology Program supports research in the nature and occurrence of earthquakes, the propagation of seismic waves within the earth, and the use of seismological data and technique to determine the internal structure and constitution of the earth.

Sample Grants Foreign travel and activity support for study of the rupture process of the March 3, 1985 Chile earthquake: implications for plate dynamics and earthquake prediction, $50,000 to the Massachusetts Institute of Technology (1986). Foreign travel and activity support for study of upper mantle and crustal seismicity and structure in the Central Andean Region of low-angle subduction, $71,400 to Cornell University (1986). Foreign travel and activity support for a portable digital seismic array experiment in the Central Andean Region of South America, $70,000 to Memphis State University (1986). Foreign travel and activity support for a study of site, path, and source-scaling effects on strong ground motion during the Michoacan earthquake of September 19, 1985, $77,000 to the University of Southern California (1986).

Eligibility/Limitations Proposals may be submitted by academic institutions, non-academic and nonprofit research organizations, and individuals.

Application Information For more information contact the Division of Earth Sciences.

Deadline(s) The program deadline dates for submission of proposals will be August 15 and January 15.

Subject Term(s) Earth Sciences; Individuals, Eligibility of; Seismology

282. National Science Foundation

Directorate for Geosciences, Division of Earth Sciences
1800 G Street, NW
Washington, DC 20550
(202) 357-7806

Stratigraphy and Paleontology

CFDA Program Number 47.050

Program Description The objective of the Division of Earth Sciences (EAR) is to achieve a greater understanding about the physical structure and chemical composition of the earth and the geological processes that have led to its evolution. The focus is primarily on the constitution of the earth's lithosphere, which includes the upper mantle, crust, continents, and plates. Emphasis is on the application of plate tectonics to the study of the origin and evolution of the continents. The Stratigraphy and Paleontology Program supports research on sedimentary rocks and fossils used as a framework to interpret past conditions and processes active on the earth's surface. Areas of research supported include sedimentology, biostratigraphy, paleolimnology, micropaleontology, paleoecology, and vertebrate and invertebrate paleontology.

Sample Grants Support for study of Late Cretaceous and Early Tertiary Molluscan faunas and biostratigraphy of the Magallanes Basin, South America, $83,600 to the University of South Carolina (1986). Foreign travel and activity support for study of Oliogocene chronology and vertebrate faunas of Bolivia, $52,400 to the University of Florida (1986). Foreign travel and activity support for a study of Cenozoic sedimentary and volcanic stratigraphy of southwestern Isla Tiburon, State of Sonora, Mexico, $15,000 to San Diego State University (1986). Foreign travel and activity support for study of stratigraphy, petrology, and structure of Permian and Triassic rocks of southern Coahuila, Mexico, $8,340 to University of Wisconsin, Oshkosh (1986). Foreign travel and activity support for a study of the evolution of neogene coastal upwelling and littoral ecosystems within Andean forearc basins: a study of the Pisco Formation (southern Peru), $48,700 to Oregon State University (1986).

Eligibility/Limitations Proposals may be submitted by academic institutions, non-academic and nonprofit research organizations, and individuals.

Application Information For more information contact the Division of Earth Sciences.

Deadline(s) The program deadline dates for submission of proposals will be August 15 and January 15.

Subject Term(s) Earth Sciences; Individuals, Eligibility of; Stratigraphy; Paleontology

283. National Science Foundation

Directorate for Geosciences, Division of Earth Sciences
1800 G Street, NW
Washington, DC 20550
(202) 357-7866

Surficial Processes

CFDA Program Number 47.050

Program Description The objective of the Division of Earth Sciences (EAR) is to achieve a greater understanding about the physical structure and chemical composition of the earth and the geological processes that have led to its evolution. The focus is primarily on the constitution of the earth's lithosphere, which includes the upper mantle, crust, continents, and plates. Emphasis is on the application of plate tectonics to the study of the origin and evolution of the continents. The Surficial Processes Program supports research on physical and chemical processes active at or near the earth's surface. Research interests include geomorphology and quaternary geology, low-temperature geochemistry, surface waters and groundwaters, glaciology, soil genesis and classification, fossil fuel generation, and the study of geologic hazards.

Sample Grants Support for research of tropical glaciers and climate, $45,102 to the University of Wisconsin, Madison (1986). Support for the Holocene history of a wet and a dry river valley and adjacent coastal zone in northern Peru as a function of geologic and human factors, $43,057 to Stanford University (1986). Support for work on the Orinoco River: a study of the relationship between river load and soil chemistry, $40,371 to Princeton University (1986). Foreign travel and activity support for a Quaternary history of Argentine Patagonia: establishment of an absolute age-controlled glacial chronology for the southern Andes, $71,400 to Lehigh University (1986).

Eligibility/Limitations Proposals may be submitted by academic institutions, non-academic and nonprofit research organizations, and individuals.

Application Information For more information contact the Division of Earth Sciences.

Deadline(s) The program deadline dates for submission of proposals will be August 15 and January 15.

Subject Term(s) Earth Sciences; Individuals, Eligibility of; Geology

284. National Science Foundation

Directorate for Geosciences, Division of Earth Sciences
1800 G Street, NW
Washington, DC 20550
(202) 357-7916

Volcanology and Mantle Geochemistry

CFDA Program Number 47.050

Program Description The objective of the Division of Earth Sciences (EAR) is to achieve a greater understanding about the physical structure and chemical composition of the earth and the geological processes that have led to its evolution. The focus is primarily on the constitution of the earth's lithosphere, which includes the upper mantle, crust, continents, and plates. Emphasis is on the application of plate tectonics to the study of the origin and evolution of the continents. The Volcanology and Mantle Geochemistry Program supports research on all aspects of volcanology and volcanic rocks, the geochemistry and petrology of mantle samples and meteorites, and extraterrestrial materials. Use is made of geochemical and isotopic techniques, modeling, and the theoretical studies to understand the origin and chemical evolution of the earth—especially its mantle—and the planets.

Sample Grants Support for geochemical and petrologic studies of recent volcanic rocks associated with plate convergence in Chile (33-42'S), $90,000 to Massachusetts Institute of Technology (1986). Foreign travel support for an emergency mission to study gasses and mudflows of Volcan Nevado Del Ruiz, Colombia, $6,800 to Louisiana State University, Baton Rouge (1986). Foreign travel support for study of the influence of magma properties on the dynamics of explosive eruptions, $3,000 to the University of Rhode Island (1986). Support for study of the petrology and volcanic evolution of the Galapagos Platform, $86,000 to the University of Oregon, Eugene (1986).

Eligibility/Limitations Proposals may be submitted by academic institutions, nonacademic and nonprofit research organizations, and individuals.

Application Information For more information contact the Division of Earth Sciences.

Deadline(s) The program deadline dates for submission of proposals are August 15 and January 15.

Subject Term(s) Earth Sciences; Individuals, Eligibility of; Geology; Volcanology

285. National Science Foundation

Directorate for Geosciences, Division of Ocean Sciences
1800 G Street, NW
Washington, DC 20550
(202) 357-7924

Biological Oceanography Program

Program Description This division supports research to improve understanding of the sea and ocean basins. A broad range of projects are supported dealing with physical, chemical, geological, and biological processes in the ocean. The Biological Oceanography Program supports research on ocean productivity; distribution, abundance, physiology, and life history of pelagic, coastal, and deep sea marine organisms, and their interactions with their environments; structures of pelagic and benthic food chains; primary and secondary production; interactions between deep sea biological processes and the ocean ecosystem; and specialization of deep sea organisms.

Sample Grants Support for a study of the ecology of Caribbean Cryptic Coral Reef communities, $40,564 to American Museum of Natural History (1986). Support for study of long distance dispersal of planktonic larvae and the biogeography of sublittoral benthic invertebrates on islands of the Central Pacific Ocean, $73,247 to Woods Hole Oceanographic Institute (1986). Support for a study of the biology of gelatinous zooplankton: comparative studies on oceanic and neritic Salps; and further investigations on mesopelagic organisms, using a submersible, $144,193 to Woods Hole Oceanographic Institute (1986). Support for a study of the physiological ecology of Radiolaria, $166,490 to Columbia University (1986).

Eligibility/Limitations Individual scientists, small groups of cooperating scientists, and some large coordinated projects are eligible to apply. Grants are awarded on the basis of competitive peer review of unsolicited research proposals.

Fiscal Information Large and small grants of several months' to several years' duration are awarded.

Application Information For additional information contact the director of the Division of Ocean Sciences.

Deadline(s) Proposals may be submitted at any time. Allow about six months for review and processing. Proposals that require the use of ships should be submitted by February 1 (preferred) or June 1, so that timely decisions can be made on ship support and schedules.

Subject Term(s) Ocean Sciences; Individuals, Eligibility of; Oceanography

286. National Science Foundation

Directorate for Geosciences, Division of Ocean Sciences
1800 G Street, NW
Washington, DC 20550
(202) 357-7924

Chemical Oceanography Program

Program Description This division supports research to improve understanding of the sea and ocean basins. A broad range of projects are supported dealing with physical, chemical, geological, and biological processes in the ocean. The Chemical Oceanography Program supports research on the physical and chemical properties of seawater, including kinetic and thermodynamic equilibria of chemical species and compounds in seawater; fluxes between seafloor sediments, their interstitial waters, and overlying seawater; fates of materials deposited on the sea floor; alterations of material moving through the ocean; interactions and interdependencies between chemical processes and marine organisms; and air-sea exchanges of manmade and naturally mobilized chemicals and chemical properties of the ocean surface.

Sample Grants Support for a study of pore water chemistry of rare earth elements in oceanic sediments, $78,674 to Woods Hole Oceanographic Institute and $40,336 to Harvard University (1986). Foreign activity support for an oceanic flux program: modes and rates of particulate transfer to the Deep Sargasso Sea, $160,593 to Woods Hole Oceanographic Institute (1986). Support for a collaborative project: calcium carbonate preservation in the deep sea, $91,128 to the University of California, San Diego (1986). Foreign activity support for biogeochemical studies of organic matter in recent and ancient sediments of organic-rich depositional environments, $235,977 to the Woods Hole Oceanographic Institute (1986).

Eligibility/Limitations Individual scientists, small groups of cooperating scientists, and some large coordinated projects are eligible to apply. Grants are awarded on the basis of competitive peer review of unsolicited research proposals.

Fiscal Information Large and small grants of several months' to several years' duration are awarded.

Application Information For additional information contact the director of the Division of Ocean Sciences.

Deadline(s) Proposals may be submitted at any time. Allow about six months for review and processing. Proposals that require the use of ships should be submitted by February 1 (preferred) or June 1, so that timely decisions can be made on ship support and schedules.

Subject Term(s) Ocean Sciences; Individuals, Eligibility of; Oceanography

287. National Science Foundation

Directorate for Geosciences, Division of Ocean Sciences
1800 G Street, NW
Washington, DC 20550
(202) 357-7924

Marine Geology and Geophysics

Program Description This division supports research to improve understanding of the sea and ocean basins. A broad range of projects are supported dealing with physical, chemical, geological, and biological processes in the ocean. The Marine Geology and Geophysics Program supports research on the structure of continental margins, oceanic rise systems, and deep sea sedimentary basins; evolution of ocean basins; processes controlling exchanges of heat and chemical elements between seawater and oceanic rocks; tectonic and volcanic activity at mid-ocean ridges; chemical and mineralogic variations in marine sediments; deposition, erosion, and distribution of marine sediments; geologic and oceanographic processes controlling sedimentary systems; past oceanic circulation patterns and climates; evolution of microfossil groups; paleoenvironmental controls on fossil groups and sediment types; and interactions of continental and oceanic geologic processes.

Sample Grants Support of study of magmatism associated with the opening of the South Atlantic Ocean, $70,133 to North Carolina State University (1986). Support for study of sedimentary facies of the Amazon Deep Sea Fan, $100,629 to Columbia University (1986).

Eligibility/Limitations Individual scientists, small groups of cooperating scientists, and some large coordinated projects are eligible to apply. Grants are awarded on the basis of competitive peer review of unsolicited research proposals.

Fiscal Information Large and small grants of several months' to several years' duration are awarded.

Application Information For additional information contact the director of the Division of Ocean Sciences.

Deadline(s) Proposals may be submitted at any time. Allow about six months for review and processing. Proposals that require the use of ships should be submitted by February 1 (preferred) or June 1, so that timely decisions can be made on ship support and schedules.

Subject Term(s) Ocean Sciences; Individuals, Eligibility of; Marine Geology; Marine Geophysics

288. National Science Foundation

Directorate for Geosciences, Division of Ocean Sciences
1800 G Street, NW
Washington, DC 20550
(202) 357-7924

Oceanographic Centers and Facilities

Program Description The National Science Foundation supports construction, conversion, acquisition, and operation of shared major-use facilities. This program supports large and expensive facilities that will aid NSF-funded research and training of oceanographers. Examples of these facilities are ships, submersibles, large shipboard equipment, and complex instruments to collect and analyze data. Funds are also available to develop research instrumentation that has potential for wide use.

Sample Grants For ship operations support (Bahamas), $1,500,000 to the University of Miami (1986). For ship operations support (Brazil), $4,000,000 to Woods Hole Oceanographic Institute (1986). For ship operations (Latin America), $4,000,000 to University of California, San Diego (1986). For planning a workshop for observation of El Nino, $15,478 to Duke University Marine Laboratory (1986).

Eligibility/Limitations Support for major oceanographic facilities is concentrated at a few suitably located institutions that have the capability to operate major facilities.

These institutions have substantial research programs in oceanography; they also support the research projects of other institutions.

Fiscal Information The foundation encourages local contributions from nonfederal funds; however, there is no fixed requirement for institutional contributions.

Application Information Before submitting a proposal for support under this program, institutions should seek advice from the Oceanographic Centers and Facilities Section. Specific instructions on how to submit proposals for ship operations, technicians, shipboard equipment, and oceanographic instrumentation are available.

Deadline(s) Proposals for ship operations and technicians are due July 1 each year. Proposals for shipboard equipment and oceanographic instrumentation are due September 1 each year. Proposals requesting support for other activities may be submitted at any time.

Subject Term(s) Equipment Acquisition; Oceanography; Ocean Sciences

289. National Science Foundation

Directorate for Geosciences, Division of Ocean Sciences
1800 G Street, NW
Washington, DC 20550
(202) 357-7924

Physical Oceanography Program

Program Description This division supports research to improve understanding of the sea and ocean basins. A broad range of projects are supported dealing with physical, chemical, geological, and biological processes in the ocean. The Physical Oceanography Program supports research on the description, analysis, and modeling of oceanic circulation and transport; effects of circulation on energy momentum transport; physical circulation processes, eddy generation, and turbulent mixing on continental shelves; mixing processes and circulation in estuaries; wind-generated tides and surface and internal waves; small-scale transport processes such as diffusion, conduction and convection, and three-dimensional turbulence; physical properties of seawater; and circulation and mixing in lakes.

Sample Grants Support of study of the geochemical cycles of 9Be and 27A1 and other reactive trace elements, $65,033 to the Massachusetts Institute of Technology (1986). Support for a hydrographic survey of the subtropical convergence front in February 1986, $425,000 to Woods Hole Oceanographic Institute (1986). Foreign activity support of study of nitrogen cycling and particle dynamics in the Sargasso Sea: the use of 15N natural abundances as an in situ tracer, $85,246 to Woods Hole Oceanographic Institute (1986).

Eligibility/Limitations Individual scientists, small groups of cooperating scientists, and some large coordinated projects are eligible to apply. Grants are awarded on the basis of competitive peer review of unsolicited research proposals.

Fiscal Information Large and small grants of several months' to several years' duration are awarded.

Application Information For additional information contact the director of the Division of Ocean Sciences.

Deadline(s) Proposals may be submitted at any time. Allow about six months for review and processing. Proposals that require the use of ships should be submitted by February 1 (preferred) or June 1, so that timely decisions can be made on ship support and schedules.

Subject Term(s) Ocean Sciences; Individuals, Eligibility of; Oceanography

290. National Science Foundation

Directorate for Geosciences, Division of Polar Programs
1800 G Street, NW
Washington, DC 20550
(202) 357-7817

Antarctic Research

Program Description The foundation manages the national program in Antarctica, including research, logistics, and operational support, to provide an active and influential U.S. presence in the region. The principal purpose of the program is to maintain and strengthen the Antarctic Treaty. The principal expression of the U.S. presence is a balanced program of scientific research. Research objectives include improving understanding of Antarctica and its role in global processes through the award of grants or contracts for projects to be performed either in the field or at home institutions. Research is supported in the fields of biology and polar-related medicine, astronomy, upper atmosphere physics, meteorology, geology and geophysics, glaciology, and oceanography. Specific objectives of the program are to understand the function, evolution, and adaptations of land and sea species and ecosystems; the geology and geologic history of the continent and its surrounding ocean basins; the structure and dynamics of the magnetosphere and the ionosphere, which are uniquely measurable at the high geomagnetic latitudes of Antarctica; Antarctica's role in past and present global climate through study of surface and upper air processes, the structure, dynamics, and chemistry of the ice sheet, and oceanic circulation; and the physical and chemical oceanography of antarctic seas.

Sample Grants Foreign activity support for an aerogeophysical survey of the basins surrounding the Antarctic Peninsula, $343,343 to Columbia University (1986). Foreign travel support for Pygoscelid Penguin population studies, $13,882 to the Point Reyes Bird Observatory (1986). Support for a study of kinematic evolution of Scotia Ridge, Antarctica and southernmost South America: a study of orogenic processes at convergent plate margins, $188,715 to University of Texas, Austin (1986). Foreign travel support for a study of the predatory feeding ecology of Euchaeta Antarctica, a marine planktonic copepod, $25,766 to the University of Hawaii, Manoa (1986). Support for a study of the physiological ecology and energetics of thermal regulation in Adelie Penguins, $65,113 to the University of California, Riverside (1986).

Eligibility/Limitations U.S. academic institutions and academically-related nonprofit organizations may submit proposals for grants or contracts for research project support. Industry and other local, state, and federal agencies are also eligible for support.

Application Information A special brochure further describes the program; sets forth research opportunities and objectives; describes facilities, logistics, and other support available to investigators; and explains how to prepare proposals. An investigator must get a copy of this brochure and a proposal preparation kit from the Division of Polar Programs before writing a proposal. Scientists must specify their logistic needs in their proposals. They also must use a proposal preparation kit containing a copy of the brochure mentioned above plus other essential forms and instructions.

Deadline(s) Requests for support of research must be received by June 1 of the year preceding the proposed commencement of field work.

Subject Term(s) Polar Research; Antarctic Research

291. National Science Foundation

Directorate for Mathematical and Physical Sciences, Division of Astronomical Sciences
1800 G Street, NW
Washington, DC 20550
(202) 357-9488

Astronomical Instrumentation and Development

CFDA Program Number 47.049

Program Description The overall objective of the Astronomical Sciences program is to increase our knowledge of the universe. Research is aimed at determining the composition, structure, and evolution of planets, stars, and galaxies, including our sun and the Milky Way. The Astronomical Instrumentation and Development Program supports development and construction of state-of-the-art detectors and data-handling equipment; procurement of detection and analysis systems for telescopes; development of interactive picture-processing systems; very-long-baseline interferometric instrumentation; and application of new technology and innovative techniques to astronomy.

Sample Grants Foreign travel and activity support for research in infrared speckle spectroscopy, $85,000 to Cornell University (1986).

Eligibility/Limitations Scientists initiate research proposals, which are usually submitted on their behalf by their employing institutions. The foundation welcomes proposals by organizations on behalf of all qualified scientists and engineers, and it especially encourages those initiated by female and minority group researchers and handicapped individuals. The most frequent recipients of support for basic scientific research projects are colleges, universities, and nonprofit research organizations. In special circumstances, grants also go to other types of institutions and to individuals. In these cases preliminary inquiry should be made to the appropriate program officer before a proposal is submitted. Support may be provided for projects involving one or more scientists.

Fiscal Information To give reasonable assurance of long-term support for continuing projects of high scientific merit, funding may be provided for periods of up to sixty months in annual increments (contingent upon the availability of funds and satisfactory progress of the research). Most support is for periods of twenty-four to thirty-six months.

Application Information For more information contact the Division of Astronomical Sciences.

Deadline(s) Submit proposals at any time during the year; allow about seven to nine months for review and processing. Proposals to be funded in a particular fiscal year (ending September 30) normally should be received by NSF no later than December of that fiscal year.

Additional Information In addition to basic and applied research projects, support may go to research workshops, symposia, conferences, the purchase of scientific equipment for research purposes, and construction of specialized research facilities.

Subject Term(s) Astronomy; Individuals, Eligibility of; Seminars and Conferences; Equipment Acquisition

292. National Science Foundation

Directorate for Mathematical and Physical Sciences, Division of Astronomical Sciences
1800 G Street, NW
Washington, DC 20550
(202) 357-9488

Extragalactic Astronomy

CFDA Program Number 47.049

Program Description The overall objective of the Astronomical Sciences program is to increase our knowledge of the universe. Research is aimed at determining the composition, structure, and evolution of planets, stars, and galaxies, including our sun and the Milky Way. The Extragalactic Astronomy Program supports theoretical and observational studies of extragalactic objects ranging from the nearest galaxies to the most distant quasars and their relevance to galactic evolution and cosmology.

Sample Grants Support for study of the non-nuclear regions of active galaxies, $20,000 to Michigan State University (1986). Support for studies of luminous stars in nearby galaxies, $100,100 to the University of Minnesota (1986). Support for observational studies of extragalactic objects, $57,000 to University of Arizona (1986). Support for studies of large scale structure in the universe and of the internal structure of galaxies, $80,000 to University of California, Berkeley (1986). Support for studies of galaxies, Seyfert nuclei and quasars, $99,500 to California Institute of Technology (1986).

Eligibility/Limitations Scientists initiate research proposals, which are usually submitted on their behalf by their employing institutions. The foundation welcomes proposals by organizations on behalf of all qualified scientists and engineers, and it especially encourages those initiated by female and minority group researchers and handicapped individuals. The most frequent recipients of support for basic scientific research projects are colleges, universities, and nonprofit research organizations. In special circumstances, grants also go to other types of institutions and to individuals. In these cases preliminary inquiry should be made to the appropriate program officer before a proposal is submitted. Support may be provided for projects involving one or more scientists.

Fiscal Information To give reasonable assurance of long-term support for continuing projects of high scientific merit, funding may be provided for periods of up to sixty months in annual increments (contingent upon the availability of funds and satisfactory progress of the research). Most support is for periods of twenty-four to thirty six months.

Application Information For more information contact the Division of Astronomical Sciences.

Deadline(s) Submit proposals at any time during the year; allow about seven to nine months for review and processing. Proposals to be funded in a particular fiscal year (ending September 30) normally should be received by NSF no later than December of that fiscal year.

Additional Information In addition to basic and applied research projects, support may go to research workshops, symposia, conferences, the purchase of scientific equipment for research purposes, and construction of specialized research facilities.

Subject Term(s) Astronomy; Individuals, Eligibility of; Seminars and Conferences; Equipment Acquisition

293. National Science Foundation

Directorate for Mathematical and Physical Sciences, Division of Astronomical Sciences
1800 G Street, NW
Washington, DC 20550
(202) 357-9488

Galactic Astronomy

CFDA Program Number 47.049

Program Description The overall objective of the Astronomical Sciences program is to increase our knowledge of the universe. Research is aimed at determining the composition, structure, and evolution of planets, stars, and galaxies, including our sun and the Milky Way. The Galactic Astronomy Program supports theoretical and observational studies of the distribution and kinematics of stars in the immediate vicinity of the sun (through determining their distances and motions with the highest attainable precision); the characteristics of binary and multiple star systems, star clusters, and the interstellar medium; and the structure and evolution of the Milky Way galaxy.

Sample Grants Support for observation of the galactic system of star clusters, $46,600 to Boston University (1986). Foreign travel support for a low-dispersion, photographic infrared search for southern red supergiants, $17,600 to Computer Sciences Corp., Silver Springs (1986). Support for observational studies of stellar evolution of intermediate-age open clusters, $31,700 to University of Kansas Main Campus (1986). Support for study of the nature of faint stellar objects discovered in a deep charge-coupled device survey, $45,000 to Rider College (1986).

Eligibility/Limitations Scientists initiate research proposals, which are usually submitted on their behalf by their employing institutions. The foundation welcomes proposals by organizations on behalf of all qualified scientists and engineers, and it especially encourages those initiated by female and minority group researchers and handicapped individuals. The most frequent recipients of support for basic scientific research projects are colleges, universities, and nonprofit research organizations. In special circumstances, grants also go to other types of institutions and to individuals. In these cases preliminary inquiry should be made to the appropriate program officer before a proposal is submitted. Support may be provided for projects involving one or more scientists.

Fiscal Information To give reasonable assurance of long-term support for continuing projects of high scientific merit, funding may be provided for periods of up to sixty months in annual increments (contingent upon the availability of funds and satisfactory progress of the research). Most support is for periods of twenty-four to thirty-six months.

Application Information For more information contact the Division of Astronomical Sciences.

Deadline(s) Submit proposals at any time during the year; allow about seven to nine months for review and processing. Proposals to be funded in a particular fiscal year (ending September 30) normally should be received by NSF no later than December of that fiscal year.

Additional Information In addition to basic and applied research projects, support may go to research workshops, symposia, conferences, the purchase of scientific equipment for research purposes, and construction of specialized research facilities.

Subject Term(s) Astronomy; Individuals, Eligibility of; Seminars and Conferences; Equipment Acquisition

294. National Science Foundation

Directorate for Mathematical and Physical Sciences, Division of Astronomical Sciences
1800 G Street, NW
Washington, DC 20550
(202) 357-9488

Solar System Astronomy

CFDA Program Number 47.049

Program Description The overall objective of the Astronomical Sciences program is to increase our knowledge of the universe. Research is aimed at determining the composition, structure, and evolution of planets, stars, and galaxies, including our sun and the Milky Way. The Solar System Astronomy Program supports theoretical and observational studies of the detailed structure and composition of planetary surfaces, interiors, atmospheres, and satellites; the nature of small bodies (the asteroids, comets, and meteors); and the relevance of this to the origin and development of the solar system.

Sample Grants Support for spectrophotometry of Comet Halley, $45,900 to Rice University (1986). Support for cometary optical spectroscopy, $61,600 to Lowell Observatory (1986).

Eligibility/Limitations Scientists initiate research proposals, which are usually submitted on their behalf by their employing institutions. The foundation welcomes proposals by organizations on behalf of all qualified scientists and engineers, and it especially encourages those initiated by female and minority group researchers and handicapped individuals. The most frequent recipients of support for basic scientific research projects are colleges, universities, and nonprofit research organizations. In special circumstances, grants also go to other types of institutions and to individuals. In these cases preliminary inquiry should be made to the appropriate program officer before a proposal is submitted. Support may be provided for projects involving one or more scientists.

Fiscal Information To give reasonable assurance of long-term support for continuing projects of high scientific merit, funding may be provided for periods of up to sixty months in annual increments (contingent upon the availability of funds and satisfactory progress of the research). Most support is for periods of twenty-four to thirty-six months.

Application Information For more information contact the Division of Astronomical Sciences.

Deadline(s) Submit proposals at any time during the year; allow about seven to nine months for review and processing. Proposals to be funded in a particular fiscal year (ending September 30) normally should be received by NSF no later than December of that fiscal year.

Additional Information In addition to basic and applied research projects, support may go to research workshops, symposia, conferences, the purchase of scientific equipment for research purposes, and construction of specialized research facilities.

Subject Term(s) Astronomy; Individuals, Eligibility of; Seminars and Conferences; Equipment Acquisition

295. National Science Foundation

Directorate for Mathematical and Physical Sciences, Division of Astronomical Sciences
1800 G Street, NW
Washington, DC 20550
(202) 357-9488

Stars and Stellar Evolution

CFDA Program Number 47.049

Program Description The overall objective of the Astronomical Sciences program is to increase our knowledge of the universe. Research is aimed at determining the composition, structure, and evolution of planets, stars, and galaxies, including our sun and the Milky Way. The Stars and Stellar Evolution Program supports theoretical and observational studies of the structure and activity of the sun; the physical properties of all types of stars; all aspects of stellar formation and evolution; the effects of mass loss, rotation, and magnetic fields; and the properties of stellar atoms and molecules of relevance to stellar astronomy.

Sample Grants Support for the analysis of cool stars using synthetic spectroscopy and photometry, $100,000 to University of Maryland (1986). Support for studies of white dwarf stars and related objects, $93,200 to the University of Arizona (1986). Support for studies of supernovae and supernova remnants, $94,900 to Harvard University (1986). Support for spectroscopic studies of stars in metal-poor systems, $50,000 in an individual award (1986). Support for study of causes and consequences of mass loss from red giant stars, $114,000 to University of California, Los Angeles (1986).

Eligibility/Limitations Scientists initiate research proposals, which are usually submitted on their behalf by their employing institutions. The foundation welcomes proposals by organizations on behalf of all qualified scientists and engineers, and it especially encourages those initiated by female and minority group researchers and handicapped individuals. The most frequent recipients of support for basic scientific research projects are colleges, universities, and nonprofit research organizations. In special circumstances, grants also go to other types of institutions and to individuals. In these cases preliminary inquiry should be made to the appropriate program officer before a proposal is submitted. Support may be provided for projects involving one or more scientists.

Fiscal Information To give reasonable assurance of long-term support for continuing projects of high scientific merit, funding may be provided for periods of up to sixty months in annual increments (contingent upon the availability of funds and satisfactory progress of the research). Most support is for periods of twenty-four to thirty-six months.

Application Information For more information contact the Division of Astronomical Sciences.

Deadline(s) Submit proposals at any time during the year; allow about seven to nine months for review and processing. Proposals to be funded in a particular fiscal year (ending September 30) normally should be received by NSF no later than December of that fiscal year.

Additional Information In addition to basic and applied research projects, support may go to research workshops, symposia, conferences, the purchase of scientific equipment for research purposes, and construction of specialized research facilities.

Subject Term(s) Astronomy; Individuals, Eligibility of; Seminars and Conferences; Equipment Acquisition

296. National Science Foundation

Directorate for Mathematical and Physical Sciences, Division of Chemistry
1800 G Street, NW
Washington, DC 20550
(202) 357-7947

Chemistry

CFDA Program Number 47.049

Program Description The Division of Chemistry supports investigations, both experimental and theoretical, of the the physical properties of chemical systems; the synthesis, structure, and reaction dynamics of carbon-based molecules, metallo-organic systems, and organized molecular assemblies; the synthesis, structure and reaction mechanisms of molecules containing metals, metalloids, and non-metals, encompassing the entire periodic table of the elements; and fundamental chemical research directed toward the characterization and analysis of all forms of matter.

Sample Grants Support for studies of molecular and radical orientation on surfaces by electron magnetic resonance, $168,120 to the University of Houston (1986). Support for biosynthetic/biomimetic studies in insect chemistry, $105,335 to SUNY Stony Brook (1986).

Eligibility/Limitations Scientists initiate research proposals, which are usually submitted on their behalf by their employing institutions. The foundation welcomes proposals by organizations on behalf of all qualified scientists and engineers, and it especially encourages those initiated by female and minority group researchers and handicapped individuals. The most frequent recipients of support for basic scientific research projects are colleges, universities, and nonprofit research organizations. In special circumstances, grants also go to other types of institutions and to individuals. In these cases preliminary inquiry should be made to the appropriate program officer before a proposal is submitted.

Fiscal Information To give reasonable assurance of long-term support for continuing projects of high scientific merit, funding may be provided for periods of up to sixty months in annual increments (contingent upon the availability of funds and satisfactory progress of the research). Most support is for periods of twenty-four to thirty-six months.

Application Information For more information contact the Division of Chemistry.

Deadline(s) Submit proposals at any time during the year; allow about seven to nine months for review and processing. Proposals to be funded in a particular fiscal year (ending September 30) normally should be received by NSF no later than December of that fiscal year.

Additional Information In addition to basic and applied research projects, support may go to postdoctoral fellowships, research workshops, symposia, conferences, the purchase of scientific equipment for research purposes, and construction of specialized research facilities.

Subject Term(s) Individuals, Eligibility of; Postdoctoral Support; Seminars and Conferences; Equipment Acquisition; Chemistry

297. National Science Foundation

Directorate for Mathematical and Physical Sciences, Division of Materials Research
1800 G Street, NW
Washington, DC 20550
(202) 357-0114

Materials Research Groups Program

CFDA Program Number 47.049

Program Description The objective of materials research is to gain deeper understanding of the properties of materials in terms of the microscopic interactions among their fundamental constituents and in terms of composition and structure. There are two aspects to this objective. First, materials research provides essential scientific underpinning for new technological advances. Second, materials research is also at the forefront of scientific research areas that are yielding major conceptual advances in scientific understanding, such as universal principles of phase transitions, the nature of the amorphous state, and the behavior of materials with submicron dimensions. Areas of research supported include: (1) solid-state physics; (2) solid-state chemistry; (3) low-temperature physics; (4) condensed matter theory; (5) metallurgy; (6) ceramics and electronic materials; and (7) polymers.

Sample Grants Support for work on coherent optical phenomena and solid state spin resonance (material research), $168,000 to the University of California, Berkeley (1986).

Eligibility/Limitations Scientists initiate research proposals, which are usually submitted on their behalf by their employing institutions. The foundation welcomes proposals by organizations on behalf of all qualified scientists and engineers, and it especially encourages those initiated by female and minority group researchers and handicapped individuals. The most frequent recipients of support for basic scientific research projects are colleges, universities, and nonprofit research organizations. In special circumstances, grants also go to other types of institutions and to individuals. In these cases preliminary inquiry should be made to the appropriate program officer before a proposal is submitted. The program provides support for collaborative, multi-investigator research within the purview of the Division of Materials Research. Proposals should normally request support for a three-year period and may come from groups at one or more institutions. Industry/university cooperative research projects are also eligible.

Fiscal Information To give reasonable assurance of long-term support for continuing projects of high scientific merit, funding may be provided for periods of up to sixty months in annual increments (contingent upon the availability of funds and satisfactory progress of the research). Most support is for periods of twenty-four to thirty-six months.

Application Information For more information contact the Division of Materials Research.

Deadline(s) Submit proposals at any time during the year; allow about seven to nine months for review and processing. Proposals to be funded in a particular fiscal year (ending September 30) normally should be received by NSF no later than December of that fiscal year.

Additional Information In addition to basic and applied research projects, support may go to research workshops, symposia, conferences, the purchase of scientific equipment for research purposes, and construction of specialized research facilities.

Subject Term(s) Materials Research; Seminars and Conferences; Individuals, Eligibility of; Equipment Acquisition

298. National Science Foundation

Directorate for Mathematical and Physical Sciences, Division of Mathematical Sciences
1800 G Street, NW
Washington, DC 20550
(202) 357-9669

Mathematical Sciences Program

CFDA Program Number 47.049

Program Description Research projects in this area aim to develop a fundamental understanding of the physical laws that govern the universe. Projects supported range from basic to applied research. Areas of research supported include: (1) classical analysis; (2) modern analysis; (3) geometric analysis; (4) topology and foundations; (5) algebra and number theory; (6) applied mathematics; (7) statistics and probability; (8) computational mathematics; and (9) special projects.

Sample Grants Foreign travel support for study of geometric methods in mathematical physics, $20,000 to Clarkson University (1986). Support for work in geometry and topology, $52,600 to the University of Illinois, Chicago (1986).

Eligibility/Limitations Scientists initiate research proposals, which are usually submitted on their behalf by their employing institutions. The foundation welcomes proposals by organizations on behalf of all qualified scientists and engineers, and it especially encourages those initiated by female and minority group researchers and handicapped individuals. The most frequent recipients of support for basic scientific research projects are colleges, universities, and nonprofit research organizations. In special circumstances, grants also go to other types of institutions and to individuals. In these cases preliminary inquiry should be made to the appropriate program officer before a proposal is submitted.

Fiscal Information To give reasonable assurance of long-term support for continuing projects of high scientific merit, funding may be provided for periods of up to sixty months in annual increments (contingent upon the availability of funds and satisfactory progress of the research). Most support is for periods of twenty-four to thirty-six months.

Application Information For more information contact the Division of Mathematical Sciences.

Deadline(s) Submit proposals at any time during the year; allow about seven to nine months for review and processing. Proposals to be funded in a particular fiscal year (ending September 30) normally should be received by NSF no later than December of that fiscal year.

Additional Information In addition to basic and applied research projects, support may go to postdoctoral fellowships, research workshops, symposia, conferences, the purchase of scientific equipment for research purposes, and construction of specialized research facilities.

Subject Term(s) Mathematical Sciences; Seminars and Conferences; Individuals, Eligibility of; Postdoctoral Support; Equipment Acquisition

299. National Science Foundation

Directorate for Mathematical and Physical Sciences, Division of Physics
1800 G Street, NW
Washington, DC 20550
(202) 357-7985

Physics Projects

CFDA Program Number 47.049

Program Description NSF-supported research projects in this area aim to develop a fundamental understanding of the physical laws that govern the universe. Areas of research supported include: (1) elementary particle physics; (2) intermediate energy nuclear physics; (3) nuclear physics; (4) atomic, molecular, and plasma physics; (5) theoretical physics; and (6) gravitational physics.

Sample Grants Support for study of relativistic quantum theory and the interactions of elementary particles, $173,000 to the University of Maryland (1986).

Eligibility/Limitations Scientists initiate research proposals, which are usually submitted on their behalf by their employing institutions. The foundation welcomes proposals by organizations on behalf of all qualified scientists and engineers, and it especially encourages those initiated by female and minority group researchers and handicapped individuals. The most frequent recipients of support for basic scientific research projects are colleges, universities, and nonprofit research organizations. In special circumstances, grants also go to other types of institutions and to individuals. In these cases preliminary inquiry should be made to the appropriate program officer before a proposal is submitted.

Fiscal Information To give reasonable assurance of long-term support for continuing projects of high scientific merit, funding may be provided for periods of up to sixty months in annual increments (contingent upon the availability of funds and satisfactory progress of the research). Most support is for periods of twenty-four to thirty-six months.

Application Information For more information contact the Division of Physics.

Deadline(s) Submit proposals at any time during the year; allow about seven to nine months for review and processing. Proposals to be funded in a particular fiscal year (ending September 30) normally should be received by NSF no later than December of that fiscal year.

Additional Information In addition to basic and applied research projects, support may go to postdoctoral fellowships, research workshops, symposia, conferences, the purchase of scientific equipment for research purposes, and construction of specialized research facilities.

Subject Term(s) Individuals, Eligibility of; Postdoctoral Support; Seminars and Conferences; Physics; Equipment Acquisition

300. National Science Foundation

Directorate for Science and Engineering Education, Division of Research Career Development
1800 G Street, NW
Washington, DC 20550

Graduate Fellowships

CFDA Program Number 47.009

Program Description This program promotes the future strength of the nation's scientific and technological base by providing recognition and support for advanced study to outstanding graduate students. Fellowships are awarded for study or work leading to master's or doctoral degrees in the mathematical, physical, biological, engineering and social sciences, and the history and philosophy of science. Fellows are selected in a national competition on the basis of actual and potential achievements in their chosen disciplines. They may pursue their studies at any appropriate United States or foreign institution of higher learning.

Eligibility/Limitations Applicants must be United States citizens or nationals. Applicants must not have completed, by the beginning of the fall term, more than twenty semester hours, thirty quarter hours, or the equivalent, of study in the science and engineering fields listed above following completion of their first baccalaureate degree in science or engineering, or its equivalent. No individual will be eligible who, at the time of application, has earned an advanced degree in science or engineering.

Fiscal Information Each fellowship gives up to three years of support for full-time graduate study. The stipend is $11,000 for a twelve-month tenure. In addition, NSF will provide fellowship institutions, on behalf of each fellow, with a cost-of-education allowance ($6,000) in lieu of all tuition costs and assessed fees.

Application Information For information and application materials write to The Fellowship Office, National Research Council, 2101 Constitution Avenue, Washington, DC 20418 or telephone (202) 334-2872. A detailed program description and guidelines for application are in the brochure "Graduate Fellowships Announcement" available from NSF.

Deadline(s) The deadline for receipt of applications is November 15.

Subject Term(s) Fellowships; Graduate Support; Predoctoral Support

301. National Science Foundation

Directorate for Science and Engineering Education, Division of Research Career Development
1800 G Street, NW
Washington, DC 20550

Minority Graduate Fellowships

CFDA Program Number 47.009

Program Description This program gives fellowship support to members of ethnic minority groups whose abilities traditionally have been untapped in the advanced levels of the nation's science talent pool. Under this program, support goes to outstanding minority graduate students for study or work toward master's or doctoral degrees in the mathematical, physical, biological, engineering, and social sciences, and in the history and philosophy of science.

Eligibility/Limitations Applicants must be United States citizens or nationals who are members of one of the following ethnic minority groups: American Indian, Black, Hispanic, Native Alaskan (Eskimo or Aleut), or Native Pacific Islander (Polynesian or Micronesian). Applicants must not have completed, by the beginning of the fall term, more than twenty semester hours, thirty quarter hours, or the equivalent, of study in the science and engineering fields listed above following completion of their first baccalaureate degree in science or engineering, or its equivalent. No individual will be eligible who, at the time of application, has earned an advanced degree in science or engineering.

Fiscal Information Each award provides up to three years of support for full-time graduate study. The stipend is $11,000 for a twelve-month tenure. In addition, NSF will provide fellowship institutions, on behalf of each fellow, with a cost-of-education allowance ($6,000) in lieu of all tuition costs and assessed fees.

Application Information For information and application materials write to The Fellowship Office, National Research Council, 2101 Constitution Avenue, Washington, DC 20418 or telephone (202) 334-2872. A detailed program description and guidelines for application are in the brochure "Graduate Fellowships Announcement" available from NSF.

Deadline(s) The deadline for receipt of applications is November 15.

Subject Term(s) Predoctoral Support; Graduate Support; Fellowships; Minorities, Eligibility of

302. National Science Foundation

Directorate for Scientific, Technological, and International Affairs, Division of International Programs
1800 G Street, NW
Washington, DC 20550
(202) 357-9537

Science in Developing Countries: Conference Grants

CFDA Program Number 47.053

Program Description The Science in Developing Countries (SDC) program is primarily directed toward improving the scientific infrastructure of developing countries. Conference grants are made to U.S. institutions that sponsor these national, regional, and international activities: (1) seminars that are research oriented and focused on developing-country problems; (2) workshops concerned with the planning and initiation of cooperative research activities; or (3) colloquia at which scientists or engineers involved with state-of-the-art research explore the application of science and technology to development problems.

Eligibility/Limitations NSF will consider proposals from universities or colleges; nonprofit, nonacademic research institutions; and private for-profit organizations. All prospective principal investigators must be professionally qualified through training and work experience and be employed by a U.S. institution. Each proposal must identify a host-country counterpart scientist or engineer and a counterpart institution. Such institutions may be local, regional, national, or international in character. Projects may have multiple sites and may involve more than one foreign institution.

Fiscal Information The SDC program makes small grants ($20,000 or less) for the life of a project.

Application Information U.S. scientists and engineers may obtain further information about this program, including program announcements, by writing to the program in care of the Division of International Programs. International programs encourage, but do not require, preliminary inquiries from scientists and engineers who intend to apply for support.

Deadline(s) Target dates for receipt of proposals are September 1 and March 1. However, proposals may be submitted at any time. Processing time averages seven months.

Additional Information Countries in Latin America (including the Caribbean) that may participate in the program include: Antigua and Barbuda, Argentina, Bahamas, Barbados, Belize, Bolivia, Brazil, Colombia, Costa Rica, Chile, Dominica, Dominican Republic, Ecuador, El Salvador, Grenada, Guatemala, Guyana, Haiti, Honduras, Jamaica, Mexico, Nicaragua, Panama, Paraguay, Peru, Saint Christopher and Nevis, Saint Lucia, Saint Vincent and the Grenadines, Surinam, Trinidad and Tobago, Uruguay, and Venezuela. Projects in Argentina, Brazil, Mexico, and Venezuela are limited to workshops in which the majority of the participants come from other countries of the region.

Subject Term(s) Developing Countries; Antigua and Barbuda; Argentina; Bahamas; Barbados; Belize; Bolivia; Brazil; Colombia; Costa Rica; Chile; Dominica; Dominican Republic; Ecuador; El Salvador; Grenada; Guatemala; Guyana; Haiti; Honduras; Jamaica; Mexico; Nicaragua; Panama; Paraguay; Peru; Saint Christopher and Nevis; Saint Lucia; Saint Vincent and the Grenadines; Surinam; Trinidad and Tobago; Uruguay; Venezuela; Seminars and Conferences

303. National Science Foundation

Directorate for Scientific, Technological, and International Affairs, Division of International Programs
1800 G Street, NW
Washington, DC 20550
(202) 357-9537

Science in Developing Countries: Dissertation Improvement Grants

CFDA Program Number 47.053

Program Description The Science in Developing Countries (SDC) program is primarily directed toward improving the scientific infrastructure of developing countries. Dissertation improvement grants are provided for the incremental support of developing-country graduate students who are enrolled at U.S. universities and qualified to undertake a dissertation research project. Only projects related to a developing-country problem and approved by a U.S. research advisor are considered for support.

Eligibility/Limitations Qualified dissertation-level students are eligible to apply.

Fiscal Information The SDC covers costs for field equipment and supplies, and for travel to and from research sites. No stipend, tuition, fees, or indirect costs are provided. SDC grants are small, $20,000 or less for the life of a project.

Application Information Potential applicants may obtain further information about this program, including program announcements, by writing to the program in care of the Division of International Programs. International programs encourage, but do not require, preliminary inquiries from students who intend to apply for support.

Deadline(s) Target dates for receipt of proposals are September 1 and March 1. However, proposals may be submitted at any time. Processing time averages seven months.

Additional Information Students from countries in Latin America (including the Caribbean) that may participate in the program may come from: Antigua and Barbuda, Bahamas, Barbados, Belize, Bolivia, Colombia, Costa Rica, Chile, Dominica, Dominican Republic, Ecuador, El Salvador, Grenada, Guatemala, Guyana, Haiti, Honduras, Jamaica, Nicaragua, Panama, Paraguay, Peru, Saint Christopher and Nevis, Saint Lucia, Saint Vincent and the Grenadines, Surinam, Trinidad and Tobago, or Uruguay.

Subject Term(s) Foreign Nationals, Eligibility of; Doctoral Dissertation Support; Developing Countries; Antigua and Barbuda; Bahamas; Barbados; Belize; Bolivia; Colombia; Costa Rica; Chile; Dominica; Dominican Republic; Ecuador; El Salvador; Grenada; Guatemala; Guyana; Haiti; Honduras; Jamaica; Nicaragua; Panama; Paraguay; Peru; Saint Christopher and Nevis; Saint Lucia; Saint Vincent and the Grenadines; Surinam; Trinidad and Tobago; Uruguay

304. National Science Foundation

Directorate for Scientific, Technological, and International Affairs, Division of International Programs
1800 G Street, NW
Washington, DC 20550
(202) 357-9537

Science in Developing Countries: Research Participation Grants

CFDA Program Number 47.053

Program Description The Science in Developing Countries (SDC) program is primarily directed toward improving the scientific infrastructure of developing countries. Research participation grants are made to U.S. institutions that sponsor SDC projects. These grants support (1) the participation of U.S. scientists or engineers in a research or science education project in an eligible developing country; (2) the participation by scientists or engineers from an eligible developing country in an appropriate U.S.-based project; or (3) a combination of these.

Eligibility/Limitations NSF will consider proposals from universities or colleges; nonprofit, nonacademic research institutions; and private for-profit organizations. All prospective principal investigators must be professionally qualified through training and work experience and be employed by a U.S. institution. Each proposal must identify a host-country counterpart scientist or engineer and a counterpart institution. Such institutions may be local, regional, national, or international in character. Projects may have multiple sites and may involve more than one foreign institution.

Fiscal Information The SDC program makes small grants ($20,000 or less) for the life of a project. Research participation grants provide only supplemental costs related to collaboration; primary research costs are not provided.

Application Information U.S. scientists and engineers may obtain further information about this program, including program announcements, by writing to the program in care of the Division of International Programs. International programs encourage, but do not require, preliminary inquiries from scientists and engineers who intend to apply for support.

Deadline(s) Target dates for receipt of proposals are September 1 and March 1. However, proposals may be submitted at any time. Processing time averages seven months.

Additional Information Countries in Latin America (including the Caribbean) that may participate in the program include: Antigua and Barbuda, Bahamas, Barbados, Belize, Bolivia, Colombia, Costa Rica, Chile, Dominica, Dominican Republic, Ecuador, El Salvador, Grenada, Guatemala, Guyana, Haiti, Honduras, Jamaica, Nicaragua, Panama, Paraguay, Peru, Saint Christopher and Nevis, Saint Lucia, Saint Vincent and the Grenadines, Surinam, Trinidad and Tobago, and Uruguay.

Subject Term(s) Developing Countries; Antigua and Barbuda; Bahamas; Barbados; Belize; Bolivia; Colombia; Costa Rica; Chile; Dominica; Dominican Republic; Ecuador; El Salvador; Grenada; Guatemala; Guyana; Haiti; Honduras; Jamaica; Nicaragua; Panama; Paraguay; Peru; Saint Christopher and Nevis; Saint Lucia; Saint Vincent and the Grenadines; Surinam; Trinidad and Tobago; Uruguay

305. National Science Foundation

Directorate for Scientific, Technological, and International Affairs, Division of International Programs
1800 G Street, NW
Washington, DC 20550
(202) 357-9563

U.S.-Argentina Cooperative Science Program

CFDA Program Number 47.053

Program Description The foundation encourages and supports U.S. participation in international science and engineering activities that promise significant benefit to the U.S. research effort. It is foundation policy to foster the exchange of information among scientists in the United States and foreign countries, initiate and support scientific activities in matters relating to international cooperation, give U.S. scientists opportunities for scientific collaboration in developing countries, and provide support to U.S. institutions for research done abroad. Three types of activities may receive support: (1) cooperative research projects designed and conducted jointly by principal investigators from the U.S. and the foreign country; (2) research-oriented seminars and workshops (meetings of small groups of researchers from the U.S. and from the foreign country) to exchange information, review the current status of a specific field of science and engineering, and plan cooperative research; and (3) scientific visits for planning cooperative activities for research. The U.S.-Argentina Cooperative Science Program is designed to support the work of U.S. scientists and engineers cooperating with Argentina in research and related activities.

Sample Grants U.S.-Argentina cooperative research on studies on the mechanism of action of aldosterone in the brain, $20,390 to Rockefeller University (1986). U.S.-Argentina cooperative research on stabilization of active phases of titanium dioxide-support catalysts, $23,315 to Yale University (1986). U.S.-Argentina cooperative research studies on the development and reproduction of subantarctic Spincula, $3,619 to Smithsonian Institution(1986). U.S.-Argentina cooperative science program study of Cenozoic basin development in the Puna Plateau, Central Andes, $7,212 to Cornell University (1986). U.S.-Argentina cooperative research on radio wavelength observations of Comet Halley from the southern hemisphere, $66,085 to the University of Puerto Rico (1986). U.S.-Argentina cooperative research on the dynamics of mima-mound grasslands in Argentina, $19,650 to San Diego State University (1986).

Eligibility/Limitations U.S. universities and colleges, professional societies, research institutes, and individual scientists and engineers affiliated with such organizations may apply for support. Principal investigators/project directors should be U.S. scientists and engineers with professional experience equivalent to at least five years of postdoctoral scientific work. A U.S. scientist or engineer is a member of the U.S. scientific or engineering community who performs scientific or engineering work chiefly in the United States.

Fiscal Information In most instances, each country pays for the costs of the participation of its own scientists and engineers. NSF usually provides only the supplemental support required to introduce an international element or broaden the international character of a research effort. Primary funding for an investigator's research may come from any U.S. funding source, including but not confined to domestic research support programs at NSF.

Application Information For cooperative research and seminars, a U.S. applicant sends a proposal to NSF; the cooperating scientist or engineer in the foreign country usually submits at the same time to the appropriate agency in that country. Activities typically require approval of both NSF and its foreign counterpart agency before funding in either country. The Division of International Programs welcomes inquiries about programs and encourages U.S. scientists and engineers to discuss their plans with the staff of the division. A program announcement and additional information are available from the Division of International Programs.

Deadline(s) Deadlines for cooperative research, long-term research visits (6-12 months), and seminar proposals are May 1 and November 1. Processing time for proposals for cooperative research, seminars, and long-term scientific visits averages six months, but seminar organizers often need to submit their proposals up to twelve months in advance for planning purposes. Proposals for short-term scientific visits (visits of about a month) should be received at NSF at least four months before desired departure date.

Subject Term(s) Exchanges; Cooperative Science Support; Argentina; Seminars and Conferences

306. National Science Foundation

Directorate for Scientific, Technological, and International Affairs, Division of International Programs
1800 G Street, NW
Washington, DC 20550
(202) 357-9563

U.S.-Brazil Cooperative Science Program

CFDA Program Number 47.053

Program Description The foundation encourages and supports U.S. participation in international science and engineering activities that promise significant benefit to the U.S. research effort. It is foundation policy to foster the exchange of information among scientists in the United States and foreign countries, initiate and support scientific activities in matters relating to international cooperation, give U.S. scientists opportunities for scientific collaboration in developing countries, and provide support to U.S. institutions for research done abroad. Three types of activities may receive support: (1) cooperative research projects designed and conducted jointly by principal investigators from the U.S. and the foreign country; (2) research-oriented seminars and workshops (meetings of small groups of researchers from the U.S. and from the foreign country) to exchange information, review the current status of a specific field of science and engineering, and plan cooperative research; and (3) scientific visits for planning cooperative activities for research. The U.S.-Brazil Cooperative Science Program is designed to support the work of U.S. scientists and engineers cooperating with Brazil in research and related activities.

Sample Grants U.S.-Brazil workshop on recent developments in organic and bioorganic NMR, Campinas, Brazil, August 18-22, 1986, $17,225 to Northwestern University (1986). U.S.-Brazil cooperative research on simple nuclear reaction studies, $9,017 to the University of Colorado, Boulder (1986). U.S.-Brazil cooperative research on physiological and anatomical study of the postnatal development of the mouse visual system, $1,736 to Purdue University (1986). U.S.-Brazil cooperative research on investigation of elevated concentrations of ozone in unpolluted areas of Brazil, $15,620 to Harvard University (1986). U.S.-Brazil cooperative research on infrared and ultraviolet problems in lattice and continuous gauge quantum field theory, $10,210 to Northeastern University (1986). U.S.-Brazil cooperative research on regional and global aspects of precipitation in the Amazon Basin, $29,964 to the University of Utah (1986).

Eligibility/Limitations U.S. universities and colleges, professional societies, research institutes, and individual scientists and engineers affiliated with such organizations may apply for support. Principal investigators/project directors should be U.S. scientists and engineers with professional experience equivalent to at least five years of postdoctoral scientific work. A U.S. scientist or engineer is a member of the U.S. scientific or engineering community who performs scientific or engineering work chiefly in the United States.

Fiscal Information In most instances, each country pays for the costs of the participation of its own scientists and engineers. NSF usually provides only the supplemental support required to introduce an international element or broaden the international character of a research effort. Primary funding for an investigator's research may come from any U.S. funding source, including but not confined to domestic research support programs at NSF.

Application Information For cooperative research and seminars, a U.S. applicant sends a proposal to NSF; the cooperating scientist or engineer in the foreign country usually submits at the same time to the appropriate agency in that country. Activities typically require approval of both NSF and its foreign counterpart agency before funding in either country. The Division of International Programs welcomes inquiries about programs and encourages U.S. scientists and engineers to discuss their plans with the staff of the division. A program announcement and additional information are available from the Division of International Programs.

Deadline(s) Deadlines for cooperative research, long-term research visits (six to twelve months), and seminar proposals are May 1 and November 1. Processing time for proposals for cooperative research, seminars, and long-term scientific visits averages six months, but seminar organizers often need to submit their proposals up to twelve months in advance for planning purposes. Proposals for short-term scientific visits (visits of about a month) should be received at NSF at least four months before desired departure date.

Subject Term(s) Exchanges; Cooperative Science Support; Brazil; Seminars and Conferences

307. National Science Foundation

Directorate for Scientific, Technological, and International Affairs, Division of International Programs
1800 G Street, NW
Washington, DC 20550
(202) 357-9563

U.S.-Latin America Regional Cooperative Science Program

CFDA Program Number 47.053

Program Description The foundation encourages and supports U.S. participation in international science and engineering activities that promise significant benefit to the U.S. research effort. It is foundation policy to foster the exchange of information among scientists in the United States and foreign countries, initiate and support scientific activities in matters relating to international cooperation, give U.S. scientists opportunities for scientific collaboration in developing countries, and provide support to U.S. institutions for research done abroad. Three types of activities may receive support: (1) cooperative research projects designed and conducted jointly by principal investigators from the U.S. and the foreign country; (2) research-oriented seminars and workshops (meetings of small groups of researchers from the U.S. and from the foreign country) to exchange information, review the current status of a specific field of science and engineering, and plan cooperative research; and (3) scientific visits for planning cooperative activities for research. In addition to activities under formal bilateral agreements with Argentina, Brazil, Mexico, and Venezuela, NSF supports U.S. participation in projects under less formal arrangements with other countries in Latin America and the Caribbean.

Sample Grants In support of a seminar and workshop on Creole languages in time, space and society, New York City, July 7-25, $8,753 to the University of Pennsylvania (1986). Foreign travel, activity, and cooperative support for a regional conference on the water resources of the Caribbean Islands, St. Croix, Virgin Islands, July 23-24, $7,390 to the University of Puerto Rico (1986). Foreign travel, activity, and cooperative support for research on predation and thermal environment as selective constraints on lizard social organization, $12,480 to Oklahoma State University (1986). U.S.-Ecuador research oriented workshop on the Galapagos Islands Marine Reserve, Puerto Ayora, Ecuador, $10,000 to Woods Hole Oceanographic Institute (1986).

Eligibility/Limitations U.S. universities and colleges, professional societies, research institutes, and individual scientists and engineers affiliated with such organizations may apply for support. Principal investigators/project directors should be U.S. scientists and engineers with professional experience equivalent to at least five years of postdoctoral scientific work. A U.S. scientist or engineer is a member of the U.S. scientific or engineering community who performs scientific or engineering work chiefly in the United States.

Fiscal Information In most instances, each country pays for the costs of the participation of its own scientists and engineers. NSF usually provides only the supplemental support required to introduce an international element or broaden the international character of a research effort. Primary funding for an investigator's research may come from any U.S. funding source, including but not confined to domestic research support programs at NSF.

Application Information For cooperative research and seminars, a U.S. applicant sends a proposal to NSF; the cooperating scientist or engineer in the foreign country usually submits at the same time to the appropriate agency in that country. Activities typically require approval of both NSF and its foreign counterpart agency before funding in either country. The Division of International Programs welcomes inquiries about programs and encourages U.S. scientists and engineers to discuss their plans with the staff of the division. A program announcement and additional information are available from the Division of International Programs.

Deadline(s) Deadlines for cooperative research or seminar proposals are May 1 and November 1. Scientific visits may not exceed one month. Processing time for proposals for cooperative research, seminars, and long-term scientific visits averages six months, but seminar organizers often need to submit their proposals up to twelve months in advance for planning purposes. Proposals for short-term scientific visits (visits of about a month) should be received at NSF at least four months before desired departure date.

Subject Term(s) Exchanges; Cooperative Science Support; Seminars and Conferences

308. National Science Foundation

Directorate for Scientific, Technological, and International Affairs, Division of International Programs
1800 G Street, NW
Washington, DC 20550
(202) 357-9563

U.S.-Mexico Cooperative Science Program

CFDA Program Number 47.053

Program Description The foundation encourages and supports U.S. participation in international science and engineering activities that promise significant benefit to the U.S. research effort. It is foundation policy to foster the exchange of information among scientists in the United States and foreign countries, initiate and support scientific activities in matters relating to international cooperation, give U.S. scientists opportunities for scientific collaboration in developing countries, and provide support to U.S. institutions for research done abroad. Three types of activities may receive support: (1) cooperative research projects designed and conducted jointly by principal investigators from the U.S. and the foreign country; (2) research-oriented seminars and workshops (meetings of small groups of researchers from the U.S. and from the foreign country) to exchange information, review the current status of a specific field of science and engineering, and plan cooperative research; and (3) scientific visits for planning cooperative activities for research. The U.S.-Mexico Cooperative Science Program is designed to support the work of U.S. scientists and engineers cooperating with Mexico in research and related activities.

Sample Grants U.S.-Mexico cooperative research in exciton dynamics in finite aggregates and in defect lattices (condensed matter theory), $23,290 to the University of California, San Diego (1986). U.S.-Mexico cooperative research in models for multispecies fisheries, $3,520 to the University of Wisconsin, Milwaukee (1986). U.S.-Mexico cooperative research in radio frequency quadrupole development (physics), $17,400 to Texas A&M Main Campus (1986). U.S.-Mexico cooperation in the operation and analysis of seismic data from the Northern Baja California Strong Motion Array, $16,962 to the University of California, San Diego (1986). U.S.-Mexico cooperative research on direct contact heat exchange in solar ponds, $17,067 to Solar Energy Research Institute (1986).

Eligibility/Limitations U.S. universities and colleges, professional societies, research institutes, and individual scientists and engineers affiliated with such organizations may apply for support. Principal investigators/project directors should be U.S. scientists and engineers with professional experience equivalent to at least five years of postdoctoral scientific work. A U.S. scientist or engineer is a member of the U.S.

scientific or engineering community who performs scientific or engineering work chiefly in the United States.

Fiscal Information In most instances, each country pays for the costs of the participation of its own scientists and engineers. NSF usually provides only the supplemental support required to introduce an international element or broaden the international character of a research effort. Primary funding for an investigator's research may come from any U.S. funding source, including but not confined to domestic research support programs at NSF.

Application Information For cooperative research and seminars, a U.S. applicant sends a proposal to NSF; the cooperating scientist or engineer in the foreign country usually submits at the same time to the appropriate agency in that country. Activities typically require approval of both NSF and its foreign counterpart agency before funding in either country. The Division of International Programs welcomes inquiries about programs and encourages U.S. scientists and engineers to discuss their plans with the staff of the division. A program announcement and additional information are available from the Division of International Programs.

Deadline(s) Deadlines for cooperative research, long-term research visits (six to twelve months), and seminar proposals are May 1 and November 1. Processing time for proposals for cooperative research, seminars, and long-term scientific visits averages six months, but seminar organizers often need to submit their proposals up to twelve months in advance for planning purposes. Proposals for short-term scientific visits (visits of about a month) should be received at NSF at least four months before desired departure date.

Subject Term(s) Exchanges; Cooperative Science Support; Mexico; Seminars and Conferences

309. National Science Foundation

Directorate for Scientific, Technological, and International Affairs, Division of International Programs
1800 G Street, NW
Washington, DC 20550
(202) 357-9563

U.S.-Venezuela Cooperative Science Program

CFDA Program Number 47.053

Program Description The foundation encourages and supports U.S. participation in international science and engineering activities that promise significant benefit to the U.S. research effort. It is foundation policy to foster the exchange of information among scientists in the United States and foreign countries, initiate and support scientific activities in matters relating to international cooperation, give U.S. scientists opportunities for scientific collaboration in developing countries, and provide support to U.S. institutions for research done abroad. Three types of activities may receive support: (1) cooperative research projects designed and conducted jointly by principal investigators from the U.S. and the foreign country; (2) research-oriented seminars and workshops (meetings of small groups of researchers from the U.S. and from the foreign country) to exchange information, review the current status of a specific field of science and engineering, and plan cooperative research; and (3) scientific visits for planning cooperative activities for research. The U.S.-Venezuela Cooperative Science Program is designed to support the work of U.S. scientists and engineers cooperating with Venezuela in research and related activities.

Sample Grants U.S.-Venezuela cooperative research support for taxonomic studies on plant pathogenic ascomycetes in Venezuela, $20,000 to the University of Georgia (1986). U.S.-Venezuela cooperative research on normal ultrafilters and ideals (mathematics), $3,735 to Smith College (1986). U.S.-Venezuela cooperative research support for numerical study of an ocean-strait-inland sea system, the Lake Maracaibo System, $30,000 to Dartmouth College (1986).

Eligibility/Limitations U.S. universities and colleges, professional societies, research institutes, and individual scientists and engineers affiliated with such organizations may apply for support. Principal investigators/project directors should be U.S. scientists and engineers with professional experience equivalent to at least five years of postdoctoral scientific work. A U.S. scientist or engineer is a member of the U.S. scientific or engineering community who performs scientific or engineering work chiefly in the United States.

Fiscal Information In most instances, each country pays for the costs of the participation of its own scientists and engineers. NSF usually provides only the supplemental support required to introduce an international element or broaden the international character of a research effort. Primary funding for an investigator's research may come from any U.S. funding source, including but not confined to domestic research support programs at NSF.

Application Information For cooperative research and seminars, a U.S. applicant sends a proposal to NSF; the cooperating scientist or engineer in the foreign country usually submits at the same time to the appropriate agency in that country. Activities typically require approval of both NSF and its foreign counterpart agency before funding in either country. The Division of International Programs welcomes inquiries about programs and encourages U.S. scientists and engineers to discuss their plans with the staff of the division. A program announcement and additional information are available from the Division of International Programs.

Deadline(s) Deadlines for cooperative research or seminar proposals are May 1 and November 1. Scientific visits may not exceed one month. Processing time for proposals for cooperative research, seminars, and long-term scientific visits averages six months, but seminar organizers often need to submit their proposals up to twelve months in advance for planning purposes. Proposals for short-term scientific visits (visits of about a month) should be received at NSF at least four months before desired departure date.

Subject Term(s) Exchanges; Cooperative Science Support; Venezuela; Seminars and Conferences

310. National Science Foundation

Directorate for Scientific, Technological, and International Affairs, Division of Research Initiation and Improvement
1800 G Street, NW
Washington, DC 20550
(202) 357-7350

Minority Research Initiation

CFDA Program Number 47.053

Program Description The Minority Research Initiation (MRI) is part of the foundation's overall effort to promote full utilization of all highly qualified scientists and engineers. The objectives of MRI are to encourage the establishment of independent research projects by minority scientists and engineers and to increase the participation of minority researchers in all programs of the foundation. The MRI program accepts research proposals in all scientific and engineering disciplines supported by the foundation.

Eligibility/Limitations Proposals may be submitted to the MRI program by minority scientists and engineers who (a) hold full-time faculty or research-related positions at colleges or universities in the United States, its possessions, and territories and (b) have not previously received federal research support as faculty members. Previous research support in such non-faculty positions as faculty associate, postdoctoral associate, or graduate research assistant does not exclude an applicant from eligibility. The term "minority" as used in this program refers to those ethnic minority groups that are significantly underrepresented in advanced levels of science and engineering, i.e., Blacks, Native Americans, Mexican Americans, Puerto Ricans, Alaskan Natives (Eskimo and Aleut), and Native Pacific Islanders (Polynesian or Micronesian). Investigators must be nationals of the United States.

Fiscal Information Research initiation projects normally will be supported for a period up to three years and may be extended for up to two additional years of support without additional peer review, if warranted by evidence of publications, invited lectures, seminars, or other outcomes demonstrating the significance and promise of the research to date. There is no upper limit on the size of MRI grants. However, the size of awards will be consistent with the general level of awards in the foundation's research programs in the relevant disciplines. Research initiation grants are non-renewable. Subsequent proposals must be submitted directly to the appropriate disciplinary research programs.

Application Information Proposals submitted to this program should be prepared in accordance with instructions in the NSF booklet "Grants for Research and Education in Science and Engineering." using copies of the forms included in its appendices. Those who have questions about their eligibility for this program should call the MRI program director at (202) 357-7350.

Deadline(s) No specific deadlines or target dates apply to proposals submitted under this announcement. Applicants are advised that reviewing and processing of proposals usually requires six to nine months.

Subject Term(s) Minorities, Eligibility of

311. National Science Foundation

Directorate for Scientific, Technological, and International Affairs, Division of Research Initiation and Improvement
1800 G Street, NW
Washington, DC 20550
(202) 357-7734

NSF Visiting Professorships for Women

CFDA Program Number 47.053

Program Description The NSF Visiting Professorships for Women (VPW) program addresses the need to develop full use of the nation's human resources for science and technology. The objectives of the program are to provide opportunities for women to advance their careers in engineering and in the disciplines of science supported by NSF and to encourage women to pursue careers in science and engineering by providing greater visibility for women scientists and engineers employed in industry, government, and academic institutions. These objectives will be furthered by awarding grants to enable women scientists and engineers experienced in independent research to serve as visiting professors at academic institutions in the United States, its possessions, and territories. The program enables a woman scientist or engineer to undertake advanced research at a host institution—a university or four-year college which has the necessary facilities. In addition to her research responsibilities, the visiting professor undertakes lecturing, counseling, and other interactive activities to increase the visibility of women scientists in the academic environment of the host institution and to provide encouragement for other women to pursue careers in science and engineering. The research must be in a field normally supported by NSF, and may be conducted independently or in collaboration with others. The instructional and other interactive activities may be at the undergraduate or graduate levels, be directed to the community at large, or involve some combination of such activities.

Eligibility/Limitations To be eligible to compete in this program an applicant must: hold a doctorate in a field of research supported by NSF, although in exceptional circumstances, experience equivalent to the Ph.D. will be accepted; have independent research experience in an academic institution, industry, or the public sector of the type normally expected of individuals with a faculty appointment; be currently or recently affiliated with an institution of higher education, research institute, government, or industry in the United States, its possessions or territories (if the affiliation is not current, or if the home institution is a foreign one, a statement must be given in the proposal describing the applicant's plan to resume a career in the United States or one of its possessions or territories); and not have a salaried position, or the promise of one, with the proposed host institution, nor be receiving funds from a research grant distributed through that institution, at the time of application to VPW. Those who received visiting professorship awards in previous years are not eligible to reapply. Each applicant may submit only one proposal to the VPW program.

Fiscal Information Awards range in size from $31,900 to $113,000. The usual award will be for twelve months for a full- or part-time professorship. Awards for one academic semester will be considered, as will proposals for periods of up to twenty-four months. In keeping with the objectives of the program, periods of time spent away from the campus for field research or similar activities should be limited.

Application Information Candidates may initiate contact with prospective host institutions, or the institutions may invite eligible candidates to apply to NSF. The applicant, together with the host institution, is responsible for developing plans and arranging for (a) fully developed independent research, which may involve collaboration with a scientist at the host institution, and (b) participation in instructional, counseling, or other interactive activities at the host institution. Applicants submit proposals as individuals, but the host institution's official authorization is required and awards are made to the host institution.

Deadline(s) Proposals must be postmarked no later than October 1. Proposals postmarked after that date will be returned.

Subject Term(s) Women, Eligibility of; Faculty Support; Individuals, Eligibility of

312. National Science Foundation

Directorate for Scientific, Technological, and International Affairs, Division of Research Initiation and Improvement
1800 G Street, NW
Washington, DC 20550
(202) 357-7734

Research Opportunities for Women Program

CFDA Program Number 47.053

Program Description This program provides opportunities for women scientists and engineers to undertake independent research. By supporting research grants for women who have not previously been principal investigators or who are reentering research careers, The Research Opportunities for Women (ROW) program responds to NSF's concern for the quality, distribution, and effectiveness of the human resource base in science and engineering.

Eligibility/Limitations Women eligible to submit proposals are (1) those who have received the doctorate at least three years prior to the submission of the proposals to NSF and have not previously served as principal investigators under a federal award for scientific or engineering research, and (2) those with doctorates whose research careers have been interrupted for at least two of the past five years and who have not served as principal investigators under a federal award for scientific or engineering research since reentering their careers. Proposals will be accepted from individuals with no institutional affiliation, provided the applicant agrees to the fiscal arrangements required by NSF.

Fiscal Information Research projects will be supported up to a maximum period of thirty-six months.

Application Information An annual program announcement gives more information on preparing proposals for submission to this program. For a copy, contact the program director.

Deadline(s) Proposals must be postmarked by January 15.

Subject Term(s) Women, Eligibility of; Individuals, Eligibility of

313. National Wildlife Federation

1412 Sixteenth Street, NW
Washington, DC 20036
(202) 797-6800

Environmental Conservation Fellowships

Program Description These fellowships for graduate students are offered annually to encourage advanced study in fields relating to wildlife, natural resource management, and protection of environmental quality. The following study topics illustrate areas of continuing interest to the National Wildlife Federation (NWF) and its affiliates. Proposals addressing these topics are encouraged: environmental education, communications, and public participation; wildlife habitat management and land use planning; systems ecology, population manipulation, and utilization of fish, wildlife, and plants, including threatened and endangered species; environmental pollution, toxic wastes, and ocean dumping; environmental law and public policy; social and economic aspects of natural resource management; and environmental aspects of energy development and utilization.

Eligibility/Limitations Applications will be accepted from citizens of the United States, Canada, and the Republic of Mexico who are pursuing degrees in a college or university graduate program or law school and have been accepted for the fall semester following the awarding of the grant. Applicants must be principally engaged in research, rather than in course work, during the period for which support is given. First-year graduate students engaged primarily in course work should not apply.

Fiscal Information Grants up to $4,000 are made for a one-year period and imply no commitment for renewal in subsequent years.

Application Information Application for the fellowships must be made on official forms which are available from September through November of each year from the executive vice president of the federation.

Deadline(s) Completed applications must be received by November 30.

Subject Term(s) Foreign Nationals, Eligibility of; Fellowships; Graduate Support; Wildlife Conservation; Environment; Natural Resources; Ecology; Canadian Nationals, Eligibility of; Mexican Nationals, Eligibility of

314. National Wildlife Federation

1412 Sixteenth Street, NW
Washington, DC 20036
(202) 797-6800

Resources Conservation Internships

Program Description The National Wildlife Federation (NWF) offers a program for interns to work in Washington, DC in its resources conservation department. Much of an intern's time is spent in researching environmental policy issues and covering Congressional activity. The federation seeks interns with experience and academic background in the areas of energy, fisheries and wildlife, international issues, pollution and toxics, public lands, and water resources, as well as economics, environmental conservation, and natural resource management.

Eligibility/Limitations The internship program is designed for college graduates and graduate students with a special interest in environmental issues.

Fiscal Information All the internships are for a six-month period. They are full-time positions, with a maximum stipend of $4,200.

Application Information No application form is required. An application consists of a personal letter indicating the applicant's special interests, a complete resume, including a list of three to five references, and a short, nontechnical writing sample.

Deadline(s) Applications for January must be received by November 16; for July, by April 9.

Subject Term(s) Graduate Support; Internships; Wildlife Conservation; Environment; Natural Resources

315. The Needmor Fund

1730 Fifteenth Street
Boulder, CO 80302
(303) 449-5801

Program Description The fund has four primary areas of grantmaking: education, individual rights, environment, and population control. Within these broad areas, the fund is particularly interested in proposals from groups with a high degree of member control working at a local level to change conditions which impact negatively on individual and family development.

Sample Grants In support of continued legal assistance in amassing documentary and testimonial evidence for use in all Guatemalan Indian asylum claims raised in the U.S., $30,000 to Florida Rural Legal Services, Bartow, Florida (1986).

Eligibility/Limitations Organizations which are tax exempt under Section 501(c)(3) of the Internal Revenue Service Code are eligible to apply. The fund does not award grants to individuals.

Fiscal Information The average grant size is between $25,000 and $30,000 for one-year grants.

Application Information Initial contact with the fund should be by letter, not telephone. We suggest applicants send a brief letter describing the project for which support is requested. If it is determined that the activity falls within the fund's guidelines, submission of a written proposal will be invited.

Deadline(s) The fund has two grantmaking cycles per year, with the deadlines for receipt of applications usually falling in December and June. The grantmaking cycle takes approximately ninety days from deadline to final action.

Subject Term(s) Education; Environment; Population Control; Social Justice; Human Rights

316. The Newberry Library

60 West Walton Street
Chicago, IL 60610
(312) 943-9090

American Society for Eighteenth-Century Studies (ASECS) Fellowships

Program Description The Newberry Library, founded in 1887 is a privately endowed independent research library located on the near north side of Chicago. Comprising more than one million volumes and five million manuscripts, it has a strong general collection embracing history and the humanities within Western Civilization from the late Middle Ages to the early twentieth century. Bibliographic holdings are extensive, and certain special collections are internationally noted. ASECS/Newberry Library Fellowships are available for one to three months in residence at the Newberry for studies in the period 1660-1815.

Eligibility/Limitations Applicants must be postdoctoral scholars no more than ten years from receipt of their Ph.D., and members in good standing of the American Society for Eighteenth-Century Studies at the time of application.

Fiscal Information Stipends are $750 per month.

Application Information For additional information and application forms, write to the Committee on Awards, The Newberry Library.

Deadline(s) Completed applications are due by March 1 or October 15.

Subject Term(s) Postdoctoral Support; Fellowships; Humanities; Library Research

317. The Newberry Library

60 West Walton Street
Chicago, IL 60610
(312) 943-9090

Columbian Quincentennial Fellowships

Program Description The Newberry Library, founded in 1887 is a privately endowed independent research library located on the near north side of Chicago. Comprising more than one million volumes and five million manuscripts, it has a strong general collection embracing history and the humanities within Western Civilization from the late Middle Ages to the early twentieth century. Bibliographic holdings are extensive, and certain special collections are internationally noted. Columbian Quincentennial Fellowships are offered for work in residence on topics related to the transatlantic exchange of ideas, products, and peoples in the period 1450-1650. Projects must be synthetic or interdisciplinary in approach, or represent new fields of study for the applicant, or aim at the creation of new classroom materials, teaching units, or courses.

Sample Grants Support to an Assistant Professor of Foreign Languages, Arizona State University, for research on the metalinguistic theme in Columbian documents (1986-1987). Support to a Professor of History, University of Illinois at Chicago, for developing a teaching unit on the world view of the age of discovery (1986-1987).

Fiscal Information Stipends are $800 per month for periods up to four months.

Application Information For information write the Transatlantic Encounters Program at the Newberry, or call 312-943-9090, extension 475.

Additional Information The fellowships are offered in conjunction with a program of summer institutes on the *Transatlantic Encounters* theme, but prior participation in an institute is not required for application.

Subject Term(s) Fellowships; Humanities; Library Research

318. The Newberry Library

60 West Walton Street
Chicago, IL 60610
(312) 943-9090

The Hermon Dunlap Smith Center for the History of Cartography Fellowships

Program Description The Newberry Library, founded in 1887 is a privately endowed independent research library located on the near north side of Chicago. Comprising more than one million volumes and five million manuscripts, it has a strong general collection embracing history and the humanities within Western Civilization from the late Middle Ages to the early twentieth century. Bibliographic holdings are extensive, and certain special collections are internationally noted. These fellowships support short-term or long-term research in the history of cartography.

Eligibility/Limitations Applicants for long-term fellowships must be established scholars.

Fiscal Information Short-term fellowships carry a stipend of $750 per month for periods not exceeding three months. Long-term fellowships are available for six to twelve months' research in residence (maximum stipend, $27,500).

Application Information For additional information and application forms, write to the Committee on Awards, the Newberry Library.

Deadline(s) Applications for long-term fellowships will be considered once a year, with a deadline of March 1. Applications for short-term fellowships will be considered twice a year, with deadlines of March 1 and October 15.

Subject Term(s) Fellowships; Cartography; Library Research

319. The Newberry Library

60 West Walton Street
Chicago, IL 60610
(312) 943-9090

Joint Fellowships with the American Antiquarian Society

Program Description The Newberry Library, founded in 1887 is a privately endowed independent research library located on the near north side of Chicago. Comprising more than one million volumes and five million manuscripts, it has a strong general collection embracing history and the humanities within Western Civilization from the late Middle Ages to the early twentieth century. Bibliographic holdings are extensive, and certain special collections are internationally noted. Scholars who desire to use collections both at the Newberry and the American Antiquarian Society may apply for a joint fellowship via a single application.

Eligibility/Limitations Applicants must have the Ph.D. or have completed all requirements except the dissertation.

Fiscal Information Awards are available for up to two months at the Newberry, and for from one to three months at the American Antiquarian Society. Stipends at the Newberry are $750 per month.

Application Information For additional information and application forms, write the Committee on Awards, The Newberry Library.

Deadline(s) Completed application forms are due by January 31 or October 15.

Additional Information Decisions will be made independently at each institution.

Subject Term(s) Postdoctoral Support; Fellowships; Humanities; Library Research

320. The Newberry Library

60 West Walton Street
Chicago, IL 60610
(312) 943-9090

Monticello College Foundation Fellowship for Women

Program Description The Newberry Library, founded in 1887 is a privately endowed independent research library located on the near north side of Chicago. Comprising more than one million volumes and five million manuscripts, it has a strong general collection embracing history and the humanities within Western Civilization from the late Middle Ages to the early twentieth century. Bibliographic holdings are extensive, and certain special collections are internationally noted. The Monticello College Foundation Fellowship is designed primarily for women at an early stage in their professional careers whose work gives clear promise of scholarly productivity and whose career would be significantly enhanced by six months of research and writing. Preference will be given to applicants whose scholarship is particularly concerned with the study of women, but study may be proposed in any field appropriate to the Newberry's collections.

Eligibility/Limitations Applicants must have the Ph.D. at the time of application, and must by U.S. citizens or permanent residents.

Fiscal Information The six-month fellowship for work in residence at the Newberry carries a stipend of $8,500.

Application Information For additional information and application forms, write to the Committee on Awards, The Newberry Library.

Deadline(s) Completed applications are due by January 15.

Subject Term(s) Fellowships; Postdoctoral Support; Women, Eligibility of; Humanities; Library Research; Women's Studies

321. The Newberry Library

60 West Walton Street
Chicago, IL 60610
(312) 943-9090

National Endowment for the Humanities Fellowships

Program Description The Newberry Library, founded in 1887 is a privately endowed independent research library located on the near north side of Chicago. Comprising more than one million volumes and five million manuscripts, it has a strong general collection embracing history and the humanities within Western Civilization from the late Middle Ages to the early twentieth century. Bibliographic holdings are extensive, and certain special collections are internationally noted. NEH/Newberry Fellowships are designed not only to encourage the individual scholar's research, but also to deepen and enrich the opportunities for serious intellectual exchange through the active participation of fellows in the Newberry community. Fellowships are available for research in residence in any field appropriate to the Newberry's collections.

Eligibility/Limitations These grants are for established scholars at the postdoctoral level, or its equivalent. Awards are open to United States citizens or nationals, and to foreign nationals who have been living in the United States for at least three years. Preference is given to applicants who have not held major fellowships or grants for three years preceding the proposed period of residency.

Fiscal Information Fellowships are available for six to eleven months' research and are for up to $27,500 for eleven months' residency.

Application Information For additional information and application forms, write to the Committee on Awards, The Newberry Library.

Deadline(s) Completed applications are due by January 15.

Subject Term(s) Fellowships; Postdoctoral Support; Library Research; Foreign Nationals, Eligibility of; Humanities

322. The Newberry Library

60 West Walton Street
Chicago, IL 60610
(312) 943-9090

Resident Fellowships for Unaffiliated Scholars

Program Description The Newberry Library, founded in 1887 is a privately endowed independent research library located on the near north side of Chicago. Comprising more than one million volumes and five million manuscripts, it has a strong general collection embracing history and the humanities within Western Civilization from the late Middle Ages to the early twentieth century. Bibliographic holdings are extensive, and certain special collections are internationally noted. These fellowships support unaffiliated scholars working on a specific research project in a field appropriate to the Newberry's collections.

Eligibility/Limitations Applicants must have held the Ph.D. at least two years and not be employed professionally as scholars. Applicants must anticipate spending at least six to eight hours a week in residence and participating fully in the intellectual life of the Newberry.

Fiscal Information The fellowships carry stipends of $250 per calendar quarter. Stipends may be renewed quarterly up to one year; after the first year fellowship status may be renewed annually, but without stipend.

Application Information For additional information and application forms, write to the Committee on Awards, The Newberry Library.

Deadline(s) Completed applications are due March 1 or October 15.

Subject Term(s) Postdoctoral Support; Fellowships; Humanities; Individuals, Eligibility of; Library Research

323. The Newberry Library

60 West Walton Street
Chicago, IL 60610
(312) 943-9090

Short-Term Resident Fellowships for Individual Scholars

Program Description The Newberry Library, founded in 1887 is a privately endowed independent research library located on the near north side of Chicago. Comprising more than one million volumes and five million manuscripts, it has a strong general collection embracing history and the humanities within Western Civilization from the late Middle Ages to the early twentieth century. Bibliographic holdings are extensive, and certain special collections are internationally noted. Short-term fellowships are designed primarily to help provide access to Newberry resources for people who live beyond commuting distance. Preference is given accordingly to applicants from outside the greater Chicago area.

Sample Grants Fellowship to an Assistant Professor, Department of History, University of Turin, for research on the Christianization of Central American Indians (1985).

Eligibility/Limitations Applicants must have the Ph.D. or have completed all requirements except the dissertation.

Fiscal Information Fellowships carry stipends of $750 per month, for periods of up to two months, or when travel from a foreign country is involved, three months.

Application Information For additional information and application forms, write to the Committee on Awards, The Newberry Library.

Deadline(s) Completed applications are due by March 1 or October 15.

Subject Term(s) Fellowships; Predoctoral Support; Individuals, Eligibility of; Library Research; Humanities; Foreign Nationals, Eligibility of; Predoctoral Support

324. Jessie Smith Noyes Foundation

16 East 34th Street
New York, NY 10016
(212) 684-6577

Program Description The Jessie Smith Noyes Foundation provides support primarily in the areas of environment and population. The environmental program focuses on three topics: tropical ecology (Western Hemisphere) and sustainable agriculture (U.S., Canada, Third World), which include preservation of genetic diversity, and water resources (U.S.). The population program is limited almost exclusively to family planning programs in Third World countries. The foundation favors projects that address the connections among those problems and their global implications, and especially those that have a widespread impact or applicability.

Sample Grants In support of a research assistantship to study the effects of the use of agrochemicals on lakes used as an important resource for food and water in Ecuador, $15,275 to Ohio State University (1985). In support of postdoctoral fellowships for inventorying tropical forests, $79,600 (first year of a two-year grant totaling $140,600) to New York Botanical Garden, Bronx, New York (1985). In support of graduate fellowships for students engaged in research vital to knowledge about the maintenance of genetic diversity and the functioning of tropical ecosystems, $57,500 (second year of a three-year grant totaling $172,000) to Organization for Tropical Studies, Durham, North Carolina (1985). In support of a study of overlooked crops of the Andes and their worldwide promise for expanding food supplies and preserving genetic resources, $31,050 (first year of a two-year grant totaling $62,100) to National Academy of Sciences and National Research Council (1985).

Eligibility/Limitations Awards are granted only to tax-exempt institutions, in the form of scholarships, fellowships, internships, or training stipends for participating students.

Application Information Institutions applying for a grant should send a letter, not exceeding two pages in length, to the program administrator at the foundation. The following information should be included: a concise description of the proposed project, including its starting date and probable duration; the total budget; and the specific amount requested from the Noyes Foundation for student aid or training. The applicant will be notified as soon as possible whether or not the foundation is able to give the proposal further consideration, and, if so, what additional information is required.

Deadline(s) Meetings of the board of directors of the foundation are held in January, May, and October. Proposals to be considered must therefore be received by the first of the preceding month.

Subject Term(s) Population; Environment; Tropical Ecology; Ecology; Agriculture; Family Planning

325. John M. Olin Foundation, Inc.

100 Park Avenue, Suite 2701
New York, NY 10017
(212) 661-2670

Grants

Program Description The general purpose of the John M. Olin Foundation is to provide support for projects that reflect or are intended to strengthen the economic, political, and cultural institutions upon which the American system of democratic capitalism is based. The foundation also seeks to promote a general understanding of these institutions by encouraging the thoughtful study of the interactions between economic and political freedoms, and the cultural heritage which sustains them. Within the context of the foundation's general purposes, the board of trustees has authorized grants in the following areas: research on the formulation, implementation, and evaluation of public policy in the economic and social fields; projects that address the relationship between American institutions and the international context within which they operate; studies of the American Constitution, the operation of American political institutions, and the moral and cultural principles underlying these institutions; and public interest law and studies related to the judicial system, jurisprudence, and the relationship between law and economics. In each of these four areas, the foundation attempts to advance its objectives through support of the following kinds of activities: research, institutional support, fellowships, professorships, lectures and lecture series, books, scholarly journals, journals of opinion, conferences and seminars, and, on occasion, television and radio programs.

Sample Grants To support educational events during the second annual commemoration of the liberation of Grenada, $10,000 to American Opportunity Foundation, Washington, DC (1985). To support educational programs which encourage the development of democracy in Central America, $40,000 to The Friends of the Democratic Center in Central America, Arlington, VA (1985). To support a conference on the Soviet Union, Nicaragua and Central America, $20,000 to University of Miami, Graduate School of International Studies, Coral Gables, Florida (1985).

Eligibility/Limitations The guidelines established by the board of trustees normally preclude funding for administrative overhead costs. In addition, grants will not be considered for endowment or building programs, annual giving programs, direct support for individuals or programs without significant impact on national affairs. Grants will be made only to institutions that provide a responsible fiscal agent and that are tax exempt under Section 501(c)(3) of the Internal Revenue Code.

Fiscal Information Grant authorizations in 1985 exceeded $20 million.

Application Information Applicants should prepare a letter which gives a brief and concise description of the project, its objectives and significance, and the qualifications of the organizations and individuals involved. Included with the letter should be a project budget, the amount of the grant sought from the foundation, and mention of other sources of support. To insure eligibility for a grant, the applicant should also submit a copy of the IRS letter confirming the organization's tax-exempt status under Section 501(c)(3) of the Internal Revenue Code.

Deadline(s) Final authority for making grants rests with the board of trustees which meets five times a year.

Subject Term(s) Economics; Law; Public Policy Studies; International Studies

326. Organization of American States

Department of Fellowships and Training
Washington, DC 20006-4499
(202) 789-3902

OAS Regular Training Program: Fellowships

Program Description The OAS Regular Training Program (PRA) is one of the instruments of development cooperation of the Organization of American States (OAS). Its fundamental objective is to further the economic, social, technical, and cultural development of the American peoples. Under the policy established by the council of the OAS, priority will be given to the studies, research, and training necessary for the expansion of man's productivity, and fellowships will be granted to candidates who give evidence of having had advanced training in the field for which the fellowship is requested. Fellowships are for research or advanced graduate study in any of the member countries of the Organization of American States.

Eligibility/Limitations Those who may apply for an OAS fellowship are citizens or permanent residents of an OAS member country, with a university degree or who have demonstrated ability to pursue advanced studies in the field chosen. Therefore, the fellowships are for advanced study or research in any field, with the exception of the medical sciences, and are not granted for undergraduate level studies nor for introductory language training. Candidates must know the language of the study country.

Fiscal Information Fellowships provide funds sufficient to cover, as a maximum, and in accordance with circumstances, travel expenses, tuition fees, study materials, and subsistence allowance (which varies from country to country). No benefits are provided to the family of the fellowship holder. Fellowships are granted for periods of not less than three months nor more than two years.

Application Information Additional information is available from the Department of Fellowships and Training. Applications should be sent to the advisory board of the OAS.

Deadline(s) Applications should be received no later than April 30 or August 31.

Subject Term(s) Fellowships Abroad; Foreign Nationals, Eligibility of; Graduate Support Abroad; Economic Development; Individuals, Eligibility of; Development

327. Pacific Coast Council on Latin American Studies

Foreign Language Department
Arizona State University
Tempe, AZ 85287
(602) 965-3752

Hubert B. Herring Memorial Awards

Program Description The annual Hubert Herring Awards of the Pacific Coast Council on Latin American Studies (PCCLAS) were established in 1965 to encourage, promote, and recognize significant research in Latin American Studies. Awards are made in the following categories: (1) best article or article-length manuscript; (2) best book or book-length manuscript; (3) best master's or senior thesis; (4) best Ph.D. dissertation; and (5) best film, videotape, or non-print media. For purposes of the award the geographic area of the PCCLAS is as follows: Canada, British Columbia and Alberta; Mexico, Baja California and Sonora; and the U.S., Washington, Oregon, California, Arizona, Nevada, Idaho, Hawaii, and Alaska.

Eligibility/Limitations Candidates need not be members of PCCLAS. The work must have been published or produced no more than two years prior to nomination. Three copies of the project must be submitted by deadline. The works of candidates must be nominated.

Application Information Contact the Hubert Herring Awards Committee at the address listed above for additional information.

Deadline(s) The deadline for submissions is June 1.

Subject Term(s) Awards and Prizes

328. The David and Lucile Packard Foundation

330 Second Street
Los Altos, CA 94022
(415) 948-7658

Conservation Program

Program Description The Conservation Program reflects the foundation's local, national, and international interests in the major areas of land use planning, the purchase of open space, wildlife and wildlife habitat preservation, and a small program concerning water conservation on agricultural land .

Sample Grants Toward development of a master plan to protect the migration system of monarch butterflies in the U.S., Canada, and Mexico, $35,000 to Monarch Project of the Xerces Society, Portland, Oregon (1984).

Eligibility/Limitations Applications for grants are accepted only from qualified tax-exempt charitable organizations. Applications cannot be accepted for the benefit of individuals or religious purposes.

Fiscal Information In 1984 the foundation authorized grants totaling $776,656 in this program area.

Application Information Foundation staff is willing, whenever possible, to offer assistance through advice and contacts, in addition to the review of proposals. Additional information and application guidelines are available on request.

Deadline(s) Although proposals shall be accepted throughout the year, applicants wishing to be considered at quarterly board meetings should forward their proposals by the following deadlines: January 7 for the March meeting, April 7 for the June meeting, July 7 for the September meeting, and October 7 for the December meeting.

Subject Term(s) Conservation; Wildlife Conservation; Natural Resources

329. The David and Lucile Packard Foundation

330 Second Street
Los Altos, CA 94022
(415) 948-7658

Health Program

Program Description The foundation's health interests are focused on programs for disabled children and adults in four California counties, and population and family planning services. The foundation's international population program has focused primarily on the training of medical and administrative personnel in developing countries. The foundation will in the future concentrate grants in Latin America.

Sample Grants To initiate a program of pregnancy termination services at the Family Medical Center near Bogata, Colombia $19,790 to the Pathfinder Fund, Chestnut Hill, Massachusetts (1983).

Eligibility/Limitations Applications for grants are accepted only from qualified tax-exempt charitable organizations. Applications cannot be accepted for the benefit of individuals or religious purposes.

Fiscal Information In 1984 the foundation authorized grants totaling $1,021,203 in this program area.

Application Information Foundation staff is willing, whenever possible, to offer assistance through advice and contacts, in addition to the review of proposals. Additional information and application guidelines are available on request.

Deadline(s) Although proposals shall be accepted throughout the year, applicants wishing to be considered at quarterly board meetings should forward their proposals by the following deadlines: January 7 for the March meeting, April 7 for the June meeting, July 7 for the September meeting, and October 7 for the December meeting.

Subject Term(s) Population; Family Planning

330. Pan American Health Organization

Pan American Sanitary Bureau, Regional Office of the World Health Organization
525 Twenty-third Street, NW
Washington, DC 20037
(212) 861-3200

Fellowships

Program Description This fellowship program is intended to assist member governments in strengthening their health services; to promote cooperation among scientific and professional groups which contribute to the advancement of health; and to improve standards of teaching and training in health, medical, and related professions. The major fields in which fellowships are given comprise public health administration, environmental health, nursing, medical social work, maternal and child health, communicable diseases, laboratory services, clinical medicine, basic medical sciences, and medical and allied education.

Eligibility/Limitations An individual, to be considered for a fellowship, should be proposed by his or her own government. Normally, fellowships are granted only to persons who are in good health and not over fifty-five years of age if the retiring age is sixty or above, and not over fifty if the retiring age is below sixty.

Fiscal Information The fellowship carries a stipend for room, board, and incidentals. Stipend rates are established by worldwide interagency agreement in order that all fellows in a country be paid uniformly.

Application Information The World Health Organization (WHO) can only accept applications for fellowships which have been duly approved and transmitted by the recognized health authority of the candidate's country. Candidates for fellowships must start by making contact with their national health administration.

Subject Term(s) Foreign Nationals, Eligibility of; Fellowships; Health; Health Care

331. Partners of the Americas

1424 K Street, NW, Suite 700
Washington, DC 20005
(202) 628-3300

Excellence Grants

Program Description Partners of the Americas is the largest private voluntary organization promoting economic and social development in the Western Hemisphere, while fostering inter-American friendship and cooperation. Through the program, U.S. states and countries of Latin America and the Caribbean are linked into "partnerships." The Partners of the Americas Foundation has announced its first annual grants program offering funds to strengthen a partnership in the pursuit of excellence.

Eligibility/Limitations Partners committees are eligible to apply. Both the northern and southern committees of a partnership need to endorse applications for the funding and their joint participation is emphasized, though not required.

Fiscal Information The grants carry an award of up to $2,000 a year in operational funds.

Application Information Additional information is available on request.

Subject Term(s) International Relations; Development; Exchanges

332. Partners of the Americas

1424 K Street, NW, Suite 700
Washington, DC 20005
(202) 628-3300

Fellowships in International Development

Program Description Partners of the Americas has established its Fellowships in International Development program to prepare young professionals for a wide variety of leadership roles in helping to solve or minimize problems affecting human well-being. Through the program, U.S. states and countries of Latin America and the Caribbean are linked into "partnerships." Partnerships exchange volunteers with professional backgrounds in a variety of fields. These volunteers directly share their knowledge and skills to conduct self-help projects at the grass-roots level. They provide training and technical assistance to help communities identify and achieve long-range goals. Forty candidates, twenty from the United States and twenty from Latin America and the Caribbean, are selected for this two-year leadership development program. These individuals take part in a series of seminars, development projects, and other learning experiences which require a four to six-week commitment each year.

Eligibility/Limitations Nominees for the fellowship program: must be twenty-five to forty-five years of age as of June 1 in the year of the first seminar; may come from any career field; must have demonstrated interest in international relations and development and work towards the ability to converse in an appropriate second or third language; must submit employer's permission in writing to participate in the program for up to six weeks per year; must be or become active members of a Partners committee; and must have demonstrated leadership potential.

Fiscal Information The fellowships cover airfare and most of the costs associated with the seminars. As an expression of commitment to the program and to help cover costs, each participant or sponsor contributes $400 (U.S.) per year to the two-year program.

Application Information The local Partners committee in a candidate's state, region, or country submits nominations for this program.

Subject Term(s) International Relations; Development; Exchanges

333. Partners of the Americas

1424 K Street, NW, Suite 700
Washington, DC 20005
(202) 628-3300

International Training Program

Program Description Partners of the Americas is the largest private voluntary organization promoting economic and social development in the Western Hemisphere, while fostering inter-American friendship and cooperation. Through the program, U.S. states and countries of Latin America and the Caribbean are linked into "partnerships." The training program is designed to provide new opportunity for Latin American and Caribbean professionals, technicians, craftsmen, and students to receive advanced training in their chosen fields in the U.S. Training areas are flexible, but fields of major importance are: agriculture and rural development; health and nutrition; urban or regional planning; business, marketing, and finance; engineering; construction trades; and crafts trades.

Eligibility/Limitations The program seeks a mix of participants in a variety of trades and professions. It is important that each candidate have: a strong professional performance and growth record; evidence of leadership ability; a commitment to work in his or her country after completing the program; and a willingness to participate in the local partnership on return home.

Fiscal Information Both short- and long-term training are available. However, there are more technically-oriented short-term (one to six months) positions available than long term (up to twenty-four months). No one can be supported for less than one month or more than twenty-four. Travel, training and tuition costs, and living expenses will be largely borne by Partners of the Americas. However, the amount of in-kind or other support that a partnership arranges for a nominee will help the individual's chances for selection to the program.

Application Information Candidates must be nominated through their local Partners committee. Interested persons can obtain information and applications through their local Partners president. This name and address can be obtained by contacting the U.S. Agency for International Development representative at the nearest U.S. mission or embassy or by writing to the Partners International Training Grant Program at the address listed above.

Subject Term(s) Foreign Nationals, Eligibility of; Development

334. The Population Council

One Dag Hammarskjold Plaza
New York, NY 10017

Graduate Study

Program Description Fellowships may be awarded for advanced training in population studies (including demography and biostatistics), or for study plans in population in combination with a social science discipline, such as economics, sociology, anthropology, geography, political science, or public administration.

Eligibility/Limitations Applications by persons who have already made considerable progress toward the Ph.D. or an equivalent degree in one of the social sciences, or who are already at the dissertation level, will be given preference. Awards are open to all qualified persons but strong preference will be given to applicants from developing countries who have a firm commitment to return to their home country upon completion of their training programs. Applications by women are particularly encouraged.

Fiscal Information Awards consist of a monthly stipend (based on place of study), tuition payments and related fees, transportation expenses, and health insurance. Some research-related costs may also be part of the award. There will be a modest supplement to stipends for up to three dependents but transportation expenses for dependents are not covered. Awards are made for up to one year. A single extension, or a nonconsecutive second award will be considered in competition with first-time applicants.

Application Information Application forms can be obtained from the fellowship secretary.

Deadline(s) Applications must be received by December 1.

Subject Term(s) Fellowships; Predoctoral Support; Foreign Nationals, Eligibility of; Population; Population Studies; Demography; Social Sciences; Anthropology; Sociology; Geography; Political Science; Public Administration; Economics

335. The Population Council

One Dag Hammarskjold Plaza
New York, NY 10017

Mid-Career Study

Program Description These awards are granted for advanced training in population studies (including demography and biostatistics), or for study plans in population in combination with a social science discipline, such as economics, sociology, anthropology, geography, political science, or public administration.

Eligibility/Limitations Mid-career Study Awards are open to persons with substantial professional experience in the population field wishing to undertake a specific plan of training and study to update and strengthen their professional skills. Awards are open to all qualified persons but strong preference will be given to applicants from developing countries who have a firm commitment to return to their home country upon completion of their training programs. Applications by women are particularly encouraged.

Fiscal Information Awards consist of a monthly stipend (based on place of study), tuition payments and related fees, transportation expenses, and health insurance. Some research-related costs may also be part of the award. There will be a modest supplement to stipends for up to three dependents but transportation expenses for dependents are not covered. Awards are made for up to one year.

Application Information Application forms can be obtained from the fellowship secretary.

Deadline(s) Applications must be received by December 1.

Subject Term(s) Foreign Nationals, Eligibility of; Population; Population Studies; Demography; Social Sciences; Economics; Sociology; Anthropology; Geography; Political Science; Public Administration

336. The Population Council

One Dag Hammarskjold Plaza
New York, NY 10017

Postdoctoral Study

Program Description These awards are granted for advanced training in population studies (including demography and biostatistics), or for study plans in population in combination with a social science discipline, such as economics, sociology, anthropology, geography, political science, or public administration.

Eligibility/Limitations Postdoctoral study awards are open to persons having the Ph.D. or equivalent degree who wish to undertake postdoctoral training and research with a population specialization. Awards are open to all qualified persons but strong preference will be given to applicants from developing countries who have a firm commitment to return to their home country upon completion of their training programs. Applications by women are particularly encouraged.

Fiscal Information Awards consist of a monthly stipend (based on place of study), tuition payments and related fees, transportation expenses, and health insurance. Some research-related costs may also be part of the award. There will be a modest supplement to stipends for up to three dependents but transportation expenses for dependents are not covered. Awards are made for up to one year.

Application Information Application forms can be obtained from the fellowship secretary.

Deadline(s) Applications must be received by December 1.

Subject Term(s) Fellowships; Foreign Nationals, Eligibility of; Postdoctoral Support; Population; Population Studies; Demography; Economics; Sociology; Anthropology; Geography; Political Science; Public Administration; Social Sciences

337. Smith Richardson Foundation, Inc.

5000 Laurinda Drive, P.O. Box 3265
Greensboro, NC 27402
(919) 288-7230

Grants-in-Aid

Program Description The Grants-in-Aid program of the foundation has two main thrusts. The first is a public affairs program, aimed at supporting and promoting those elements necessary to a vigorous economy and a free society. It does this through: support of specific projects which encourage competent scholars and organizations to study public policies that affect business and the economy; seed-money grants for innovative educational programs that appear to have a substantial promise of success; support of carefully conceived projects that illuminate the degree of consensus necessary for a free society; and support of scholarship and educational projects which encourage competent scholars and organizations to examine foreign policy and national security issues of greatest importance to the United States. The second major thrust of the foundation is to aid in developing the qualities of leadership that will make society fully responsive to the great demands being placed upon it in today's world through support of the Center for Creative Leadership in Greensboro, North Carolina.

Sample Grants To provide support for the Instituto Libertad y Democracia of Lima, Peru, $40,000 to Atlas Economic Research Foundation, San Francisco, California (1985). To provide support in establishing its Center for Caribbean and Central American Studies, $5,302 to Freedom House, New York, New York (1985). To provide support for its Central American speakers program, New York, New York $25,000 to PRODEMCA—Citizens' Committee for the Pro-Democratic Forces in Central America (1985). To provide support for a public information program on Central America, $38,012 to United States Strategic Institute, Cambridge, Massachusetts (1985). To provide support for publicizing domestic problems and international activities of Castro's regime, $15,000 to Cuba Independiente Y Democratica, Miami, Florida (1985).

Eligibility/Limitations Grants are normally made to organizations which are tax-exempt under the Internal Revenue Code.

Fiscal Information Grants-in-aid totaled over $7.2 million in 1985. Grants are not normally provided for deficit funding, projects relating to construction, programs relating to the arts, historic preservation projects, research in the physical sciences, or community or regional health, recreation, welfare, and employment programs.

Application Information The foundation has no specific forms for requesting grants nor does it require a specific presentation format. A letter of application is sufficient and should include the following: a brief statement of the purpose and desirability of the project; a brief description of the applicant organization; a detailed schedule of work and budget for the project; evidence that the proposed project has not been earlier and adequately carried out; and a description of the audience for which the project is intended. All requests should be submitted to the coordinator.

Deadline(s) Grants are normally approved quarterly.

Subject Term(s) Public Policy; Foreign Affairs

338. Rockefeller Archive Center

Pocantico Hills
North Tarrytown, NY 10591
(914) 631-4505

Research Grant Program

Program Description During the twentieth century, organizations founded and supported by the philanthropies of the Rockefeller family have influenced the development of education, science, medicine, social science, agriculture, economics, conservation, and cultural affairs throughout the world. Material relating to these activities, plus the personal papers of family members and other individuals associated with their endeavors, total some twenty million documents to date and comprise an invaluable and irreplaceable reference source for historians and other scholars. To ensure the protection of these unique collections and to assemble them under one roof, the Rockefeller Archive Center of the Rockefeller University was established. The center is a permanent repository that offers convenient access and assistance to qualified scholars. To foster research, a modest grant-in-aid program was established to support students or scholars engaged in projects based substantially on the holdings of the center.

Sample Grants A 1986 research grant was awarded for a study of Daniel Cosio Villegas, The Rockefeller Foundation, and the professionalization of Mexican history.

Eligibility/Limitations Applicants of any discipline who are engaged in projects that require substantial use of collections at the center are eligible.

Fiscal Information Grants carry awards up to $1,500. The exact size of the grant is dependent upon the travel and research needs of the applicant.

Application Information Additional information and application guidelines are available on request.

Deadline(s) The deadline for application is December 31 of each year.

Subject Term(s) Individuals, Eligibility of; Graduate Support; Postdoctoral Support; Archives, Research

339. Rockefeller Brothers Fund

1290 Avenue of the Americas
New York, NY 10104

Global Interdependence Grants

Program Description The Rockefeller Brothers Fund (RBF) seeks to achieve its major objective of improving the well-being of all people through support of efforts in the United States and abroad that contribute ideas, develop leaders, and encourage institutions in the transition to global interdependence and that counter world trends of resource depletion, militarization, protectionism, and isolation which now threaten to move humankind everywhere further away from cooperation, trade and economic growth, arms restraint, and conservation. The basic theme of interdependence presupposes a global outlook and, hence, internationally-oriented activity. While United States problems and grantees will receive considerable attention, this will be in the context of global concerns and not simply national ones. The fund makes grants in four general areas. The first, "One World", is made up of two components, Sustainable Resource Use and World Security, which will receive the major portion of grant funds. The other three areas are New York City, Nonprofit Sector, and Special Concerns.

Sample Grants For continued core support for the eco-development programs of its Eastern Caribbean Natural Area Management Program and Marine Resources Program for the Eastern Caribbean which encourage economic growth using natural resources in ways consistent with sustained productivity and environmental limitations, $75,000 to Caribbean Conservation Association, St. Michael, Barbados (1985). For continued core support for the school's Wildland Management Center, which cooperates with the Eastern Caribbean Natural Area Management Program of the Caribbean Conservation Association, Barbados, in promoting economic development in ways that encourage efficient and sustainable use of natural resources, $55,000 to the School of Natural Resources, University of Michigan, Ann Arbor, Michigan (1985).

Eligibility/Limitations To qualify for a grant from RBF a prospective grantee must be either a tax-exempt organization or an organization seeking support for a project that would qualify as tax exempt. A grantee must also be engaged in work that fits generally within the fund's new program, Global Interdependence. The fund does not make grants to individuals, nor does it, as a general rule, support research, graduate study, or the writing of books or dissertations by individuals.

Fiscal Information Although the RBF has made substantial gifts to organizations and programs in which it has considerable interest, most grants run between $10,000 and $75,000, the average between $25,000 and $35,000.

Application Information A preliminary letter of inquiry is recommended for an initial approach to the fund, although the submission of detailed proposals is also appropriate. Additional information and application guidelines are available on request.

Deadline(s) Grants are awarded by the trustees, who meet regularly throughout the year.

Subject Term(s) Peace; Conservation; International Affairs; International Studies; Arms Control

340. The Rockefeller Foundation

1133 Avenue of the Americas
New York, NY 10036
(212) 869-8500

Fellowships in Population Sciences

Program Description Fellowships are awarded for advanced training in reproductive biology/medicine and in population studies in demography or for studies of population in combination with a social science discipline. Program components focus on: (1)

reproductive biology including research in reproductive biology and contraceptive technology and (2) policy studies which are designed to improve understanding of fertility determinants, with an emphasis on the status and role of women; delineate the determinants and consequences of population growth in developing countries; and explore selected population issues in the United States.

Eligibility/Limitations Postdoctoral applicants must be thirty-five years of age or under and have a recent Ph.D. Graduate awards are intended for persons thirty-five years of age or under and are restricted to persons who have completed all work, except the dissertation, toward the Ph.D. or an equivalent in one of the social sciences with a specialization in population. Preference will be given to persons from developing countries who have a firm commitment to return to their home countries upon completion of training.

Fiscal Information Awards consist of a monthly stipend (based on the type of fellowship and place of study), tuition payments and related fees, transportation expenses, and health insurance. A family allowance may be granted to appointees who have dependents in their immediate family for whom they are financially responsible.

Application Information Additional information and application guidelines are available on request.

Deadline(s) Applications should be received by the foundation no later than November 15.

Subject Term(s) Foreign Nationals, Eligibility of; Postdoctoral Support; Predoctoral Support; Fellowships; Population; Population Studies; Reproductive Biology; Demography; Social Sciences; Contraception; Women; Developing Countries; Fertility

341. The Rockefeller Foundation

1133 Avenue of the Americas
New York, NY 10036
(212) 869-8500

Gender Role Program

Program Description The Rockefeller Foundation announces support for projects that will improve the understanding and recognition of changing gender roles in the work place and within the family. The foundation's purpose is to encourage attention to changes in gender roles by supporting projects that address the social, psychological, political, and economic phenomena associated with the rapidly changing status of women. Projects should examine factors underlying such changes, or analyze ways in which policy could respond to these changes.

Sample Grants A grant was awarded in support of a study to examine the changing nature of women's work in Brazil from 1850 to 1920 (1985).

Eligibility/Limitations The competition is open to women and men around the world who have completed their professional training. Scholars and practitioners from the social sciences, humanities, law, journalism, health, and the natural sciences are encouraged to apply. Awards cannot be made for the completion of degree training. Applicants need not have an academic or institutional affiliation.

Fiscal Information The foundation seeks to support projects with small and moderate budgets. Most grants will be in the range of $15,000 to $30,000. Grant funds may be requested for salary and honoraria, secretarial or research support, or travel. Overhead payments cannot be provided. The grant may be made through a tax-exempt institution or self-administered.

Application Information Additional information and application procedures are available from the Gender Roles Program, The Rockefeller Foundation.

Deadline(s) Deadlines for submission of proposals are March 15 and September 15.

Subject Term(s) Individuals, Eligibility of; Foreign Nationals, Eligibility of; Gender; Gender Roles; Family; Women

342. The Rockefeller Foundation

1133 Avenue of the Americas
New York, NY 10036
(212) 869-8500

Grants

Program Description The foundation largely concentrates its efforts in selected areas with well-defined goals. It tries to keep its overall program flexible and dynamic through periodic reappraisals and changes in the light of new needs and opportunities. At present, program interests are as follows: (1) In the agricultural sciences, foundation grants are made to encourage research and action programs that are dedicated to providing adequate food supplies and distribution in the developing world. The foundation is focusing on three specific objectives: strengthening food and agricultural systems in sub-Saharan Africa; supporting research and practical application of genetic engineering methods to improve crop and animal productivity; and promoting institutional cooperation to address critical agricultural issues. (2) In the arts and humanities, the foundation has as its fundamental purposes the encouragement of creative work by artists, scholars, and teachers, and the channeling of that work into the broader society. (3) The foundation attempts to assure full participation of minorities in the benefits as well as the obligations of American citizenship by expanding economic opportunity, broadening career opportunities, and supporting and protecting basic rights. (4) The foundation considers the vigorous pursuit of humane, wise, and peaceful relations among countries an important corollary to its objectives in other programs. Two broad issues warrant sustained attention: How might threats to peace arising from the intersection of local tensions and the competition for security or influence between the United States and the Soviet Union be reduced, and how can political and institutional obstacles to sound management of economic relations among countries by overcome? (5) Since 1963 the foundation has been striving toward the goal of population stabilization through support of research, training, and experimental programs in a broad range of fields related to population. (6) Medicine and health have been concerns of the foundation since its inception. The foundation is interested in great neglected diseases, the health of populations, and projects focused on coping with biomedical information. In addition to these areas of interest, the foundation, under its Special Interests and Explorations program, allows itself the flexibility to examine for possible support proposals that do not fall within the existing programs.

Sample Grants Toward improving their laboratory facilities for use of rice anther culture technology, $40,300 to the International Center for Tropical Agriculture, Cali, Colombia (1985). For use by its Department of Agriculture and Applied Economics in a study of the Cuban agricultural research system, $12,900 to the University of Minnesota, St. Paul (1985). Toward the costs of a lithography project and exhibition by nine Mexican artists, $17,500 to the University of New Mexico for use by the Tamarind Institute and the Latin American Studies Institute (1985). For the study of the pathogenesis of invasive amebiasis, onchocerciasis, and American trypanosomiasis, $30,000 to the Center for Research and Advanced Studies, National Polytechnic Institute, Mexico City, Mexico (1985). Toward the costs of a study, in Peru, on the pathogenesis of measles and its attendant immune deregulation, $10,914 to Johns Hopkins University (1985). For the analysis of a study of the factors contributing to the good health of the poor rural population of the Puriscal region in Costa Rica, to be administered by Harvard University, $30,000 to the University of Costa Rica (1985). Toward the costs of a meeting of Latin American scientists engaged in research on human reproduction, $10,000 to Catholic University of Chile, Santiago, Chile (1985).

Eligibility/Limitations To accomplish lasting results with finite resources, the foundation must necessarily concentrate its support on projects that fall within defined program areas.

Fiscal Information The foundation does not give or lend money to individuals; appraise or subsidize cures or inventions; contribute to the establishment of local hospitals, churches, schools, libraries, or welfare agencies, or to their building and operating funds; or, normally, provide general institutional support.

Application Information No special form is required in making a request for foundation aid. An application should be addressed to the assistant secretary of the foundation. It should include a description of the project; a comprehensive plan for the total funding of the project; and a listing of the applicant's qualifications and accomplishments. Additional information and application guidelines are available upon request.

Deadline(s) Grant appropriations are approved by an independent board of trustees which meets three times a year, in April, September, and December.

Subject Term(s) Agriculture; International Security; Population Studies; Arts, Support of; Peace; Medicine; Health; Humanities; Biomedical Sciences

343. The Rolex Awards for Enterprise

P.O. Box 178
CH-1211 Geneva 26 Switzerland

The Rolex Awards for Enterprise

Program Description The Rolex Awards for Enterprise were conceived to encourage the "Spirit of Enterprise" in individuals throughout the world by rewarding outstanding personal efforts or contributions made in selected categories of human behavior. The 1987 Selection Committee invites applications in any of the following three categories: (1) Applied Sciences and Invention, projects in this category will be concerned primarily with science and technology and should be aimed at innovative progress in experimental or applied research; (2) Exploration and Discovery, projects in this category will be concerned primarily with ventures or expeditions and should be aimed at inspiring our imagination or expanding our knowledge of the world we live in; and (3) The Environment, projects in this category will be concerned primarily with our environment and should be aimed at protecting, preserving, or improving the world around us.

Sample Grants Awards have been granted for: a study of pre-Columbian musical instruments of the south and central-south Andes; a study of small cetaceans of the South American sector of the Antarctic and Subantarctic; research on vision substitution for congenitally blind children in Mexico; research on unlocking the mystery of the underwater columns of the lost city of Nueva Cadiz; work in maritime archeology and the search for shipwrecks in the Cape Verde Islands; exploration of the caverns of the Maya Mountains of Belize and Guatemala; and a study of geoglyphs in the Iquique Province of northern Chile.

Eligibility/Limitations Applications for the awards may be submitted by anyone except: previous Rolex laureates; Rolex employees; Rolex agents and retailers and their employees; employees of advertising and public relations agencies acting for Rolex; members of the immediate families of the above; and any other person closely connected with Montres Rolex S.A.

Fiscal Information Five laureates chosen by the selection committee who will receive The Rolex Awards for Enterprise. The five individual laureates will receive 50,000 Swiss francs and a gold Rolex chronometer.

Application Information To be considered, applications must: be submitted on the official application form; be full and complete; be signed by the applicant; and, be typewritten in English.

Deadline(s) Applications must be received by March 31.

Subject Term(s) Field Research, Support of; Environment; Science and Technology; Awards and Prizes

344. Rosenberg Foundation

210 Post Street
San Francisco, CA 94108-5172
(415) 421-6105

Grants

Program Description The Rosenberg Foundation makes grants in four major fields. In early childhood development, it supports new programs which appear to have unusual promise of encouraging the normal, healthy development of young children both as individuals and as members of a diverse society. For adolescent and older youth, it supports new programs in which young people have joint responsibility for planning and implementation and which will strengthen their relationship with the community. In rural development, it supports programs designed to enhance the quality of life for children and their families in rural areas of California. In immigration policy, it supports projects which identify and address policy issues in the immigration field with particular emphasis on migration from Mexico and its consequences for both children and their families in both countries.

Sample Grants In support of a study of how Mexican immigration is changing the United States, $40,000 to Pacific News Service of the Bay Area Institute, San Francisco, California (1983). In support of a study of government attempts to regulate the use of Mexican labor in the California economy, $43,900 to Center for U.S.-Mexican Studies, University of California, San Diego (1983).

Eligibility/Limitations The foundation does not make grants for programs outside California. Support is given to tax-exempt groups or organizations, public or private. No grants are made to individuals, nor for construction, scholarships, operating expenses of ongoing programs, or for support of basic research.

Fiscal Information The foundation's policies preclude grants to continue or expand projects started with funds from other sources or to match grants from other sources. The foundation made grants for over $1.1 million in 1983.

Application Information The foundation does not use application forms but prefers brief letters of inquiry which describe the proposed project, the applicant agency, and the estimated budget. If, after preliminary review, the proposal appears to fall within the foundation's narrow program priorities, the foundation will request an application.

Deadline(s) Grants are authorized by the foundation board at monthly meetings. Because of the large number of requests, there is usually a waiting period of two to three months before an application can be considered by the board.

Subject Term(s) Immigration; Mexico

345. The Rotary Foundation

1600 Ridge Avenue
Evanston, IL 60201
(312) 328-0100

Grants for University Teachers

Program Description The trustees of The Rotary Foundation announce a grant program for university teachers to teach at universities in countries other than their own, especially developing countries. The fields taught must have international applications in the general areas of economic, political, social, or cultural sciences. Teachers will have an obligation to act as ambassadors of goodwill in their host countries.

Eligibility/Limitations Applicants must hold (or have held, if retired) a university appointment at a rank equivalent to associate professor or higher, and must have held a university teaching or research appointment for at least three years prior to the year in which the grant is to be used. Applicants may not be Rotarians or Rotary employees, their spouses, parents, grandparents, children (including legally adopted), or grandchildren, or their spouses. Awards are not restricted by gender, age, or marital status of the applicant. The country of the applicant's present academic appointment and the prospective host country must contain at least one Rotary club (there are Rotary clubs in more than 150 countries). Applicants may not have previously received a Grant for University Teachers from the Rotary Foundation. Proficiency in the language of the host country may be a factor in selection.

Fiscal Information Grant awards are in the amount of U.S. $10,000 each for periods of six to ten months.

Application Information Application forms may be obtained from any Rotary club, district, or from The Rotary Foundation.

Deadline(s) Applications must be received no later than June 15 of the year preceding the proposed teaching year.

ect Term(s) Faculty Support Abroad; Foreign Nationals, Eligibility of; International Studies

346. The Rotary Foundation

1600 Ridge Avenue
Evanston, IL 60201
(312) 328-0100

Rotary Foundation Scholarships

Program Description The purpose of Rotary Foundation Scholarships is to further international understanding and friendly relations among peoples of different countries. Scholarships are designed to support one year of academic training or study in another country where Rotary clubs are located. A scholarship may be used for almost any field of study. However, it may not be used by a person intending to do unsupervised research.

Eligibility/Limitations Graduate scholarships are available for those who will have received a bachelor's degree or its equivalent before commencement of scholarship duties. Applicants may not be Rotarians or Rotary employees, their spouses, parents, grandparents, children (including legally adopted), or grandchildren, or their spouses. Awards are not restricted by gender, age, or marital status of the applicant. A candidate whose native language is other than that of the proposed study institution and country must submit evidence of the ability to read, write, and speak the host language(s).

Fiscal Information The basic period of the scholarship is the regular academic year at the assigned study institution. Scholarships include round-trip transportation between the scholar's home and study city, all required academic fees, some necessary educational supplies, room and board, limited educational travel during the award year, and limited contingency expenses.

Application Information Application must be made through a Rotary club in the district of the applicant's legal or permanent residence, or place of employment or study. In order to be considered for a scholarship, a candidate must be sponsored by both the Rotary club through which the application is made and the sponsoring club's district. Additional information and application guidelines are available on request.

Deadline(s) Applications must be received by The Rotary Foundation by December 1.

Additional Information Additional scholarships are available for undergraduates, vocational students, teachers of handicapped students, and journalists. Contact the Rotary Foundation for applications and additional information.

Subject Term(s) Foreign Nationals, Eligibility of; Graduate Support Abroad; International Studies; Undergraduate Support Abroad; Journalism

347. Russel Sage Foundation

112 East 64th Street
New York, NY 10021
(212) 750-6000

Social Science Research Support

Program Description The Russel Sage Foundation is the principal American foundation devoted exclusively to research in the social sciences. The foundation is dedicated to support of social science research as a means of improved social policies. Russel Sage directs its efforts not only toward inquiries that contribute to more informed and rational policy formulation, but also to basic research on improvements in methodology, data, and social science theory. The foundation maintains contact with a wide range of disciplines, fields, and topics within the area of social science. While its support of scholars has tended to reflect this broad view of social research, its limited resources require that it give special attention to a few research topics at a time. These topics change from time to time and the foundation makes a strong effort to assure that the attention given to these special research problems does not prevent it from seeing and supporting promising work in other areas of social research. At present, the foundation is actively encouraging proposals on the changing role of gender in American institutions—that is, changes in American society and institutions that are coming about in response to changes in the traditional view of women's and men's opportunities and roles. While not actively seeking proposals, the foundation also remains interested in innovative research in an area recently prominent on its research agenda—risk perception as a social phenomenon. Areas of more traditional concern to the foundation include political institutions and the democratic process, social science development and methodology, and social conditions in New York City. Over the next few years, the foundation will also allot a steady flow of funds to high quality social science research.

Eligibility/Limitations Grants are not made for the support of undergraduate or graduate degree work, nor for institutional support. Grantees are generally expected to produce, and to offer to the foundation first refusal rights on, book-length research reports.

Fiscal Information Grant awards vary depending on the project proposed.

Application Information There is no application form; a brief letter of inquiry is advisable to determine whether the foundation's present interests and funds permit consideration of a proposal for research or residence at the foundation. Grant applications should summarize the project's objectives, the work plan, the qualifications of persons engaged in the work, and an estimated budget. After consideration of this letter, the foundation will indicate whether or not a detailed proposal should be submitted.

Deadline(s) Applications are considered throughout the year.

Additional Information At its headquarters in New York City, the foundation has established a small center for advanced study, where scholars can pursue their research. This professional community consists of full-time resident scholars, social scientists who engage in their own research and help administer foundation policies and projects; visiting scholars, who work in fields of interest to the foundation for periods ranging from a few months to two years, continuing their own research and writing and occasionally helping the foundation with its activities; visiting postdoctoral fellows, young social scientists selected in a national competition and appointed for one year to pursue a program of research on topics of their own choosing; and a few social scientists who are affiliated with nearby universities and who serve part-time as advisors and consultants. Contact the foundation for information about the Visiting Postdoctoral Fellows Program.

Subject Term(s) Fellowships; Social Sciences; Postdoctoral Support

348. School of Advanced International Studies

The Johns Hopkins University
1740 Massachusetts Avenue, NW
Washington, DC 20036
(202) 785-6200

Program Description The School of Advanced International Studies (SAIS) of The Johns Hopkins University provides graduate training to men and women planning careers in government, international public service, and in the private sector in business, banking, journalism, teaching, and research. Since its founding SAIS has pursued three primary goals: to provide professional education that adheres to the highest standard of scholarship and is at the same time relevant to contemporary problems in international affairs; to conduct scholarly research that addresses the concerns of the United States and public and private institutions in their relations with the governments and institutions of other countries, and to disseminate the research findings to a broad audience concerned with foreign relations; and to offer mid-career educational opportunities for those already working in international affairs. Students the school can specialize in several regional studies programs (including Latin Amer and in American foreign policy.

Fiscal Information SAIS awards aid in several categories and for varying amou Contact SAIS for detailed information about types of available aid.

Application Information Additional information and application guidelines are available from the school.

Deadline(s) Confirm application deadlines with the schools.

Additional Information The SAIS Center of Brazilian Studies opened in 1978 as the first U.S. institution devoted exclusively to the study of Brazilian economics, politics, and international affairs.

Subject Term(s) International Affairs; Foreign Relations; Graduate Support

349. School of American Research

P.O. Box 2188
Santa Fe, NM 87504
(505) 982-3583

Resident Scholar Fellowship Program

Program Description The Resident Scholar Fellowship Program at the School of American Research (SAR) provides support for scholars pursuing advanced study in anthropology and related fields. While the program stresses southwestern studies, scholars in other areas are urged to apply. The major benefit of the resident scholar program is an opportunity to work with no other responsibilities and with the stimulus of intellectual interaction with fellow resident scholars, visiting anthropologists, and SAR staff.

Eligibility/Limitations Funding for this program is provided by the Weatherhead Foundation and NEH. Weatherhead scholarships are awarded to Ph.D. candidates, postdoctoral scholars, and retired scholars. NEH fellowships are awarded only to postdoctoral scholars.

Fiscal Information The length of tenure is usually eleven months and begins on September 15. Preference will be given to those whose field work is complete. Additional benefits of the program include: a furnished apartment for Weatherhead scholars and a rental allowance for NEH scholars; a $650 stipend for each month in residence; a separate office on the school campus; medical insurance; and assistance from the school's part-time librarian in obtaining books to supplement the school's limited anthropological collection.

Application Information For additional information contact the school.

Subject Term(s) Fellowships; Postdoctoral Support; Anthropology; Archeology

350. Sigma Xi, The Scientific Research Society

Committee on Grants-in-Aid Research
345 Whitney Avenue
New Haven, CT 06511
(203) 624-9883

Grants-in-Aid of Research

Program Description Research awards are made to support scientific investigation in any field.

Eligibility/Limitations Priority is usually given to applicants who are in an early stage of their scientific careers. The committee attaches a low priority, however, to support for applicants holding postdoctoral or junior faculty appointments.

Fiscal Information Awards are made in amounts up to a maximum of $1,000. However, most awards do not exceed $600. All funds must be expended directly in support of the proposed investigation.

Application Information Additional information and application forms are available on request.

Deadline(s) The committee normally meets three times a year; closing dates for receipt of applications and supporting letters are February 1, May 1, and November 1.

Subject Term(s) Faculty Support; Graduate Support

351. The L. J. Skaggs and Mary C. Skaggs Foundation

1330 Broadway, 17th Floor
Oakland, CA 94612
(415) 451-3300

Grants

Program Description The foundation presently makes grants under six program categories: performing arts, social and community concerns, projects of historic interest, folklore/folklife, international grants, and special projects. Where necessary, as new program areas arise, new funding categories may be opened.

Sample Grants For preparation of a comprehensive survey of projects concerned with the preservation/conservation of Caribbean cultural and historic structures, programs, and traditions, $10,000 to Partners for Livable Places, Washington, DC (1985). To create a team of art historians and photographers to assemble a guide to the pictoral repositories of Mexico, $2,500 to Latin-American Library, Tulane University, New Orleans, Louisiana (1985).

Eligibility/Limitations The foundation makes grants to qualified tax-exempt charitable organizations. No grants are made to individuals, or for capital fund, endowment fund or annual fund drives, sectarian or religious purposes. With very special exceptions, grants to programs in the social and community concerns category will only be made in Northern California.

Fiscal Information The foundation set a grant budget for 1985 of over $1.8 million.

Application Information Telephone inquiries regarding program eligibility are not encouraged. Requests for grants are initiated by a brief letter of intent to apply for funding during the following calendar year. This letter should briefly describe the applying organization and the purpose for which funds are sought. Information concerning the organization's income and expenses, and material outlining the experience and expertise of key personnel should also be included. When a letter of intent is received, the foundation's staff determines whether the proposed project meets current guidelines and interests. The foundation then invites a full proposal.

Deadline(s) Letters of intent are accepted by the foundation from January 1 to June 1; full proposals, if invited, must be received by the foundation no later than September 1.

Subject Term(s) Folklore; Conservation; Historic Preservation

352. Smithsonian Institution

Office of Fellowships and Grants
3300 L'Enfant Plaza
Washington, DC 20560
(202) 287-3271

Fellowships: Faculty Fellowships for Minority Scholars

Program Description The Smithsonian Institution offers fellowships for support of research and study in fields which are actively pursued by the museums and research organizations of the institution. At present these fields are: anthropology, including archeology; astrophysics and astronomy; earth sciences and paleobiology; ecology; behavioral and environmental sciences, including an emphasis on the tropics; evolutionary and systematic biology; history of science and technology; history of art; social and cultural history and folklife of the United States; and social and cultural history and folklife of Burma, Guinea, India, and Pakistan. Faculty fellowships for minority scholars are awarded to provide opportunities for minority faculty members to conduct research in residence in association with members of the Smithsonian professional research staff, using facilities and collections of the institution.

Fiscal Information Awards may be for from two to four months and stipends are determined by the appointee's faculty status.

Application Information Additional information and application forms are available on request from the Office of Fellowships and Grants. Some opportunities for research are available on a limited or irregular basis. Contact the Office of Fellowships and Grants for complete, current information on Smithsonian Institution fellowships.

Deadline(s) Deadlines for receipt of application are June 1, September 1, and February 15 of each year.

Additional Information The Smithsonian Institution is planning a series of diverse exhibits and public and scholarly publications and programs commemorating the 500th anniversary of Columbus' voyage to the Americas. The Smithsonian Quincentenary will focus on four contiguous themes: Magnificent Traditions, The Cultures of Spain and the Americas; The Dynamic of the Encounter; The Continuity of the Encounter; and The Next 500 Years. The majority of the programs will occur in 1991 and 1992. For more information, contact the Smithsonian.

Subject Term(s) Fellowships; Faculty Support; Minorities, Eligibility of; Museums

353. Smithsonian Institution

Office of Fellowships and Grants
3300 L'Enfant Plaza
Washington, DC 20560
(202) 287-3271

Fellowships: Graduate Student Fellowships

Program Description The Smithsonian Institution offers fellowships for support of research and study in fields which are actively pursued by the museums and research organizations of the institution. At present these fields are: anthropology, including archeology; astrophysics and astronomy; earth sciences and paleobiology; ecology; behavioral and environmental sciences, including an emphasis on the tropics; evolutionary and systematic biology; history of science and technology; history of art; social and cultural history and folklife of the United States; and social and cultural history and folklife of Burma, Guinea, India, and Pakistan. Graduate student fellowships are offered to students to study and conduct research in residence under the guidance of Smithsonian staff members.

Eligibility/Limitations Applicants must be students actively engaged in graduate study at any level and must submit a proposal for research in a discipline which is pursued at the Smithsonian.

Fiscal Information Graduate student fellowships are awarded for ten weeks and carry a stipend of $2,000.

Application Information Applications for fellowships are available from the Office of Fellowships and Grants in the early fall. Some opportunities for research are available on a limited or irregular basis. Contact the Office of Fellowships and Grants for complete, current information on Smithsonian Institution fellowships.

Deadline(s) The deadline for receipt of applications is January 15.

Additional Information The Smithsonian Institution is planning a series of diverse exhibits and public and scholarly publications and programs commemorating the 500th anniversary of Columbus' voyage to the Americas. The Smithsonian Quincentenary will focus on four contiguous themes: Magnificent Traditions, The Cultures of Spain and the Americas; The Dynamic of the Encounter; The Continuity of the Encounter; and The Next 500 Years. The majority of the programs will occur in 1991 and 1992. For more information, contact the Smithsonian.

Subject Term(s) Fellowships; Graduate Support; Museums

354. Smithsonian Institution

Office of Fellowships and Grants
3300 L'Enfant Plaza
Washington, DC 20560
(202) 287-3271

Fellowships: Postdoctoral Fellowships

Program Description The Smithsonian Institution offers fellowships for support of research and study in fields which are actively pursued by the museums and research organizations of the institution. At present these fields are: anthropology, including archeology; astrophysics and astronomy; earth sciences and paleobiology; ecology; behavioral and environmental sciences, including an emphasis on the tropics; evolutionary and systematic biology; history of science and technology; history of art; social and cultural history and folklife of the United States; and social and cultural history and folklife of Burma, Guinea, India, and Pakistan. Postdoctoral fellowships are offered to investigators who wish to conduct research in areas in which the Smithsonian institution has particular research strengths.

Eligibility/Limitations Applicants must have completed the doctoral degree and submit a detailed research project, indicating clearly why the Smithsonian Institution is the appropriate place to conduct the proposed study.

Fiscal Information Postdoctoral fellowships are awarded for not less than six months and not more than twelve months and carry a stipend of $18,000 per year plus allowances.

Application Information Applications for fellowships are available from the Office of Fellowships and Grants in the early fall. Some opportunities for research are available on a limited or irregular basis. Contact the Office of Fellowships and Grants for complete, current information on Smithsonian Institution fellowships.

Deadline(s) The deadline for receipt of applications is January 15.

Additional Information The Smithsonian Institution is planning a series of diverse exhibits and public and scholarly publications and programs commemorating the 500th anniversary of Columbus' voyage to the Americas. The Smithsonian Quincentenary will focus on four contiguous themes: Magnificent Traditions, The Cultures of Spain and the Americas; The Dynamic of the Encounter; The Continuity of the Encounter; and The Next 500 Years. The majority of the programs will occur in 1991 and 1992. For more information, contact the Smithsonian.

Subject Term(s) Fellowships; Postdoctoral Support; Museums

355. Smithsonian Institution

Office of Fellowships and Grants
3300 L'Enfant Plaza
Washington, DC 20560
(202) 287-3271

Fellowships: Predoctoral Fellowships

Program Description The Smithsonian Institution offers fellowships for support of research and study in fields which are actively pursued by the museums and research organizations of the institution. At present these fields are: anthropology, including archeology; astrophysics and astronomy; earth sciences and paleobiology; ecology; behavioral and environmental sciences, including an emphasis on the tropics; evolutionary and systematic biology; history of science and technology; history of art; social and cultural history and folklife of the United States; and social and cultural history and folklife of Burma, Guinea, India, and Pakistan. Predoctoral fellowships are offered to investigators who have completed preliminary course work and examinations and are engaged in dissertation research

Eligibility/Limitations Applicants must have the approval of their universities to conduct their doctoral research at the Smithsonian Institution.

Fiscal Information Predoctoral fellowships are awarded for not less than six months and not more than twelve months, and carry a stipend of $11,000 per year plus allowances.

Application Information Applications for fellowships are available from the Office of Fellowships and Grants in the early fall. Some opportunities for research are available on a limited or irregular basis. Contact the Office of Fellowships and Grants for complete, current information on Smithsonian Institution fellowships.

Deadline(s) The deadline for receipt of applications is January 15.

Additional Information The Smithsonian Institution is planning a series of diverse exhibits and public and scholarly publications and programs commemorating the 500th anniversary of Columbus' voyage to the Americas. The Smithsonian Quincentenary will focus on four contiguous themes: Magnificent Traditions, The Cultures of Spain and the Americas; The Dynamic of the Encounter; The Continuity of the Encounter; and The Next 500 Years. The majority of the programs will occur in 1991 and 1992. For more information, contact the Smithsonian.

Subject Term(s) Fellowships; Predoctoral Support; Museums

356. Smithsonian Institution

Office of Fellowships and Grants
3300 L'Enfant Plaza
Washington, DC 20560
(202) 287-3271

Internships

Program Description The Smithsonian Institution offers internships for support of research and study in fields which are actively pursued by the museums and research organizations of the institution. At present these fields are: anthropology, including archeology; astrophysics and astronomy; earth sciences and paleobiology; ecology; behavioral and environmental sciences, including an emphasis on the tropics; evolutionary and systematic biology; history of science and technology; history of art; social and cultural history and folklife of the United States; and social and cultural history and folklife of Burma, Guinea, India, and Pakistan. An internship at the institution is a prearranged, structured learning experience scheduled within a specific time frame. The experience must be relevant both to the intern's stated academic or professional goals and to disciplines and research and museum professions represented at the institution.

Fiscal Information Internships may range from a few weeks to a year or more. Internships may be with stipend (which vary according to assignment and length of stay) or without stipend.

Application Information Academic internships, offering research-related experience, can be arranged in most of the bureaus of the Smithsonian. Additional information and application guidelines are available from the Office of Fellowships and Grants.

Deadline(s) Usually applications can be made at any time of the year.

Additional Information Internships for minority students, either graduate students or upper division undergraduates, are available. Appointments are usually for a nine to twelve-week period, and carry a stipend of $150 per week (undergraduate) or $200 per week (graduate). Deadlines for application are July 1, October 15, and March 1 of each year.

Subject Term(s) Internships; Museums; Graduate Support; Minorities, Eligibility of

357. Smithsonian Institution

Office of Fellowships and Grants
3300 L'Enfant Plaza
Washington, DC 20560
(202) 287-3271

Short-Term Visits

Program Description The Smithsonian Institution offers support for research and study in fields which are actively pursued by the museums and research organizations of the institution. At present these fields are: anthropology, including archeology; astrophysics and astronomy; earth sciences and paleobiology; ecology; behavioral and environmental sciences, including an emphasis on the tropics; evolutionary and systematic biology; history of science and technology; history of art; social and cultural history and folklife of the United States; and social and cultural history and folklife of Burma, Guinea,

India, and Pakistan. Short-term visit support is available for scholars and students seeking access to the Smithsonian facilities.

Fiscal Information Financial support up to $350 is available.

Application Information For additional information and application forms contact the Office of Fellowships and Grants.

Deadline(s) Applications are accepted throughout the year.

Additional Information The Smithsonian Institution is planning a series of diverse exhibits and public and scholarly publications and programs commemorating the 500th anniversary of Columbus' voyage to the Americas. The Smithsonian Quincentenary will focus on four contiguous themes: Magnificent Traditions, The Cultures of Spain and the Americas; The Dynamic of the Encounter; The Continuity of the Encounter; and The Next 500 Years. The majority of the programs will occur in 1991 and 1992. For more information, contact the Smithsonian.

Subject Term(s) Internships; Museums; Collections Study, Museums

358. Social Science Research Council

605 Third Avenue
New York, NY 10158
(212) 661-0280

Fellowships for International Doctoral Research

Program Description Fellowships are offered for doctoral dissertation research in the social sciences and the humanities to be carried out in Africa, Asia, Japan, Korea, Latin America and the Caribbean, the Near and Middle East, Russia and the Soviet Union, South Asia, Southeast Asia, or Western Europe. Fellows must plan to carry out research in the geographical region that is the setting of their doctoral dissertation.

Sample Grants 1987 fellowships were awarded for: research in Brazil on free labor in the slave society of rural Bahia, 1790-1860; research in Peru on the relationship between social integration and architectural function at the site of Pacatnamu; research in Mexico on the emergence of the national railways; research in Costa Rica on the origins of democracy in Costa Rica; research in Argentina, the U.S., and Venezuela on the *cronicas* of Jose Marti; and research in Mexico on the writing systems of southwest Mesoamerica.

Eligibility/Limitations Program purposes and eligibility vary from one area to another, but all programs are designed to support scholars who intend to become specialists in the area of research. Applicants should consult the relevant program description, available from the council.

Fiscal Information The fellowships support nine to eighteen consecutive months of field research in the relevant area. Awards differ from country to country; they normally include maintenance stipends and transportation expenses for the fellow and financial dependents, health insurance for the fellow and dependents, and a research allowance. Applicants may request up to six months of support for specialized preparatory training in disciplinary, language, or methodological skills essential to the successful undertaking of the dissertation research. Support is not provided for the completion of normal academic requirements for the Ph.D.

Application Information Application forms are furnished in response to written requests. In requesting forms, the applicant should give the following information: a brief statement of the proposed research; geographical area or areas of interest; proposed site of research; occupation or current activity; university or other affiliation; country of citizenship and/or permanent residence; academic degrees, specifying disciplines or fields of study; the date for completion of all requirements for the doctoral degree except the dissertation; and proposed date for beginning tenure of the award and the duration requested. Application forms will be sent after preliminary determination of eligibility by the council staff.

Deadline(s) The application deadline for fellowship programs is November 1.

Subject Term(s) Fellowships; Doctoral Dissertation Support Abroad; Foreign Nationals, Eligibility of; Social Sciences; Humanities

359. Social Science Research Council

605 Third Avenue
New York, NY 10158
(212) 661-0280

Grants for Advanced International Research

Program Description Grants for advanced international research are offered to scholars whose competence for research in the social sciences or humanities has been demonstrated by their previous work. These programs are designed to support research in one country, comparative research between countries in any area, and comparative research between areas. Research under these program grants may be conducted in Africa, Japan, Korea, Latin America and the Caribbean, the Near and Middle East, Russia and the Soviet Union, South Asia, and Southeast Asia.

Sample Grants 1987 grants were awarded for: research in Bolivia on the representation of ethnicity and domination in Bolivian calendrical feasts; comparative research in Venezuela and the U.S. on the effects of personal attributes and lifestyles on criminal victimization; research in Mexico on ideology and society in ancient Mexico; research in Chile on the search for feminine identity in the writings of Chilean writers Maria Luisa Bombal, Marta Brunet, and Gavriela Mistral; research in Bolivia on the relationship between the socioeconomic and cultural conditioning of fertility and modalities and causes of mortality in three Bolivian rural communities; research in Argentina on 19th century photography in the province of Santa Fe; and research in Brazil on comparative and long-range historical study of the Indian peoples of the northwest Amazon region.

Eligibility/Limitations Eligibility requirements vary from country to country. Generally, applicants must be citizens or permanent residents of the United States (there is no citizenship requirement for work in Latin American and the Caribbean) and must hold the Ph.D. or equivalent professional experience. These grants are not for training and candidates for academic degrees are not normally eligible.

Fiscal Information Grants are normally for periods of two months to one year, and awards range up to $25,000. Grants may be used for travel and research expenses as well as for partial maintenance. Grants may be held concurrently with grants from other organizations.

Application Information Application forms are furnished in response to written requests. In requesting forms, the applicant should give the following information: a brief statement of the proposed research; geographical area or areas of interest; proposed site of research; occupation or current activity; university or other affiliation; country of citizenship and/or permanent residence; academic degrees, specifying disciplines or fields of study; proposed date for beginning tenure of the award and the duration requested; and the approximate amount of support needed. Application forms will be sent after preliminary determination of eligibility by the council staff.

Deadline(s) The application deadline is December 2.

Additional Information Some countries offer special funding for collaborative research, allow support for revision of the doctoral dissertation, and have prioritized research interests. Contact the council for current information on all Advanced International Research Grants.

Subject Term(s) Social Sciences; Humanities; Foreign Nationals, Eligibility of

360. Social Science Research Council

Program in International Peace and Security
605 Third Avenue
New York, NY 10158
(212) 661-0280

MacArthur Foundation Fellowships in International Security: Dissertation Training and Research

Program Description The Social Science Research Council (SSRC) administers a program of fellowships for training and research in international security with funds provided by the John D. and Catherine T. MacArthur Foundation. Dissertation training and research fellowships add one year of training to the normal graduate program. During this year, fellows have an opportunity to combine their previous disciplinary skills with specialized training in international peace and security. A second year of support is provided for dissertation research which should reflect the broadened perspectives acquired during the training year. Training may occur at an institution of the applicant's choice and may consist of formal course work, tutorials, or supervised study with relevant faculty.

Eligibility/Limitations There are no citizenship or nationality requirements. However, only scholars in a recognized field of the physical and biological sciences or the social/behavioral sciences, including history and foreign area studies may apply. Applicants must be candidates for the Ph.D. or its equivalent in any one of these disciplines, who have completed all requirements for the degree except the dissertation or who will have met these requirements when the fellowship commences.

Fiscal Information An award of $15,000 per year is provided to cover living expenses, travel, and research costs. Additionally, funds are available for the payment of fees at institutions hosting a fellow's training or research.

Application Information For further information and application materials contact the Program in International Peace and Security, SSRC.

Deadline(s) Applications are due March 31 and July 31.

Subject Term(s) Predoctoral Support; Security Studies; Foreign Nationals, Eligibility of; International Security; Doctoral Dissertation Support

361. Social Science Research Council

Program in International Peace and Security
605 Third Avenue
New York, NY 10158
(212) 661-0280

MacArthur Foundation Fellowships in International Security: Postdoctoral Training and Research

Program Description The Social Science Research Council (SSRC) administers a program of fellowships for training and research in international security with funds provided by the John D. and Catherine T. MacArthur Foundation. Postdoctoral training and research fellowships include support for one year of advanced training and one year of research applying knowledge gained during the training year. For scholars entering the field of international peace and security studies, the year of advanced training must be in a specific area of peace and security studies that will inform the research to be conducted during the second year. For scholars who have previously specialized in international peace and security studies, the year of advanced training must be in a specific area of the physical and biological sciences or the social/behavioral sciences, including history and foreign area studies, that will inform the research to be conducted during the second year. Training may occur at an institution of the applicant's choice and may consist of formal course work, tutorials, or supervised study with relevant faculty.

Sample Grants 1987 fellowships were awarded for: training in international security studies and research which will identify threats to Mexican security and will define Mexican national security interests as distinct from those of the U.S. and other nations; the study of the economic and technical aspects of development strategies followed by the Third World after 1945 and an examination of typical problems of several small-debtor nations in Latin America, focusing on links between economic malaise, social decomposition, and revolutionary activity in an effort to identify the components essential to a successful development strategy; and the study of international security, moral aspects of peace and war, and recent Central American political history and an examination of the ways in which organized violence has been justified in Latin American thought on development and social progress since 1945 and the influence of Latin American "just war" theories upon conceptions of national and international security in Central America.

Eligibility/Limitations There are no citizenship or nationality requirements. However, only scholars in a recognized field of the physical and biological sciences or the social/behavioral sciences, including history and foreign area studies may apply. Applicants must hold or will hold (when the fellowship commences) a Ph.D. or its equivalent in any one of these disciplines.

Fiscal Information An award of $30,000 per year is provided to cover living expenses, travel, and research costs. Additionally, funds are available for the payment of fees at institutions hosting a fellow's training or research.

Application Information For further information and application materials contact the Program in International Peace and Security, SSRC.

Deadline(s) Applications are due March 31 and July 31.

Subject Term(s) Fellowships; Postdoctoral Support; Security Studies; International Security; Foreign Nationals, Eligibility of; Peace

362. The Spencer Foundation

875 North Michigan Avenue
Chicago, IL 60611
(312) 337-7000

Grants

Program Description The Spencer Foundation supports research that gives promise of yielding new knowledge leading to the improvement of education. The foundation is interested in a wide variety of disciplinary and interdisciplinary approaches, though by direction of its charter it gives emphasis to the behavioral sciences and it defines education broadly to include all the situations and institutions in which education proceeds, across the entire life span, in the U.S. and around the world. The foundation is also interested in a wide variety of research areas, including what the anthropologist might call cultural knowledge, what the political scientist might call socialization, and what the economist might call the production and distribution of knowledge. Finally, the foundation is interested in a wide variety of research formats, from relatively low-cost individual efforts extending over a few months to more expensive collaborative efforts extending over several years.

Sample Grants To support a study of income returns to education in Brazil, $115,000 ($229,500 in 1985) to University of Wisconsin, Madison (1986). To support research on the transition from high school to employment in Jamaica, $11,234 to State University of New York at Albany (1986). For the study of education and society in the Creole Caribbean, $348,550 over three years to the Research Institute for the Study of Man, New York (1986).

Eligibility/Limitations The foundation rejects, as a matter of policy, requests for any of the following purposes: capital funds, operating and ongoing program expenses, support for service, training, or curriculum development programs, and grants for travel fellowships or sabbatical supplements.

Fiscal Information During the fiscal year ended March 31, 1986, over $2.6 million was authorized for grants.

Application Information An informal letter of inquiry or a brief preliminary proposal is usually sufficient for the foundation to determine whether a proposed study falls within the foundation's scope. A curriculum vitae of the principal investigator is expected with the initial inquiry to inform the foundation staff concerning the individual's qualifications for conducting the research suggested. If the proposed research appears to be of potential interest, three copies of a more detailed proposal will be requested.

Deadline(s) Full proposals, not the initial inquiry, must be received by the first of February, May, August, or November for consideration at the following meetings of the program committee and of the board of directors.

Additional Information The foundation also conducts a Small Grants Program within the domains of its concerns, which is intended to facilitate scholars in pursuing exploratory research, problem-finding research, pilot research, modest research projects, and the initial phases of larger investigations. Grants made under the program may range from $1,000 to $7,500. The principal investigator must have an earned doctorate in an academic discipline or in the field of education and must hold an appointment in a college or university, a research facility, or a cultural institution; and the research topic must be clearly relevant to the field of education. Projects under the Small Grants Program may not extend beyond a year in duration. Inquiries concerning this program should be addressed to the administrator of the Small Grants Program.

Subject Term(s) Education; Behavioral Sciences

363. Stanford Humanities Center

Stanford University
Mariposa House
Stanford, CA 94305-8630
(415) 497-3052

External Faculty Fellowships

Program Description The general aims of the Stanford Humanities Center are to promote humanistic studies and interests in three main ways: by operating a fellowship program mainly concerned with research; by supplementing and otherwise strengthening humanistic teaching at Stanford; and by conducting studies of problems in the area of the humanities broadly defined, and of their relationships to other disciplines. The fellowship program is primarily concerned with offering research opportunities both for members of humanities departments as traditionally defined and for all other scholars seriously interested in humanistic issues.

Sample Grants Research interests of faculty fellows have included: cultural expressions in developing societies, an analysis of authors and fiction in African and Caribbean nations (1984-85); claiming the Americas, the making of Third World and ethnopoetic literature (1985-86).

Eligibility/Limitations External fellowships are awarded in three categories: (1) fellowships for already well-established and usually tenured scholars; (2) fellowships for junior, usually untenured, scholars who teach at colleges or universities which do not have major graduate schools or do not have doctoral programs in their own departments; and (3) fellowships for U.S. ethnic minority scholars (Blacks, Chicanos/Mexican-Americans, Native Americans, Puerto Rican Americans) and for scholars from Third World countries who either now reside in a Third World nation or who intend to return and resume their professional careers there. Persons on temporary teaching appointments or without academic affiliation may apply, but their applications can only be considered under category one (1). The external fellowship is not intended either for students who are now finishing, or who, with the exception of those who might qualify under category three (3), have recently completed, their doctorates.

Fiscal Information Fellows will receive stipends based on their expected academic salary for the coming year. The funding of the center, however, is limited. Applicants are expected to seek supplementary financial support. External Fellows will also receive necessary travel allowances for themselves and their families, and some other benefits.

Application Information Forms of application and further information are available from the center.

Deadline(s) The deadline for applications is December 1.

Subject Term(s) Faculty Support; Minorities, Eligibility of; Foreign Nationals, Eligibility of; Humanities; Individuals, Eligibility of

364. The Tinker Foundation Incorporated

55 East 59th Street
New York, NY 10022
(212) 421-6858

Field Research Grants

Program Description These awards, open to centers or institutes of Ibero-American or Latin American Studies, are to be used for brief periods of research only in Iberia or

Latin America. The purpose of the program is to make it possible for people of ability to work in specific regions of Ibero-America, Portugal, and Spain. The awardees will be able to acquire as comprehensive a knowledge as possible of language, terrain, and culture; to gather research data; and to develop contacts with scholars and institutions in their field.

Sample Grants In 1986 the followin institutes received renewals of their 1985 awards: Council on Latin American Studies, Duke University; Latin American Institute, University of New Mexico; Latin America Area Center, University of Arizona, Tucson

Eligibility/Limitations Field Research Grants are intended to be used by graduate students and junior faculty in recognized centers or institutes of Ibero-American or Latin American Studies with graduate doctoral programs at accredited United States universities.

Fiscal Information Grants carry awards of up to $15,000 per year. These grants must be matched by the university in the amount of $10,000.

Application Information There are no formal application forms. Interested institutions should contact the foundation for complete application procedures.

Deadline(s) Applications must be received by the foundation before October 1.

Additional Information Graduate students and junior faculty from Latin American and Iberian countries may use the award to conduct research in their home countries

Subject Term(s) Area Studies

365. The Tinker Foundation Incorporated

55 East 59th Street
New York, NY 10022
(212) 421-6858

Institutional Grants

Program Description In order to qualify for consideration by the Tinker Foundation, proposals must be concerned with topics or activities related to Ibero-America, Spain, or Portugal. Priority is given to work in the broad field of the social sciences with particular emphasis on areas such as international relations, urban and regional studies, education, communications, management, and economics. Support is also offered for projects focusing on natural resource development, the training of specialists at the post-graduate level, and for programs designed to further the education of Spanish- or Portuguese-speaking people of the United States.

Sample Grants To support the Institute of Andean Research project entitled "Ecological complementarity and long-distance maritime exchange in the Chincha area, Peru", $39,400 (final payment of a two-year $77,700 grant) to The American Museum of Natural History, New York, New York (1985). For a study entitled "U.S. and Brazilian computers: consequences of core country industrial organization and state policy for high technology sectors in newly industrialized countries", $33,000 (first payment on a two-year $57,000 grant) to Brown University, Providence, Rhode Island (1985). To support a project on debt in developing countries, $45,000 (first allocation of a two-year grant of $45,000 per annum) to National Bureau of Economic Research, Inc., Cambridge, Massachusetts (1985).

Eligibility/Limitations Proposals must be written in English. The foundation will not consider requests for annual fundraising appeals, the construction of buildings, requests from private individuals, or proposals concerned with health/medical issues.

Fiscal Information Grant awards range from $3,500 to $70,000 for one year of support. Grants may be renewable for up to three years.

Application Information Additional information and application guidelines are available from the foundation.

Deadline(s) Applications are considered biannually by the board of directors in mid-June and mid-December. The deadline for the receipt of proposals for the summer meeting is March 1; for the winter meeting it is October 1.

Subject Term(s) Social Sciences; Area Studies; International Relations; Natural Resources

366. The Tinker Foundation Incorporated

55 East 59th Street
New York, NY 10022
(212) 421-6858

Postdoctoral Fellowship Program

Program Description Tinker Postdoctoral Fellowships are offered to further understanding among the peoples of the United States, Latin America, Spain, and Portugal by providing professionals interested in Latin American and Iberian Studies with the opportunity to do research in areas of the foundation's interests: social sciences, natural resource development, and international relations. The principal objective of the fellowship is to foster intellectual growth by encouraging field research which will have significant theoretical implications within or between disciplines or for public policy.

Sample Grants Fellowships in 1985 were awarded in support of the following projects: a study of sexuality and illegitimacy in colonial Spanish America; elite strategies for control, industrialization, worker training, and social assistance in Brazil, 1920-64; appropriateness of coastal resources management strategies for Argentina, a normative study.

Eligibility/Limitations Applicants must have completed their doctoral studies less than three years, but no more than ten years prior to the time of application. Citizens and permanent residents of the United States, Canada, Spain, Portugal, and the Latin American countries are eligible to apply. United States citizens and others with a Ph.D. from a United States university may hold the fellowship in a country of their choice justified by their research project; non-United States citizens who do not hold a United States doctorate may use the fellowship at a United States institution only.

Fiscal Information The award carries an annual stipend of $25,000. The fellowship is awarded for one year. A request for a second year of support may be made but must be documented by a report detailing scholarly achievement and accomplishment during the initial award. The fellowship may not be held concurrently with other awards nor may it be used to fulfill "matching" requirements.

Application Information Although there are no formal application forms, for ease of administration, it is asked that a standard format be followed. The necessary application instructions may be obtained from the foundation.

Deadline(s) Applications must be submitted by December 15. Applications for renewal must be submitted by March 1 of the subsequent year.

Additional Information The 1987 fellowship competition will be the final year for this program. Successful applicants will be eligible for a second and final year of support. A request for renewal must be received no later than March 1, 1988.

Subject Term(s) Postdoctoral Support; Fellowships; Foreign Nationals, Eligibility of; Canadian Nationals, Eligibility of; Spanish Nationals, Eligibility of; Portuguese Nationals, Eligibility of; Social Sciences; International Relations; Natural Resources

367. The Twentieth Century Fund

41 East 70th Street
New York, NY 10021

Research Program

Program Description The Twentieth Century Fund is an operating foundation which sponsors and supervises research on significant economic, social, and political issues. Fund research projects are designed to produce analytic book-length manuscripts containing public policy recommendations. They are aimed at an audience that includes the informed public, the press, policymakers, and the academic community. The fund commissions individual scholars to carry out its research projects, and the book-length manuscripts that result are edited by the fund and then placed by the fund with commercial publishers or university presses. The objective of the fund's program, which supports research and writing on issues of public policy, is publishable books. The fund rarely supports large-scale data-gathering efforts or research designed primar-

ɇlop theory or methodology. Although the fund does not define its program ɩ currently concentrates on the following areas: domestic policies, politics, and ɹics; urban and social issues; communications, science, and technology, and U.S. ɏ in the international area. The fund welcomes project proposals within these ɹad areas for consideration.

Sample Grants In 1985 support was awarded for a study of U.S. policy in the Caribbean.

Eligibility/Limitations Under the terms of the Tax Reform Act of 1969, the fund is an operating rather than a grant-making foundation, which means that the fund directly administers its own programs. The fund does not participate in projects initiated or administered under other auspices, nor does it award fellowships or scholarships, or support dissertation research. Except under extraordinary circumstances, the fund does not make grants to individuals or institutions.

Fiscal Information The fund finances all reasonable costs associated with its research projects and the drafting and editing of the manuscripts that result from them. It directly administers its projects; it does not pay university or other institutional overhead. The director of the fund negotiates budgets with prospective researchers prior to submitting proposals to the board of trustees.

Application Information An individual interested in working under the fund's auspices should submit a letter or a preliminary proposal, of no more than a page or two in length, describing the policy problem to be investigated, the approach to be taken in research, and how the work will differ from other work being done in the field. If the preliminary proposal appears promising, the fund staff may then ask the applicant to develop a proposal and to supply additional materials for a full-scale presentation to the board of trustees. Inquiries about the fund's research program and the administration of its projects should be addressed to the director or to members of the program staff. The fund's annual report is available upon request.

Deadline(s) The fund's board of trustees meets twice a year to consider proposals, usually in early May and in early November, but proposals are reviewed throughout the year. To be considered for the spring meeting, proposals must be submitted by early March, and for the fall meeting, by late August. Specific deadlines for submissions will be supplied by the fund on request.

Subject Term(s) Public Policy Studies

368. United States Information Agency

Bureau of Educational and Cultural Affairs, Academic Exchanges Division: American Republics Branch
301 Fourth Street, SW
Washington, DC 20547
(202) 485-7365

University Affiliations Program

Program Description The Bureau of Educational and Cultural Affairs of the United States Information Agency (USIA) announces a program of support for institutional partnerships between U.S. and non-U.S. institutions of higher education. The goal of the program is to facilitate bilateral institutional relationships which promote mutual understanding through faculty and staff exchanges. In the American Republics only proposals noted after each country will be accepted. Eligible are: Antigua, Argentina, Aruba, The Bahamas, Barbados, Bermuda, Bolivia, Chile, Colombia, Curacao, Dominica, The Dominican Republic, Grenada, Guyana, Haiti, Jamaica, Mexico, Paraguay, Peru, St. Lucia, Trinidad and Tobago, Uruguay, and Venezuela in the fields of economics, history, law, and political science (political behavior and methods of analysis); Brazil in the fields of fine arts and/or performing arts (exchange activities should have an academic focus); and Belize, Costa Rica, El Salvador, Guatemala, Honduras, and Nicaragua in the fields of communications, primary and secondary education, and the social sciences.

Eligibility/Limitations Accredited, degree-granting two-year and four-year undergraduate and/or graduate-level U.S. institutions of higher education are eligible to apply.

Participants traveling under USIA grant support must be U.S. citizens (or nationals) if representing the U.S. partner institution, and nationals of the country or area of the foreign partner. Proposals will be accepted either for the establishment of new affiliations or for the development of programs in new areas for existing affiliations not previously funded by USIA's Affiliations Program.

Fiscal Information The maximum amount for each grant is $50,000. Support may be requested for a minimum of two years and a maximum of three years. USIA funds may be used only for participant travel costs and modest supplements for maintenance expenses. Institutional overhead is not allowable and all other costs related to the exchange program must be borne by the participating institutions. Proposals for funding ad hoc research projects, technical assistance projects, and feasibility studies to plan affiliations will not be considered under this program.

Application Information Application forms, instructions, and additional information are available upon request.

Deadline(s) Complete proposal packages must be received by USIA on or before January 29.

Additional Information In Fiscal Year 1987, approximately twenty grants were available world-wide through the regular competition for specific countries and themes.

Subject Term(s) Exchanges; Faculty Support Abroad

369. United States Information Agency

Bureau of Educational and Cultural Affairs, Office of Private Sector Programs
301 Fourth Street, SW
Washington, DC 20547
(202) 485-7319

Grants Program for Private, Nonprofit Organizations in Support of International Educational and Cultural Activities

Program Description The United States Information Agency (USIA) announces a program of limited grant support for nonprofit U.S. institutions and organizations in the private sector which fosters long-term communication and understanding between the U.S. and other countries through educational and cultural exchange. Projects proposed for grant support should be designed to increase mutual understanding between the people of the U.S. and other countries and to strengthen the ties which unite our societies. Projects should include an international people-to-people component. The Office of Private Sector Programs works with U.S. not-for-profit organizations on cooperative international group projects which introduce American and foreign participants to one another's traditions, arts, social and political structures, and international interests.

Eligibility/Limitations Nonprofit U.S. institutions and organizations in the private sector are eligible to apply. Grants are not ordinarily given to support research projects, youth or youth-related activities, or to fund publications or student exchanges.

Fiscal Information USIA grant assistance will constitute only a portion of total project funding. Proposals should list other anticipated sources of support—both financial and in-kind. The project should be completed during the duration of the grant, which does not normally exceed one year. Most funding assistance is limited to participant travel and per diem requirements with only modest contributions to cover administrative costs.

Application Information For further information, organizations interested in participating should contact the program.

Deadline(s) Grant proposals are reviewed on a regular basis and should be submitted in final written form a minimum of four months prior to the commencement of the proposed program to be eligible for consideration. Inquiries are welcome prior to submission of formal applications.

Subject Term(s) Education; International Education; Exchanges

370. University of Cincinnati

Graduate Studies and Research
ML 627
Cincinnati, OH 45221

Charles Phelps Taft Postdoctoral Fellowships

Program Description Application are invited for Taft Postdoctoral Fellowships intended to afford scholars who have demonstrated unusual ability for creative research the opportunity to enhance their education through additional study and research in the following areas: anthropology, economics, English and comparative literature, Germanic languages and literatures, history, mathematics, philosophy, political science, Romance languages and literature, and sociology.

Eligibility/Limitations Each applicant must have been awarded the Ph.D. during the past five years, or have completed all the requirements for the degree by September 1 of the year in which the tenure of the fellowship begins.

Fiscal Information The fellowship carries a stipend of $15,000 per year. The fellow is expected to devote full time to research during the tenure of the fellowship. The recipient may not accept other compensation or supplementation from employment or from another fellowship, scholarship, or grant. However, as part of his or her activities, subject to departmental instructional needs, the fellow may be offered the opportunity to teach one course as lecturer, and for those duties may receive, in addition to the stipend, compensation not to exceed $2,500 per year.

Application Information Additional information and application guidelines are available from the Dean for Graduate Studies and Research, University of Cincinnati.

Deadline(s) Applications must be received by February 1.

Subject Term(s) Postdoctoral Support; Fellowships; Anthropology; Economics; History; Philosophy; Sociology; Political Science; Literature; Languages

371. University of Florida

Center for Latin American Studies
Linton E. Grinter Hall, Room 319
Gainesville, FL 32611
(904) 392-0375

Library Travel Grants

Program Description The Center for Latin American Studies of the University of Florida offers library travel grants for summer research at the extensive resources of the Latin American Collection in the University of Florida Libraries.

Eligibility/Limitations Researchers from other U.S. universities are eligible to apply.

Fiscal Information Awardees are expected to remain in Gainesville for at least one week and present one informal seminar at the center during their residence.

Application Information Applicants should send a letter of intent, brief library research proposal, travel budget, and curriculum vitae.

Deadline(s) Application materials must reach the center no later than March 15 to be considered.

Subject Term(s) Library Research

372. University of Florida

Center for Latin American Studies
Linton E. Grinter Hall, Room 319
Gainesville, FL 32611
(904) 392-0375

Vining Davis Field Research Grants

Program Description The Center for Latin American Studies at the University of Florida, Gainesville, announces the Vining Davis Field Research Grants competition to support field work in Latin America. Proposed projects must display an interdisciplinary approach to studies within Latin America.

Eligibility/Limitations This competition is open only to graduate students, with priority given to MALAS students and students in the Latin American Studies certificate programs. Those who have received a Tinker or Amazon Research and Training Program Award are not eligible to apply.

Fiscal Information Funds up to $1,200 are available only to support international travel to Latin America.

Application Information Additional information is available on request.

Deadline(s) The deadline for receipt of proposals is March 1. Fieldwork must be completed by September 1 of the following year.

Additional Information Amazon Research and Training Program Seed Grants are available for summer field work by graduate students in the Amazon Basin. Applicants are expected to enroll in the center's Amazon Seminar. The grants provide travel expenses and a modest per diem. Deadline for application is March 20. Contact the center for additional information.

Subject Term(s) Graduate Support Abroad; Field Research, Support of

373. University of Florida

School of Forest Resources and Conservation
Gainesville, FL 32611
(904) 392-1792

Dickinson Award in Tropical Agriculture

Program Description These awards are intended to provide summer travel expenses to enable holders to spend a summer in the tropics, engaged in structured work or other training related to tropical agriculture from an ecological perspective.

Eligibility/Limitations Two awards are available: one for undergraduate and one for graduate students.

Fiscal Information The awards are $500.

Application Information Additional information is available on request.

Deadline(s) The deadline for receipt of applications is March 20.

Subject Term(s) Agriculture; Ecology; Undergraduate Support Abroad; Graduate Support Abroad; Field Research, Support of

374. University of Pittsburgh

Center for Latin American Studies
4E04 Forbes Quadrangle
Pittsburgh, PA 15260

Mellon Visiting Professorship in Latin American Studies at the University of Pittsburgh

Program Description Since 1981 the Center for Latin American Studies of the University of Pittsburgh has awarded visiting professorships to distinguished experts in the field of Latin American Studies. Each year the fellowship will be awarded to an individual who has made a significant contribution to the field of Latin American scholarship.

Eligibility/Limitations The search is world-wide, but the applicant must be fluent in English.

Fiscal Information The visiting professorship offers a monthly stipend, health insurance, and roundtrip airfare. The visiting professor will be requested to teach one course and will spend the majority of his or her time at the university concentrating on a research project.

Application Information To apply, send a current curriculum vitae, a short (three to five pages) description of the research project to be conducted, and a sample syllabus for the proposed course to the director of the center.

Deadline(s) The deadline for receipt of application is April 1.

Subject Term(s) Faculty Support; Foreign Nationals, Eligibility of

375. U.S. Army Center of Military History

Washington, DC 20314-0200
(202) 272-0293

Dissertation Year Fellowships

Program Description To stimulate scholarly research and writing among qualified civilian graduate students preparing dissertations in American military history, especially U.S. Army history, the U.S. Army Center of Military History offers dissertation year fellowships. For purposes of this program, American Army history will be broadly defined. Biography, military campaigns, military organization and administration, policy, strategy, tactics, weaponry, technology, training, logistics, and the evolution of civil-military relations are areas of study within the scope of the awards.

Eligibility/Limitations Applicants to become visiting research fellows of the center must be civilian citizens or nationals of the U.S. They must demonstrate professional potential and must have completed by September of the award year all requirements for the Ph.D., except for the dissertation. Any student who has held or accepted an equivalent fellowship from any other department agency is not eligible for these awards.

Fiscal Information The stipend of $5,000 for the fellowship is provided in two payments. A principal objective of the program is to promote the use of the main federal archival centers in and around the nation's capital. Accordingly, fellows are expected to spend a portion of their fellowship year in Washington. Fellows will receive desk space at the center if requested and will be assisted in gaining access to archival and library sources in the Washington area, as well as to the U.S. Army Military History Institute at Carlisle Barracks, Pennsylvania, as necessary.

Application Information Applications may be obtained from the Chief Historian of the center.

Deadline(s) Applications and all supporting documents must be postmarked no later than January 12, and none will be accepted when mailed after that date.

Subject Term(s) Military History; Doctoral Dissertation Support; Archives, Research; Library Research

376. U.S. Army Military History Institute

ATTN: Assistant Director for Historical Services
Carlisle Barracks, PA 17013
(717) 245-3611

Advanced Research Program in Military History

Program Description The United States Army Military History Institute (USAMHI) announces an "Advanced Research Program in Military History" in order to stimulate research and study at the Army's major repository for materials in the history of military affairs. For purposes of this program, the field of military history can be broadly interpreted to include wars, institutions, organization and administration, policy, biography, civil affairs and civic action activities, civil-military relations, weaponry and technology, manpower training and education, strategy, tactics, and logistics, as well as the interaction of diplomatic, political, economic, social, and intellectual trends in society with military affairs during and between wars. The Military History Institute (MHI) collects materials from libraries throughout the Army as well as from individual donors. In addition to purely military matters, these volumes include coverage of many allied fields such as law, science and technology, sociology, medicine, religion, exploration, economics, geography, and political science. Many relate to military and diplomatic affairs of foreign nations, for the military history of the U.S. has been closely intertwined with that of other nations.

Eligibility/Limitations Applicants must be persons with graduate level education or equivalent professional experience pursuing research topics of interest in the discipline of military history. Interdisciplinary topics are encouraged and awards are not limited to topics dealing solely with American military history.

Fiscal Information The payment of a stipend of $750 will be made to associates upon completion of their research tour at the institute.

Application Information An applicant must submit a signed application form describing the subject, scope, and character of the project; the time estimated for residency at MHI; and how MHI facilities, materials, and professional personnel will aid in this research. Applications may be obtained from the institute.

Deadline(s) All documents must be submitted by January 1.

Subject Term(s) Military History; Archives, Research; Library Research

377. Vatican Film Library

Saint Louis University, The Pius XII Memorial Library
3655 West Pine Boulevard
Saint Louis, MO 63108

The Andrew W. Mellon Fellowship Program

Program Description The Andrew W. Mellon Foundation has made available a grant for a continuing postdoctoral fellowship program to assist scholars wishing to conduct research in the manuscript collections in the Vatican Film Library at Saint Louis University. Projects proposed for support under the fellowship program can be in such areas as classical languages and literature, paleography, scriptural and patristic studies, history, philosophy and sciences in the Middle Ages and the Renaissance, and Romance literature. There are also opportunities for supported research in the history of music manuscript illumination, mathematics and technology, theology, liturgy, Roman and canon law, and political theory.

Eligibility/Limitations Scholars with well-defined research projects which require the collections of the library are eligible to apply.

Fiscal Information The program provides travel expenses and a reasonable per diem for periods of research at the library ranging from two full weeks to eight weeks.

Application Information Applications should be submitted in the form of a project description including a precise statement of the project, an account of current research, a bibliography of the applicant's publications in areas related to the project, a curriculum vitae, a statement of the length of time for which support is requested, and letters from three persons qualified to judge the applicant's manuscript research skills in the project area.

Deadline(s) Fellowship projects can be scheduled only within one of the following periods: January 15 to May 15, June 1 to July 31, and September 1 to December 22. Persons wishing to apply for research support within one of these periods should first write to indicate the exact dates during which support is desired. These persons will be notified whether facilities are still available for the desired dates; and if facilities are available these persons will be given a deadline by which project descriptions must be submitted.

Additional Information The library possesses on microfilm perhaps the most extensive collection in this country of documents on Jesuit work in Latin America, mainly in the colonial period. These documents have been filmed in the Jesuit Archives in Rome and in various other collections, chiefly in Spain, Italy, France, Mexico, Canada, and the United States.

Subject Term(s) Fellowships; Postdoctoral Support; Library Research; Catholicism

378. Wenner-Gren Foundation for Anthropological Research

1865 Broadway
New York, NY 10023-7596
(212) 957-8750

Developing Country Training Fellowships

Program Description Wenner-Gren's sphere of interest is the support of research in all branches of anthropology and in related disciplines pertaining to the sciences of man. Projects supported use cross-cultural, historical, biological, and linguistic approaches towards understanding man's origins, development, and variation. Special consideration is given to projects integrating two or more subfields of anthropology or related disciplines, particularly when combined with theoretical or methodological issues.

Sample Grants A 1986 fellowship was awarded to aid education and training in physical anthropology in pursuance of research on human population structure in Venezuela. A 1986 fellowship was awarded to aid training and education in pursuance of anthropological research in Argentina.

Eligibility/Limitations Developing Country Training Fellowships are awarded to qualified scholars or students from developing countries. These fellowships are designed primarily to support younger scholars who need training unavailable in their home country and who cannot meet the costs of such training elsewhere.

Fiscal Information Fellowships of up to $12,500 are awarded annually. Foundation aid does not support: large-scale projects, salary and/or fringe benefits, tuition, non-project personnel, travel to national meetings, dissertation publication, institutional overhead, intermediary funding agencies, or building material and construction.

Application Information Additional information and application materials for Developing Country Training Fellowships are mailed on request. Applicants may submit a brief description of the proposed project, including anticipated starting date and required funding. If a project is considered eligible, a formal application will be invited and the appropriate forms and guidelines supplied.

Deadline(s) Applications must be submitted no less than nine months prior to starting date of training.

Subject Term(s) Individuals, Eligibility of; Fellowships; Foreign Nationals, Eligibility of; Anthropology

379. Wenner-Gren Foundation for Anthropological Research

1865 Broadway
New York, NY 10023-7596
(212) 957-8750

Foundation-Administered Conferences

Program Description Wenner-Gren's sphere of interest is the support of research in all branches of anthropology and in related disciplines pertaining to the sciences of man. Projects supported use cross-cultural, historical, biological, and linguistic approaches towards understanding man's origins, development, and variation. Special consideration is given to projects integrating two or more subfields of anthropology or related disciplines, particularly when combined with theoretical or methodological issues. In addition to awarding direct grants-in-aid for conferences, the foundation accepts proposals from accredited scholars for conferences to be administered by the foundation under its conference program.

Fiscal Information Foundation assistance varies with the size and location of each conference.

Application Information Additional information and application materials concerning foundation-administered conferences are mailed on request. Applicants may submit a brief description of the proposed conference, including anticipated starting date and required funding. If a conference is considered eligible, a formal application will be invited and the appropriate forms and guidelines supplied.

Deadline(s) Applications must be submitted at least eighteen months in advance of a conference.

Subject Term(s) Seminars and Conferences; Anthropology

380. Wenner-Gren Foundation for Anthropological Research

1865 Broadway
New York, NY 10023-7596
(212) 957-8750

Postdoctoral Fellowships

Program Description Wenner-Gren's sphere of interest is the support of research in all branches of anthropology and in related disciplines pertaining to the sciences of man. Projects supported use cross-cultural, historical, biological, and linguistic approaches towards understanding man's origins, development, and variation. Special consideration is given to projects integrating two or more subfields of anthropology or related disciplines, particularly when combined with theoretical or methodological issues. Postdoctoral fellowships are intended to allow recent Ph.D.'s in the anthropological sciences to train in a related field or fields outside anthropology. The program of study must be designed to broaden interdisciplinary skills relevant to a particular problem or project within the candidate's area of specialization.

Eligibility/Limitations Recent Ph.D.'s in the anthropological sciences may apply. Postdoctoral fellowships are not designed to support fieldwork. Formal enrollment or association with a non-anthropological department or research laboratory is required.

Fiscal Information Fellowships carry an award up to $15,000. Foundation aid does not support: large-scale projects, salary and/or fringe benefits, tuition, non-project personnel, travel to national meetings, dissertation publication, institutional overhead, intermediary funding agencies, or building material and construction.

Application Information Application materials for postdoctoral fellowships are mailed on request. Applicants may submit a brief description of the proposed project, including anticipated starting date and required funding. If a project is considered eligible, a formal application will be invited and the appropriate forms and guidelines supplied.

Deadline(s) Applications must be postmarked no later than June 1.

Subject Term(s) Fellowships; Postdoctoral Support; Anthropology

381. Wenner-Gren Foundation for Anthropological Research

1865 Broadway
New York, NY 10023-7596
(212) 957-8750

Senior Scholar Research Stipends

Program Description Wenner-Gren's sphere of interest is the support of research in all branches of anthropology and in related disciplines pertaining to the sciences of man. Projects supported use cross-cultural, historical, biological, and linguistic approaches towards understanding man's origins, development, and variation. Special consideration is given to projects integrating two or more subfields of anthropology or related disciplines, particularly when combined with theoretical or methodological issues. Senior scholar stipends provide support for writing and study integrating a scholar's past research with his or her current interests.

Eligibility/Limitations Scholars who have established records of research and publication may apply. Priority consideration will be given to retired scholars, to those about to retire, or to those who have no facilities at the time of application.

Fiscal Information Stipends up to $15,000 are available. Foundation aid does not support: large-scale projects, salary and/or fringe benefits, tuition, non-project personnel, travel to national meetings, dissertation publication, institutional overhead, intermediary funding agencies, or building material and construction.

Application Information Application materials for senior scholar research stipends are mailed on request. Applicants may submit a brief description of the proposed project, including anticipated starting date and required funding. If a project is considered eligible, a formal application will be invited and the appropriate forms and guidelines supplied.

Deadline(s) Application materials must be postmarked no later than June 1.

Subject Term(s) Individuals, Eligibility of; Anthropology

382. Wenner-Gren Foundation for Anthropological Research

1865 Broadway
New York, NY 10023-7596
(212) 957-8750

Small Grants Program: Regular Grants

Program Description Wenner-Gren's sphere of interest is the support of research in all branches of anthropology and in related disciplines pertaining to the sciences of man. Projects supported use cross-cultural, historical, biological, and linguistic approaches towards understanding man's origins, development, and variation. Special consideration is given to projects integrating two or more subfields of anthropology or related disciplines, particularly when combined with theoretical or methodological issues. Small grants are geared to seeding innovative or untried approaches and ideas, and provide material support to encourage aid from other funding agencies. Regular Grants are awarded to individual scholars from anywhere in the world who are affiliated with an accredited institution or organization.

Eligibility/Limitations Accredited scholars may apply.

Fiscal Information Regular grant awards usually range from $500 to $7,000 and are primarily for basic research. Foundation aid does not support: large-scale projects, salary and/or fringe benefits, tuition, non-project personnel, travel to national meetings, dissertation publication, institutional overhead, intermediary funding agencies, or building material and construction.

Application Information Applicants are required to submit project description forms, which are available on request. Project description forms will be accepted only in accordance with the current deadline schedule, available from the foundation. Applicants may submit a brief description of the proposed project, including anticipated starting date and required funding. If a project is considered eligible, a formal application will be invited and the appropriate forms and guidelines supplied.

Deadline(s) Applications must be postmarked by June 1.

Subject Term(s) Individuals, Eligibility of; Foreign Nationals, Eligibility of; Anthropology

383. Wenner-Gren Foundation for Anthropological Research

1865 Broadway
New York, NY 10023-7596
(212) 957-8750

Small Grants Program: Richard Carley Hunt Memorial Postdoctoral Fellowships

Program Description Wenner-Gren's sphere of interest is the support of research in all branches of anthropology and in related disciplines pertaining to the sciences of man. Projects supported use cross-cultural, historical, biological, and linguistic approaches towards understanding man's origins, development, and variation. Special consideration is give to projects integrating two or more subfields of anthropology or related disciplines, particularly when combined with theoretical or methodological issues. The Richard Carley Hunt Memorial Postdoctoral Fellowships are awarded to aid completion of specific studies or for preparation for publication of field manuals.

Eligibility/Limitations Postdoctoral scholars may apply.

Fiscal Information The fellowship carries a stipend of $4,000 and is non-renewable.

Application Information Applicants are required to submit project description forms, which are available on request. Project description forms will be accepted only in accordance with the current deadline schedule, available from the foundation. Applicants may submit a brief description of the proposed project, including anticipated starting date and required funding. If a project is considered eligible, a formal application will be invited and the appropriate forms and guidelines supplied.

Deadline(s) Applications must be postmarked by June 1.

Subject Term(s) Fellowships; Postdoctoral Support; Anthropology

384. Wenner-Gren Foundation for Anthropological Research

1865 Broadway
New York, NY 10023-7596
(212) 957-8750

Small Grants Program: Student Grants

Program Description Wenner-Gren's sphere of interest is the support of research in all branches of anthropology and in related disciplines pertaining to the sciences of man. Projects supported use cross-cultural, historical, biological, and linguistic approaches towards understanding man's origins, development, and variation. Special consideration is given to projects integrating two or more subfields of anthropology or related disciplines, particularly when combined with theoretical or methodological issues. Small grants are geared to seeding innovative or untried approaches and ideas, and provide material support to encourage aid from other funding agencies. Student grants are awarded to individuals at the advanced predoctoral level for research.

Eligibility/Limitations Students at the advanced predoctoral level are eligible. Anyone enrolled in a degree program at the time of application must be considered by the foundation to be in the student category.

Fiscal Information Student grant awards usually range from $500 to $7,000 and are primarily for basic research. Foundation aid does not support: large-scale projects, salary and/or fringe benefits, tuition, non-project personnel, travel to national meetings, dissertation publication, institutional overhead, intermediary funding agencies, or building material and construction. Whenever possible student applicants from North America, Western Europe, and Japan should demonstrate the availability of matching funds. However, any worthy project will be taken under consideration despite lack of such funds, regardless of the citizenship of the applicant.

Application Information Applicants are required to submit project description forms, which are available on request. Project description forms will be accepted only in accordance with the current deadline schedule, available from the foundation. Applicants may submit a brief description of the proposed project, including anticipated starting date and required funding. If a project is considered eligible, a formal application will be invited and the appropriate forms and guidelines supplied.

Deadline(s) Applications must be postmarked by June 1.

Subject Term(s) Foreign Nationals, Eligibility of; Doctoral Dissertation Support; Predoctoral Support; Anthropology

385. Woodrow Wilson International Center for Scholars

Smithsonian Institution Building
Washington, DC 20560
(202) 357-2841

Latin American Program

CFDA Program Number 60.020

Program Description The center seeks to commemorate through its residential fellowship program of advanced research both the scholarly depth and the public concerns of Woodrow Wilson. The center welcomes from individuals throughout the world outstanding project proposals representing a wide diversity of scholarly interests and approaches. Projects are encouraged from the whole range of the humanities and social sciences. The Latin American Program supports advanced research by social scientists and humanists on Latin America, the Caribbean, and inter-American affairs. Although proposals on any subject will be carefully reviewed, there is particular interest in research on a number of central themes: (1) the interplay between cultural traditions and political institutions; (2) the history of ideas in Latin America; (3) the prospects for democracy; and (4) in exceptional cases, novels or poetry related to larger cultural themes.

Sample Grants 1985 fellows conducted research on: the political economy of recovery, Brazil's emergence from its deepest recession in sixty years; democracy and broadcasting in a Third World country, the Jamaica Broadcasting Corporation, a test case; varieties of faith—religion and politics in Nicaragua, 1965-1985; social dynamics and ethnicity in Peru; the Marsh-Darien expedition and the Kuna Revolution of 1925; pre-Colombian political organization in the Central Andes; and perceptions of the Inca empire, 1532-1650.

Eligibility/Limitations Applicants from any country are eligible. Men and women with outstanding capabilities and experience from a wide variety of backgrounds (such as academia, journalism, government, labor, business, and the professions) are eligible for support. For academic participants, eligibility is limited to the postdoctoral level, and normally it is expected that academic candidates will have demonstrated their scholarly development by the publication of some major work beyond the Ph.D. dissertation. For participants from other fields, an equivalent degree or professional achievement is expected. While English is the working language of the center, research and writing may be pursued in any language. The center's program is residential in character and fellows are expected to devote full time to the major research project proposed in the application.

Fiscal Information Because the center has a limited amount of fellowship support it strongly encourages applicants to seek concurrent sources of funding: other fellowships, foundation grants, sabbaticals, or other funding from their home institutions. Within this limitation and under a ceiling established by the board of trustees ($35,000 per twelve-month period), the center attempts to meet a fellow's previous year's earned income. For scholars from abroad, the center attempts to approximate, but does not exceed, the salaries of U.S. scholars of comparable experience and position. Certain travel expenses for a fellow and accompanying spouse and younger children may also be provided. Appointments normally extend for from four months to a year.

Application Information Additional information and application procedures are available from the center.

Deadline(s) The center holds one round of competitive selection per year. The deadline for receipt of applications and all supporting materials is October 1.

Subject Term(s) Foreign Nationals, Eligibility of; Individuals, Eligibility of; Postdoctoral Support; Fellowships; Humanities; Social Sciences

386. Woodrow Wilson National Fellowship Foundation

Box 642
Princeton, NJ 08540
(609) 924-4666

Charlotte W. Newcombe Doctoral Dissertation Fellowships

Program Description The Charlotte W. Newcombe Doctoral Dissertation Fellowships are designed to encourage original and significant study of ethical or religious values in all areas of human endeavor.

Sample Grants A 1986 fellowship was awarded for a study in the basketry and symbolism of the Makiritare Indians of Venezuela.

Eligibility/Limitations Students must be candidates for Ph.D., Ed.D., or Th.D. degrees, enrolled in doctoral programs in the humanities and social sciences at graduate schools in the United States, and expect to complete all doctoral requirements except the dissertation by January.

Fiscal Information Winners will receive $9,000 for twelve months of full-time dissertation research and writing. The award does not include tuition, but small fees may be covered. Forty-seven fellowships will be awarded with funds from the Charlotte W. Newcombe Foundation.

Application Information Application forms are available from the Woodrow Wilson National Fellowship Foundation.

Deadline(s) Applications must be requested by December 11. Completed applications must be postmarked by January 1.

Subject Term(s) Fellowships; Doctoral Dissertation Support; Values; Religion; Humanities; Social Sciences

387. Woodrow Wilson National Fellowship Foundation

Box 642
Princeton, NJ 08540
(609) 924-4666

Mellon Fellowships in the Humanities

Program Description The Mellon Fellowships in the Humanities have two objectives: to attract annually 100 to 125 exceptionally promising students into preparation for careers in humanistic teaching and scholarship by providing top-level, competitive, portable awards tenable for as many as three years; and to contribute thereby to the continuity of teaching and research of the highest order in America's colleges and universities. Fields eligible are the traditional humanities disciplines, including history, but not the creative or performing arts. American studies, other area studies, and interdisciplinary programs are also eligible if the emphasis in subject and method is substantially humanistic.

Eligibility/Limitations Any college senior or recent graduate who is a U.S. or Canadian citizen, can present evidence of outstanding academic promise, and wishes to begin graduate work in preparation for a career of teaching and scholarship in a humanistic field of study is eligible for consideration. Individuals who have been candidates in a previous year, however, are normally not eligible.

Fiscal Information The stipend for fellows entering graduate school in the fall will be $8,500 plus payment of tuition and standard fees to their graduate schools. Fellowships will be renewed for a second year on recommendation of the graduate school concerned. In that year, the graduate school is expected to cover one-third of tuition and fees; the Mellon Fellowships will cover the remainder. In addition, fellows who have performed with distinction will be eligible for stipends (but not tuition and fee support) in the final year of work on their dissertations. Normally, the support will not extend beyond the fifth year of graduate study, but in special circumstances it may be available later at the discretion of the director.

Application Information Candidacy must be initiated by nomination from a faculty member to the program's appropriate regional chairman or the central office if the nominee is overseas or expects to be there in January-February.

Deadline(s) Nominations must reach the regional chairman by November 2. Applications must reach the regional chairman by December 7.

Subject Term(s) Humanities; Graduate Support; Canadian Nationals, Eligibility of; Fellowships

388. Woodrow Wilson National Fellowship Foundation

Box 642
Princeton, NJ 08540
(609) 924-4666

Woodrow Wilson Women's Studies Research Grants

Program Description These research grants are designed to encourage original and significant research about women on such topics as the evolution of women's role in society and particularly contemporary America, women in history, the psychology of women, and women as seen in literature.

Eligibility/Limitations Eligible applicants are students in doctoral programs who have completed all pre-dissertation requirements in any field of study at graduate schools in the United States.

Fiscal Information Winners will receive grants averaging $1,200 to be used for research expenses connected with the dissertation. These may include travel, books, microfilming, photocopying, taping, and computer services. The number of awards will be determined by available funds.

Application Information Application forms are available on request. Applications must be endorsed by the candidate's dissertation director and graduate dean.

Deadline(s) Deadline for receipt of applications is November 13.

Subject Term(s) Social Sciences; Humanities; Predoctoral Support; Women's Studies

389. Woods Hole Oceanographic Institution

Dean of Graduate Studies
Education Office, Clark Laboratory
Woods Hole, MA 02543
(617) 548-1400

Research Fellowships in Marine Policy and Ocean Management

Program Description The Woods Hole Oceanographic Institution offers fellowships to individuals in social sciences, law, the humanities, or natural sciences to apply their training to the legal, political, social, or economic problems or issues involved with the use of the oceans. Present research in the center includes marine policy problems and opportunities in developing countries; policy and management issues concerning fisheries, marine minerals, and coastal zone use; implications of the Law of the Sea Treaty for ocean activities; Arctic and Antarctic resource issues; and the use of scientific information in decision making and policy planning. Other research topics are also appropriate. Previous policy fellows have been trained in fields such as law, economics, anthropology, political science, sociology, international relations, engineering, marine science, and geography. The objective of the fellowship program is to provide an opportunity for research in marine policy problems which may require the interdisciplinary application of natural science, technology, and social science.

Eligibility/Limitations Applicants to the center must have completed a doctoral level degree or possess equivalent professional qualifications through career experience. The center also welcomes experienced professionals who can arrange a leave or sabbatical.

Fiscal Information Recent doctorates will receive a stipend of $23,100 for a period of one year and are eligible for group health insurance. In addition, modest research and travel funds will be made available. Recipients are initially appointed for one year; however, depending upon the nature and scope of the recipient's effort, opportunities may be available to continue their professional affiliation with the institution.

Application Information A complete application consists of an application form, transcripts of college and university records, at least three personal references, and a preliminary but precise proposal for the research project to be undertaken while in residence in Woods Hole.

Deadline(s) Applications should be made no later than January 15.

Subject Term(s) Fellowships; Marine Policy; Antarctica; Marine Research; Oceanography

390. The Carter G. Woodson Institute for Afro-American and African Studies

University of Virginia
1512 Jefferson Park Avenue
Charlottesville, VA 22903
(804) 924-3109

Postdoctoral Fellowships

Program Description The Carter G. Woodson Institute for Afro-American and African Studies at the University of Virginia announces the availability of residential research fellowships in Afro-American and African Studies. These fellowships are for the support of projects in those disciplines of the humanities and social sciences which concern themselves with Afro-American and African Studies. For the purpose of this competition, Afro-American and African Studies is considered to cover Africa, Africans, and peoples of African descent in North, Central, and South America, and the Caribbean, past and present.

Eligibility/Limitations Applicants for postdoctoral fellowships must have been awarded their Ph.D. by the time of the application or must furnish proof that it will have been received prior to June 30. Fellows will receive the status of visiting scholars in their respective fields at the University of Virginia.

Fiscal Information The fellowship is for one year and carries a stipend of $25,000.

Application Information Additional information and application guidelines are available on request.

Deadline(s) Applications must be received no later than December 1.

Subject Term(s) Postdoctoral Support; Fellowships; Afro-American Studies; Humanities; Social Sciences

391. The Carter G. Woodson Institute for Afro-American and African Studies

University of Virginia
1512 Jefferson Park Avenue
Charlottesville, VA 22903
(804) 924-3109

Predoctoral Fellowships

Program Description The Carter G. Woodson Institute for Afro-American and African Studies at the University of Virginia announces the availability of residential research fellowships in Afro-American and African Studies. These fellowships are for the support of projects in those disciplines of the humanities and social sciences which concern themselves with Afro-American and African Studies. For the purpose of this competition, Afro-American and African Studies is considered to cover Africa, Africans, and peoples of African descent in North, Central, and South America, and the Caribbean, past and present.

Eligibility/Limitations Applicants for predoctoral fellowships must have completed all requirements for the Ph.D. except the dissertation prior to August 1. Fellows will become visiting graduate students at the University of Virginia attached to their respective disciplinary departments.

Fiscal Information The fellowship is for two years and carries a stipend of $12,500 per year.

Application Information Additional information and application guidelines are available on request.

Deadline(s) Applications must be received no later than December 1.

Subject Term(s) Predoctoral Support; Fellowships; Afro-American Studies; Social Sciences; Humanities

392. World Bank

McNamara Fellowships Program, Economic Development Institute
1818 H Street, NW
Washington, DC 20433
(202) 477-4446

Robert S. McNamara Fellowships

Program Description Fellowships are awarded for full-time work at the post-graduate level in fields related to economic development and institution building.

Eligibility/Limitations Applications are considered from individuals as well as from small groups (up to five persons) for work on a joint project. Applicants must be a national of a World Bank member country, be under thirty-five years of age, hold a Master's degree or its equivalent, and propose work which will be carried out in a country other than his or her own. These fellowships are not intended to support work leading to an advanced degree.

Fiscal Information Fellowships include a stipend to cover maintenance, travel, and an allowance for books and the cost of research.

Application Information Additional information and application guidelines are available upon request.

Deadline(s) Applications must reach the bank's Economic Development Institute by December 1.

Subject Term(s) Foreign Nationals, Eligibility of; Fellowships; Individuals, Eligibility of; Economic Development

393. World Wildlife Fund

WWF International
World Conservation Center
CH-1196 Gland Switzerland
022/64 71 81

The World Conservation Center

Program Description The World Wildlife Fund (WWF) is a private, international conservation foundation. Its scope is the conservation of nature and the natural environment in all its forms: fauna, flora, landscapes, soils, water, air, and other natural resources. WWF mobilizes, on a world-wide basis, the strongest possible moral and financial support for safeguarding the living world and seeks to convert such support into action based on scientific priorities.

Sample Grants For a coordinator for a wildlife program in Central America, $28,275 (1986). For primate conservation in the Atlantic Forest region of eastern Brazil, $36,200 (1986). For a project on land-use and human carrying capacity in the Amazon Basin, Brazil, $20,000 (1986).

Fiscal Information Since its founding in 1961, WWF has channeled over $95 million into more than 4,200 projects in some 130 countries.

Application Information Additional information is available from the WWF.

Subject Term(s) Conservation; Wildlife Conservation

Subject Index

Sponsor Type Index

Museum/Library

Nonprofit Organization

Professional Society

University

List of Sponsoring Organizations

Agency for International Development
320 Twenty-first Street, NW
Washington, DC 20523

American Alpine Club
113 East 90th Street
New York, NY 10028

American Association for the Advancement of Science
1776 Massachusetts Avenue, NW
Washington, DC 20036

American Association of University Women Educational Foundation
2401 Virginia Avenue, NW
Washington, DC 20037

American Council of Learned Societies
228 East 45th Street
New York, NY 10017-3398

American Heart Association
7320 Greenville Avenue
Dallas, TX 75231

American Institute of Nutrition
9650 Rockville Pike
Bethesda, MD 20814

American Museum of Natural History
Central Park West at 79th Street
New York, NY 10024

The American Musicological Society
201 South 34th Street
Philadelphia, PA 19104-6313

The American Numismatic Society
Broadway at 155th Street
New York, NY 10032

American Philosophical Society
104 South Fifth Street
Philadelphia, PA 19106

Amoco Foundation
200 East Randolph Drive
Chicago, IL 60601

The Annenberg/CPB Project
1111 Sixteenth Street, NW
Washington, DC 20036

The Arca Foundation
1425 Twenty-first Street, NW
Washington, DC 20036

Association for Women in Science, Inc.
2401 Virginia Avenue, NW, Suite 303
Washington, DC 20037

Leo Baeck Institute
129 East 73rd Street
New York, NY 10021

Bancroft Prize
202A Low Library
New York, NY 10027

Benton Foundation
1776 K Street, NW, Suite 900
Washington, DC 20006

Bermuda Biological Station
Ferry Reach 1-115,
Bermuda

Boehm Foundation
500 Fifth Avenue
New York, NY 10110-0296

The Brookings Institution
1775 Massachusetts Avenue, NW
Washington, DC 20036

John Carter Brown Library
Box 1894
Providence, RI 02912

Mary Ingraham Bunting Institute of Radcliffe College
34 Concord Avenue
Cambridge, MA 02138

Business and Professional Women's Foundation
2021 Massachusetts Avenue, NW
Washington, DC 20036

Carnegie Corporation of New York
437 Madison Avenue
New York, NY 10022

Center for Advanced Study in the Behavioral Sciences
202 Junipero Serra Boulevard
Stanford, CA 94305

The Center for Field Research
680 Mount Auburn Street, Box 403
Watertown, MA 02172

The Edna McConnell Clark Foundation
250 Park Avenue
New York, NY 10017

Columbia Foundation
1090 Sansome Street
San Francisco, CA 94111

Compton Foundation
10 Hanover Square
New York, NY 10005

Corporation for Public Broadcasting
1111 Sixteenth Street, NW
Washington, DC 20036

Council for International Exchange of Scholars
Eleven Dupont Circle, NW, Suite 300
Washington, DC 20036-1257

Council on Foreign Relations
58 East 68th Street
New York, NY 10021

Council on International Educational Exchange
205 East 42nd Street
New York, NY 10017

Cummins Engine Foundation
Mail Code 60814, Box 3005
Columbus, IN 47202-3005

Eben Demarest Fund
111 Yorkshire Road
Pittsburgh, PA 15208

Department of Education
Seventh and D Streets, SW, ROB-3
Washington, DC 20202

Department of State
1400 Key Boulevard
Washington, DC 22209

The William H. Donner Foundation, Inc.
630 Fifth Avenue, Room 2452
New York, NY 10111

Dumbarton Oaks Center for Byzantine Studies
1703 Thirty-second Street, NW
Washington, DC 20007

Explorers Club
46 East 70th Street
New York, NY 10021

Exxon Education Foundation
111 West 49th Street
New York, NY 10020-1198

The Film Fund
80 East 11th Street
New York, NY 10003

Fogarty International Center
National Institutes of Health, Building 38A, Room 615
Bethesda, MD 20892

Folger Shakespeare Library
201 East Capitol Street, SE
Washington, DC 20003

The Ford Foundation
320 East 43rd Street
New York, NY 10017

Foreign Policy Research Institute
3508 Market Street, Suite 350
Philadelphia, PA 19104

Foundation for Field Research
787 South Grade Road
Alpine, CA 92001-0380

General Service Foundation
P.O. Box 4012
Boulder, CO 80306

The Geological Society of America
P.O. Box 9140
Boulder, CO 80301

The Getty Center for the History of Art and the Humanities
401 Wilshire Boulevard, Suite 400
Santa Monica, CA 90401-1455

The J. Paul Getty Trust
1875 Century Park East, Suite 2300
Los Angeles, CA 90067

Global Perspectives in Education, Inc.
218 East 18th Street
New York, NY 10003

Graham Foundation
4 West Burton Place
Chicago, IL 60610

The Harry Frank Guggenheim Foundation
527 Madison Avenue
New York, NY 10022-4301

John Simon Guggenheim Memorial Foundation
90 Park Avenue
New York, NY 10016

Harvard University
Lamont Library 202
Cambridge, MA 02138

The H. John Heinz III Charitable Trust
301 Fifth Avenue, Suite 1417
Pittsburgh, PA 15222-2494

Howard Heinz Endowment
301 Fifth Avenue, Suite 1417
Pittsburgh, PA 15222-2494

The Herb Society of America
300 Massachusetts Avenue
Boston, MA 02115

The William R. and Flora L. Hewlett Foundation
525 Middlefield Road
Menlo Park, CA 94025

Hewlett-Packard Company Foundation
3000 Hanover Street
Palo Alto, CA 94304

Hoover Institution on War, Revolution and Peace
Stanford University
Stanford, CA 94305

The George A. and Eliza Gardner Howard Foundation
42 Charlesfield Street, Box 1867
Providence, RI 02912

The Hudson Institute
5395 Emerson Way, P.O. Box 26-919
Indianapolis, IN 46226

Institute for Development Anthropology
99 Collier Street, Suite 302, P.O. Box 2207
Binghamton, NY 13902

Institute for Intercultural Studies, Inc.
145 East 74th Street, Suite 1C
New York, NY 10021

Institute of Current World Affairs—The Crane-Rogers Foundation
Wheelock House, 4 West Wheelock Street
Hanover, NH 03755

Institute of International Education
809 United Nations Plaza
New York, NY 10017

Inter-American Foundation
1515 Wilson Boulevard
Rosslyn, VA 22209

Interamerican Press Association
2911 Northwest 39th Street
Miami, FL 33142

International Center for Reseach on Women
1717 Massachusetts Avenue, NW, Suite 501
Washington, DC 20036

Inter-University Program for Latino Research
Student Services Building 4.120
Austin, TX 78712

The Johns Hopkins University
The Johns Hopkins University
Baltimore, MD 21218

W. Alton Jones Foundation
433 Park Street
Charlottesville, VA 22901

The Helen Kellogg Institute for International Studies
University of Notre Dame
Notre Dame, IN 46556

W. K. Kellogg Foundation
400 North Avenue
Battle Creek, MI 49017-3398

Samuel H. Kress Foundation
221 West 57th Street
New York, NY 10019

L.S.B. Leakey Foundation
Foundation Center 1-7
Pasadena, CA 91125

The Charles A. Lindbergh Fund, Inc.
Box O
Summit, NJ 07901

London School of Hygiene and Tropical Medicine
Keppel Street
London WC1E 7HT
England

J. Roderick MacArthur Foundation
9333 North Milwaukee Avenue
Niles, IL 60648

The John D. and Catherine MacArthur Foundation
140 South Dearborn Street
Chicago, IL 60603

The Andrew W. Mellon Foundation
140 East 62nd Street
New York, NY 10021

The Metropolitan Museum of Art
Fifth Avenue and 82nd Street
New York, NY 10028

National Association for Foreign Student Affairs
1860 Nineteenth Street, NW
Washington, DC 20009

National Cancer Institute
Bethesda, MD 20205

National Endowment for Democracy
1156 Fifteenth Street, NW, Suite 304
Washington, DC 20005

National Endowment for the Arts
1100 Pennsylvania Avenue, NW
Washington, DC 20506

National Endowment for the Humanities
1100 Pennsylvania Avenue, NW
Washington, DC 20506

National Eye Institute
Bethesda, MD 20892

National Geographic Society
Seventeenth and M Streets, NW
Washington, DC 20036

National Heart, Lung, and Blood Institute
7550 Wisconsin Avenue
Bethesda, MD 20892

National Humanities Center
7 Alexander Drive
Research Triangle Park, NC 27709

National Institute of Allergy and Infectious Diseases
Extramural Activities Program, Westwood Building, Room 703
Bethesda, MD 20892

National Institute of Arthritis, Musculoskeletal and Skin Diseases
Building 31, 9000 Rockville Pike
Bethesda, MD 20892

National Institute of Child Health and Human Development
9000 Rockville Pike
Bethesda, MD 20892

National Institute of Dental Research
Westwood Building, 5333 Westbard Avenue
Bethesda, MD 20892

National Institute of Diabetes and Digestive and Kidney Diseases
Westwood Building, 5333 Westbard Avenue
Bethesda, MD 20892

National Institute of Environmental Health Sciences
P.O. Box 12233
Research Triangle Park, NC 27709

National Institute of General Medical Sciences
9000 Rockville Pike
Bethesda, MD 20892

National Institute of Mental Health
5600 Fishers Lane
Rockville, MD 20857

National Institute of Neurological and Communicative Disorders and Stroke
Building 31, 9000 Rockville Pike
Bethesda, MD 20892

National Institute on Aging
Building 31, 9000 Rockville Pike
Bethesda, MD 20892

National Institute on Alcohol Abuse and Alcoholism
5600 Fishers Lane
Rockville, MD 20857

National Institute on Drug Abuse
5600 Fishers Lane
Rockville, MD 20857

National Research Council
2101 Constitution Avenue, NW
Washington, DC 20418

National Science Foundation
1800 G Street, NW
Washington, DC 20550

National Wildlife Federation
1412 Sixteenth Street, NW
Washington, DC 20036

The Needmor Fund
1730 Fifteenth Street
Boulder, CO 80302

The Newberry Library
60 West Walton Street
Chicago, IL 60610

Jessie Smith Noyes Foundation
16 East 34th Street
New York, NY 10016

John M. Olin Foundation, Inc.
100 Park Avenue, Suite 2701
New York, NY 10017

Organization of American States
Washington, DC 20006-4499

Pacific Coast Council on Latin American Studies
Arizona State University
Tempe, AZ 85287

The David and Lucile Packard Foundation
330 Second Street
Los Altos, CA 94022

Pan American Health Organization
525 Twenty-third Street, NW
Washington, DC 20037

Partners of the Americas
1424 K Street, NW, Suite 700
Washington, DC 20005

The Population Council
One Dag Hammarskjold Plaza
New York, NY 10017

Smith Richardson Foundation, Inc.
5000 Laurinda Drive, P.O. Box 3265
Greensboro, NC 27402

Rockefeller Archive Center
Pocantico Hills
North Tarrytown, NY 10591

Rockefeller Brothers Fund
1290 Avenue of the Americas
New York, NY 10104

The Rockefeller Foundation
1133 Avenue of the Americas
New York, NY 10036

The Rolex Awards for Enterprise
P.O. Box 178
CH-1211 Geneva 26
Switzerland

Rosenberg Foundation
210 Post Street
San Francisco, CA 94108-5172

The Rotary Foundation
1600 Ridge Avenue
Evanston, IL 60201

Russel Sage Foundation
112 East 64th Street
New York, NY 10021

School of Advanced International Studies
1740 Massachusetts Avenue, NW
Washington, DC 20036

School of American Research
P.O. Box 2188
Santa Fe, NM 87504

Sigma Xi, The Scientific Research Society
345 Whitney Avenue
New Haven, CT 06511

The L. J. Skaggs and Mary C. Skaggs Foundation
1330 Broadway, 17th Floor
Oakland, CA 94612

Smithsonian Institution
3300 L'Enfant Plaza
Washington, DC 20560

Social Science Research Council
605 Third Avenue
New York, NY 10158

The Spencer Foundation
875 North Michigan Avenue
Chicago, IL 60611

Stanford Humanities Center
Mariposa House
Stanford, CA 94305-8630

The Tinker Foundation Incorporated
55 East 59th Street
New York, NY 10022

The Twentieth Century Fund
41 East 70th Street
New York, NY 10021

United States Information Agency
301 Fourth Street, SW
Washington, DC 20547

University of Cincinnati
ML 627
Cincinnati, OH 45221

University of Florida
Linton E. Grinter Hall, Room 319
Gainesville, FL 32611

University of Pittsburgh
4E04 Forbes Quadrangle
Pittsburgh, PA 15260

U.S. Army Center of Military History
Washington, DC 20314-0200

U.S. Army Military History Institute
ATTN: Assistant Director for Historical Services
Carlisle Barracks, PA 17013

Vatican Film Library
3655 West Pine Boulevard
Saint Louis, MO 63108

Wenner-Gren Foundation for Anthropological Research
1865 Broadway
New York, NY 10023-7596

Woodrow Wilson International Center for Scholars
Smithsonian Institution Building
Washington, DC 20560

Woodrow Wilson National Fellowship Foundation
Box 642
Princeton, NJ 08540

Woods Hole Oceanographic Institution
Education Office, Clark Laboratory
Woods Hole, MA 02543

The Carter G. Woodson Institute for Afro-American and African Studies
1512 Jefferson Park Avenue
Charlottesville, VA 22903

World Bank
1818 H Street, NW
Washington, DC 20433

World Wildlife Fund
World Conservation Center
CH-1196 Gland
Switzerland

Bibliography

GENERAL FUNDING AND GRANTSMANSHIP:

Printed Source Materials

Academic Research Information Service (ARIS). San Francisco: Academic Research Information System. Monthly newsletters (*Biomedical Sciences Report, Creative Arts and Humanities Report, Social and Natural Sciences Report, The Student Report*) detailing grant information and deadlines of federal programs, foundations, associations, organizations, and universities.

Annual Register of Grant Support 1986-1987. 20th ed. Wilmette, IL: National Register Publishing Co., 1986. Lists 3,000 grant programs offered by the federal government, foundations, and professional and educational associations. Includes support for research, travel, exchanges, and information about prizes and awards.

Catalog of Federal Domestic Assistance. 21st ed. Washington, DC: U.S. Office of Management and Budget, 1987. Lists federal grants, loans, technical assistance, programs, and other service and information activities. Includes information on program purpose, eligibility, deadlines, and points of contact for additional information.

Chronicle of Higher Education. Washington, DC: The Chronicle of Higher Education, Inc. A weekly publication which includes grant and fellowship information and deadlines.

The CISP International Studies Funding Book. 4th ed. Walter T. Brown, Robert Cassani, David Dembo, eds. New York: Council on International and Public Affairs, 1986. Lists information on funding and other sources of support for college and university international/intercultural education.

Commerce Business Daily. Washington, DC: Superintendent of Documents, Government Printing Office. A daily publication, Monday through Friday, which includes information about grants and contracts from the federal government.

Computer Resource Guide for Nonprofits. 3rd ed. San Francisco: Public Management Institute, 1985. Lists foundations, corporations, and federal agencies that award grants for computer hardware, software, and training.

Corporate 500: The Directory of Corporate Philanthropy. 5th ed. San Francisco: Public Management Institute, 1986. Contains information on corporate direct-giving programs and foundation giving programs. Includes information on funding areas, eligibility, points of contact, and listings of former grant recipients.

Corporate Foundation Profiles. 4th ed. New York: The Foundation Center, 1986. Provides information on 230 of the largest company-sponsored foundations in the United States.

The Corporate Fund Raising Directory. 1985-1986 ed. Hartsdale, NY: Public Service Materials Center, 1984. Lists information on the application procedures, areas of interest, and grantmaking activities of over 600 corporations.

Directory of Biomedical and Health Care Grants, 1987. Phoenix, AZ: The Oryx Press, 1986. Lists 1,358 health-related funding sources. Includes information on program goals and interests, eligibility, points of contact, deadlines, and grant amounts.

Directory of Financial Aids for International Activities. 4th ed. Prepared by the Office of International Programs, University of Minnesota. Minneapolis, MN: University of Minnesota, 1985. Contains information on 455 individual awards for research, study, travel, and teaching abroad.

Directory of Financial Aids for Minorities, 1986-1987. Gail Ann Schlachter. Los Angeles: Reference Service Press, 1985. Lists funding sources available to Asian Americans, Black Americans, Hispanic Americans, Native Americans, and other minorities.

Directory of Financial Aids for Women. 3rd ed. Gail Ann Schlachter. Santa Barbara, CA: ABC-CLIO, Inc., 1984. Lists over 1,100 funding sources in support of postsecondary education for and research by women.

Directory of Grants in the Humanities, 1987. Phoenix, AZ: The Oryx Press, 1987. Lists approximately 2,000 funding sources in the humanities, including federal sources, state sources, university-sponsored programs, corporate, and foundation sources.

Directory of Grants in the Physical Sciences, 1987. Phoenix, AZ: The Oryx Press, 1986. Lists over 1,500 grant programs covering the physical sciences and technology including federal, state, corporate, and foundation sources of funding.

Directory of Research Grants, 1987. Phoenix, AZ: The Oryx Press, 1987. Lists over 3,000 funding sources including the federal government, foundations, and other private-sector sources.

Federal Grants & Contracts Weekly. Arlington, VA: Capitol Publications, Inc. Published weekly; lists grant and contract announcements, RFPs and RFAs of the federal government of interest to the academic community.

Federal Register. Washington, DC: Superintendent of Documents, U.S. Government Printing Office. Published daily and includes public regulations and legal notices issued by federal agencies, as well as RFAs and RFPs.

Federal Research Report. Silver Spring, MD: Business Publishers, Inc. Published weekly; lists federal contract and grant opportunities.

The Foundation Directory. 11th ed. New York: The Foundation Center, 1987. Profiles 4,403 foundations, including over 700 corporate foundations.

Foundation Grants Index. 16th ed. New York: The Foundation Center, 1987. Identifies over 40,000 foundation grants of $5,000 or more awarded by 460 major U.S. foundations. *The Foundation Grants Index Bimonthly* is a bimonthly update of the *The Foundation Grants Index*.

Foundation Grants to Individuals. 5th ed. New York: The Foundation Center, 1986. Lists foundation funding programs for individual applicants.

Funding for Anthropological Research. Karen Cantrell and Denise Wallen, eds. Phoenix, AZ: The Oryx Press, 1986. Lists over 700 sources of support for anthropological research, broadly defined.

The Grant Advisor. Arlington, VA: Toft Consulting. Published monthly; lists grant opportunity information on federal and non-federal sources of support.

Grant Seekers Guide. Jill R. Shellow, ed. Mount Kisco, NY: Moyer Bell Ltd., 1985. Lists programs which support projects in the areas of social and economic justice.

Grants and Fellowships of Interest to Historians. Thelma Schwartz, ed. Washington, DC: American Historical Association, 1986. Lists over 180 funding programs in support of historical projects.

Grants in the Humanities, A Scholar's Guide to Funding Sources. 2nd ed. William E. Coleman, ed. New York: Neal-Schuman Publishers, 1984. Lists 197 programs for scholars in the humanities.

Grants Magazine. New York: Plenum Publishing Corporation. Quarterly publication containing information on corporation, foundation, and government grants, and information on current funding trends and programs.

The Grants Register, 1987-1989. Roland Turner, ed. New York: St. Martin's Press, 1986. Lists support from international and national government agencies and private organizations including scholarships, fellowships, research grants, exchange programs, and study and travel grants.

Guide to Financial Aid for Latin American Studies. Prepared by the Center for Latin American Studies, University of Pittsburgh, PA. This frequently updated photocopied list includes information on grants, fellowships, and other financial support for teaching, research, and study related to Latin American Studies for faculty and graduate students.

Guide to Grants and Fellowships in Languages and Linguistics, 1983-1984. Washington, DC: Linguistic Society of America, 1983. Lists funding sources of interest to academicians and researchers in linguistics and languages.

Guide to Research Support. 2nd ed. Ralph Dusek, et al, eds. Washington, DC: American Psychological Association, 1984 Lists research funding sources for behavioral scientists, including federal agencies, foundations, and private sector sources.

Guide to Research Support Addendum. 2nd ed. Marti E. Burke, ed. Washington, DC: American Psychological Association, 1986. Provides updated information on federal and nonfederal sources of behavioral science research support covered in the 2nd edition.

How to Get Money for Research. Mary Rubin and the Business and Professional Women's Foundation. Old Westbury, NY: The Feminist Press, 1983. Lists research funding opportunities for and about women at the pre- and postdoctoral levels.

Humanities. Washington, DC: Superintendent of Documents, U.S. Government Printing Office. A bimonthly review of NEH programs and deadlines.

The International Foundation Directory. 4th ed. H.V. Hodson, consultant ed. Detroit, MI: Gale Research Co., 1986. Lists 770 foundations worldwide (including the U.S.) which provide transnational service.

International Funding Guide: Resources and Funds for International Activities at Colleges and Universities. Washington, DC: American Association of State Colleges and Universities, 1985. A listing of public and private sources of funds for international education.

National Data Book. 11th ed. New York: The Foundation Center, 1987. Lists names, addresses, principal officers, and fiscal data on approximately 24,000 U.S. foundations.

NIH Extramural Programs. Bethesda, MD: National Institutes of Health, 1985. Lists funding for research and research and training at the various institutes of NIH.

NIH Guide. Bethesda, MD: National Institutes of Health. Published at irregular intervals to announce scientific initiatives and to provide policy and administrative information to individuals and organizations who need to be kept informed of opportunities, requirements, and changes in grants and contract activities administered by the NIH.

NSF Bulletin. Washington DC: National Science Foundation. Issued monthly (except July and August) and provides news about NSF programs, deadline dates, publications, meetings, and other sources of information.

Source Book Profiles 1987. New York: The Foundation Center, 1987. Provides profiles and analyses of the grantmaking patterns and activities of the 1,000 largest U.S. foundations.

Taft Corporate Directory. Washington, DC: The Taft Group, Inc. , 1985. Lists over 350 corporate foundations and profiles and analyzes their grantmaking activities. The *Corporate Giving Watch* provides monthly updates.

Taft Foundation Information System. Washington, DC: The Taft Group, Inc. Includes the *Taft Foundation Reporter* and 12 issues each of *Foundation Giving Watch* and *Foundation Updates* ; profiles U.S. foundations and lists grantmaking activities.

GENERAL FUNDING

Online Databases

Budgetscope. Washington, DC: Data Resources, Inc. Computer searchable through Data Resources, Inc. Includes federal budget information.

CBD-Online. Silver Springs, MD: United Communications Group. The complete, online equivalent of the *Commerce Business Daily*.

DBD Plus. Greenwich, CT: DMS, Inc. Computer searchable through Data Resources, Inc. Provides contract information of federal government sources.

Federal Assistance Programs Retrieval System. Washington, DC: General Services Administration. Computer searchable through Control Data Corporation Business Information Services. Provides details on federal programs. Corresponds to the *Catalog of Federal Domestic Assistance*.

Federal Research Report. Silver Spring, MD: Business Publishers, Inc. Computer searchable through NewsNet. Includes information on federal contract and grant opportunities. Corresponds to *Federal Research Report* newsletter.

Foundation Directory. New York: The Foundation Center. Computer searchable through Dialog Information Services, Inc. Includes profiles of grantmaking foundations with assets of $1,000,000 or more who have given $100,000 or more in the year of record. *The Foundation Directory* is the corresponding printed source.

Foundation Grants Index. New York: The Foundation Center. Computer searchable through Dialog Information Services, Inc. Details grants of $5,000 and over awarded by major U.S. foundations. *Foundation Grants Index* and *Foundation Grants Bimonthly* are the corresponding printed sources.

Grants. Phoenix, AZ: The Oryx Press. Computer searchable through Dialogue Information Services, Inc. Includes information on grant sources in support of research and study in all fields. *The Directory of Research Grants* is the corresponding printed source.

Grants and Contracts Weekly/Grants and Contracts Alert. Arlington, VA: Capitol Publications, Inc. Computer searchable through NewsNet. Includes federal grant and contract funding information in the social sciences, education, and health. The corresponding printed source is *Federal Grants & Contracts Weekly* and *Health Grants & Contracts Weekly.*

Illinois Researcher Information Service (IRIS). Prepared by Campuswide Research Services Office. Urbana, IL: University of Illinois at Urbana-Champaign. Contains over 4,000 funding opportunities sponsored by federal agencies, private and corporate foundations, and other organizations which support research and scholarship activities. Identifies potential sponsors for faculty, staff, and graduate students' research, teaching, travel, equipment, advanced study, and other activities.

National Foundations. New York: The Foundation Center. Computer searchable through Dialog Information Services, Inc. Lists 22,500 grantmaking foundations in the U.S., including those with total assets less than $1,000,000. The *National Data Book* is the corresponding printed material.

National Scholarship Research Service. San Rafael, CA: National Scholarship Research Service. Lists information for college students to the doctoral level on scholarships, fellowships, grants, and loans.

Research Monitor News. Washington, DC: National Information Service. Computer searchable through NewsNet. Includes funding information from the *Commerce Business Daily* and the *Federal Register.*

Sponsored Programs Information Network (SPIN). Albany, NY: The Research Foundation of SUNY. Lists funding opportunities (federal, nonfederal, and corporate) designed to assist faculty and administrators in the identification of external support for research, education, and development projects.

LATIN AMERICA AND THE CARIBBEAN

Printed Source Materials

A Directory of Latin American Studies in the United States. David B. Bray and Rich E. Greenleaf, eds. Center for Latin American Studies, Tulane University, 1986. A descriptive listing of Latin American Studies programs in 111 institutions of higher education in the U.S.

GIST. Washington, DC: U.S. Department of State, Bureau of Public Affairs. A quick reference guide to U.S. foreign relations that often contains information on Latin America and the Caribbean. Published monthly.

LASA FORUM. Latin American Studies Association, University of Pittsburgh. A newsletter published four times a year by the Latin American Studies Association (LASA).

National Directory of Latin Americanists. Washington, DC: Superintendent of Documents, Government Printing Office, 1985. Contains information of 4,915 individuals with specialized knowledge of Latin America.

Scholars' Guide to Washington, DC for Latin American and Caribbean Studies. Michael Grow. Washington, DC: Smithsonian Institution Press, 1979. Lists Latin American Studies programs, organizations, and agencies involved in Latin American concerns, and other resources of interest to Latin Americanists.